THE COMPLETE BOOK OF VAMPIRES

OTHER BOOKS BY LEONARD R. N. ASHLEY

George Alfred Henty and the Victorian Mind
Turkey: Names and Naming Practices
The Complete Book of Spells, Curses, and Magical Recipes
The Complete Book of the Devil's Disciples
The Complete Book of Devils and Demons
The Complete Book of Magic and Witchcraft
The Complete Book of Superstition, Prophecy, and Luck
What's in a Name?
Elizabethan Popular Culture
Colley Cibber
Authorship and Evidence in Renaissance Drama
George Peele: The Man and His Work
Ripley's "Believe It Or Not" Book of The Military
The Air Defence of North America (NORAD)
Nineteenth-Century British Drama
Mirrors for the Man: 26 Plays of World Drama
The History of the Short Story
Other People's Lives
Tales of Mystery and Melodrama

editor

Phantasms of the Living
Reliques of Irish Poetry
The Ballad Poetry of Ireland
Shakespeare's Jest Book
Soohrab and Rustum
A Narrative of the Life of Mrs. Charlotte Charke

co-editor

British Short Stores: Classics and Criticism
Geolinguistic Perspectives
Language in Contemporary Society
Constructed Languages and Language Construction
Geolinguistics 1997
Geolinguistics 1998
Language and Communications in the New Century

The Complete Book of

VAMPIRES

Leonard R.N. Ashley

**Professor *Emeritus*, Brooklyn College
of The City University of New York**

BARRICADE BOOKS / NEW YORK

Published by Barricade Books Inc.
150 Fifth Avenue
New York, NY 10011

Printed in the United States of America.

Library of Congress Cataloging-in-Publication Data

Ashley, Leonard R. N.
    The complete book of vampires / Leonard R.N. Ashley.
        p.   cm.
    Includes index.
    ISBN 1-56980-125-8

Designed by Cindy LaBreacht
First printing

Here begins a very cruel, frightening story about a wild, bloodthirsty man, Dracula the Vovoid. How he impaled people and roasted them, and how he skinned people and hacked them to pieces like a head of cabbage.

Vlad "The Impaler" feasts as he watches his enemies staked. This woodcut of the historical Dracula errs in showing how the impaling was done. In fact, sharpened stakes were inserted in the vaginas of women and the anuses of men. When he wished to torture victims longer, Dracula ordered blunter stakes to be used.

This is as strange a maze as e'er men trod,

And there is in this business more than nature

Was ever conduct of. Some oracle

Must rectify our knowledge.

—William Shakespeare, *The Tempest*

FOR MARK

Lon Chaney, Jr., as Count Alucard, in *Son of Dracula* (1943).

Table of Contents

Read This First

I know that people seldom or never read the introductions to books. I keep on hoping that they will read mine, because an introduction helps to put a book in context. This introduction will be brief.

The Complete Book of Vampires is the sixth book in a series on the occult which I have published with Barricade Books. The earlier books in the series, each able to stand on its own but the set adding up to something like a planned encyclopedia of the supernatural, are: *The Complete Book of Superstition, Prophecy, and Luck* (1995), *The Complete Book of Magic and Witchcraft* (1995), *The Complete Book of Devils and Demons* (1996), *The Complete Book of the Devil's Disciples* (1996), and *The Complete Book of Spells, Curses and Magical Recipes (1997)*. The seventh book in the series will be *The Complete Book of Ghosts and Poltergeists*.

The sixth and seventh books in the series address the subject of whether the dead survive in some fashion. This is the question which every civilization has asked. It is one which some have answered in rather fantastic ways. In 1759, in a hurry to pay the expenses of his mother's funeral (it was said), Dr. Samuel Johnson of dictionary fame wrote another book which deserves to be remembered. It was the short philosophical novel of *Rasselas, Prince of Abyssinia*. In it, the philosopher Imlac says:

> "That the dead are no more. . . I will not undertake to maintain
> against the concurrent and unvaried testimony of all ages, and of
> all nations. There is no people, rude or learned, among whom

apparitions of the dead are not related and believed. This opinion, which, perhaps, prevails as far as human nature is diffused, could become universal only by its truth; those, that never heard of one another, would not have agreed on a tale which nothing but experience can make credible. That it is doubted by single cavillers can very little weaken the general evidence, and some who deny it with their tongues confess it with their fears."

The Complete Book of Vampires, begun in the year which marked the centenary of the publication of Bram Stoker's *Dracula* (1997), is written even for those "single cavillers who doubt" an afterlife punishment for evil of this life—and for the innumerable, dedicated fans of The Count and the long vampire tradition. It must be admitted that there are far more skeptics in the twentieth century than there were even in the Age of Reason, the eighteenth century, not just about vampires but about any kind of survival of human personality after the death of the body. This book is also written for the vast majority who more or less believe. The book attempts, as do all the other books in my series, to bring scholarly research to all readers in a user-friendly sort of way and to entertain as it educates. I hope it is as well received as the others have been. I do not expect everyone to share my personal views, but I do want as many as possible to share the interesting materials I have, as you might say, dug up about vampires.

On the advice of researchers and librarians, who have praised the bibliographical features of previous books, being so kind as to call them extraordinarily expert and helpful, I continue and somewhat expand the guides to further reading. Those who do not wish to read more than I have presented for them can simply ignore book lists. They can take them simply as evidence of the widespread popularity of the subject. I continue to write in a popular style because, despite all the scholarship, this is a popular book. While some may think a more sombre tone would be preferable, I, and almost all of the readers I have heard from, do not. They like to be amused as well as amazed.

Dracula is a book (like its main character) that will not die! The vampire is a superstition and a metaphor known to everyone, whether in terms of actual "bloodsuckers" or in terms of the greedy landlord, the taxman, bitterly contested divorce, or other problems of modern life. In their sexual aspect, vampires also connect to matters of feminism, another popular subject of heated discussion. If feminist Jenny Uglow is right, "seeing a ghost pushes men into conventional female roles, timid, nervous." Seeing a vampire is worse.

As usual, in presenting my book to the public I have to thank uncounted and consequently unnamable authors whose works I have consulted. I am grateful to all of them. Those writers whose works I believe the reader may wish to consult I have taken care to mention (with full author's name) in the text. I am equally grateful to helpful librarians at Brooklyn College of The City University of New York and at libraries elsewhere in this country and abroad. They have directed me to, or provided through interlibrary loans, many obscure volumes I might otherwise never have seen. I owe much to my publishers and to my patient editor. Most of all I must thank the readers who have welcomed my earlier books and sometimes written to me to commend or to correct me. It is they who have encouraged me to offer still another volume in the series.

God Bless, and Blessed Be.

The Feast of St. Guthlac, 1998

1

The Vampire's Deathless Appeal

INTRODUCING THE VAMPIRE

There can be nobody in civilized society who has not seen a vampire presented on television, in the cinema, in comic books, in the toy store, on the box of breakfast food, and so on. And in uncivilized societies around the world this terrifying creature, or some predator very like it, has been feared since time immemorial.

In the first chapter there is a *pot pourri* of vampire lore, to whet the appetite. Later chapters will deal with the vampire in ancient and modern times in Europe, the United States and around the world, under various headings.

CHARACTERISTICS OF THE VAMPIRE

From Roxana Stuart's highly recommended *Stage Blood: Vampires of the 19th-Century Stage* (1994):
1. The true vampire is a dead body, not a ghost, spectre, or demon.
2. Vampires can be either victims of a contagious disease similar to rabies, or they can be a separate species from man; they are not necessarily connected with Satan and the powers of hell.
3. They have superhuman strength, and are most powerful at night.
4. They feed on the blood of living persons.
5. Barring accident, they can "live" forever.

6. They have command over lower animals, and can change into wolves or bats (a recent development; when vampire bats were discovered in South America in the 1770s, they were quickly grafted onto the persona of Old World vampire).
7. Vampires live in graves and shun the light.
8. Since they are already dead, they are exceedingly difficult to destroy.

THE DEAD ARE WITH US

Portraits made in the old days and now photographs and films and videos keep the dead with us in some way. Painted and very realistic faces are found on mummies of Roman times. In olden days, wax effigies of the dead were used in funeral processions and later were kept in the churches. Paintings of the nobility of Eastern Europe in the seventeenth century—and later— were often commissioned in advance to be used in funeral rites. Poland, where in the seventeenth century a tenth of the whole population was noble, was famous for such portraits. (Bosena Grabowska writes of "Portraits after Life" in *History Today* [October 1993] and her article is important.)

Friends in New York ask me how I can live with ancestral portraits on the wall: "all those dead people looking down at you all the time." I like them. They are not all inferior art, and they naturally mean more to me than they would to most other people. They helped make me what I am, through genes. I even have a few "dead people" not related to me hanging around. I suppose they are ghosts of a sort. They do have some kind of impact. William of Orange and Queen Anne are both in one of my living rooms, and perhaps they are annoyed that neither enjoys the place of honor over the principal fireplace. There hang portraits of Sir John Wentworth and his second wife, Mary, a Yorkshire couple of the 1690s, looking very satisfied with themselves. They had hired themselves a fashionable painter to preserve them for posterity. It has worked.

THE OUTSIDER

Sir John and Lady Wentworth were, in their day, no more out of society than other country gentry in the wilds of Yorkshire. They showed themselves to the *beau monde*.

Vampires, however, usually are outsiders, though they like titles. True, Dr. John Polidori's vampire, Lord Ruthven, moves in fashionable society, but he does much to wreck it by giving money to the unworthy and leading them to destruction that way. His charity is a weapon against society. As the author says, "all those on whom it was bestowed inevitably found that there was a curse upon it, for they were all either led to the scaffold or sunk to the lowest and most abject misery."

You might be interested to know that in British society, for political punishment, certain surnames were once banned. Macgregor was one, which is why we have approximations of it like Magruder. Another banned named was Ruthven (pronounced "Rivven"). It was not chosen for his vampire without cleverness on the part of Dr. Polidori. Or it may have come from Byron's first attempt at the story, for Polidori was Byron's personal physician and, at that house party in the Alps which also produced Mary Shelley's *Frankenstein*, Byron seems to have created the germ of Polidori's tale. Goethe went so far as to say it was Byron's best work, which goes to show great writers are often poor literary critics. In any case, the vampire certainly appealed to Byron. He was romantically dedicated to regarding himself as standing apart. Byron flamboyantly played the role of the talented misfit, devilishly deviant as he became society's darling.

In the television series *Dark Shadows*, the estranged Barnabas Collins is a reluctant vampire. He wishes he could be a part of normal life.

But Dracula "lives" apparently alone in that gruesome castle in Transylvania in most versions, unless a bevy of female vampires is thrown in for a little extra sexual excitement. (He doesn't take any female companions to cook for him when he goes on a trip to England. If he gets hungry, he'll just grab a bite.) Vampires without crumbly castles at their disposal reside most of the time in lonely coffins. They do not appear to have undead neighbors in nearby vaults or graves.

In some modern vampire stories the undead one is not compelled to rest (in a coffin) by day, prowl by night, like the kids of clubland. He or she moves among ordinary people by day and night, mostly indistinguishable from others. The vampire's dark designs and malicious predatory qualities are mostly hidden, as with lawyers.

Pseudo-vampires, on the other hand—persons who because of some anemia or mania like to suck blood—boast of their peculiarity in selected circles where it is tolerated. They tend to get together for support, as do (with great caution) even sexual deviants such as pedophiles and necrophiles. Some of these people may not really be attracted to deviance but are so lonely that they will pretend to an obsession simply to get friends, like some Trekkies who could care less about *Star Trek* but have found a pretended interest can be the key to companionship. The role of loneliness in depravity has never been sufficiently weighed.

Ray Bradbury has an amusing short story called "Homecoming". In it what you might call a dysfunctional family of vampires and other weirdos gets together for a little rejuvenation before they disperse again to face a not understanding, even hostile, world.

VAMPIRE USED LOOSELY

The term gets used loosely, as when, in the decadent days of the Weimar Republic, the case of Peter Kürten, so shocking it confirmed public opinion in favor of capital punishment, put the phrase "The Vampire of Düsseldorf" on every German's lips. This man was a sexual psychopath, like the "Vampire of Hanover" and Jeffrey Dahmer in our own day. "The Vampire of Düsseldorf" belonged in an insane asylum, not a courtroom or a prison. Besides, if a criminal actually were a vampire, how could you try the dead? If the prisoner were convicted of murder, would you sentence the dead to capital punishment?

We have in English the French word *revenant* (one who comes back). It covers both ghosts and vampires as spirits of the dead who return. Throughout this book we omit werewolves. Those are fearsome creatures

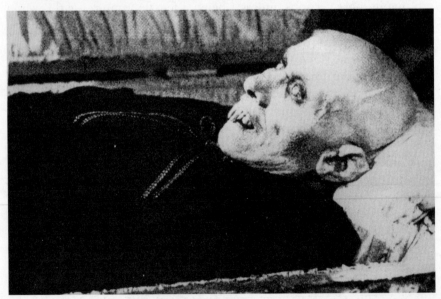

Reggie Nalder in *Salem's Lot*, Tobe Hooper's TV movie of 1979. Then came *Return to Salem's Lot*.

of superstition, too, but they are different from ghosts and vampires in that they are not produced out of dead human beings but, it is claimed, out of live ones. They resemble vampires only in that they are bloodthirsty and supernatural.

The term "vampire" gets kicked around a lot. Lately Transylvanian Imports has been selling in the US Romanian wines labelled Vampire. At about seven dollars a bottle, people buy them mostly for the label. From the scariest movies to comedies such as *Love at First Bite*, everyone loves a vampire, or loves to hate them. I think they even contemplated a sequel, *Love at Second Bite*, but it may not have been made.

INCUBUS

The *incubus*, as the Latin name suggests, lies heavily on top of a person, usually in sleep. It creates dread, inability to breathe easily, and a sense of helplessness. It resembles the nightmare. The Greeks believed the sensation came from too much to eat or drink and treated it as a medical problem, but the Jews superstitiously considered the *incubus* a kind of demon that wanted illicit sex with women. The female version, called a *succuba* or *succubus*, stole the semen of men—providing an explanation, or excuse, for erotic dreams. There is a modern, pornographic vampire film in which the vampires seek semen, not blood.

Early Christians, who mortified the flesh, had lots of trouble with lustful temptations. Celibacy (which one writer has defined as "an overemphasis on sex") is not easy, even with the consolations of religion. St. Anthony in the desert was believed to have been tempted by sexual demons, and as Judeo-Christianity elaborated its demonology these evil forces were connected with witchcraft. They were prosecuted actively by The Holy Inquisition, a lot of which was in the hands of sex-starved clergy.

Here we do not consider devils and demons. However, these imaginary sexual creatures are worth noting as equated with vampires by Ernest Jones in *On the Nightmare* (1931). It is useful to reiterate as often as possible that the vampire is but one way of discussing certain sexual drives and fears. What lies at the heart of it all is the deeply-rooted Jewish antipathy toward any and all forms of sexual activity that do not produce offspring. That aversion lumps together intercourse with *incubi*, *succubæ*, vampires, etc., with masturbation, the sin of Onan (premature withdrawal and "spilling the seed on the ground"), homosexuality, and (presumably) DINKism: double-income-no-kids, deliberately unfruitful marriage.

THE ORIGIN OF VAMPIRES

Though the name *vampire* did not come into use until Early Modern Europe, from the earliest times people have feared predators that might come in the dark. We humans have always been fearful of night creatures, natural or supernatural. Early civilizations such as those of Assyria and Chaldea yield us records of magic and superstitions about vampire-like threats, but they do not explain where these ideas came from.

The burial of people naturally suggested that some of them might rise again, especially if they had left earthly things undone or were prompted by revenge. So, many rituals were created to attempt to put the dead to permanent rest. When it came to be believed that there is a spirit which survives the death of the physical body, ghosts were possible. When the body itself was thought capable of coming back supernaturally with that spirit, for evil deeds, we had vampires. When it came to be believed that the good go on to a better world, a corollary was that the evil could not break with this world.

Vampires do not really "come back"; they are not ghosts because they have real bodies and they are not revenants because they never left in the first place. They are not demons but do resemble the spirits of Psalm 91 that are "the terror by night."

How did they get to be as they are? Explanations are numerous. They may have led evil lives and ended them by suicide. If priests, they may have said Mass while in the state of mortal sin. If lay people, they may have been excommunicated, or they may never have been baptized. They may have been born at an inauspicious time—between Christmas and Epiphany is especially bad, some say—or to cursed parents or at the new moon or just to a mother who did not eat enough salt when pregnant. They may have had a sibling who sleepwalked. They may have been born with teeth or suckled after weaning or fed on sheep that a wolf had killed and taken in thereby a touch of the werewolf. They may have drunk blood when alive or stolen the ropes by which someone's corpse was lowered into the grave or desecrated a church or dabbled in the black arts. They may have been bitten by another vampire.

Once they were dead, their corpses may have had a candle or a cat pass over them or been exposed to moonlight. The corpses may not have been buried, or buried wrong, or simply put into unhallowed graves or graves across which evil winds blew.

There are many other ways that superstition records for one to become a vampire. It is amazing there are so few vampires. *Or are there?*

THE ORIGIN OF BELIEF IN VAMPIRES

Carl Jung in *Flying Saucers* (1959) denied that UFOs existed but posited that what was interesting was that people sincerely believed in spaceships manned by extraterrestrials. UFOs must, he said, answer some deep need or reflect some deep fear in people.

One might suggest that the belief in vampires betrays something in the unconscious and fills some need people have to imagine a world in which the rapacious undead stalk the living. Think about what belief in vampires might reveal about human psychology.

As anciently and in many cultures mankind created gods and goddesses, monsters and demons in our own likeness, embodying in them human traits and terrors, so we may in our superstitions about vampires be seeking a way to recognize the usefulness of faith in the supernatural, faith in survival (if not a pleasant survival) after death, faith in the possibility that at another level of existence there could be predators and thieves of energy, soul destroyers, similar to certain real-life individuals we know.

THE VAMPIRE MYTH

Traditionally they are gaunt and hideous; with red and glowing eyes, long nails, and sharp teeth and even fangs (or extra-long canine teeth). In Poland, people say their tongues are pointed. In Bulgaria, people say they have but one nostril. They stink of corruption; this is strange, because everyone knows that in the grave they remain frighteningly incorrupt. Because they are dead, or because blood is their food, their breath is foul. You might say they have mourning breath. They have, says some folklore, gray eyes and black hair or, in other traditions, blue eyes and red hair.

The vampire myth was fortified by ancient superstitions, by catalepsy and premature burial, by unusual but not supernatural preservation of the unembalmed corpse, by porphyria (a blood disease that accounted for the insanity of George III), by bloodlust psychosis, and most of all (I must say) by the fact that they comfort us by suggesting that life exists after death and that evil cannot harm the pure in heart (a vampire cannot harm you unless you invite him in). They offer a way of discussing forbidden secrets of sexuality. They reek not only of the grave but of sexual fantasies. They cater to our morbid sadomasochistic and necrophiliac imaginings. They are Eros and Thanatos combined. As with most supernatural things, if you dig deep enough you will see in them connections with the perfectly ordinary and mundane. They have real-life parallels in psychological parasitism.

The anthologist of the Gothic, D. P. Varma, writes:

> Like all true myths the vampire legend has been subjected to man-
> ifold interpretations, but surely it is logical within the realms of
> fantasy . . . . Sin must follow temptation. Evil may be terrible, but
> it is also irresistible. Even a loathsome embrace marks the naked
> cruelty of passion. The vampire's embrace may plumb the bot-
> tomless pit of damnation; nonetheless, it ravages the heights of
> heaven with rage and rapture.

The Vampire by Edvard Munch

THE VAMPIRE IN EUROPE IN THE EIGHTEENTH CENTURY

It is often remarked that the vampire craze suddenly struck in Transylvania in the eighteenth century. The fact is that vampires had been discussed
in Europe for centuries before this. In England, for instance, there was an
Anglo-Saxon poem now called *The Vampire of the Fens*. Of course that title
was given later, because the term "vampire" did not enter English until
the eighteenth century, when we picked it up from Eastern Europe, probably through German reports. I have seen the term—at first often spelled
vampyre, a practice which lasted well into the nineteenth century—in English use as early as 1745: here is a quotation from the Harleian Miscellany
(papers collected by Robert Harley, first Earl of Oxford, 1661 - 1724, who

bought up the libraries of such early historians as John Stow and others). This is a piece that records "Travels of Three English Gentlemen" in Laubach, Carniola, on The Continent, early in the eighteenth century. That was a time when gentlemen made a Grand Tour of Europe as part of their education and sometimes wandered well off the beaten track, bringing back strange news to their countrymen.

> These Vampyres, said to infest some part of this Country . . . are supposed to be the Bodies of deceased Persons, animated by evil Spirits, which come out of Graves, in the Night-time, suck the Blood of many of the Living, and thereby destroy them.

You could not ask for a clearer definition of *vampire* than that. As a cynic might say, it is simple, clear, and wrong. Note that these vampires are essentially demonic: diabolical powers are reanimating the corpses. For more on diabolical forces, see *The Complete Book of Devils and Demons*. I do not discuss vampires there because in the standard view vampires are evil human undead, not demons possessing human corpses.

Here are the titles of half a dozen learned dissertations regarding the vampire from eighteenth-century scholars (who generally Latinized their German names). These men seem to have been convinced of the reality of vampirism and even lectured in the university on the feeding of the dead:

Karl Ferdinand Schertz, *Magia posthuma* (1706)

Michael Ranftius, *De Masticatione mortuorum in tumulus liber* (Book of the Dead Feeding in the Tomb, 1728)

Johann Christian Stock, *Dissertatio de cadaveribus sanguisugis* (Dissertation on Bloodsucking Cadavers, 1732)

Johann Christoff Rohlius, *Dissertatio de hominibus post mortem sanguisugis, vulgo dictic Vampyrea* (Dissertation on Blood-sucking Men after Death, Commonly Called Vampires, 1732)

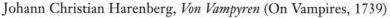

Johann Heinrich Zopfius, *Dissertatio de Vampyris Serviensibus* (Dissertation on Serbian Vampires, 1733)

Johann Christian Harenberg, *Von Vampyren* (On Vampires, 1739)

IS A VAMPIRE A DEMON?

No. John Boyer Noss (author of *Man's Religions*) wrote in an *Encyclopædia Britannica* article on "Demons" (7, 1971) that vampires are "demons or evil spirits," but he is wrong to lump them with goblins and "wraiths or ghosts and *specters* [italics mine]." By definition, vampires were once human and are "undead." They must be differentiated both from never-human supernatural creatures (some of whom are said to assume human shape on occasion) and from vengeful ghosts (in classical times thought to be the result of violent, tragic deaths) and lemures (evil dead humans from unquiet graves). Noss says that in India's long list of supernatural terrors "a special class is the *vetala* or vampire," but those are also not human and do not qualify as vampires. He connects the Chinese demons (collectively *kuei*) with "man-eating spectres, the ghouls and vampires, and the gigantic devils with horned foreheads, long fangs and fuzzy red hair." All that vampires really have in common with these other predators is that they have a fear of sunlight (which represents life not death, God not the Evil One), and fangs (some say). Noss is as inconsistent in dealing with vampires as he is in the spelling *specter/spectre*.

This series includes *The Complete Book of Devils and Demons* and *The Complete Book of the Devil's Disciples*, but I omitted vampires there. Vampires are a distinct category worthy of particular consideration; hence the present study. *The Complete Book of Ghosts and Poltergeists* will follow.

DEUTERONOMY: THE BLOOD IS THE LIFE

Reay Tannahill's *Sex in History* (1992) is a concise statement of facts that appear in a great many forms, usually less readable than this:

> It is easy enough to understand . . . the conclusion not only that blood was essential to life, but that it was the essence of life itself. There was blood at the moment of birth, and blood, very often, at the moment of death. To early man it seemed to have a positive, intrinsic power, and because it was thought of as a vitalizing (and revitalizing) agent, it was used in may magical rituals, most cults of the dead, and most dealings with the gods and spirits.

WHAT YOU CAN DO ABOUT VAMPIRES

Put up garlic flowers and crucifixes and make crosses with tar on buildings and place three wishbones (open side up) over your bed. Keep vampires away with water or salt, sweet-smelling incense, and prayer. Seek out their graves with white horses allowed to roam in the cemetery, then destroy the vampires. Look for graves with small holes in them. You could pour scalding water or vinegar down the holes. Look for people buried facing North/South rather than East/West. Shoot vampires; but lead cannot kill them, only a silver bullet. Dig them up and deprive them of their native soil. Expose them to sunlight. Strike off their heads—with a single blow only. Burn the corpse and cast the ashes into flowing water. Catch them before they are vampires for seven years, for after that they can walk about like regular human beings, breed, and create children who will become vampires when they die.

What you can do most effectively is to stay holy yourself. As the old poem goes:

Mans Danger lyes in Satan, sin, and selfe.

VAMPIRES IN ANCIENT DAYS

The first wife of Adam was Lilith, says the Talmud. We have seen from recent films, if not from personal experience, that rejected first wives can be dangerously hostile. Lilith was a demon. She and other such diabolical creatures you can read about in an earlier book in this series, *The Complete Book of Devils and Demons*. Some of these horrors from early pagan and later, Judeo-Christian, times had vampiristic aspects, despite the fact that the term *vampire*, originating in Eastern Europe, as already noted, did not make its way into common usage until just a couple of hundred years ago. After all, vampires are after your souls! The Babylonians and Hittites, the Greeks and Romans, and many other civilizations—not to mention uncivilized tribes and nations—believed in fearsome female vampire and male vampire creatures that flew by night. Some were created evil and some stalked the night because they were not given what we might now call closure by receiving proper burial. They had what recent horror films called *The Hunger* or *The Addiction*.

ANCIENT FABLES

In *The Aeneid*, Palinurus, the helmsman, falls asleep at the wheel. He is washed overboard, is cast up on the shores of Africa, and is murdered by the locals. He comes back as a ghost, not a vampire, because he has not had a proper burial. His unquiet grave, however, may have contributed something to vampire legend. So also may have the phoenix, fabled bird of Egypt. The phoenix is supposed to have built itself a nest of fragrant wood, burned itself up, and then risen from its ashes. The resurrected are reported by Herodotus. There are also the *empusa* or the *lamia*, not vampires but demons of possession. The lustful *faunus* likewise is vaguely connected to the sexuality of the vampire. Myths are often mosaics.

THE PREDATORY FEMALE

Bram Dijkstra argues that the most authentic vampires were all women, not "effete foreigners" who were sexually ambiguous and "unmanly." His views on predatory females are to be found in books such as *Idols of Perversity* (1988) and its update, *Evil Sisters* (1997). *New York Times* critic Michael Sherry comments that the latest book shows "the contested field of cultural studies at its best and worst: powerfully exposing malevolent, taken-for-granted assumptions about gender; needlessly overstating the case." It might be added that in the same way that sociology bolsters its observation with numbing statistics because what it so scientifically has discovered is often little more than what everyone has more or less noticed already to be true. Cultural studies tend to overdramatize rather obvious conclusions, perhaps anxious to make us face what we have often suspected but basically try to avoid accepting. In fact, the aggressiveness of predatory females is little different from the aggressiveness of predatory males, whether it be in the practice of law or the pursuit of lawlessness, the greed for money or for power or for blood. A touch of perversity seems inherent in our humanity. Male and female vampires are evidence of the desires for domination apparently possible in human beings of all sexual orientations. S&M (sado-masochism, or sex and manipulation) is not sex-specific. Any two can play.

Discussions of top and bottom, violence and masochism, and other sorts of gender topics are all the rage now, and certainly the vampire—of any of the four sexes (heterosexual male or female, homosexual male or female)—fits right into the trendy cultural studies mode. Whether the

A Victorian female vampire. Painting by Burne-Jones, 1897.

predator can be regarded as essentially masculine or, what Dr. Dijkstra considers its opposite, "effeminate," is debatable. It seems clear to me that female vampires are to be regarded as aggressively masculine; many of them are portrayed as lesbian in recent literature and films. What is also clear is that in the figure of the vampire we have long had and will continue to have a symbol of, and way of talking to the general public about, enduring problems in sex and society, civilization and its discontents, the war between the sexes, and other deathless matters.

Movies with female vampires include: *Black Sunday, Blood and Roses, Brides of Dracula, Countess Dracula, Dance of the Vampires, Daughters of Darkness, Dracula, Dracula's Daughter, The Hunger, Lifeforce, Lust for a Vampire, Mark of the Vampire, Nightlife, Twins of Evil, Vampire Lovers.* We have a whole chapter on film later on.

THE VAMPIRE AS MODERN METAPHOR

The vampire appears in many disciplines (as we like to say in Academe) and so was a perfect choice for an interdisciplinary seminar which I gave twice in the City University of New York, bringing together students of literature and folklore, opera and pop music, sociology and psychology, even hard science and popular culture in general.

In an anthology on the vampire in contemporary culture, *Blood Read* (1997), editors Joan Golden & Veronica Hollinger write a typically academic—watch for the jargon use of *inscribe*—but usefully succinct paragraph of interest:

> The figure of the vampire, as metaphor, can tell us about sexuality, of course, and about power; it can also inscribe more specific[ally] contemporary concerns, such as relations of power [different from "power"?] and alienation, attitudes toward illness, and the definition of evil at the end of an unprecedentedly secular century. And it can help to clarify the nature of the fantastic realities [oxymoron?] that seem occasionally to overwhelm the empirical. In recent decades, [no comma after brief introductory prepositional phrase] the vampire has re-affirmed [hyphen?] its power as an icon of popular culture—for example, in the incredible [why not believable?] popularity of Rice's Vampire Chronicles (1976 - 1994), in the appearance of Forever Knight (1992—) as a regular TV series, in the success of films like Near Dark (1987), The Lost Boys [date?], Francis Ford Coppola's Bram Stoker's Drac-

ula (1992), and [forename?] Jordan's version of Interview with the Vampire (1994), in new revisions of Dracula by authors such as Fred Saberhagen (The Dracula Tape, 1975) and Brian Aldiss Dracula Unbound, 1991), and in the proliferation of vampire literature that continues to spread [redundant] throughout the horror sections of bookshops and comic book stores. So familiar a part of our everyday culture has the vampire become that, most appropriately, it provided the subject of director [writer? actor?] Mel Brooks's most recent parody of popular taste, Dracula: Dead and Loving It (1995).

Just to make fun of academic writing, or perhaps to point up the failure of university presses to edit the books they publish, I nitpick as a pedant would the text here.

In the matter of style I want to say that I have tried in my series of books on the occult to write in a reader-friendly fashion, entertainingly, not pompously, though my subjects have been serious and seriously researched. The relaxed style has been welcomed by all but one correspondent. In writing to point out several typos in a total of 700 or 800 pages (he read two books in the series), and most especially to tell me that I was a fool to think anyone believes in such old-fashioned ideas as good and evil and was evil for not showing respect for the Church of Satan. He expressed rage that a university professor would ever use *impact* as a verb.

Well, so many people do that I have joined them, though I hold out against obviously wrong uses of *disinterested, hopefully*, etc. (Abandon *hopefully* all ye who enter here.) I do believe that a correct and appropriate style is always important. Texts such as *Blood Read* should not have to be tinkered with or translated by the reader. The reader should be able to concentrate on the subject, which is interesting and includes, in *Blood Read*'s case, a lot about the vampire in science fiction in works such as Stableford's *Empire of Fear*. Of that, more later.

FROM VOLTAIRE'S PHILOSOPHICAL DICTIONARY

François-Marie Arouet (1694 - 1778), "Voltaire," called upon The Enlightenment to "crush" superstition. His friend, Frederick the Great, told him this would never be possible. Here is "Voltaire" in his *Dictionnaire philosophique* (1764), written just as rationalist Europe is trying to recover from tales of vampires in Transylvania.

What! is it in our eighteenth century that vampires exist? Is it after the reigns of [philosopher John] Locke, [Locke's pupil Anthony

Ashley Cooper, 3rd earl of] Shaftesbury, Trenchard, and [theologian Anthony] Collins? Is it under those of [Jean Le Rond] d'Alembert, [Denis] Diderot, [Jean François de] St. Lambert, and [Charles-Pinot] Duclos, that we believe in vampires, and that the reverend father Dom [Augustin] Calmet, Benedictine priest of the congregation of St. Vannes and St. Hidulphe, abbé of Senon,—an abbey of a hundred thousand livres a year, in the neighborhood of two other abbeys of the same revenue,—has printed and reprinted the history of vampires, with the approbation of the Sorbonne, signed with the imprimatur of Marcilli?

These vampires were corpses, who went out of their graves at night to suck the blood of the living, either at their throats or stomachs, after which they returned to their cemeteries. The persons so sucked waned, grew pale, and fell into consumptions; while the sucking corpse grew fat, got rosy, and enjoyed an excellent appetite. It was in Poland, Hungary, Silesia, Moravia, Austria, and Lorraine, that the dead made this good cheer.

We never heard speak of vampires in London, nor even at Paris. I confess that in both these cities there were stock-jobbers, brokers, and men of business, who sucked the blood of the people in broad day-light; but they were not dead, though corrupted. These true suckers lived not in cemeteries, but in very agreeable palaces.

Monks are the Only True Vampires

The kings of Persia were, said they, the first who caused themselves to be served with viands after their death. Almost all the kings of the present day imitate them, but they are the monks who eat their dinner and supper, and drink their wine. Thus, properly speaking, kings are not vampires: the true vampires are the monks, who eat at the expense of both kings and people.

It is very true, that St. Stanislaus, who had bought a considerable estate from a Polish gentleman, and not paid him for it, being brought before King Boleslas, by his heirs, raised up the gentleman; but this was solely to get quittance. It is not said that he gave a single glass of wine to the seller, who returned to the other world without having eaten or drunk. They afterwards treated of the grand question, whether a vampire could be absolved who died excommunicated, which comes more to the point. I am not profound enough in theology to give my opinion on this sub-

ject, but I would willingly be for absolution, because in all doubtful affairs we should take the mildest part.

There are Now No More!

The result of all this is, that a great part of Europe has been
infested with vampires for five or six years, and that there are now
no more; that we have had convulsionaries in France for twenty
years, that we have them no longer; that we
have had demoniacs for seventeen hundred
years, but have them no longer; that we have
had demoniacs for seventeen hundred years,
but have them no longer; that the dead have
been raised ever since the days of Hippolytus,
but that they are raised no longer; and lastly,
that we have had Jesuits in Spain, Portugal,
France, and the two Sicilies, but that we have
them no longer.

Bram Stoker:
Dracula
Ein Vampirroman

CONTAGION

Vampirism is a perfect fit for the romantic and decadent interest in contagion, disease, and death. David Farrell Krell in *Contagion* (1998) discusses
Novalis, Schelling, and Hegel in terms of these destructive powers as
viewed in German Romanticism. Michael O'Neill's bibliographical guide
to *Literature of the Romantic Period* (1998) will open up to you similar trends
in other literatures, 1790 - 1830.

Now in the Age of AIDS we have still more frightening connections
to make, or connections to fear. Vampires suggest the spread of some terrible disease of the blood (soul) transmitted through sexual contact. It is
no accident that gay and lesbian fiction should have recently contributed
notably to a rise in the number of vampires in fiction.

THE VAMPIRE AND GAY PORNOGRAPHY

Of all places, Canada—whose laws on gay and lesbian and even "straight"
pornography are far more stringent than those of the United States—produced in 1996 a homosexual comic book, *Canadian Male*, and its premier
issue had a "vampire" on the cover and a featured article on "Blood Lust:
Vampire Sexuality Unleashed." Whether a second issue, from the pub-

lishers of *Xtra!*, a Canadian gay weekly newspaper, ever appeared, or whether the Royal Canadian Mounted Police stepped in, I don't know.

The cover art in question shows a nude male being attacked by another male in a chain-mail and leather outfit, presumably the uniform for these "vampire" games. If blood is drawn or any physical damage done, even the rather broadminded European Union laws about consensual sex condemn it, let alone the conservative Canadians. All of this bears no closer relation to the standard vampire myth than, say, 1997's summer blockbuster movie, *Batman and Robin*. It does, however, demonstrate the hold of the vampire myth on the public imagination and its continued connection with predation.

MODERN VAMPIRES

Neil Straum has an interesting short story, "Vanishing Breed", in the collection edited by M. L. Carter, *The Curse of the Undead* (1970). It speaks of the decline in the old-school vampires and the new generation of those who "blended into the background, became respected commoners, upheld the UN and hated the perverts" and in most ways were accepted as a norm for their particular subculture.

There is here what William J. Mann in an article in *Frontiers* 14 (3 November 1995, 62-68) calls "the natural connection between horror films and gay audiences." That is thoroughly studied in a University of Southern California doctoral dissertation, *Monsters in the Closet: Homosexuality and the Horror Film* (1996), by Henry Morgan Benshoff; he suggests a parallel with the homosexual lifestyle, "deviant but accepted and permitted."

As Straum's story ends, however, the "human" vampires flee the earth in a spaceship because the "psych-proctors" (the twenty-second century equivalent of twentieth-century psychiatrists) have turned against them as threats to society and have set out to have them destroyed.

Benshoff notes that about this time *Time* and *Newsweek*, reacting to the Stonewall Riots, alerted America to the "newly visible, newly understood" homosexual culture. Benshoff quotes *Time* (31 October 1969, 65):

> At their fullest flowering, the Persian, Greek, Roman, and Moslem civilizations permitted a measure of homosexuality; as they decayed, it became more prevalent.

Of all Benshoff's homosexual characters in modern films, the most striking may be the lesbian vampires. "During the 1980s," he writes, "les-

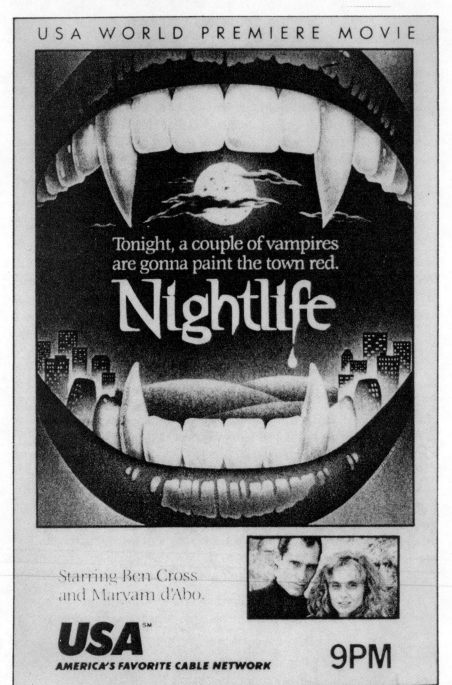

Cable televison ropes in vampire fans.

bian vampires were enjoying a vogue on the continent, but many of these films never received a wide release in the United States, and today they remain difficult to view." Have you seen any of these: Roger Vadim's *Blood and Roses* (1960), Mario Bava and Antonio Margheriti's *Black Sunday* (1960) and *La Danza macabra* (Dance Macabre, 1960), Jean Rollin's *La Vampire nue* (The Naked Vampire, 1969), Hammer's *The Vampire Lovers* (1970, based on "Carmilla") and *Lust for a Vampire* (1971, ditto) and *Twins of Evil* (1972, "Carmilla" once more), Hammer's *Countess Dracula* (1971), the Belgian-French (English-language) *Daughters of Darkness* (1971)? See Benshoff and also Bonnie Zimmerman's essential "Daughters of Darkness: Lesbian Vampires" in *Jump Cut* 24 (Fall 1980) and the resources carefully listed by Benshoff.

The gay predator seeking if not blood, blood products—and in the recently quite widespread sado-masochistic mode perhaps blood as well—and the female vamp seducing and subjecting victims, with a hatred of men (also prominent in S&M "games"), both easily lend themselves to comparison as a subculture with the underground vampire heritage. For all the role-playing and costume aspects of gaunt and gothic youth in the age of punk, piercing, and perversion, the vampire motif offers something more than a mere pose to disaffected young people out to outrage.

THE VAMPIRE ON THE CONCERT STAGE

From *The Economist* for 17 May 1997 (p. 92): "Audiences have heard Alban Berg's violin concerto performed by a mock punk in a Dracula costume...."

STAMP OUT VAMPIRES

In 1997, the United States Postal Service included the vampire in its series of stamps commemorating the popularity of monsters in the movies.

SEXUAL DEVIANCE AMONG VAMPIRES

Joseph Sheridan LeFanu (1814 - 1873), whose novels include the chilling *Uncle Silas* (1864), published a collection of short stories entitled *In a Glass Darkly* (1872). It included a vampire tale with lesbian overtones, so it looks very modern now. Today lesbian and gay colorations are frequently added to give spice to the vampire tales, always connected, of course, with a kind of rape, and often involving (Nina Auerbach and other feminists now insist) a way of escaping from the confines of patriarchy. Now we have *Gaycula*, *Dracula Sucks*, and other non-heterosexual pornography as well as gay and lesbian vampires in fiction and—at least as role-playing—in fact. There are publicized clubs for them in New York City's East Village and in SoHo, and perhaps covert ones in less open cities.

Raymond McNally takes up about a third of his cut-and-paste *A Clutch of Vampires* with the lesbian vampire tale of "Carmilla", by LeFanu, and still does not print all of this long story. The story was the basis for Carl Dreyer's admired horror film, *Vampyr* (1932). It still can thrill. When they open the vampire's coffin in "Carmilla", though she has been dead 150 years, the well-preserved body is floating in seven inches of fresh blood!

In comedy, the corny classic *The Rocky Horror Picture Show* (1975) features a transsexual transvestite from Transylvania, but he is more of a Dr. Frankenstein than a Dracula. He wants to "make me a man." Midnight showings of this cult film continue to this day (or night).

Often described as vampires but simply sexual psychopaths are such horrendous creatures of real life as Franz Haarmann, "The Vampire of Hanover." Born in 1879, he and his boyfriend (Hans Grans) preyed on youthful strays in the dislocation after World War I. Haarmann was executed in 1925. By then he had molested and murdered (and maybe eaten some of) twenty-seven boys. That did not put him in the same league with the notorious friend of Joan of Arc, Gilles de Rais, whose Satanic murders of youths ran into the hundreds, but "The Vampire of Hanover" was frightening enough.

There is something cannibalistic about many pedophiles, if only symbolically so; they are driven to consume the youth of their victims, whom they sometimes call "chicken" and "twinkies" and by other names for food. There was an obsessive Werner Rainer Fassbinder film about Haarmann. There are vampire overtones in the film *M* (1931) and its remake. Pedophiles and vampires are linked as the public's most despised outsiders.

THE CAPED CROSS-HATER

The vampire in formal dress with a cape derives from the nineteenth-century popularity of the myth and its first appearances on the stage (in a dramatization of Bram Stoker's *Dracula*), its first film version, and a top-hatted Lon Chaney in *London after Midnight* (1927). From the time Europeans discovered the so-called vampire bats of the Americas, the vampire and the bat were closely associated. Naturally, the cape often suggests a bat, as it does even with *Batman*. Vampires do not change into bats, hang upside down, operate by sonar, or fly.

This has not obviated cheap-shot vampire stories with bats in them. One of the best of boy-meets-bat bits of popular fiction is Richard Matheson's *Drink My Red Blood* (1951). This author wrote much more imaginatively in *The Omega Man (1954)*, filmed as *The Last Man on Earth* (1964, with Vincent Price in an unaccustomed sympathetic role) and with a little more flair as *The Omega Man* (1971, in which Charlton Heston played the last *non*-vampire in the world). The novel was republished as *I Am Legend* (1971).

ASSYRIAN VAMPIRES

The ancient Assyrians not only had flying demons but also vampire-like monsters. From these the Jews appear to have derived some ideas about terrifying creatures of the night. Robert S. McCully describes a representation of a vampire on an old Assyrian bowl, in his discussion of "a case of auto-vampirism," in the *Journal of Nervous and Mental Disease* 139 (November 1964): 440-452.

BLOOD TRANSFUSION

Inherited wealth enabled "Projecting Prock," an amusing inventor in Ireland (1690 - 1759), to try all sorts of schemes, from his Angelic Organ (musical glasses, improved in Benjamin Franklin's Armonica) to his method of rejuvenation by blood transfusion. Of course nobody in the eighteenth century understood blood types and details like that—nor does vampirism ever worry about that, apparently—but "Projecting Prock" Pokrich was so sure that new blood was the answer to long life and renewed vigor that he also suggested that a law be passed that limited a human life to 999 years.

How to live almost a thousand years? Blood transfusion.

Take an inflex tube in the nature of a syphon, fix it to the extreme ends of the veins of two different persons to be opened to receive them, the one youthful, adult, and sanguine, the other aged, decrepit, and withered. The redundant fermenting blood of the one will immediately flow like wine decanted into the shriveled veins of the other. The effects will be found no less surprising— the wrinkled skin braces, the flesh pumps up and softens, the eyes sparkle.

A remarkably boring label for a Transylvanian wine, considering it calls itself Vampire. But then Count Dracula has said, "I never drink—wine."

As far as I know, no one has ever connected this odd Irishman's theories, in his day considered insane, with features of later vampire stories. To Pokrich, tales that blood drinkers might be immortal were only exaggerations.

VAMPIRES SIGHTED

The movies probably must take the blame for the popular idea that vampires slink around in opera capes. Why don't they stalk, like ghosts, in the clothes, or shrouds, in which they were buried? Or in outfits that do not make them so conspicuous? Vampires have to eat out regularly and they have opportunities to shop (if stores stay open very late). If that is so, why the dated fashion sense?

Connected to this is the fact that anyone seen slinking around in a cape, especially near graveyards, must be a vampire. More and more people are being cremated these days. This obviates some potential vampire problems, naturally. However, there still are enough burials to mean lots of cemetery plots. So when some kook in a cape is seen regularly around cemeteries in Jai (CA) or Highgate (London), there are reports of a vampire. Same, too, of Lerici (near La Spezia, down the west coast of Italy from Genoa). I visited Lerici in 1998 and they were still talking about a vampire in a cape seen about a quarter of a century ago. (Actually, there isn't much else in Lerici to talk about.)

"Vampire sighted" is for slow news days. Now, a New York *Daily News* headline such as BODY FULL OF ALCOHOL, DRAINED OF BLOOD, IN TOPLESS BAR—that would be news.

"THE VAMPIRES COME TO US FROM ENGLAND"

The English vampire tales not only impressed Germans such as Goethe but also the French. Charles Nodier and others produced vampire melodramas for the theatres of the boulevards—in a way this was an origin of the bloody spectacles of the later *Guignol*—and the *vaudevilles* hopped on the hot topic and presented burlesques. In 1820, for example, a team of writers (Brazier, Gabriel, and Armand) put together a burlesque one-acter for the *Varieties* in Paris; it was called *Les trois Vampires; ou, Le Clair de lune* (The Three Vampires; or, The Light of the Moon).

The flimsy plot is that M. Gobetout has been reading far too many vampire tales and his mind is adversely affected. This borrows something from Don Quixote, who goes crazy because he read too many romances of chivalry. In the farce here, M. Gobetout sees his three daughters dancing in the moonlight with three males and M. Gobetout foolishly assumes they are dancing with three vampires. Actually it is a couple of boyfriends and a valet.

You could break up a Parisian house with a line about the vampires coming from England: *"Les vampires...ils nous viennent d'Angleterre!"*

Throughout the first part of the century England and France traded all sorts of plays, including vampire plays. It was so much easier, in those days without copyright, to translate and adapt a play than think one up for yourself. Dickens fans may recall that one of his characters is put to the task of producing a text this way when a theatrical company needs a play in a hurry.

At the *Ambigù* in Paris in 1851, to cite another example, Alexandre Dumas and a collaborator (Marquet) presented *Le Vampire*, which was nothing more than a ripoff of Charles Nodier's play of a generation before, itself a ripoff of Dr. John Polidori's tale of *The Vampyre*.

INTERVIEW WITH A VAMPIROLOGIST

Dr. Jeanne Keyes Youngson is the guiding spirit of The Count Dracula Fan Club and author of *Private Files of a Vampirologist* and many other books in the field. She has kindly given me permission to print here an interview with her by Donald A. Best, journalist and photographer of big game in Africa, who traces his interest in The Count to the time he first read *Dracula* in a tent at the foot of Mt. Kilmanjaro.

DB: I read *Private Files* through in one sitting. I assume these are actual people—but are they really real or are they just putting you on?

JY: They certainly are real. Just ask Eric Held (Director of the Vampire Information Exchange). He has been contacted by a lot of wannabe vampires. Elizabeth Miller (Transylvanian Society of Dracula) and McNally & Florescu *In Search of Dracula* have also heard from several of the people in the book. They're real, alright.

DB: I can appreciate the desire to live forever, but what would possess any-one to want to live in a coffin and go out and bite human beings in order to suck their blood?

JY: Well, in order to become a real vampire, you have first to be dead. As far as I know, no one has gone that far. Some try to be vampire-like—which is about the best they can do without actually dying.

DB: But what's the attraction?

JY: There's no easy answer to that. The middle-aged woman in Florida who wants to have an affair with Dracula has a lot in common with the 21-year-old college girl who says she would give up everything, home, family, career, if we could find a good-looking vampire for her to run away with. Many of these people have lost touch with reality. They're dissatisfied with their lives. They are looking for some mag-ical way to escape. Vampires seem to fill the bill.

DB: I was intrigued by the choices you made for inclusion in the book. You obviously had a lot of material to work from.

JY: Don't forget I've been talking to, and hearing from, "vampires" since 1979. Once the word got around that I was a sympathetic listener, a lot of people started writing and calling. Not all of them were seri-ous. Some realized they were being rather silly. It was almost a game to them. Then there were the ones who were exchanging blood with willing partners. A 30-year-old woman in California had a live-in donor who allowed her to take his blood twice a week. Someone else, a man in Philadelphia, claimed to be part of a 'tribe' that drank cows' blood from a slaughterhouse. They had certain rituals they followed, including having sex with a virgin—with her consent. I had the feel-ing this guy was indeed putting me on, especially the part about the virgin. I did believe "Cathy," whom I interviewed in 1980 for Olga Hoyt's *Lust for Blood*. She said she had gone to a blood-cult meeting on New York's Upper West Side where they slit a mangy old (her words) Doberman pincher's throat and drank its blood. They then smeared blood all over their bodies and had an orgy. I believed her story because Bernhardt J. Hurwood of *Vampires* had already men-tioned this group to me.

DB: What about those who dress in black and wear white makeup and fangs?

JY: Many of them are kids. I get a lot of letters written on lined paper that follow the same general pattern: "Dear Dr. Youngson: My name is _____ and I am ____ years old. I think I am turning into a vampire. I am allergic to the sun, I dress in black, and I have this tremendous desire to drink blood...."

DB: Have you met any of these "vampires"?

JY: I've met quite a few of the people in the book and I've appeared on some TV and radio shows with a number of "wannabes". They are mainly blood-fetishists, whether they like to be called that or not.

DB: Getting back to why people are so fascinated by the idea of becoming a vampire, I believe you said there were no easy answers....

JY: That's true. I'd be hard-pressed to try and explain the popularity of vampires. As I said, in some cases people are unhappy with their lives and think if they become vampires they won't have any more problems. Others are fixated on drinking blood. Still others want to impress their peers by being different, more exotic. A few years ago when I was in England, I met a young couple who came from a small village outside London. They told me they had nothing in common with the people there and were looked down on because they always wore black and had matching silver rings in their noses. They also both had skull earrings. They wanted to get married their way. They had found a minister with mail-order credentials who said he would be glad to perform the ceremony for a few pounds. They planned to have four attendants, everyone wearing black. All the food and drink would be red. None of their families would be at the ceremony, but they didn't seem to care. They were having a double coffin made for their bedroom and were going to name their first-born either 'Dracula' or 'Draculita'. They planned to contact one of the tabloids to cover the wedding. I had to return to the States so I never heard what happened after that. I'm not sure if they were the same people Rosemary Guiley interviewed, but they may well have been.

DB: What about you, Dr. Youngson? I know you've been active within the vampire genre for a long time. In fact, my research shows that you founded The Count Dracula Fan Club seven years before Stephen Kaplan appeared on the scene. He seemed always to be promoting himself, but very little was heard of The Count Dracula Fan Club.

JY: That's true. We were always low-key. That's the way I wanted it. It says in our handbook, "The Count Dracula Fan Club has, through the years, successfully continued to maintain a balance between the serious aspects of the subject and a light-hearted approach, thus appealing to all age groups." We've never gone out of our way to get publicity and I think that approach has paid off.

DB: You've certainly done a remarkable job with The Count Dracula Fan Club, the Dracula Museum, the Bram Stoker Memorial Association—

and now these two extremely timely books, *The Bizarre World of the Vampire* and *Private Files of A Vampirologist*. What next, now that you've covered both the vampire of folklore and the New Age "wannabe"?

JY: I may do one last piece, *In the Company of Vampires*, after I finish *Vampires from A to Z*. After that, who knows? I'll certainly stay with the genre. I'm as fascinated by The Undead as the next guy. Don't ask me why!

"I WON'T EAT PEOPLE!"

So sings the antisocial member of a cannibal tribe in Michael Flanders & Donald Swann's comic song. "Eating people," says this rebel, "is wrong."

Elsewhere we mention the *gúl* or ghoul, the inhuman monster that in Muslim mythology feeds on human corpses. In other mythologies there are similar cannibals. Saturn ate his children. More connected to the subject of vampires is the real human cannibal who tries to consume the spirit with the flesh of the dead.

People in various cultures have long believed in a sympathetic magic by which, for instance, eating the heart of a slain enemy might confer some of his courage on the victor. (Courage like love is often supposed to reside in the heart. Think of "disheartened", "You Gotta Have Heart" in *Damn Yankees*, and the Cowardly Lion in *The Wizard of Oz* in search of a heart.) The Indians of North and South America dried and powdered the hearts of slain enemies and consumed them for courage, and the worshippers of the African god Ogun among the Yoruba still do. The Inuit (formerly called Eskimos or "meat-eaters") used to eat a bit of the heart and drink the blood of their first victims in war, says Sir James Frazer in *The Golden Bough*, and he cites other examples from the Efugaos of The Philippines, and various peoples of Australia, Indo-China, etc. Other peoples ate brains for wisdom or drank blood.

Similarly, people have eaten parts of their dead relatives to confer some kind of immortality on them (they live on in the living, becoming part of them) or just to show respect lest the ghosts come to bother the living. In Papua-New Guinea as late as the middle of this century, cannibals ate their dead relatives. This produced a disease similar to mad cow disease (the brain of the sufferer being found at autopsy to be spongy) which in Papua-New Guinea killed one percent of the population every year and still broke out (the incubation period being very long) decades after this gruesome feasting was stopped. The incidence of ghosts, it is reported, has risen there since cannibalism was repressed. But if the corpse is eaten the vampire is going to find it hard to come back.

The vampire legend depends upon the belief that one can consume the soul or virtues of the victim, a belief which, without desiring to be blasphemous, I must say is identical to The Eucharist in the Christian religion: communicants symbolically consume the body and blood of the sacrificed God. Reports of the madness of alleged vampires may have some connection with the ill effects of drinking contaminated blood. At least the Christian communicants eat the sacrificial victim only magically transubstantiated, not human flesh and blood. The health hazard in passing the chalice is negligible compared to the terrible diseases transmitted by the ingestion of human flesh and blood.

Some people may say that holding superstitions is bad for the brain whether it kills you or not. Do you think you have "holes in your head?"

THE BIMBO MEETS THE MUMMY

The vamp, very much alive, is not a vampire in any but the metaphorical sense. She is, however, worth mentioning to illustrate how the myth of the seductive predator is applied. The mummy, as in Boris Karloff's film of that title of 1932 and many imitations that followed, is indeed a reanimated corpse and dangerous, but it is not a vampire, either.

The mummy and other horror characters sometimes have appeared with vampires in horror gala films. *I Walked with a Zombie, Devil Doll, Invasion of the Body Snatchers, Blood Feast*, and *I Was a Teenage Werewolf* are related to the vampire movie. They indicate a need to bolster a declining interest in the basic vampire story, just as fresh elements are introduced to jazz up one of the latest films, *Bordello of Blood* (1996). Really terrible movies have had the vampire "meet" the Marx Brothers, Abbott & Costello, and other comedy teams, even Mickey Mouse and other cartoon characters. The vampire adds spice to any entertainment dish.

Similarly, vampires play minor roles in works by Piers Anthony (such as *Robot Adept*, 1988), Richard Bach (*Illusions*, 1977), Ray Bradbury (*The Illustrated Man*, 1951), Lawrence Durrell (*Balthazar*, 1958), John M. Ford (*The Dragon Waiting*, 1983), Ron Goulart (*The Prisoner of Blackwood Castle*, 1984), Robert E. Howard (*Conan the Conqueror*, 1950), James Howe (*Howliday Inn*, 1982), Stephen King (*IT*, 1986), Dean Koontz (*The Haunted Earth*, 1973), T. C. Rypel (*The Deathwind of Vedun*, 1982), Jessica Amanda

Salmonson (*Tomoe Gozen*, 1980), Kathleen Sky (*Death's Angel*, 1981), Florence Stevenson (*The Curse of the Concullens*, 1972), and J. R. R. Tolkein (*The Silmarillion*, 1977), additionally appearing in many short stories and dramas. All these are conveniently presented along with vampire-featured works in Margaret L. Carter's invaluable labor of love, *The Vampire in Literature* (1989).

National Lampoon Class Reunion (1982) suggests that there may have been a vampire in the average high-school class. What about yours?

MANANANGGAL

That's the Filipino vampire, the one with a long tongue that can suck a baby right out of a pregnant woman's womb (unless she sleeps with a bullet on a string around her neck and a little coal dust on her abdomen).

When reports of sightings and horrors were bruited about Manila, Ascunción Albór was shocked. "They usually live in the provinces," was the comment. Alderman Alfonso Bernardo "saw the manananggal fly from her house" and set authorities on Teresita Beronqui, but Bob Tamarkin's lively *Rumor Has It* (1993) reports Ms. Beronqui says she was attacked by the monster (which is why she had too few toes on one foot), that she herself was not the monster. Tamarkin adds:

A teenage wonder woman tackles vampires on TV with a mixture of horror and humor. Can an acrobatic Jewish American Princess defeat the Undead? Can a show like this sell airtime for advertisements? Yes, about 24 minues of the show's hour.

Manananggal experts among the villagers [of the suburb of Quezon City] were unimpressed. She obviously had changed back into human form in such a rush that she forgot her three toes, they said.

Tamarkin goes on to discuss appearances of The Blessed Virgin in Quezon City and psychic surgeons in The Philippines. Of US vampires he writes:

A public vampire exorcism was also employed in Manchester, Vermont, in 1793. A man there had repeated bad luck with wives: Captain Isaac Burton married one woman in 1790, and she died of tuberculosis. He married another woman who also fell ill after the nuptial[s]. Determined not to lose this wife too, the Captain planned to rid himself and his wife of their vampire relatives. A ceremony was held in which over one thousand people watched the body of the Captain's old [i.e., first] wife dug up. Her organs were removed and burned. This didn't change the Captain's luck, however, his second wife also died.

In the sixties and seventies there was a rash of vampire movies from the Philippines which were incredibly bad. Here's a dozen of them. What a Trash Festival they could make if all shown together!

Batman Fights Dracula
  (1967)
Blood Drinkers (1966)
Blood Thirst (1965)
The Bloodless Vampire (1965)
Curse of the Vampires (1970)
Malikmata (1967)
*Men of Action Meet Women
  of Dracula* (1969)
Ng manugang ni Drakila
  (Secrets of Dracula,
  1964)
The Thirsty Dead (1974)
Tore ng diabolo
  (Devil's Tower, 1969)
Vampira (1961)
Vampire Hookers (1979)

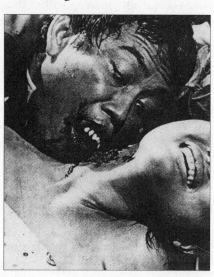

Filipino vampire in *The Blood Drinkers*, 1966.

UNDEAD CREATURES

Some people in the Balkans believed that the undead could return in the shape of totemic animals, such as wolves. The Swedish gypsies said that the undead could appear as birds or horses, and the gypsies of what once was Yugoslavia said that even vegetables such as watermelons and pumpkins could contain the spirits of the undead.

A FEW EASY WAYS OF COPING WITH THE VAMPIRE

✠ Cross the arms of a corpse as you are burying it (at a crossroads, I suspect).
✠ Watch out noon to midnight for these are the hours of operation according to the superstitions of Russia and some countries of Central Europe.
✠ Force the vampire to swear "by my shroud" he or she will never return. Not easy.
✠ Put a lemon in the mouth of a corpse. It will not then become a vampire.
✠ Nail the corpse to the coffin, face down.

SUPERSTITIONS OF OLD RUSSIA

The Kashoubes say that when a Vieszy as they call the Vampire, wakes from his sleep within the grave, he begins to gnaw his hands and feet; and as he gnaws, one after another, first his relations, then his other neighbours, sicken and die. When he has finished his own store of flesh, he rises at midnight and destroys cattle, or climbs a belfry and sounds the bell. All who hear the ill-omened tones will soon die. But generally he sucks the blood of sleepers. Those on whom he has operated will be found next morning dead, with a very small wound on the left side of the breast, exactly over the heart. The Lusatian Wends hold that when a corpse chews its shroud or sucks its own breast, all its kin will soon follow it to the grave. The Wallachians say that a murony—a sort of cross between a werewolf and a vampire, connected by name with our nightmare—can take the form of a dog, a cat, or a toad, and also of any blood-sucking insect. When he is exhumed, he is found to have long nails of recent growth on his hands and feet, and blood is streaming from his eyes, ears, nose and mouth.

—W.R.S. Ralston (1873)

About the beginning of the nineteenth century there occurred in Russia one of the most frightful cases of vampirism on record. The governor of the province of Tch– was a man of about sixty years old, of a cruel and jealous disposition. Clothed with despotic authority, he exercised it without stint, as his brutal instincts prompted. He fell in love with the pretty daughter of a subordinate officer. Although the girl was betrothed to a young man whom she loved, the tyrant forced her father to consent to his having her marry him; and the poor victim, despite her despair, became his wife. His jealous disposition soon exhibited itself. He beat her, confined her to her room for weeks together, and prevented her seeing anyone except in his presence. He finally fell sick and died. Finding his end approaching, he made her swear never to marry again, and with fearful oaths threatened that if she did he would return from his grave and kill her. He was buried in the cemetery across the river, and the young widow experienced no further annoyance until, getting the better of her fears, she listened to the importunities of her former lover, and they were again betrothed.

On the night of the customary betrothal feast, when all had retired, the old mansion was aroused by shrieks proceeding from her room. The doors were burst open, and the unhappy woman was found lying on her bed in a swoon. At the same time a carriage was heard rumbling out of the courtyard. Her body was found to be black and blue in places, as from the effects of pinches, and from a slight puncture in her neck drops of blood were oozing. Upon recovering, she stated that her deceased husband had suddenly entered her room, appearing exactly as in life, with the exception of a dreadful pallor; that he had unbraided her for her inconstancy, and then beaten and pinched her most cruelly. Her story was disbelieved; but the next morning the guard stationed at the other end of the bridge which spans the river reported that just before midnight a black coach-and-six had driven furiously past without answering their challenge.

The new governor, who disbelieved the story of the apparition, took nevertheless the precaution of doubling the guards across the bridge. The same thing happened, however, night after night, the soldiers declaring that the toll-bar at their station near the bridge would rise of itself, and the spectral equipage would sweep past them, despite their efforts to stop it. At the same time every night the watchers, including the widow's family and the servants, would be thrown into a heavy sleep; and every morning the young victim would be found bruised, bleeding, and swooning as before. The town was thrown into consternation. The physicians had no explanations to offer; priests came to pass the night in prayer, but as midnight approached, all would be seized with the same terrible lethargy. Finally the archbishop of the province came and performed the ceremony of exorcism in person. On the following morning the governor's widow was found worse than ever. She was brought to death's door.

The governor was finally driven to take the severest measures to stop the ever-increasing panic in the town. He stationed fifty Cossacks along the bridge, with orders to stop the spectral carriage at all hazards. Promptly at the usual hour it was heard and seen approaching from the direction of the cemetery. The officer of the guard and a priest bearing a crucifix planted themselves in front of the toll-bar and together shouted: "In the name of God and the Czar, who goes there?" Out of the coach was thrust a well-remembered head, and a familiar voice responded: "The Privy Council of State and Governor C—!" At the same moment the officer, the priest, and the soldiers were flung aside, as by an electric shock, and the ghostly equipage passed them before they could recover breath.

The archbishop then resolved as a last expedient to resort to the time-honoured plan of exhuming the body and driving an oaken stake through its heart. This was done with great religious ceremony in the presence of the whole populace. The story is that the body was found gorged with blood, and with red cheeks and lips. At the instant that the first blow was struck upon the stake a groan issued from the corpse and a jet of blood spouted high into the air. The archbishop pronounced the usual exorcism, the body was reinterred, and from that time no more was heard of the vampire.

—Helena Petrovna Blavatsky (published 1910)

VAMPIRE SONG

Not "the music of the night" (the howling of wolves) but a French music-hall song that celebrated the infamous Sgt. Bertrand, who was caught in 1849 desecrating corpses in Parisian graveyards and was popularly referred to as a vampire. Long after the event of mid-century came a *chanson complainte* popular in the music halls of Paris and composed by Jean Bal. It was *Le Vampire de Muy; ou, Le Violeur de cadavres* (The Vampire of Muy; or, The Violator of Corpses).

Le Vampire of Charles Nodier is often described as if it were opera or a usual melodrama. Actually this dramatic collaboration—Nodier wrote it, after he had been annoyed at being charged with writing what he considered an inferior vampire piece, along with Pierre Carmouche and Achille Jouffrey—contained only one song, a warning of impending disaster. This is it, with my translation.

Quand le soleil de ces déserts,	When the sun deserted mountain
Des monts ne dore plus le cime,	Peaks no longer bathes in light,
Alors lese anges des enfers	And the angels of the underworld
Viennent caresser leur victime.	Their victim come to blight,
Si leur douce voix vous endort,	Fear their sweet hypnotic voices.
Reculez!...leur main est glacée!...	Flee their icy hands and breath.
Gardez-vous, jeune fiancée,	Save yourself, young bride, from evil.
De l'amour qui donne la mort.	Flee the love that brings you death.

PROTECTION AGAINST EVIL

Sir Henry Rawlinson and Edwin Norris in *Cuneiform Inscriptions of Western Asia* (1866) give us this amuletlike message for their twenty-second example:

> The phantom, child of heaven,
> which the gods remember,
> the *Innin* [demon] prince
> of the lords
> the [*something missing here*]
> which produces painful fever,
> the vampyre which attacks man,
> the *Uruku* [more demons] multifold
> upon humanity
> may they never seize him!

If this is a prayer, it may work like this, unless (of course) you think the gods to whom it was directed are mere superstitions. If it is a magical formula, assuming (of course) you believe in magic, the missing bit might render it wholly ineffective. Plenty more on amulets and talismans in *The Complete Book of Spells, Curses, and Magical Recipes.*

TWO ROMANIAN FOLKTALES

Collected from the oral tradition, these two reveal the pride the peasantry took in Dracula as a wise if strict ruler and also the contempt in which they held outsiders, such as the Greeks. Dracula was long regarded in Wallachia not as a monster but as a national hero. Dracula was the man who terrified the Turks and turned back the Muslim forces of the Ottoman Empire.

In modern times the government of Romania for quite a while resisted visits to Dracula sites by vampire-lovers. They preferred to think of Dracula as a hero of the faith and a defender of his country.

Here are two out of many stories the peasantry handed down from one generation to another. In that oral tradition, I have created my own adaptions of the tales. The essence of each, however, is preserved.

BAT WORSHIPPERS

Back in the days when Dracula was the ruler of Wallachia there was a merchant from Florence who traveled all over the country and with him he took much merchandise and much money.

At Tirgoviste [the capital] the merchant went directly to Dracula's palace and asked for servants to look after himself, his merchandise, and the money he was carrying with him.

Dracula told him he was welcome to sleep in the palace but that he must leave his merchandise and his money right in the middle of the public square in his carriage. From such a ruler such an order, however insecure it made the merchant, had to be obeyed, and it was.

During the night someone stole 160 gold ducats from the money in the carriage. The merchant next morning found his merchandise undisturbed but that sum missing and he went to Dracula and told him about the theft. Dracula told him that there was no need for concern, that the thief and the gold would soon be found. Secretly, he ordered his servants to place 160 gold ducats in the carriage—plus one.

He publicly ordered the citizens of Tirgoviste to find the thief, saying that if the thief were not found the whole capital would be destroyed.

The merchant went back to his carriage and counted his money only to discover that the gold ducats had reappeared but that there was one ducat too many. He returned to Dracula and thanked him, saying that all his money had been returned—and that there was one ducat more.

At that very moment the thief was brought before Dracula and summarily ordered to be impaled. Then Dracula turned to the merchant and said, "If you had not told me about that extra ducat his fate would also have been yours."

That is the way that Dracula conducted himself both with his subjects and with strangers who passed through his domains.

The story is told in Wallachia of a Greek monk, crafty like all of his kind, who as he traveled met a poor Orthodox priest, an honest and God-fearing man. They argued theology fiercely, the Greek attacking all the Romanians and all their beliefs.

"If you think we are all so stupid and uncouth," said the priest, "why don't you go back to where you came from, back to the wily and sophisticated Greeks?"

Dracula heard of their disputes and ordered both of them to come before him.

On the appointed day they arrived and Dracula gave them audience in two separate rooms. The Greek monk was proud to have been received by the prince and did not know that the Orthodox priest had also been summoned. The priest, for his part, in his humility could not understand why the prince would want to see him but determined he would do his best and take the opportunity to put in a good word for his flock.

Dracula had his own ideas. He was going to find out as much as he could from these two different sources.

To the Greek monk Dracula said: "Reverend Sir, you have traveled widely in my country. Please tell me what you have heard from my people about me."

"Your Highness," replied the conniving monk, "from one end of the country to the other the people have nothing but praise for you. They say a more just man never ruled in Wallachia. All I would ask of Your Highness is that you show your generosity of spirit, that your subjects enjoy, to the holy monks who come from Greece to minister to the spiritual needs of people as you minister to their temporal needs."

"You lie," retorted Dracula. "I know what my people think of the way I must keep order in these domains. You are a deceitful and not a holy man at all, and you insult me by your insincere flattery." And Dracula called the guards and had the monk taken out and impaled.

Human blood flows freely as Aztecs dedicate their temple to Hutziloplchli (1486).

Then Dracula went to the Orthodox priest and asked the same question, "What do my people think of me?"

"It is difficult to answer that question," said the priest, "for the people do not all speak with one voice. But in truth I have to say to Your Highness that some of your people complain of your rigor and claim that you are not addressing their needs. Those people say that life was easier for them under Your Highness' predecessor."

"You are brave to speak thus to a ruler," replied Dracula. "I shall consider what you say and what they say. As for you, you will be my confessor from this day forward. In my court I must have men who have the courage to tell me the truth."

HEMATOMANIA

Bloodlust is not always connected with vampires. But see:

Philip Carden & Ken Mann, *Vampirism: A Sexual Study* (1969)
Beverly Miller, *Blood Lust* (1969)
Richard Noll, *Vampires, Werewolves & Demons* (1992)
Reay Tannahill, *Flesh and Blood: A History of the Cannibal Impulse* (1975)
Charles K. & Myrna Zinck, *Psychological Studies on the Increase of Lycanthropy and Vampirism in America, 1930 - 1941* (1952)

UNUSUAL VAMPIRE BOOKS

Jean Marigny, *Vampires: Restless Creatures of the Night* (1993)
William Myers, *Vampires or Gods?* (1993)
Steven Moore, ed., *Vampires in Verse* (1985)

THE VAMPYRE IN VERSE

The vampire as a Romantic cliché attracted many bad poets, among them "Owen Meredith," as the son of Lord Lytton signed his early work. The father, the first Baron Lytton, was known as a practitioner of the black arts as well as a novelist and dramatist. The son, Edward Robert Bulwer (1831-1891), was a diplomat, a viceroy of India, and, among other writings penned "The Vampyre". It begins:

> I found a corpse, with golden hair,
> Of a maiden seven months dead,

and it ends with wishing she were not a vampire and had lips "Not so very terribly red." You'll find the complete text in Kathryn Petras & Ross Petras' anthology *Very Bad Poetry* (1997), if you want it. There is vampire verse in many languages, if you want that.

VAMPIRES IN THE CLASSROOM

I have mentioned a college course in which the vampire has been seriously studied. The subject certainly lends itself to discussions of important trends in literature and art, psychology and sociology; but, unfortunately, it can be trivialized, and this feeds the resistance to popular culture studies that has, for instance, divided the academic community on the subject of such offerings as "Madonna 101," an extremely popular course on the pop music icon offered at the University of Amsterdam, courses on Marilyn Monroe in the United States, etc.

College professors who attempt to enliven their classes by arriving in historical costume to discuss this or that have long been seen as weird. For instance, when as an adjunct in sociology and education, Gladys G. Palma de Schrynemakers turned up in 1996, in a class at Long Island University, dressed as a vampire for Halloween, her predictable discourse on how women are presented in vampire literature, light even for LIU, was perhaps more damaged than bolstered by the getup. She did not, however, wear fangs; she considered that they "distract people," *The Chronicle of Higher Education* reported.

The fact is that bringing any legitimate but novel popular culture element into the traditional curriculum disturbs the conservatives and must be done with dignity. There is much to be learned about the public mind from the vampire and similar topics. Film departments now take their place almost without apology beside departments of theater and literature and other entertainments. Folklore is a thoroughly respectable subject now. Ray Browne and other pioneers have done yeoman service toward establishing popular culture as an equally respectable academic pursuit. But the study of parapsychology has not reached the level of respectability even of psychology, and courses in vampires are best taught without the black cape. Students having fun make humorless administrations uneasy. Also, many academics feel they must be doing something too easy if the students are enjoying themselves. To them, a popular course of any kind, let alone any kind of course in popular culture, must have something wrong with it.

The book you hold in your hand is far more scholarly, much better researched, than some others I have published on pop culture (among which

I include the plays Shakespeare wrote for the groundlings), but my academic colleagues may well look down their noses at the subject. Don't let them know you *enjoyed* reading it. If you do, my stodgy reputation for immense erudition, built on bulky tomes with footnotes in many languages and specialist articles in literary encyclopedias largely devoted to minor writers about whom no one should give a damn, will go right down the drain.

DRACULA RIDDLES FOR THE UNDER TENS

What's The Count's favorite holiday? (*Fangsgiving*.)

Where did they put Dracula when he was arrested? (*In a red blood cell.*)

What does Dracula say when he is ready for another victim? (*Necks!*)

What did Dracula rob? (*A blood bank*.)

What is Dracula's state of mind? (*He's batty*.)

What do you call two vampires who have a friendly relationship? (*Best Fiends.*)

Al Lewis, as Grandpa, left *The Munsters* to host his own horror show, run a restaurant, and run for governor of New York State. On *The Munsters* he was supposed to be 350 years old, but looked somewhat younger.

DRACULA JOKE

He can't sleep nights. His work is draining.

DRACULA LIQUEUR

A decade after its introduction in 1987, the Dracula Liqueur, blood-red, in a black bottle with a fanged cap, sold with a rack of test tubes for drinking it, seems not to have been deathless.

WHAT DOES COUNT DRACULA LOOK LIKE?

Vampires are supposed to be gaunt, pale, a lot more evil-looking than (say) George Hamilton, who is perpetually tanned, but in all the modern representations of The Count one thing that Stoker insisted upon about Dracula's

Béla Lugosi in a publicity shot for Tod Browning's *Dracula* (1931). The essential US Dracula.

appearance is most often neglected. Where is his moustache? Stoker describes him at one point as having a moustache and a beard, both dark, and at another time wearing a moustache that is white (presumably because he has not drunk blood lately and is weakening). I can recall only a few instances—the cover of a foreign translation of *Dracula* is one, Leonard Wolf's *Annotated Dracula* another, Dell's paperback edition a third.

UNUSUAL VAMPIRES

Playing around with the traditions is necessary, even though people appear to be able to tolerate one repetitive vampire movie or one vampire paperback after another with little innovation. But writers get bored with writing what happened to Mina after Stoker's story ends, or what came before it, or ringing the obvious changes on the same old stuff. Their vampires may not come from Transylvania anymore. Now they may be cyberpunks. Among unusual vampires has been a professor at a university in Los Angeles, a San Francisco policeman, New York undead who are followers of Zen and don't want to kill to survive, a vampire called Weyland who has no fangs but a sting under his tongue, reluctant and sadly lonely and romantic vampires (a recent trend in the fiction), vampires in black leather, a vampire overlord (Master of The City) who nonetheless saves the life of the official vampire-killer of the state of Missouri, non-Christian vampires (who are not afraid of the crucifix), a vampire reanimated by pouring blood onto dust in a coffin (Instant Vampire, just add blood and stir—this is my favorite, and I have mentioned it several times in print), and Robert Bloch's faked but staked vampire in *The Living Dead*.

NOT VAMPIRES

History has accused some people of being vampires who were not so, however strange or bloodthirsty they were. One is the Countess Elizabeth

Bàthory, of seventeenth-century Hungary. She had some 600 young girls murdered over a period of years because she believed bathing in their blood would help her complexion. Her rank kept her from physical harm; she was walled up in her castle in 1611. She was no more a vampire than Vlad *Tepeş* "Vlad the Impaler." She does turn up in movies, though, as Countess Dracula.

There are—how can we put this politely?—*unusual* real people who like to drink blood and have their social and/or sex lives closely tied up with blood lust and vampire costumes. They find willing blood donors and companionable poseurs. You see them in their black costumes, often with black lipstick and painted eyesockets, hanging around the clubs and discos and after-hours sex joints—if you happen to frequent such places yourself. They won't bother you unless you want them to do so.

BEDSIDE READING

The vampire in literature and legend will rise again in our last chapter, but those who cannot wait can start immediately on the rich harvest of desmodic bedtime stories:

Leonard R. N. Ashley, ed., *Tales of Mystery and Melodrama* (1977)
E. F. Benson, *The Room in the Tower and Other Stories* (1912)
Algernon Blackwood, *The Empty House and Other Ghost Stories* (1906)
Sir Richard Francis Burton, *Vickram and the Vampire* (1869)
Italo Calvino, *The Tale of the Vampires' Kingdom*
Ronald Chetwynd-Hayes, *The House of Dracula* (1987)
F. Marion Crawford, *Uncanny Tales* (1911)
Tony Faivre, *Les Vampires* (1962)
Nancy Garden, *Vampires* (1977)
Joe L. Hensley, *Argent Blood* (1967)
Montague Rhodes James, *A Thin Ghost and Others* (1919)
Gordon Linzer, *The Spy Who Drank Blood* (1984)
Robert Lory, *Dracula Returns!* (1973)
Prosper Merimée, *La Guzla* (1827)
Richard Matheson, *Drink My Red Blood* (1951)
Raymond T. McNally & Radu Florescu,
    In Search of Dracula (1972)
Marilyn Ross, *Barnabas Collins* (1968)
Ossip Schubin, *Vollmondzauber* (1899)
H. G. Wells, *The Stolen Bacillus* (1894)

FOR ADVANCED ITALIAN STUDENTS

G. Davanazati, *Dissertazione sopra i vampiri* (2nd edn. Napoli, 1789)
G. Strafforello, *Errori e pregiudizi volgari* (2nd edn., Milano, 1901)
Z. Zanetti, *La Medicina della nostre donne* (*Città di Castello*, 1892)

OBSCURITIES FOR HISPANICISTS

N. Oñeca, *Los Vampiros* (a *zarzuelo*, music by A. Rubio, 1894)
Miguél Tercuate, *El Vampiro de la autopista* (1967)
José Seoane, *Cuento de aparecidos* (1963)
Dalton Trevisan, *O Vampiro de Curitaba* (1965)

This exotica is included simply to remind readers that, particularly concerning vampires, there is a vast foreign literature, not only in the classical Greek and Latin and scholarly Germanic and Slavic languages, in which
the vampire is a notable subject. Elsewhere I shall list a lot of foreign vampire flicks for you, because even if you do not command foreign languages
movies usually can get a lot across. In fact, there is (or was, because lots
of the old celluloid has perished) a considerable number of vampire movies
made in the teens of this century which though silent managed to entertain and even frighten very effectively. Words are not so important in the
cinema. Cinema, after all, puts dialogue and music to good use but means,
essentially and most powerfully, *moving pictures*. The vampire makes a very
striking icon.

101 DALMATIANS

Just a joke. Far more residents of Dalmatia than that believed in vampires,
if we are to credit the Abbot Giovanni Battista Alberto Fortis (1740-1803),
whose *Viaggio in Dalmazia* was translated into English in 1778. He
recorded belief in "the reality of witches, fairies, enchantments, nocturnal apparitions, and sortileges, as if they had seen a thousand examples
of them" and:

> Nor do they make the least doubt about the existence of Vampires;
> and attribute to them, as in Transylvania, the sucking the blood
> of infants. Therefore when a man dies suspected of becoming a
> vampire, or Vukodlak, as they call it, they cut his hams, and prick
> his whole body with pins; pretending that after this operation he
> cannot walk about.

THE NIGHT STALKER

The old Television series of that name lives again on e-mail MSKolchak@ suba.com and PO Box 4000, Venter Line, MI 48015.

SOME VAMPIRE CONNECTIONS

Bram Stoker International Youth Club, 42 Grange Park Grove, Raheny, Dublin 5, Ireland

British Vampire Society, Allen J. Gittens, 38 Westcroft, Chippenham, Wiltshire, 5N4 OLY, England

Club Vampyre, Riyn Gray, 1764 Lugonia, Suite 104 # 223, Redlands, CA 92374

Count Dracula Fan Club, Penthouse North, 29 Washington Square West, New York, NY 10011

P. N. Elrod Fan Club, PO Box 100362, Fort Worth, TX 76185

International Society of Vampires, Michelle Belanger, PO Box 474, Hinckley, OH 44233

Nox, PO Box 2467, Grand Central Station, New York, NY 10163

Shadows of the Night, PO Box 17006, Rochester, NY 14617

Translyvania Society of Dracula, Nicolae Padararu, 47 Primaverii Blvd., Bucharest 1, Romania

Transylvanian Society of Dracula, PO Box 91611, Santa Barbara, CA 93190

Vampire Guild, Phill White, 82 Ripcroft, Southwell, Portland, Dorset DT5 2EE England

Vampire's Crypt, Margaret Carter, 105 Phipps Lane, Annapolis, MD 21403

Vampire Research Institute, PO Box 21067, Seattle, WA 98111

LIFE ENERGIES SUCKED OUT

Mary E. Wilkins Freeman, *Luella Miller*

Fritz Lieber, *The Girl with the Hungry Eyes*

Harlan Ellison, *Try a Dull Knife*

THE TABLOID PRESS

VAMPIRE KILLINGS SWEEP U.S.

A terrifying wave of vampire killings is sweeping the nation and experts believe that the bloodthirsty murderers may be responsible for as many as 6,000 deaths a year.

Police are investigating dozens of eerie murders which have left pale, broken bodies of victims drained of blood—sometimes horribly mutilated and bearing the evidence of ghoulish Satanic rituals. They include:

✠ A double murder in New York City in which the victims were so completely drained of blood that the medical examiner couldn't get enough for a sample.

✠ Six Sacramento, Calif., people who were murdered by a man who later admitted drinking the blood of his victims.

✠ A 7-year-old Bronx, N.Y., boy who was found hanging upside down, the blood drained from his horribly mutilated body.

✠ Nine hobos who were killed in California, each on the night of the full moon, by a murderer who also drank their blood.

"There is no doubt that some of these creatures need as much human blood as a pint a day," said Dr. Stephen Kaplan, chief of the Vampire Research Center in Elmhurst, N.Y. "They can't buy it. It requires a prescription. I believe that these people sometimes grab hitchhikers to satisfy their blood lust."

Martin V. Riccardo, president of the Vampire Studies Society based in suburban Chicago, said interviews with people who have survived vampire attacks have convinced him that "there is definitely something to the legends of the undead. There are too may things in common," he said. "People will describe a ball of light, a cloud, or mist before an attack."

Riccardo cited the Rev. Dr. Donald Omand of Devon, England, an exorcist who was attacked and bloodied by one of three vampires he admits to having encountered.

He was preparing to exorcise a 25-year-old Swede when the man suddenly leaped at him. Spitting and snarling, the blood-mad creature began tearing at this throat. The vampire had to be dragged off the priest by half-a-dozen burly attendants.

"One of the most interesting things the Rev. Omand discovered," said Riccardo, "is that when people are bitten by one of these creatures they develop the vampire symptoms themselves."

—*Weekly World News*, 2 December 1980

IF YOU ARE GOING TO TRANSYLVANIA

Before you fly to Bucharest (which like some other capitals of Central Europe recently freed from the controls of communism is chock-a-block with pickpockets and other thieves that make tourism these days an adventurous gamble), contact the Translylvanian Dracula Society at Petru Rareş Square No. 7A, 4400 Bistria, Romania (40-63-73-98-03). They have information on guided tours of Dracountry, but you are best off assembling a little party to rent a car. Why not take your itinerary from Jonathan Harker in Stoker's *Dracula*? Don't miss what Stoker calls the Borgo (that is Bîrgau) Pass, but do not expect to see Dracula's castle. There isn't one. What is called Dracula's Castle is a hotel Zacharary Margoulis and other visitors have described kindly as "cheesy." The locals believe in ghosts (such as *ieli* and *strigoi*) but not in vampires. Surely they would know!

MORE STRANGE VAMPIRES

The oddest I can think of are: the one blown up with a grenade by a fellow American soldier in 'Nam (Douglas Drake's *Something Had to Be Done*, (1976), the one who is not dead (Suzy McKee Charnas' *The Vampire Tapestry*, (1980), the real-life monster Peter Kürten ("I need blood as others need

The British pantomine Dame (man in drag) tradition produced Arthur Lucan as Old Mother Riley from *Old Mother Riley's Ghosts* (1941) to *My Son, the Vampire* (1952). Béla Lugosi is a criminal who believes he is a vampire but the cleaning lady does him in.

Christopher Lee in his first outing as a vampire, a part that he was to play more times than any other actor. Although on television he played every kind of role from Prince Philip to a Neo-Nazi leader, he never played a vampire there.

alcohol"), and the ones who are only actors pretending to be vampires (to frighten a murderer into a confession in the old film of *London after Dark*).

WEBLIOGRAPHY

An ugly new word, but there has to be some concept of keeping track of all the websites, of which there are thousands upon thousands dedicated to vampires. As I write, hundreds are being added daily. Good search engines are available. Log on and start looking on the World Wide Web. Besides *Vampire Pages* check (say) *Role Playing Games*, etc. There are also reference lists of horror writers (http://www.cat.pdx.educaseyh/horror/author /index.html) and other sites with names as awkward, including booksellers with lists of vampire organizations and publications, filmographies, homepages for Dracula and others, and much more.

A PROBLEM

"How do you kill something already dead, or 'undead'?" *Dracula* (1931).

From *Midi-Minuit Fantastique* 4–5; a rare 1963 Dracula issue.

Liberty Hall.

MANAGER, - - - - - - - - J. C. MYERS.
STAGE MANAGER, - - - - - ASA CUSHMAN, Jr.

SPLENDID ATTRACTION.
Another Great Drama.

This Evening will be presented the grand Legendary Drama of the

VAMPIRE!

This strange monster is well authenticated—chiefly known in Germany. It is said that if a dead person be exposed to the first rays of the rising moon which touch the earth, a false life is installed into the corpse, which possesses movement and all signs of ordinary existence, except that there is no pulsation in the heart. This creature, living against the will of Heaven, eats not, drinks not, nor does he require the refreshment of sleep. This Phantom recruits his life by drawing the life blood from the veins of the living, but more especially it chooses victims from amongst maidens pure and spotless. As the body of this monster is bloodless, so his face is said to be as pale as death. The Vampire can be destroyed by fire or by bullet, which must pierce his heart.

LUCY PEVERYL, ADA RABY,	MISS ANNIE SENTER.
THE VAMPIRE, ALAN RABY,	MR. HARRY LANGDON,

Thursday Evening, May 29th, 1862,

Will be presented for the first time in this city the Legendy Drama in 2 acts entitled the

VAMPIRE!

Or, The Spectre of Mount Snowden!

The Vampire,	Mr. Harry Langdon
LORD ALBERT CLAVERING,	MR. C. E. BIDWELL
SIR HUGH NEVILLE,	MR. W. C. RAYMOND
SIR GUY MUSGROVE,	MR. A. CUSHMAN
RALPH SWINE,	MR. M. HURLEY
DAVY ROEBECK,	MR. H. F. STONE
Lucy Peveryl,	Miss Annie Senter
MAUDE OF GREYSTOCK,	MISS MINNIE JACKSON
JANET,	MRS. H. F. STONE

100 years are supposed to have elapsed between the 1st and 2d. acts.

Alan Raby,	Mr. Harry Langdon
COLONEL RABY,	MR. W. C. RAYMOND
EDGAR, (his son,)	MR. C. E. BIDWELL
DR. REESE,	MR. J. MURRAY
CORPORAL STUMP,	MR. H. F. STONE
CURATE,	MR. M. HURLEY
Ada Raby,	Miss Annie Senter
JENNY,	MISS ANNIE HYATT

Favorite Songs,	Mrs. H. F. Stone.
Grand Pas Seul,	Miss Minnie Jackson.

To conclude with the drama in one act, entitled

ROBERT MACAIRE!

Or, The Two Murderers!

ROBERT MACAIRE,			MR. HARRY LANGDON.
Jaques Strop,	Mr. H. F. Stone	Charles,	Mr. M. Hurley
Mons. Dumont,	Mr. J. Murray	Francois,	Mr. Merewether
Germeuil,	Mr. W. C. Raymond	Marie,	Miss Annie Hyatt
Pierre,	Mr. C. E. Bidwell	Clementina,	Mrs. H. F. Stone

☞ Friday Evening, May 30, Benefit of J. C. MYERS, and last night of the season.

Admission 15 and 25 Cents. : : : Reserved Seats 35 Cents.
DOORS OPEN AT 7—TO COMMENCE AT 7 3-4 O'CLOCK.

☞ Seats can be procured at the Box Office from 10 to 12 o'clock, and from 2 to 4 ☜

2

The Vampire in European Tradition

BLOOD RITES

The feasts of the goddess Cybele in ancient times involved sacrifices of blood from the priests and on the last day of the festival devotées sometimes cut off fingers or otherwise shed blood in her honor. This is but one of many primitive ceremonies in which persons shed their own blood, and there were many sacrifices to deities which involved the shedding of the blood of animals—the Jews eventually turned to offering bread and wine instead—and even humans (often captured in war expressly for this purpose). These rites contributed something to the bloody myth of the vampire, stealing the soul and the life of victims.

VAMPIRES IN ANGLO-SAXON BRITAIN

Among the many demons and marauding mares (as in nightmares) that the Anglo-Saxons feared was the violent nightstalker who devoured human beings. The fear went back to the dark, Teutonic woods that these people left to invade Britain. One of these monsters was the ferocious Grendel. He terrorizes the mead hall in the epic *Beowulf*. Scholar Raymond McNally wants to classify Grendel as a vampire, but Grendel is not after the souls of the humans. They are just food to him (and presumably to his mother, Grendel's Dam). Those whom he tears and eats do not become nightstalkers themselves, just leftovers.

Such monsters may recall collective memories of early man's fear of wild animals—bears and, earlier, saber-toothed tigers—snatching unprotected sleeping humans. Animal or semi-animal creatures that come by night are not full-fledged vampires. I know that in movies, where metamorphosis is so easy to accomplish and so dramatic—whether it be Dr. Jekyll turning into Mr. Hyde or an American teenager turning into a wolf (of the non-slang sort)—vampires turn into bats, but self-respecting vampires are animated human corpses. They would not think of changing into any other form. If they could, surely they would choose a form harder to battle than a corpse that can easily be seen, traced to its coffin if necessary, and staked or burned. On the other hand, the difficulty of getting out of sealed and buried coffins—the better class of vampires in movies always seem to have mausoleums—has caused some vampires to be portrayed as spirits that can leave the corpse and materialize elsewhere. That, I suppose, could be bat form, just as demons can take animal form as familiars of legend.

Most vampires are, like living humans, stuck with a human body. Heinrich von Wlislocki (1893) and others say that Transylvanians believed a vampire could transform himself or herself into a beetle, a black dog, a butterfly, even a piece of straw. But that, along with the idea that vampires can mate with humans or that they are invariably heterosexual, has since been said to be mere superstition.

VAMPIRES IN TWELFTH-CENTURY BRITAIN

The British have always been afraid of ghosts, goblins, bogeys, and other creatures of the night. From their earliest youth there is always something under the bed or in the wardrobe. As Coleridge says, some frightful fiend "doth close behind them tread." The British enjoy a high if not preeminent place in the history of fiction suffused with the supernatural. They certainly have the best ghost stories, even if they have no equivalent of Transylvania.

Vampires are mentioned in various monkish manuscripts from Britain. In early days, rumors, if not news, traveled pretty effectively. People who were in isolated communities were more than ready to believe visitors who arrived with tales of people who existed elsewhere with (say) heads below their shoulders. The credulous did not doubt at all stories of giants and supernatural monsters. History, never more than a kind of lie agreed upon, mingled the actual and the marvelous. In the histories of Gildas, Nennius, and Geoffrey of Monmouth, fact and legend are difficult or impossible to separate. Geoffrey (for instance) claimed to be translating a Welsh history from a manuscript found among the Britons on The Continent (in Brittany) but most likely his is a great work of fiction. The real warlord Arthur in Geoffrey's imagination becomes the King Arthur who stands at the center of what used to be called The Matter of Britain, the great source of enduring legend and national inspiration. Geoffrey's *Historia regum Britanniæ*, finished just before the middle of the twelfth century, influenced centuries of prose and verse and dramatic works that carried on and developed the leads he created. To him we owe a lot of King Arthur and a lot of Spenser, King Lear and Cymbeline and a lot of Shakespeare, much more.

William of Newburgh (*c.* 1135–*c.* 1200) was the principal author of the chronicle kept in his priory. Many religious institutions of the time kept up chronicles and wrote histories. In his *Historia rerum anglicanum* (edited by Hamilton in 1856) one of the subjects he addressed was vampires, for he had heard stories from a couple of other clergymen. He cites several cases. At the same time that he damned Geoffrey of Monmouth for lying "saucily and shamelessly," William of Newburgh wrote down the incredible tales that others told him with a straight face, probably believing.

Stephen told William of a man who had come back from the dead on several occasions and thrown himself violently on his wife and family, but he does not seem to have been after their blood. One can understand completely why Christians would be ready to believe that a man could come back from the dead. One can understand equally well why Christian mercy and forgiveness may often be lacking, and why the first thing that occurred to people was to get this guy totally out of the picture—by violent means if necessary but right away in any case.

The bishop of Lincoln refused requests to have the body burned. He wrote the corpse a sort of note he could take to God. The absolution in the bishop's own handwriting was placed in the tomb with the corpse and there was no further disturbance in the neighborhood. The reluctance to burn a corpse was enlightened. However, it was not to be found all over the country in the twelfth century.

A monk of Melrose Abbey told William of a dead man from Alnwick Castle who was said to have risen from his grave on a number of occasions, passed among the populace, and spread contagion by the odor of the grave, of which many died. He seems also to have been a vampire, because when the townspeople dug up the corpse to destroy it, the body was gorged with blood. They burned it. The plague ceased. The people he killed had not been bitten and so they did not become vampires. Thus the destruction of the one vampire full of blood was sufficient and not, as we might say, a drop in the bucket.

Walter Map or Mapes (*c.* 1137-1209) was of Welsh extraction like Geoffrey of Monmouth. Geoffrey became bishop of St. Asaph. Walter rose in the English church to be archdeacon of Oxford. McNally gets this all wrong; he calls Map "Archbishop of Oxford," but England has only two archbishops, of course, Canterbury and York. Montague Rhodes James, whose name we encounter whenever we delve into matters of the occult in Britain, edited in 1915 Map's record of court gossip of his time, *De Nugis curialium*. Map was at one time a member of the royal household and a charming gossip. In that work there is a female vampire (or, better, a woman possessed of a demon). A church key pressed against her face seared the skin, much like the crucifix seared the flesh of vampires in the movies until the faith of the audiences waned so much that they could no longer be asked to credit the power of the cross.

Of the twelfth-century cases and a few in the thirteenth century, Jean Marigny, in "*La Tradition légendaire du vampire au Europe*" (in a University of Grenoble publication, 1987), remarks that "contrary to what one might expect, [these] are not set in remote parts of Europe, but in England and Scotland."

THE ARMY OF GOD

Perhaps because they thought themselves better armed, in a spiritual way, to battle the forces of evil than secular authorities might, battalions of The Church Militant, monks, nuns, and priests of the Roman Catholic Church, in the Middle Ages and later, actively took on the fighting of vampires and other horrors. Dr. Van Helsing, in *Dracula*—for all his scientific training—carries one of their weapons against the Undead, the crucifix.

St. Catherine of Siena was a good example of the confidence of the holy in their approach to fighting evil: she drank the water in which she had washed the sores of lepers and she invited The Devil to a *mano a mano*. She was unafraid both physically and spiritually. While some ecclesiastical authorities preached caution and humility and said "do not tempt God" and "be very afraid" of The Devil and all forms of evil, the heroines and heroes of righteousness often boldly and bravely confronted any evil they could. It was not just The Society of Jesus that thought of itself as God's army, disciplined and devout.

My former colleague in The City University of New York, Jo Anne Kay McNamara, calls her ground-breaking history of Catholic nuns *Sis-*

ters in Arms (1996). She writes of many brave women who confronted evil head-on in the faith of their times.

IMMIGRANTS' FEAR OF VAMPIRES LED TO DEATH

That was a headline in the staid *Times* of London in January 1973 when it was discovered that a retired potter of Polish descent in Britain's potteries area, in Stoke-on-Trent, was hoisted (as you might say) by his own precautions. He had locked himself in his room, which was full of salt and other protections, even stuffing a clove of garlic into the keyhole. His Polish landlady called the police when he was not heard of for some time. He was found by Constable John Pye, who broke into the room. The Pole had choked to death in his sleep on another clove of garlic. He had put it under his tongue to ward off evil.

THE VAMPIRE OF LONDON

The term is used loosely. Think of "The Vampire of Muy" (Victor Ardisson), "The Vampire of Düsseldorf" (Peter Kürten), "The Vampire of Montparnasse" (Sgt. Bertrand), "The Vampire of Treautenau" (Stephen Hubvner), and other criminals, "The Vampire of London" was better described in the sensational press at the time as "The Acid Bath Murderer," because that is how he disposed of awkward corpses.

He was John George Haigh, ex-choirboy, church organist, compulsive attendee at cathedral services (as many as three a day), a madman who from an early age had terrible dreams in which vampires urged him to drink blood. Mad or not he was tried at the Sussex Assizes and was hanged in 1949. He had murdered 9 people. At his death he left his clothes to Madame Tussaud's, and you can see his waxwork there, looking quite ordinary and unfrightening—which in itself is scary.

LONDON BY DAY

When you are in London take a Dracula tour on your own. (Dracula walked London streets by day, and so can you.) Check 138 Piccadilly, where he stayed (but before the Hard Rock Cafe was next door). See the Regent's Park Zoo, where he visited a wolf. See Hampstead Heath, where Lucy attacked children, and Highgate Cemetery, where she would most likely be buried.

Christopher Lee in *The Horror of Dracula*. The essential British Dracula.

Bram Stoker wrote *Dracula* outside London, but the Lyceum Theatre where he worked so long is still in London. He first lived at 27 Cheney Walk in Chelsea and later moved to 17 St. Leonard's Terrace, a few doors away from where I myself lived for a year or so in the sixties. By then people spoke of "Mark Twain" and Oscar Wilde as if they had just moved out of the neighborhood but seldom thought of Stoker. He died at 5 Fernshaw Mansions, Chelsea.

There is no need to sit on the Stoker bench at Whitby or to go elsewhere to get a connection with *Dracula* or its author. He was a Dublin and London man chiefly.

IRISH VAMPIRES

Vampire women variously named—*dearg-due* is one version—are said to rise from their graves, especially at the New Year, to drink the blood of the living. The Irish used to build cairns on the graves, hoping the stones would keep these monsters from rising from their coffins, it is alleged. More likely, the stones were designed to keep wild animals from digging up the corpses.

Several scholars have noted the contribution to the vampire legend by such Irishmen as Maturin, LeFanu, Wilde, and Stoker.

A POLTERGEIST VAMPIRE

Perhaps the story of Johannes Cuntze of Silesia (1592) could to be told in this book under the rubric "Vampires" or equally well in the next book in the series under "Ghosts and Poltergeists," because he is said to have been both. In this series, we separate the categories in two books. In his life, or death, Cuntze appears to have brought the two together.

An alderman of the town of Pentschen, Cuntze was on his way to dinner with the mayor when his horse developed some trouble with a shoe.

Cuntze dismounted and, in trying to examine the horse, was kicked. He seemed to have been kicked in the head, because immediately he went wild and confessed himself to be a great sinner and complained his body was being consumed with the fires of hell.

He was put to bed and a priest, perhaps even a doctor, was called. A black cat came into the room and jumped on his face and scratched him. Soon after that, he died. There were rumors that this was proof he had been in league with The Devil, a rumor only exacerbated by the sudden terrific storm that accompanied his burial (although old superstition suggests rain at a funeral is a good sign).

Soon his house had a ghost or poltergeist. It was not only haunted by Cuntze, whose ghost tried to get in bed with his widow, but objects were thrown around, noisome smells were evident, doors mysteriously slammed, and the local priest complained that in his sleep Cuntze's ghost came to sit on him heavily or squeeze the life out of him. These disturbances went on for months.

Five months after his internment, Cuntze's tomb was opened. His blood flowed freshly. His body was bloated and heavy.

His corpse was beheaded and burned, and the predations ceased.

VRYKOLAKAS

This is the Greek vampire, a myth stretching back to *keres* and fierce monsters of antiquity. Such tales are still quite alive. Vampires are still much spoken of in Greece.

On Mykonos in 1701 a visiting French botanist reported the exhumation of a murdered man, thought to be a vampire, and the rather inexpert tearing out of his heart (which the local butcher, given the job, rummaged among the intestines to find). The traditional boiling of the heart in vinegar or oil was not followed. The heart was burned, and eventually so was the whole body.

"I have never viewed anything so pitiable as the state of this island," wrote the botanist (M. Pitton de Tornefort) as he left Mykonos in disgust. "Everyone's head was turned; the most sensible people were as stricken as the others."

AN ANTIDOTE AGAINST ATHEISM

Belief in vampires at least helps, in a way, belief in God, and so Henry More (1614-1687), the Cambridge Platonist and theologian, included the fol-

"Good Lady Ducayne" was even older than she looks in this illustration for Mary E. Bradden's vampire tale of this title in *The Strand* magazine (1896).

lowing vampire tale in *An Antidote against Atheism: or, An Appeal to the Natural Faculties of the Mind of Man, whether there be a God* (1653):

A certain shoemaker in one of the chief towns of *Silesia*, in the year 1591, *September*, 20, on a Friday betimes in the morning, in the further part of his house where there was adjoining a little Garden, cut his own Throat with his Shoemaker's knife. The family, to cover the foulness of the fact, and that no disgrace might come upon his Widow, gave out, that he died of an Apoplexy, declined all visits of friends and neighbours, in the meantime got him washed, and laid Linens so handsomely about him, that even they that saw him afterwards, as the Parson, and some others, had not the least Suspicion but that he did die of that disease; so he had honest Burial, with a funeral Sermon, and other circumstances becoming one of his rank and reputation. Six weeks had not past, but so strong a rumour broke out, that he died not of any disease, but had laid violent hands upon himself, that the Magistracy of the place could not but bring all those that had seen the corpse, to a strict examination. They shuffled off the matter as well as they could at first, with many fair Apologies, in behalf of the deceased, to remove all suspicion of so heinous an act: but it being pressed more home to their Conscience, at last they confessed, he died a violent death, but desired their favour and clemency to his widow and children, who were in no fault; adding also, that it was uncertain but that he might be slain by some external mishap, or, if by himself, in some irresistible fit of phrency or madness.

Hereupon the Council deliberate what is to be done. Which the Widow hearing, and fearing they might be determining something that would be harsh, to the discredit of her Husband, and herself, being also animated there to by some busy bodies, makes a great complaint against those that raised these reports of her Husband, and resolved to follow the Law upon them, earnestly contending that there was no reason, upon mere rumours and idle defamations of malevolent people, that her Husband's body should be digged up, or dealt with as if he had been either *Magician*, or *Self-murther*. Which boldness and pertinacity of the woman, though after the confession of the fact, did in some measure work upon the Council, and put them to a stand.

But while these things were in agitation, to the astonishment of the Inhabitants of the place, there appears a *Spectrum* in the exact shape and habit of the deceased, and that not only in the night, but at mid-day. Those that were asleep it terrified with horrible visions; those that were waking it would strike, pull, or press, lying heavy upon them like an *Ephialtes*: so that there were perpetual complaints every morning of their last night's rest through the whole Town. But the more freaks his *Spectrum* play'd, the more diligent were the friends of the deceased to suppress the rumours of them or at least to hinder the effects of those rumours; and therefore made their addresses to the President, complaining how unjust a thing it was, that so much credit should be given to idle reports and blind suspicions, and therefore beseech'd him that he would hinder the Council from digging up the corpse of the deceased, and from all ignominious usage of him: adding also that they intended to appeal to the Emperor's Court, that their Wisdoms might rather decide the Controversy, than that the cause should be determined from the light conjectures of malicious men.

But while by this means the business was still protracted, there were much stirs and tumults over the Town, that they are hardly to be described. For no sooner did the Sun hide its head, but this *Spectrum* would be sure to appear, so that every body was fain to look about him, and stand upon his guard, which was a sore trouble to those whom the Labours of the Day made more sensible of the want of rest in the night. For this terrible *Apparition* would sometimes stand by their bed-sides, sometimes cast itself upon the midst of their beds, would lie close to them, would miserably suffocate them, and would so strike them and pinch them, that not only blue marks, but plain impressions of his fingers would be upon sundry parts of their bodies in the morning. Nay, such violence and impetuousness of this Ghost, that when men forsook their beds, and kept their dining-rooms, with Candles lighted, and many of them in company together, the better to secure themselves from fear and disturbance; yet he would then appear to them and have a bout with some of them, notwithstanding all this provision against it. In brief, he was so troublesome, that the people were ready to forsake their houses, and seek other dwellings, and the Magistrates so awakened at the perpetual complaints of them, that at last they resolved, the President agreeing thereto, to dig up the body.

He had lain in the ground near eight months, *viz.* from *Sept.* 22, 1591, to *April* 18, 1592. When he was digged up, which was in the presence of the Magistracy of the Town, his body was found entire, not at all putrid, no ill smell about him saving the mustiness of the Grave-cloaths, his joints limber and flexible, as in those that are alive, his skin only flaccid, but a more fresh grown in the room of it, the wound of his throat gaping, but no gear of corruption in it; there was also observed a Magical mark in the great toe of his right foot, *viz.* as Excrescency in the form of a Rose.

His body was kept out of earth from *April* 18, to the 24th, at what time many both of the same town and others came daily to view him. These unquiet stirs did not cease for all of this, which they after attempted to appease, by burying the corpse under the Gallows, but in vain; for they were as much as ever, if not more, he now not sparing his own Family: insomuch that his Widow at last went her self to the Magistrate, and told them, that she should be no longer against it, if they thought fit to fall upon some course of more strict proceedings touching her husband.

Wherefore the seventh of *May* he was again digged up, and it was observable, that he was grown more sensibly fleshy since his last internment. To be short, they cut off the Head, Arms, and Legs of the Corpse, and opening his Back, took out his heart, which was as fresh and intire as in a Calf new kill'd. These, together with his Body, they put on a pile of wood, and burnt them to Ashes, which they carefully sweeping together, and putting into a Sack (that none might get them for wicked uses) poured them into the River, after which the *Spectrum* was never seen more.

As it also happen'd in his Maid that dy'd after him, who appeared within eight days after her death, to her fellow servant, and lay so heavy upon her, that she brought upon her a great swelling of the eyes. She so grievously handled a Child in the cradle, that if the Nurse had not come to his help, he had been quite spoil'd; but she crossing her self, and calling upon the Name of *Jesus*, the Spectre vanished. The next night she appeared in the shape of a *Hen*, which, when one of the Maids of her house took to be so indeed, and followed her, the Hen grew into an immense bigness, and presently caught the Maid by the throat, and made it swell, so that she could neither eat nor drink of a good while after.

She continued these stirs for a whole month, slapping some so smartly, that the stroke were heard of them that stood by, pulling the bed also from under others, and appearing sometime in one shape, sometimes in another, as of a Woman, of a Dog, of a Cat, and of a Goat. But at last her body was being digged up, and burnt, the Apparition was never seen more.

UPDATE ON THE COUNTESS BÁTHORY

Whether it is because of the lesbianism or the sanguine aspects of the story I cannot tell, but this horrific woman continues to fascinate. This is evidenced by recent books such as Elaine Bergstrom's *Baroness of Blood* (1995) and André Codrescu's *The Blood Countess* (1995). No wonder, when the story has scenes such as this one (in the words of William Seabrook's *Witchcraft*, 1970) in which

Wrinkles? No problem. Just bathe in the blood of slaughtered virgins, like Countess Báthory did in history or Ingrid Pitt did in the Hammer production, *Countess Dracula* (1970).

on December 30th, 1610, Count Gyorgy Thurzo, her own cousin, the governor of the province, accompanied by soldiers, gendarmes, and the village priest, raided the castle and arrested everybody in it. They had interrupted an orgy of blood. In the main hall of the castle they found one girl drained of blood and dead, another living girl whose body had been pierced with tiny holes, another who had just been tortured. In the dungeons and cellars they found and liberated a number of other girls, some of whose bodies had already been pierced and 'milked,' others intact, plump, well-fed, like well-kept cattle in their stalls. The dead bodies of some fifty more were subsequently exhumed.

The countess, by the way, haughtily refused to attend her trial. Her servants were killed and by order of King Matthias II the countess was walled up in her own castle for the rest of her life.

BASTARDS

It's easy to become a vampire. We have already noted some ways. Some further information: if a (black) bird flies over your corpse, if a nun steps over your corpse, as when you are the victim of a vampire's bite, that's it. If your mother is well along in pregnancy and a vampire just looks at her (with his steely grey eyes), you might be born a vampire. One other cause of vampirism has always been said to be illegitimacy. The illegitimate children of parents themselves illegitimate are believed to be vampires. Were this true, we should be in a great peril where I live (New York City). Here *most* children today are born out of wedlock and soon this will be, like welfare dependency, a problem that society will be forced to confront more effectively than it has done. Already bastardy has become a tradition stretching over generations. We may have to stop calling such births illegitimate.

I. Otescu (whom Montague Summers calls a "prominent authority") in *Credentele Taranului Román despre Cer Și Stele* (Beliefs of the Peasantry of Romania concerning the Sky and the Stars, cited in *Folk-Lore* 37:4, 321) claims that mythical creatures include those that eat the sun and moon and are "the souls of unbaptized children, or of children of unmarried parents, cursed by God and turned into *vârcolaci*," vampires.

A BULGARIAN CUSTOM

Finding the hole by which the vampire entered and exited his or her grave, the Bulgarians used to put there a dish of human excrement and poison it. Human excrement was thought to be a vampire's favorite food—next to blood, of course.

MORE ON GREEK VAMPIRES

The Greek word meaning ghost over the centuries came to mean vampire, and certain Greek islands eventually were said to be especially infected with *vrykolakas*. In 1645 at Cologne was published Leo Allatius's opinions on Greek folklore of the day in *De Græcorum hodie quorundam opiniatibus*. Here is my English approximation of what Alliatus writes:

> The *vrykolakas* is a man of evil and debauched life, very often one excommunicated by a bishop. The corpses of men like this do not undergo decomposition after burial as those of other dead men do

nor do they turn to dust, but having, it appears, a skin of extreme toughness, they swell up and become distended to the extent that the joints can hardly be bent; the skin becomes tight as the head of a drum, and when struck yields a similar sound. The Devil enters into such a body and it comes out of the tomb, chiefly by night, knocking on the doors [of its former home] and calling for someone from the household [to let it in]. If any such answers it, he dies the next day. However, a vampire never calls twice, and so the citizens of Chios protect themselves by always waiting for a second summons after nightfall before they will respond. This monster is said to be so destructive to mankind that, actually appearing in the daytime, even at high noon, and not only in homes but also in fields and along the roads and in the enclosed vineyards, it attacks them as they go, and the mere sight of it without even addressing them or laying a hand on them kills them. Thus it is that whenever any sudden deaths occur without any known cause, the people open the tombs and usually find such a corpse. They then take it out of its grave, the priests recite prayers over it, and it is thrown upon a burning pyre. Before the prayers are even finished the joints of the body gradually unloose. All the remains are burned to ashes. This superstition is not a novel and recent belief in Greece; in ancient and modern times alike pious [priestly] men have heard the confessions of Christians and have attempted to extirpate the belief from the public imagination.

SERBIAN VAMPIRES

In Ornella Volta & Valeria Riva's anthology, *The Vampire* (1963), appears a letter to Dom Augustin Calmet, the French historian of the subject, regarding an investigation by the governor of Serbia, Duke Charles Alexander of Würtemburg, in 1732. This was a time when vampirism in Slavic countries was a sensation all over Europe. The duke, reacting to complaints of the peasantry, sent

a deputation [led by a] public prosecutor of the kingdom, to a village where a notorious vampire, dead many years since, was ravaging his kinsmen; for it is notable that the blood-suckers seek to destroy only their own families. This deputation was composed of respected persons... [and] they were put on oath and accompanied by a lieutenant of the grenadiers... and twenty-four of his men.

Many reputable citizens accompanied the deputation, even the duke himself... in order to have definite proof of the strange occurrences.

When they reached the village they discovered that the vampire had already dispatched three of his nieces and nephews and one of his own brothers within the past two weeks. He had just commenced on his fifth victim, his young and beautiful niece, and had sucked her blood twice when [further] tragedy was averted in the following manner.

At dusk some members of the deputation went to the grave [of the alleged vampire] along with a crowd of people.... The vampire had been buried three years earlier, now they saw a light over his tomb like a flickering lamp.

The grave was opened and [the corpse of] a man was revealed, as whole and apparently as healthy as anyone present; his hair, and the hair on his body, his nails, teeth and eyes (which were half-open) were all perfect as in life, and his heart was beating.

He was taken from his coffin; the body was not truly flexible, but no particle of bone or flesh was missing; his heart was then pierced through with a species of sharp iron bar; a whitish fluid issued, mixed with blood, but the blood predominating, and the whole without any foul odor; next the head was cut off with the kind of ax that is used in England for executions; the same fluid and blood flowed out as before, but more copiously.

The body was put into the ground, covered with quicklime to consume it as rapidly as possible, and from this time onwards the girl who had been sucked twice began to recover. A bluish patch forms on the spot where these people have been sucked; but the spot is not precise[ly dictated], it can show up in different places in different cases.

As always, it is extraordinary that finding such a creature—"the heart was beating"—authorities did not think of keeping it for careful examination. They immediately "killed" it and disposed of the body as quickly as possible. This looks a lot more like a show put on to allay the fears of the populace than a serious investigation to increase the knowledge of science. Likewise, it raises the question of how many times a victim has to be bitten by a vampire before becoming a vampire, or indeed if a victim ever does. There is no mention of fear of the niece who was twice bitten nor of the four relatives who were killed, buried, and left in the grave.

ROMANIAN VAMPIRES

Anthony Masters in his essential *The Natural History of the Vampire* (1972) quotes from "Dr. Tudor Panfile, a Rumanian scholar, who published many vampire legends in *Ion Creanda*, a magazine devoted to peasant culture":

> Some twenty or thirty years ago [from 1914] in the commune Afu-mati in Dolj, a certain peasant, Mârin Mirea Ociscisc, died. It was noticed that his relations also died, one after the other. A certain Badea Vrajitor [Badea the Wizard] dug him up. Badea himself, going later into the forest up to the frontier on a cold wintry night, was eaten by wolves. The bones of Mârin were sprinkled with [sacramental?] wine, a church service was read over them, and [they were] replaced in the grave. From that time there were no more deaths in the family.
>
> Some fifteen years ago, in Amárásti, in the north of Dolj, an old woman, the mother of the peasant Dinu Gheorghiţa, died. After some months the children of her eldest son began to die, one after the other, and, after that, the children of her youngest son. The sons became anxious, dug her up one night, cut her in two, and buried her again. Still the deaths did not cease. They dug her up a second time, and what did they see? The body was whole with-out a wound. It was a great marvel. They took her and carried her into the forest, and put her under a great tree in a remote part of the forest. There they disemboweled her, took out her heart, from which blood was flowing, cut it in four, put it on hot cinders, and burnt it. They took the ashes and gave them to children to drink with water. They threw the body on the fire, burnt it, and buried the ashes of the body. Then the deaths ceased.
>
> Some twenty or thirty years ago, a cripple, an unmarried man, of Cuşmir, in the south of Mehedinţi, died. A little time after, his relations began to die, or fall ill. They complained that a leg was drying up. This happened in several places. What could it be? "Perhaps it is the cripple; let us dig him up." They dug him up one Saturday night, and found him red as red, and all drawn up into a corner of the grave. They cut him open, and took the cus-tomary measures. They took out the heart and liver, burnt them on redhot cinders, and gave the ashes to his sister and other rela-tions, who were ill. [The relatives] drank them with water, and regained their health.

In the Cuşmir, another family began to show very frequent deaths, and suspicion fell on a certain old man, dead long ago. When they dug him up, they found him sitting [cross-legged] like a Turk, and as red as red, just like fire; for had he not eaten up a whole family of strong, young men? When they tried to get him out he resisted, unclean and horrible. They gave him some blows with an ax, they got him out, but they could not cut him with a knife. They took a scythe and an ax, cut out his heart and liver, burnt them [to ashes], and gave them to the sick folk to drink. They drank, and regained their health. The old man was reburied, and the deaths ceased.

GNAWING FEAR

There are many instances in the literature of "vampires" being unearthed whose shrouds or clothes are torn and bloody, whose flesh is gnawed, who have struggled in the grave. The possibility of premature burial must be considered. In earlier centuries, if not in this, people have greatly feared waking up from a coma to find themselves screwed into a coffin. In *The Table-Rappers* (1972), Ronald Persall writes:

> The novelist Wilkie Collins always left a letter on his dressing-table adjuring anyone finding him dead to call a doctor and make certain, Harriet Martineau left her doctor ten pounds to see that her head was amputated before burial, the actress Ada Cavendish willed that her jugular vein be cut before interment, and the journalist Edmund Yates did likewise.... Lady Burton [widow of Sir Richard Burton] provided for her heart to be pierced with a needle, while [the composer] Meyerbeer arranged to have bells tied to his extremities when he was dead.
>
> Franz Hartmann collected seven hundred cases of burial alive and narrow squeaks, and in 1889 the *Undertaker's Journal* stated unequivocally: "It has been proved beyond all contradiction that there are more burials alive than are generally supposed. Stories of these cases are numerous." By 1896, there were nearly two hundred books on premature burial. It was small wonder that people who had been buried alive were believed by the superstitious to return as vampires to revenge themselves on the living, or, as Hartmann maintained, to sustain themselves.

SELLING YOUR SOUL TO THE DEVIL

There is, naturally, a good deal about this unnatural sort of thing in *The Complete Book of Devils and Demons*, but it is not mentioned there—nor is it often noted anywhere—that selling one's soul to The Devil can make one into a vampire. Still, this is the plot of Smyth Upton's novel *The Last of the Vampires* (1845). With every retelling the vampire legend becomes more complicated, even contradictory.

HIGHJINKS AT HIGHGATE

Inevitably, the press on slow news days is tempted to report sightings of ghosts and even vampires at cemeteries. London's famed Highgate is no exception. A typical, if overblown, time was around 1970, when David Farrant got in trouble charged with disturbing the neighbors if not the corpses and trespassing (though Highgate is a public place, I think) and the now late Sean Manchester (self-appointed President of The British Occult Society) turned up to look for "newly dead" in ancient vaults, coffins that vampires may have vacated in order to roam, and more. His so-called exorcism

The Undead (1957) died the death. No amount of bad vampire movies could kill the Count.

of the cemetery was attended by as many press and television reporters as he could muster for the event.

I never met Sean Manchester, but Dr. Jeanne Youngson thinks little of his work in a field she knows in and out and Carol Page, who interviewed him for print, says he was a "bore." (She also objected to his claiming to be a descendant of Lord Byron and disagreed strongly with Manchester's opinion that he looked just like Byron did.)

Manchester founded not only The British Occult Society but also the unusually named International Society for the Advancement of Irreproducible Vampire and Lycanthropy Research. I suggest it might have produced a more apt acronym as Vampire and Occult Manchester International Trickery. ISAIVLR briefly published a self-promoting newsletter called *The Cross and the Stake*. For vampire fans it is a collectors' item.

I mention the Highgate activities not because there was anything in them *per se* but so that this example can stand for many attempts of publicity seekers to attach themselves to the vampire legend. There's a huge public out there for vampire newsletters and clubs as well as for the likes of *100 Vicious Little Vampire Stories* (1995), etc.

DAYVILLES FLAVOR OF THE MONTH

BLACK FOREST GATEAU

To get the recipe for this month's flavor, Dayvilles journeyed all the way to a castle in a dark forest in a remote part of Europe for a moonlight meeting with Count Dracula.

At the stroke of midnight, Dracula rose from his coffin and showed us how to make Black Forest Gateau, just the way he likes it — full of blood red cherries, their stones gouged out and thrust into rich, thick vanilla ice cream, blended with chocolate pieces.

Then the Count sunk his fangs deep into this delicious concoction and gave a blood-curdling shriek, of ecstasy. We simply couldn't control him.

Dracula tells us he couldn't live without it! — Can you?

CARRY HOME A CARTON

America has Count Chocula breakfast food, Drac Snacks candy, and more. Here is an "advert" for an ice cream flavor from London in the seventies.

SOME BRITISH VAMPIRE LOCATIONS

Croglin Lower Hall (if really the site of the Croglin vampire)
Eastbury (a Vanbrugh mansion of 1753 at Tarrant Gunnville, Dorset)
St. Andrew's at Dent (a church in Dentdale, Yorkshire)

AM FEAR LIATH MÓR

That is Gaelic for "The Big Gray Man," said to be the ghost of a local poet, who haunts a mountain—well, it's less than 4,300 feet high, but in Scotland that's a mountain, not a hill—called Ben Macdhui. There have been a few suggestions that it may be a bloodthirsty giant ghost, but it is probably not a vampire. It is just the inheritor of a mixture of legends similar to Big Foot with the addition of a touch of the cannibalism of certain Highland dwellers of the past, such as the dreadful Sawney Beane family.

VISUM ET REPERTUM

"Seen and reported," and testified to by a number of Austrian officers, is the following extraordinary statement, worth reproducing in full because unknown even to most vampirologists. It is signed and sealed ("*L.S.*" means "place of the seal") and describes horrific events in a village near Belgrade in 1732. I'll translate it for you:

> After reports in the village of Medvegia that alleged vampires had killed some people by sucking their blood, I was, by high decree of a local Honorable Supreme Command, sent to investigate the matter thoroughly, along with [other] officers detailed for that purpose and two subordinate medical officers, and I therefore conducted and heard the present inquiry in the company of the captain of the Stalluth company of *haiduks*, *Hadnack* Gorschiz, ensign and senior *haiduk* of the village. Unanimously [reported] as follows:
>
> Some 5 years ago a local *haiduk* named Arnold Paole broke his neck in a fall from a haywain. He had while alive often described how, near Gossova in the Ottoman area of Serbia, he had been vexed by a vampire, to counter which he had eaten from the earth of the vampire's grave and smeared himself with the blood of the vampire in order to free himself from the vexation he had suffered. Twenty or thirty days after his death some people complained that they were being bothered by this same Arnold Paole and that, in fact, four people had been killed by him. To put an end to this evil, they exhumed Arnold Paole forty days after his death, on the advice of their *hadnack* (who had been present at such actions previously) and they found that he [Paole] was quite complete and undecayed, and that fresh blood had flowed from his eyes, nose, mouth and ears; that his shirt and the covering of the coffin were completely

bloodied; that the nails of his hands and feet, and the skin, had fallen off and that new growth had occurred. And since they determined from this that he was an authentic vampire, they drove a stake into his heart, as was their custom, at which he uttered a groan and bled copiously. Thereupon they burned the body to ashes without delay and threw the ashes into the grave. These same people likewise assert that all those who have been tormented and killed by vampires inevitably become vampires themselves.

In similar fashion they exhumed the four people mentioned. They also state that the said Arnold Paole attacked cattle as well as people, sucking blood. Because people ate the flesh of those cattle, it seems that vampires have been created here [thereby], for, over a period of three months, seventeen young and old people died with no previous history of illness and in two or at most three days [in each case]. Moreover, the *Haiduk* Jovitza reports that his stepdaughter, Stanaka, lay down to sleep perfectly healthy fifteen days ago but that at midnight she woke from sleep with a terrible scream, fearful and trembling, and complained that she was being throttled by the son of a *haiduk*, named Milloe, who had died nine weeks earlier. She had terrific pains in her chest, and these got worse by the hour, and within three days she was dead.

Hearing this, we proceeded that same afternoon to the cemetery, along with the *haiduks* of the village already mentioned, to cause the suspected graves to be opened and the bodies within examined. That being done, all of those [corpses] being examined, we found the following:

1. A woman named Stana, aged twenty, who had died in childbirth two months previous, after three days' illness and after saying she had smeared herself [for protection] with a vampire's blood, because of which both she and the baby which had died at birth, and because of inadequate burial had been half eaten by dogs, became vampires. She was whole and undecayed. Opening the body, we found in the chest cavity a quantity of extravascular blood. The arteries, like the ventricle of the heart, were not clogged as they should have been with coagulated blood, and the viscera (lungs, liver, stomach, spleen, intestines) were quite fresh, as they would be in a living person. The uterus, however, was much enlarged and very inflamed on the outside, for the placenta and

lochia had remained attached and they had putrefied. The skin of her hands and her nails had fallen off but new nails and fresh new skin on the hands were visible.

2. There was a woman named Melitsa, aged sixty, who had died after three months' illness and had been buried about ninety days earlier [than the exhumation]. Much liquid blood was found in the chest, and the viscera were, like those mentioned above, pristine. At her dissection, all the *haiduks* standing around marveled at her plump and perfect body, all of them stating that they had known her from her youth and that in life she had always been scrawny and dried up, stressing that only in the grave had she filled out so surprisingly. They also blamed her vampirism at this time [on her] eating the meat of sheep which had been killed by earlier vampires.

3. There was an eight-day-old child which had lain the grave for ninety days and which also was in vampire condition.

4. The son of a *haiduk*, named Milloe [the same as complained of by Stanaka], was exhumed, having lain in the earth nine weeks, dead of a three-day illness, and was found to resemble the other vampires.

5. Joachim, likewise the son of a *haiduk*, aged seventeen, died of a three-day illness. He had been buried eight weeks and four days, and being dissected was found in a similar [vampire] condition.

6. A woman named Ruscha who died after a ten-day illness and was buried six weeks earlier [was exhumed and found to have] much fresh blood not only in her chest but at the bottom of her ventricles. The same was seen in her child, eighteen days old, which had died five weeks earlier.

7. So equally did a girl aged ten who had died two months earlier exhibit the same condition . . . .

8. The wife of the *haiduk* was exhumed with her child. She had died seven weeks earlier and the baby, eight weeks old, twenty-one days earlier, and the mother and child were found to be utterly decomposed despite the fact that the earth and the graves were similar to those of the nearby [undecomposed] vampires.

9. A servant of the local corporal of the *haiduks*, named Rhadu, aged twenty-three, died after a three-month illness and after being buried for five weeks was completely decomposed.

10. The wife of the local ensign and her child were completely decomposed.

11. With Stance, a *haiduk* aged sixty, who had died six weeks before, I noticed he exhibited profuse liquid blood, like the others, in chest and stomach. The whole body was in the above-described vampire condition.

12. Milloe, a *haiduk*, aged twenty-five, who had lain six weeks in the grave, was also found in vampire condition.

13. Little Stanaka, the wife of a *haiduk*, aged twenty-three, died after a three-day illness and had been buried eighteen days. At the autopsy I found her face very red and vivid, as was mentioned above she [had complained that in sleep she] had been throttled by Milloe, a *haiduk's* son, and there was noticeable under her right ear a bruise the length of a finger. As her corpse was being taken from the grave, a quantity of fresh blood streamed from her nose. In dissecting I found, as so often stated above, a regular fragrant fresh flow of blood, not only from the chest cavity but also from the ventricle of the heart. All the viscera were in fine, healthy condition. The entire epidermis and nails on hands and feet were as in life.

After the examinations had been conducted, the heads of the vampires were cut off by the local gypsies and then burned along with the bodies, the ashes then being thrown into the River Morava. The decomposed bodies, on the other hand, were returned to their graves. This I attest along with the assistant medical officers attendant on me. Testifying to the above [with signatures]:

L.S. Johannes Fluchinger, Regimental Medical Officer of the Infantry
Regiment of the Hon. B. Furstenbush.

L.S. J. H. Siegl, Medical Officer of the Hon. Morall Regiment

L.S. Johann Friedrich Baumgarten, Medical Officer of the Infantry
Regiment of the Hon. B. Furstenbush.

We the undersigned hereby testify that everything which the Regimental Medical Officer [Fluchinger] observed in the matter of vampires—along with the two medical officers who signed with him—is in every detail accurate and has been undertaken, observed, and examined in our own presence. In witness whereof, here is our signature in our own hand and of our own making Belgrade, 26 January 1732.

L.S. Buttener, Lieutenant-Colonel of the Hon. Alexandrian Regiment

L.S. J. H. von Lindenfels, Officer of the Hon. Alexandrian Regiment

My sharper readers may have already concluded that medical men ought to have ascribed these cases of "vampirism" to an infectious disease which regularly produced blood in the chest and not the drinking of blood, which would have been found in the stomach. The doctors do not address the chemistry of undecomposed bodies and still liquid blood nor the physics of how these corpses—whose coffins had to be dug up and opened—managed get out to "throttle" and otherwise attack the live local inhabitants. Strangely, undecomposed bodies are often taken as proof of the saintliness of the deceased. Canonization processes have frequently remarked on the preservation of the bodies examined. St. Teresa of Ávilá, supposedly unembalmed, lasted in a perfect state of preservation for well over 150 years.

THE ABBÉ CALMET

Augustin Calmet (1672-1757), Benedictine abbot of Sénones, a respected biblical scholar, gave the greatest impetus to vampire lore until another (possibly false) priest, Montague Summers, emerged in the twentieth century with such works as *The Vampire in Europe* and *The Vampire, His Kith and Kin*.

Calumet's epoch-making work was his *Traité sur les apparitions des espirites, et sur les vampires* (Treatise on the Apparitions of Spirits, and on Vampires, 1751). He cited many alleged cases from Hungary, Moravia, Silesia, Poland, etc., asking (without offering a definitive answer) "how is it that these incidents are so frequent in this part of the world?" Throughout he tries to be exact and at one with the Age of Reason, although Voltaire mocked his credulity and excoriated the Sorbonne for giving Calmet's book its *imprimatur*.

As with the opinions of any other forthcoming writer of any period of the past, major or minor, what is always interesting is not only who was right and who was wrong about this or that but how what the writer says illuminates his time and what we can learn from the writer about something more than the passing parade—what evidence is presented about human nature. As Pete Smith used to say, "People are funnier than anybody." How and why people act the way they do is of never-ending fascination.

TWO WRITERS WELL WORTH LOOKING UP

Readers of *The Complete Book of Spells, Curses, and Magical Recipes* will already be familiar with Montague Rhodes James (1862-1936) of *Casting the Runes*. He might appear in this book for his beautifully crafted vampire tales. His command of atmosphere is remarkable and his construction of plot riveting. His *Count Magus* is a classic.

More prolific and popular in tone than the scholarly James (Provost of Eton) was Algernon Blackwood (1869-1951). Also born in mid-Victorian England, unlike James he led no sheltered existence: he farmed in Canada, worked in a dried milk factory, ran a hotel in Toronto, and was a newspaperman in New York. His long fiction list includes: *The Listener and Other Stories* (1907*)*, *John Silence, Physician Extraordinary* (1908), *The Human Chord* (1910), *The Centaur* (1911) and so on to *The Doll and One Other* (1946). Some of his stories are unforgettable.

Both of these writers challenge the best of European workers in the same literary vineyards.

THE MOST FAMOUS EUROPEAN VAMPIRE STORY

That must be that of *Dracula*, of course, but here is another version of the most famous nonfictional story. It concerns Arnold Paole, who returned from military service in Greece to his native village of Meduegna (near Belgrade), bought a small farm, settled in, and soon died. You have some of his story already. Here is what one broadcaster likes to call "the rest of the story." It comes from another source than the one already cited.

Shortly after Paole's death, his body was dug up, because there had been rumors of a vampire in the neighborhood and Paole's fiancée, Nina, claimed that Paole had told her that while in Greece he had desecrated the grave of a vampire and was worried what might happen to him. Here is the scene as described by Dr. Mayo (*Popular Superstitions*, 1851 edition) as quoted in Montague Summers's *The Vampire in Europe:*

> The party consisted of two officers, military representatives from Belgrade, two army surgeons, *Unterfeldscheren*, a drummer boy who carried their cases of instruments, the authorities of the village, the old sexton, and his assistants. Dr. Mayo thus reconstructs the scene. "It was early on a grey morning that the commission visited the quiet cemetery of Meduegna.... The graves were, for the most part, neatly kept.... Before very long the coffin [of Paole] was rather roughly dragged out of the ground, and the grave-digger's assistant soon knocked off the lid. It was seen that the corpse had moved to one side, the jaws gaped wide open, and the blue lips were moist with new blood which had trickled in a thin stream from a corner of the mouth. All unafraid the old sexton caught the body and twisted it straight. "So," he cried, "you have not wiped your mouth since last night's work."

At this point they might have paused to consider how, if Paole had been roaming around the night before, he got out of the buried coffin and back into it; they had just dug six feet deep to get to him. Surely the first reaction ought to have been that the blood was Paole's own. This does not seem to have occurred to Dr. Mayo or to the Rev. Mr. Summers, who continues:

> Even the officers accustomed to the horrors of the battlefield and the surgeons accustomed to the horrors of the dissecting room shuddered at so hideous a spectacle. It is recorded that the drummer boy swooned upon the spot. Nerving themselves to their awful work they inspected the remains more closely, and it was soon apparent that there lay before them the thing they dreaded—the vampire. He looked, indeed, as if he had not been dead a day. On handling the corpse the scarfskin [epidermis] came off, and below these were new skin and new nails.

Ignore the dangling modifier there; stick with the horror. They sprinkled garlic around, drove whitethorn stakes into the corpses of Paole and four of his supposed victims that they dug up, burned all five to ashes, and buried the ashes "in consecrated ground."

This does not seem to have worked. Six years later there was another local outbreak of vampirism.

THE COUNT OF ST. GERMAIN

This was the title assumed by a flamboyant figure who turned up in the highest social circles of Europe in the eighteenth century. He was rumored to have lived for hundreds of years. He also was reported to be alive in California in the twentieth century, but that imposter was a pitiful and obvious fake. We meet the count in another book in this series, as a magician.

Probably because of his alleged long life, though he dabbled in alchemy and elixirs and not blood-drinking, the Count is presented as a vampire by Chelsea Quinn Yarbro in her pop pastiche, *Hotel Transylvania* (1978), and its many sequels. Despite his dapper dress and passion for diamonds, Yarbro's creation is not among the most truly elegant or most interesting portraits of the noble vampire.

Other historical characters, from Vlad Ţepéş to a son of Queen Victoria, have been falsely presented in literature as vampires. The count, however, would probably not have minded; he always liked to surround himself with an air of mystery and glamour.

TURKISH VAMPIRES

The Ottoman Empire stretched over a vast area at its height, and in some of its dependencies the Turk was regarded with fear and hatred. Though Muslims will not even touch pork, let alone eat it, avoiding it much more assiduously than Jews do, in various Ottoman countries such as Bulgaria and the former Yugoslavia the Turk was said to turn into a wild boar when he died—if not sooner. In Albania, the Turk was said to become a vampire, a *liou(v)gat*. In J. G. v. Hahn's *Albanesischen Studien* (Albanian Studies, 1854), we read of "dead Turks, with huge nails, who wrapped in their winding sheets devour whatever they encounter and throttle men." The Turks have made a couple of vampire films but today vampires are not commonly reported in Turkey.

THE VAMPIRE AND THE WEREWOLF

The vampire is in human form, but dead, or "undead"; the werewolf is a human that gets as hairy as it is rapacious, and is alive. We must keep stressing that. Both are supernatural predators. In some Balkan mythologies, the living werewolf becomes a vampire after death. We are planning to write a follow-up to Montague Summers's *The Werewolf* (reprinted 1966) but in the format of this present series. In the meantime, we must omit lycanthropy from our considerations except for this one note to suggest that we have not forgotten the werewolf or *loup-garou*, just avoided him. Vampires and werewolves do get linked together in some myths and some movies.

CHILDREN OF JUDAS

Vampires have been called the Children of Judas and, like Judas, are supposed to have red hair. It is even said in Eastern Europe that the bite of a vampire looks like XXX, suggesting the 30 pieces of silver Judas was paid to betray Christ. As "S.L.", Julian Osgood Field published *The Kiss of Judas* (1894).

ROMANY ROAMERS

Among the Roma, which is what European gypsies like to be called, there are various vampire traditions, some originating with these people (originally from India, not Egypt as English suggests or Flanders as Spanish says) and some with accretions picked up on their travels. The *mollo* vampire is the best known but permit me to introduce Bibi.

Renfield (played by Dwight Frye) casually takes up a crucifix, but Dracula (played by Bela Lugosi in his stagey style), does a big take.

Bibi appears as a ragged old woman accompanied by two skinny children and, sometimes, two white lambs. If you take her in out of pity you will regret it. Your children will die, as of cholera. (Connecting vampires and demons with disease is an age-old habit).

KUKUTHI

I was once foolish enough to say that there was no significant literature from some countries and I singled out Albania. I thereupon heard from a number of Albanians, some of whom I am now proud to number among my most intellectual friends, and I have been given all sorts of wonderful information on the folklore particularly. In that I learned of the *kukuthi*, one of the most terrible vampires of Eastern Europe. This creature is very hard to burn in the traditional way of dispatching vampires but the Albanians say that if a wolf eats off the leg of one of these vampires the creature crawls back to its grave and is no further trouble.

GREEK VAMPIRE CURE

The Greeks have been especially plagued by vampires, presumably because anyone excommunicated from the Greek Orthodox Church has a good chance of becoming a vampire. They paint a certain blue around window and door openings, use garlic and tiny seeds (scattered for vampires and witches to count before entering), and employ other defenses. The most striking I have heard of is this: cut off the hands and feet, nose and ears of the corpse and tie them to the corpse's elbow. This is said to work well.

WALLACHIAN VAMPIRE DEFENSE

On the Feast of St. Ignatius (not Loyola but the martyr of Antioch who died for the faith in 107 A.D.), celebrated on 17 October in the church calendar of the West, kill a pig—vampires often appear as pigs in this part of the world—and smear the lard on your body. This prevents vampire attacks and prevents anyone from becoming a vampire.

VLAD IN ROMANIAN

In addition to histories of the country, see such books as these (all published in Bucharest):

Dimitrie Bolintineanu, *Viata lui Vlad Țepeș Voda si Mircea cel Batrin* (1863)
Ion Bogdan, *Vlad Țepeș ...* (1896)
G. Mavrodollu, *Vlada Țsepeshu, drama istorica* (historical drama, 1858)
Grigore Popescu, *Vlad Țepeș* (1964)
Victoria Rogoz, *Vlad fiul Dracului* (1970)

VAMPIRES AND WITCHES

Vampires resemble witches in various ways but most of all, perhaps, because witches have long been thought to be able to eat by black magic the vitals of a human being and vampires drink the vital fluid. A complete understanding of vampire superstitions requires a familiarity with European witchcraft and related topics.

THE VAMPIRE AND THE ORIGINS OF POPULAR SUPERSTITION

T. Sharper Knowlton in *The Origins of Popular Superstitions* about the turn of the century revised Brand's *Popular Antiquities* (1841) and referred to a number of British scholars, one of them being Herbert Mayo, MD, author of *On the Truths Contained in Popular Superstitions* (1851). Another was J.G. Fraser of *Psyche's Task*. Knowlton wrote about vampirism:

> The origin of vampire superstitions must be sought in the ignorance of early races who buried their dead in the earth, for it is singular that the races which cremate their dead have been practically free from vampire legends. Earth burial has never been free from the possibility of premature interment, and although there is no reason to believe that a man buried alive will not die in his coffin of suffocation, an ignorant peasantry seemed to imagine that he could live, issue forth at night, and keep himself alive by sucking the blood of the living. It is notable that as disbelief in this notion assumed large proportions, owing to the advance of education and refinement, the phenomena disappeared. Visitations as recorded in history have borne the marks of an epidemic, and even Dr. Mayo was not averse to the proposition that a man who had a wasting disease, or was threatened with one, could imagine himself vampirised and thus spread the contagion to others. Vampirism is only another proof of the power of the mind over the body. It

is the *fixed idea* that does the work. Mr. Stanley Redgrove quotes an illustration from J. G. Fraser's *Psyche's Task:*—

"In illustration of the Maori superstition of the Taboo. According to the Maoris, any one who touches a tabooed object being a sort of 'anti-talisman.' Professor [later Sir James] Frazer says:— 'Cases have been known of Maoris dying of sheer fright on learning that they had unwittingly eaten the remains of a chief's dinner, or handled something that belonged to him,' since such objects were *ipso facto* tabooed. He gives the following case on good authority: 'A woman, having partaken of some fine peaches from a basket, was told that they had come from a tabooed place. Immediately the basket dropped from her hands and she cried out in agony that the *atua* or godhead of the chief, whose divinity had been thus profaned, would kill her. That happened in the afternoon, and next day by twelve o'clock she was dead.' For us the power of the taboo does not exist; for the Maori, who implicitly believes in it, it is a very potent reality, but this power of the taboo resides, not in the external objects, but in his own mind." Very true. And the power of the vampire is the power of the idea.

AN EPISODE IN CATHEDRAL HISTORY

This is the restrained title of a typical short story by the great master of British horror tales, Montague Rhodes James, already mentioned. The following passage illustrates the subtle way he handles the vampire skulking about in Southminster. He makes the vampire sound disconcertingly credible in this unnerving "ghost story of an antiquary," to use a phrase that provided a title for two of James' collections. A brief sample:

The season was undoubtedly a very trying one. Whether the church was built on a site that had once been a marsh, as was suggested, or for whatever reason, the residents in the immediate neighbourhood had, many of them, but little enjoyment of the exquisite sunny days and the calm nights of August and September. To several of the old people—Dr. Ayloff among others, as we have seen—the summer proved downright fatal, but even among the younger, few escaped either a sojourn in bed for a matter of weeks, or at the least, a brooding sense of oppression, accompanied by hateful nightmares. Gradually there formulated itself a suspicion—which grew into a conviction—that the alterations in the Cathedral had something to say in the matter. The widow of a former old verger, a pensioner of the Chapter of Southminster, was visited by dreams, which she retailed to her friends, of a shape that slipped out of the little door of the south transept as the dark fell in and flitted—taking a fresh direction every night—about the Close, disappearing for a while in house after house, and finally emerging again when the night sky was paling. She could see nothing of it, she said, but that it was a moving form: only she had an impression that when it returned to the church, as it seemed to do in the end of the dream, it turned its head: and then, she could not tell why, but she thought it had red eyes.

BURNING VAMPIRES IS NONSENSICAL

It was the eighteenth century in Europe, the century in which vampirism was most sensationally reported, but Dr. Gérard van Swieten, physician to the Empress Maria Theresa, could hardly contain his anger at the stupidity of the vampire superstition. A letter of his may serve as witness to the fact that many people are astounded and annoyed that the vampire superstition should have persisted so long and spread so widely in the world. Translated, Swieten's letter runs something like this:

Some months back I perused an English pamphlet printed in London in which one could read of a notable and well-attested fact. In the month of February 1750 the vault of an ancient family in the county of Devon in England was opened, and among many bones and decaying coffins was found an intact wooden box; opened out of curiosity, it contained the whole body of a man; his flesh still retained its natural firmness; the shoulder joints, neck, and fingers were completely supple; when the cheek was pressed down it gave under the finger but immediately sprang back to its shape once the pressure was released; the same was tried on the whole body [which also proved similar]; the beard was black and four inches long. The corpse had not been embalmed, for no sign of an incision could be found. There you have an English vampire which for eighty years had lay in its tomb peacefully, bothering no one.

Let us examine the allegations offered as proof of vampirism. Rosina Jolakin, died 22 December 1754, was disinterred 19 January 1755 and declared to be a vampire fit for the fire because she was found intact in her tomb. In the wintertime anatomists keep cadavers in the open air for six weeks or even two months without putrefaction. And it is worth adding that this winter [1754-1755] has been particularly cold.

Most of the bodies of the other corpses unearthed had already decomposed, but it was enough that they had not completely rotted, so—into the fire! What ignorance!... Two specialists in sterilization, so-called surgeons who had never seen a dried-up corpse and who knew nothing at all about the anatomy of the human body, as they themselves confessed to the commissioners, were the witnesses who were empowered to pass the sentence of fire....

It is on the basis of evidence like this that the entire story [of vampires] has been concocted, that sacrileges are being committed [against the dead], that the sanctuary of tombs is being violated, that calumny has been heaped on the reputations of the deceased and their kin, who have only the same sort of outrages to look forward to unless such abuses do not gradually disappear. Into the hands of executioners are given the corpses of children who died in all innocence; men whose manner of life raised not the slightest suspicion have the misfortune of being dug up simply because there is a rumor that some witch has been buried nearby.

They are declared to be witches; their corpses are handed over to the executioner to be burned to ashes; but their sentence indicates that they are being disgraced more severely than if they still lived; and their bodies are burned in infamy as a lesson to their supposed accomplices.

Where are the laws that permit such judgments? It is patent that no such laws exist, but it is asserted that custom demands such [outrages]. What a shower of disasters! Things like this upset me so much and put me into such a fury that I must here conclude my account before I overstep the bounds of propriety.

GALICIAN VAMPIRES

Galician vampires not only suck blood from humans but attack cattle, stop cows from giving milk, and can foretell the future. They can take human or animal form or be invisible.

ISTRIAN VAMPIRES

The peasants of Istria believed (and to some extent some still believe) that each clan has its own *vukodlak* (vampire) and its own *krsnik* (vampire killer) and that the two, one black and one white, one representing the forces of darkness and one the forces of light, battle. Istrians have a quick way of stopping the vampire from walking. They cut the tendons at the back of the knees of any corpse that looks suspicious. Better safe than sorry.

MONEY FOR THE TRIP

My grandmother, I often recall, used to use the expression "he'd steal the money off a dead man's eyes," and I remember how she explained to me the custom of putting pennies on the eyes of a corpse. It was her English version of the old Roman custom of putting a coin or two into the mouth of a corpse so the fare would be available for Charon, the person in the underworld who ferried the dead across the River Styx. My grandfather was buried, in the nineteen-twenties, with pennies on his eyes. (They also planted, at his request, two rowan trees at his gravesite, I am told. This was before I was born.)

In Germany the coin in the mouth has long been used to keep corpses from coming back as vampires. They come back if they do not have the fare to go, the Germans say, and they sometimes come back as pigs.

SPLASH!

In some parts of Eastern Europe it is the custom to cover the corpse of a vampire with a hide before staking it. The belief is that the corpse of a vampire will bleed and that if the blood happens to fall on you you may become a vampire.

In some other places the blood issuing from a staked corpse is rubbed on the onlookers to cure them of the effects of vampirism or to prevent them from becoming vampires.

JEAN-JACQUES ROUSSEAU

In 1763, right in the middle of The Age of Reason, Rousseau wrote to Archbishop Christophe de Beaumont of Paris:

> If there is in the world one documented story it is that regarding vampires. Nothing is lacking: court records, certificates from

notaries, surgeons, priests, magistrates. The legal proof is utterly complete. In the face of all this, who believes in vampires? Do you think we'll all be damned for not having believed?

Though he died insane (perhaps by suicide) in 1778, Rousseau could, when he wanted to, be calm, cool, collected, and penetratingly brilliant.

EUROPEAN VAMPIRE TRADITIONS

It is interesting to contrast folk traditions with the literary conventions in connection with vampires. There will be more in the last chapter—on literature and folklore—but here we can introduce the subject.

In folklore, vampires can come from any class but are most likely to be peasants who have recently become "undead" and who confine their depredations more or less to family or places close to home. They may attack their widows or young girls, but there is more violence than sex involved. They are variously caused and variously treated, often with remedies that lie outside the Christian religion and are part of the pagan heritage.

In literature, the vampire is often a distinguished or alienated individual, rather noble (in the Romantic tradition of Charles Maturin's *Melmoth the Wanderer* or Byron's *Manfred*), frequently a count (like Dracula, Count Alucard, Count Magus, or Count Yorga), devilishly clever with the wisdom accrued from centuries of vampirism. He is mysteriously connected with some secret sorrow or crime or pact with The Devil. Such vampires are conventionally found residing in some castle or other great house, preferably isolated and gloomy. The vampire is, however, able to travel to big cities. The aristocratic literary vampire may have a low-class henchman. The vampire usually pursues strangers of the opposite sex with a sensual and seductive manner. Though the vampire is Satanic, he

The vampire metamorphosed from hideous to handsome, from "Max Schreck" to Louis Jourdain, George Hamilton, Frank Langella. Here, in *Dracula, Prince of Darkness* (1966), Hammer Films presents Christopher Lee as noble looking.

is not under the control of The Devil—and yet he can be thwarted by Christian means. The literary vampire can actually play on our sympathies and sometimes is melancholy about what one might call his or her life.

Scholars of Scandinavia have remarked that The Devil, so devious and sophisticated in the rest of European folklore, is (like the folklore vampire) rather stupid in the folk traditions of the North. People who believe in trolls and elementals generally refuse to believe in vampires.

Traditions vary from one culture to another, despite striking similarities in terms of fundamentals. For instance, some vampires can walk by day. Bram Stoker's can, though he is weaker than at night. Some appear at certain times (in Eastern Europe at Easter, around St. George's Eve, on Saturdays, at the full moon). Some cannot cross running water. Some must be staked with whitethorn or aspen only. Some must have boiling vinegar poured over their graves. Some are created as a result of witchcraft, some not. Some take animal forms. Some materialize out of vapors issuing from the grave. Some can vanish. Many cannot be seen in mirrors or cast shadows. Some never eat human food. Some are driven off by icons. Some areas are apparently more likely to suffer plagues of vampirism than others.

AMONG THE SLAVS

The British folklorist W. R. S. Ralston translated the three volumes of Alexander Afanasief's *Poeticheskiya Vozzryeniya Slavyan na Prirodu* (Poetic Views of the Slavs about Nature, 1865-1869). There is a wealth of information there. Ralston can be briefly quoted for a few details:

> The Kashoubes say that when a *Vieszcy*, as they call the Vampire, wakes from his sleep within the grave, he begins to gnaw his hands and feet; and as he gnaws, one after another, first his relations, then his other neighbours, sicken and die. When he has finished his own store of flesh, he rises at midnight and destroys cattle, or climbs a belfry and sounds the bell. All who hear the ill-omened tones will soon die. But generally he sucks the blood of sleepers. Those on whom he has operated will be found the next morning dead, with a very small wound on the left side of the breast, exactly over the heart. The Lusatian Wends hold that when a corpse chews its shroud or sucks its own breast, all its kin will soon follow it to the grave. The Wallachians say that a *murony*—a sort of cross between a werewolf and a vampire, connected by name with our night-

mare—can take the form of a dog, a cat, or a toad, and also of any blood-sucking insect. When he is exhumed, he is found to have long nails of recent growth on his hands and feet, and blood is streaming from his eyes, ears, nose, and mouth.

Once again, the gnawing on the self suggests premature burial. In days past people who were afraid of waking up in the grave left instructions in their wills that actions be taken, as you have read about above, really extreme precautions, though of course painless, to be certain they were dead before being interred or entombed. This particular Slavic horror can be kept in the grave by burying with the corpse pieces of iron, placed in the heart or just between the knees, under the armpits, between the toes, etc., or by putting an iron fence around the grave.

Need one go to that trouble? See if the left eye of the corpse fails to shut. If it stays open, better invest in some iron, for safety.

For the vampire legends of Romania and Eastern Europe in general, see Dorothy Nixon's "Vampire Lore and Alleged Cases...," *Miorita* 6 (1979), 14-28, and such other authorities as Lichener Klenman Babener (dissertation, 1976), Senn, Summers, *et al*.

MULLOS

These are the vampires among the Romany people. The gypsy vampires are odd in that they do not rise until they have been in the grave forty days, and they do not walk more than three to five years.

The forty days aspect may be connected to the ancient Hebrew, in which the words for "forty days" meant simply "a considerable period of time." Thus, the Flood lasted "forty days and forty nights" and Christ was "forty days" in the desert. In Turkish belief I encountered the idea that certain stone sarcophagi ("flesh eaters") could consume the flesh off the bones in exactly forty days. The decomposed body releases the soul.

SCANDINAVIA

The vampire is rather rare in the folklore of Scandinavia except in cases where the German influence has been felt, but in the *Eyrbyggja Saga* 24, the dead Thorold is said to walk. When his grave is opened he is found to be incorrupt, like a vampire. Sinners are uneasy in the grave.

GREECE

There are many stories of the vampire superstition in Greece, I repeat for it is held by the Greek Orthodox Church that anyone who dies outside the church, whether unbaptized, apostate, or excommunicated, cannot rot. The islands of Santorini and Hydra are often mentioned as being particularly infested at one time or another with vampires. It is said that the backward state of medicine in some areas of Greece accounted for the burial of persons who were only comatose, not dead, and that some of these were later found to have struggled to escape being buried alive and failed while others did escape from the tomb and terrorized the vicinity.

Even today some Greeks wear amulets to protect them not only from the dreaded Evil Eye but from vampires. I have mentioned earlier the blue paint around the doors and windows of peasant cottages; it is not to make them more photogenic for tourists. Blue keeps off vampires. Holy icons are said to drive off or kill vampires. Blowing out the light burning in front of an icon might well invite them.

LA STREGA CHI SUCCIA IL SANGUE

"The witch who sucks blood" is a vampire mentioned in DeNino's *Usi e Costumi Abruzzesi* (Uses and Customs of the Abruzzi) and discussed by Montague Summers in *The Vampire in Europe* as a possible source of a story Summers repeats from Gabriele D'Annunzio's *Trionfo della morte* (Triumph of Death). A child fading slowly and likely to die has his distraught parents engaged in all sorts of efforts to thwart the vampire. The translation of the Italian passage in Summers's text is:

> The priest had come and, after covering the child's head with the end of his stole, had repeated verses from the Gospel. The mother had hung up a wax cross, blessed on Ascension Day, over a door, and had sprinkled the hinges with holy water and repeated the Creed three times in a loud voice; she had tied up a handful of salt in a piece of linen and hung it round the neck of her dying child. The father had "done the seven nights"—that is, for seven nights he had waited in the dark behind a lighted lantern, attentive to the slightest sound, ready to catch and grapple with the vampire. A single prick with the pin sufficed to make her [here the vampire seems to be confused with the witch] visible to the naked eye. But the seven nights' watch had been fruitless, for the child wasted away and grew more hopelessly feeble from hour to hour. At last, in

despair, the father had consulted with a wizard, by whose advice he had killed a dog and put the body behind the door. The vampire could not then enter the house till she counted every hair on its body.

The superstitions of the Abruzzi and of the old Kingdom of the Two Sicilies are of special interest to Americans, because most Italian-Americans trace their ancestry back to those areas. It was chiefly from those areas Italian immigrants brought to the New World many old beliefs and customs. My own travels in Sicily in the fifties made it clear to me that vampires were still undead in folk belief there and explained to me some odd ideas of Italian-Americans. They, of course, are but one source of superstitions still prevalent in the United States. It must be said that as a group they tend to rely on the exorcisms of their church more than on pre-Christian remedies, unlike some other ethnic groups here. Some Hispanics write on their bodies with blue chalk before going to bed at night, to keep off vampires, as has been remarked. Italian-Americans do not do this. They often wear blessed medals, or even pieces of coral or other pagan charms.

Recent books have tried to assert that Italians in general add so much superstition to their religion that the Roman Catholic Church has had to turn a blind eye to many common practices and is embarrassed at street-corner shrines that punished bad language, at weeping statues, liquefying blood of saints, incorruptible bodies of the holy, and images of The Virgin mysteriously appearing on everything from concrete walls to road signs. My opinion is that Italians, and Italian-Americans, are not nearly as superstitious as some other ethnic groups. They are less likely to believe in ghosts or to claim abduction by enemy aliens, and on the whole they do not seem to be bothered by vampires.

MAURICE ROLLINAT

Rollinat, whom Mario Praz once called "a sort of diluted Baudelaire, a methodical collector of horrors...[Felicien] Rops, the Belgian artist of woman as predator translated into verse," used to dash off rather hysterical poetry in his study decorated with skulls and such and recite it, banging out a wild accompaniment on the piano, at *Le Chat Noir* (The Black Cat), a low Parisian cabaret of the eighteen-nineties. He wound up in an insane asylum, where he died (1903), but not before contributing his bit to the Decadence which described women (and even cats) as vicious and vampiristic, if at least giving pleasure to masochistic men who wanted to be degraded and destroyed. *"Insulte moi!"* pleads a victim in Rollinat's poem to a "modern Circe."

As Tom Lehrer puts it in his satiric *Masochism Tango*, "My heart is in your hands—*yuck!"* An earlier, as far as I know anonymous, satiric song writer perpetrated:

> Violate me in violet time
> On the vilest way that you know....

The misogyny of French sensualist and satanist and sadist and plain sick decadents, who turned the vampire into the vamp, shocks us still. Now, the French were not alone in their folly. Algernon Charles Swinburne, English poet and pervert, uttered a phrase almost as famous his "art for art's sake" when he said man desires to be "the powerless victim of the furious rage of a beautiful woman." But the French, maybe more *poseurs* than perverts (and maybe not), at least seem to be more "off the wall." Of these, Rollinat is an adequate example. Also, to him may be ascribed perhaps the earliest hint of what was to become The Cat Woman in horror films. He and his friends may strike the average person as weird. I will not say not *normal* in an age when that appears to be nothing more than a setting on the washing machine, but as so extreme as to verge on the hilarious. However, they were not joking.

THE LEGENDS OF EUROPEAN VAMPIRES

Those scholars who read French might want to look into *La Tradition légendaire du vampire en Europe* (University of Grenoble, 1987) in *Les Cahiers du Groupe d'Études et de Recherche sur la Fantastique* and other French studies of the fantastic. We have in America an annual conference on the fantastic in literature but French scholars seem to have some of the best publications.

NON-GERMAN EXPERTS

Giuseppi Davanzati (1665 - 1755) is a good person to note in order to counteract the misconception that it was German-speaking reporters who, getting into new lands given to them by treaties of the very early eighteenth century, created the entire vampire craze by bringing to notice the peasant beliefs regarding vampires rife in Eastern Europe. In fact, it was not Protestant writers in Germany so much as Roman Catholic writers in Italy such as Davanzati (*Dissertazione sopra i vampiri*, Dissertation on Vampires, 1744) and the monk Dom Calmet in France who publicized these sensational superstitions.

By the time Davanzati wrote, the word *vampyr* had been in use in English for at least a decade. The concept of vampire-like creatures had been around in Europe since ancient times. It was just that Eastern Europe put a name on it that stuck.

AN ODD KIND OF VAMPIRE?

In Bosnia and Serbia and environs, myths describe the *vukodlak*, which if Serbo-Croatian (the two languages of recent times were once one) ought to be translated as "werewolf," not "vampire." Some authorities, nonetheless, say this was a kind of vampire, a creature supposed to be able to eat the sun or moon and thus responsible for eclipses. Peasants made a din by banging on pots and pans when eclipses occurred, the idea being that the noise would drive away this creature.

LENORE

This famous name, known to Americans chiefly through its use in the morbid verses of Edgar Allen Poe, functions as the title of a poem that was all the rage with German Romantics in the eighteenth century and for some time afterwards. *Lenore* (1773) was written by Gottfried August Bürger (1747-1794). It was based on an old ballad called *Sweet William's Ghost* and included in Bishop Percy's collection, *Reliques of Ancient English Poetry* (1765).

In *Dracula*, one of Jonathan Harker's traveling companions quotes a refrain from the German poem, *"Denn die Toten reiten schnell,"* "For the dead ride fast." This refers to the story of Lenore, mooning over the absence of her lover, Wilhelm, who is suddenly confronted with his arrival, on horseback. He sweeps her up and off they go on a wild midnight ride. It soon becomes clear that Lenore is in the clutches of a ghost, for Wilhelm has been killed in the wars.

Stoker, by the way, got the line a little wrong. It never is exactly *"Denn die Toten reiten schnell,"* though that is pretty close to what Bürger wrote.

SODOMY AND SADISM

Related to the necrophilia of Poe's *Lenore* are other perversions.

Wallachia was a vassal state paying tribute to the empire of the Ottoman Turks and, during the Crusade of Varna (1443-1444), in which the Turkish armies destroyed the Christian forces in bloody frays, Wallachia's boy prince (born 1431), who was to become Vlad *Ţepeş* (Dracula), was sent off to the court of the Turkish Sultan, Murad II, as a hostage. Norman Davies (in *Europe: A History*, 1996) is frank to opine that "the buggery to which he was subjected can be considered the likely psychiatric source of his later obsessions."

Those obsessions included a determination to keep the country of which he became *vovoid* (as Vlad III in 1456) free of the fate of Constantinople. Sultan Mehmet II captured that city in 1453, his troops outnumbering the defenders more than 10 to 1, and the Turks turned one of the greatest churches of Christendom into a mosque. Vlad defended his people and the Christian cause by tyranny and terror until at last the horrified king of Hungary, his neighbor, captured and silenced him.

The staking of thousands of victims, whence his epithet "The Impaler," was a torture Vlad had learned of in Turkey. He did not hesitate to employ on a vast scale. It is impossible to separate in this the political from the perverse or to be certain what was terror tactics and what was sexually-driven revenge.

ITALIAN BATTALION

The French vampire melodramas and translations and transformations of *Dracula* are comparatively well known, but perhaps you are unaware of the extent to which the subject has captured the imaginations of the young people in Italy today. The bookshops are full of publications about the vampire (even comic books), the werewolf (Gael Milin's *Il Licantropo*, 1998, is recommended), and death (see Fabio Giovanni's *Necrocultura*, 1998, among recent books). Some clubs feature Goth getups. The Milan vampire exposition (mentioned earlier here) drew crowds of disaffected or disconcerting young people; they were seen afterwards at the nearby McDonald's, still in costume. In Rome there is an active vampire underground. In Viterbo the *Teatro San Leonardo* in March 1998 featured an adaptation of *Dracula* written and directed by Maurizio Annesi and starring Marco Paoli and Cristina Caldani. Italians love *l'eterno conflitto tra il bene e il male*, and Dracula's story is an exciting part of "the eternal conflict between good and evil"—and a scary spectacle, to boot. It is amazing that there has not been a major opera on the subject, but, if there were, the grand outdoor venues (such as the vast Roman amphitheater at Verona) would not suit *Dracula*; it requires a more confined space despite its grand gestures.

BOSNIAN VAMPIRES

From M. Edith Durham in *Man* 23 (1923), an anthropologist's report:

In Bosnia there was, I found, plenty of belief in vampires. Here they are called "lampir" and or "vukodiak" (lit.: wolf's hair). I was told by several of the local Austrian governors that when the Austrians first occupied the country (1878) the cases of disinterring bodies and burning them were numerous. The Government forbade the practice. A recent case (told me in 1906) was when there was an outbreak of typhus (they always called enteric, typhus, I never saw spotted typhus) in a village near Vlasenitza. A young man was the first to die. His wife sickened and swore that her husband had returned in the night and sucked her blood, and said "He is a lampir!" The neighbours, filled with fear, begged the authorities to permit them to dig up and burn his body. Permission was refused and a panic ensued. The lampir was seen and heard by many people and there were fifteen deaths. It would be interesting to know how many of these died because they believed they must die, owing to the lampir. The peasants all through Albania and Macedonia are extraordinarily affected mentally if they believe they must die, and seem to make no effort whatsoever to live...

During the last few weeks a case of burning a vampire's body has been reported from Bosnia.

"IT IS ILLYRIA, LADY"

It would be difficult now to meet with an example of the most barbarous of all those superstitions, that of the Vrukolaka. The name being Illyric, seems to acquit the Greeks of the invention, which was probably introduced into the country by the barbarians of the Slavonic race. Tournefort's description is admitted to be correct. The Devil is supposed to enter the Vrukolaka, who, rising from the grave, torments first his nearest relations, and then others, causing their death or loss of health. The remedy is to dig up the body, and if after it has been exorcized by the priest, the demon still persists in annoying the living, to cut the body into small pieces, or if that be not sufficient, to burn it. The metropolitan Bishop of Larissa lately informed me, that when metropolitan of Greneva, he once received advice of a papas [priest] having disinterred two bodies, and thrown them into the *Haliacmon*, on pretence of their being Vrukolakas. Upon being summoned before the bishop, the priest confessed the fact, and asserted in justification, that a report prevailed of a large animal having been seen to issue, accompanied with flames, out of the grave in which the two bodies had been buried. The bishop began by obliging the priest to pay him 250 piastres (his holiness did not add that he made over the money to the poor). He then sent for scissors to cut off the priest's beard, but was satisfied with frightening him. By then publishing throughout the diocese, that any similar offense would be punished with double the fine and certain loss of station, the bishop effectually quieted all the vampires of his episcopal province.

—William Martin Leake, *Travels in Northern Greece* (1835)

THE UNINVITED

Note that while demonology asserts that demons can assail you whether you call them or not, folklore says that vampires cannot. In *The Complete Book of Devils and Demons* and *The Complete Book of the Devil's Disciples* I mention a number of precautions that black magicians take in calling demons. In *The Complete Book of Spells, Curses, and Magical Recipes* I add various amulets and talismans and other ways of keeping them off. Women, chiefly, if we are to believe the movies, make the mistake of inviting vampires. The vampire is overjoyed. He is, after all, unafraid of what men have always been rather fearful of and the Jews especially regard as unclean, which is female blood. Say what you like about the vampire, he is no male chauvinist pig, no misogynist.

IF YOU READ GERMAN

Leonard R. N. Ashley, *Der Welt der Magie* (1988)
Christoph Daxelmüller, *Aberglaube, Hexenzauber, Höllenängst* (1996)
Enzyklopädie des Märchens (1977*ff.*)
Dieter Harmening, *Der Anfang von Dracula* (1983)

Egon v. Petersdorff, *Daemonen, Hexen, Spiritisten, Mächte der Finsternis einst und jetzt* (1960)

Aribert Schroeder, *Vampirismus: Seine Entwicklung vom Thema zum Motif* (1973)

ROMANIA

Andrew MacKenzie proffers a tour of *Dracula Country: Travels and Folk Beliefs in Romania* (1977). It is somewhat better than the studies of McNally & Florescu on the historical and literary Dracula. There is inevitably much about Romanian folklore and the vampire in the many books on Bram Stoker and his *Dracula*. Here are a dozen:

Margaret L. Carter, *Dracula: The Vampire and the Critics* (1988)
Daniel Farson, *The Man who Wrote Dracula* (1975)
Donald F. Glut, *The Dracula Book* (1975)
Peter Haining, *The Dracula Centenary Book* (1987)
Clive Leatherdale, *Dracula: The Novel and the Legend* (1985)
———, *The Origins of Dracula* (1987)
Harry Ludlam, *A Biography of Dracula* (actually of Stoker, 1962)
Grigore Nandris, "The Historical Dracula . . .," *Comparative Literature Studies* 3:4 (1966), 367-396
Gabriel Ronay, *The Truth about Dracula* (1972)
Phyllis A. Roth, *Bram Stoker* (1982)
Leonard Wolf, *The Annotated Dracula* (1975)
———, *A Dream of Dracula* (1972)

Romania has something of a reputation for vampires not paralleled in most non-European countries. This may derive from the strong presence in Romania, at least in times past, of gypsies. They were easily connected to the vampire as outsider. Worldwide, however, rampant evil spirits fill the imagination of the common people.

T.P. COOKE AND THE MELODRAMA

Thomas Potter Cooke (1786-1864) was very important in establishing the vampire in melodrama in England, starring for fifty years in popular entertainment, and was the first to play Lord Ruthven, the granddaddy of all English vampires.

Cooke was in the navy between the ages of 8 and 10 and then went on the stage, learning the tricks from the great Edmund Kean himself.

Cooke often starred in nautical melodrama such as *The Pilot, The Flying Dutchman, and Black-Ey'd Susan*. He deserves mention here, however, for being the first English actor to bring monster English melodrama to Paris:

Ariel (Miss Worgman.

Unda (Miss Love.

WESTS. *Characters* in THE VAMPIRE.
as performed at the Theatre Royal.

ENGLISH OPERA HOUSE.

Strand

In 3 Plates.   — Plate 1st.   Price 1d. Plain.

London, Published oct. 17, 1820. by B. West, at his Theatrical Print Warehouse.
— Exeter Street Strand. —

Lady Margaret (Mrs. W.S. Chatterley.

The Vampire (Mr. T.P. Cooke.

With penny-plain prints by West and toy theaters from Pollock, Victorian children could play with the characters and stories of the great stage successes such as *The Vampire*. That starred the hero of the nautical melodramas, T.P. Cooke, and in this case a lady called (really) Chatterley. The English Opera House in The Strand specialized in plays with music and fantastic effects, and *The Vampire* had those aplenty.

he starred in Charles Nodier's *Le Monstre et le magicien* (1826) after his success in London in Peake's *Presumption* (which featured Frankenstein). He painted himself blue and "monster blue" became all the rage in Parisian clothes.

Cooke could add a light touch to Harry Hallyard and such salty characters but never kidded the vampire character the way the French did in these farces and burlesques all produced in 1820 in reaction to Nodier's *Le Vampire: Cadet Buteux* (Desaugiers), *Le Vampire* (Martinet), *Encore un vampire* (Balisson de Rougemont), and *Les Entrennes d'un vampire* (Rousseau). He played in the style of *The Castle Spectre*, which H. Chance Newton called "old crusted grisly skeleton melodrama."

THE REV. MONTAGUE SUMMERS ON "THE VAMPIRE OF HANOVER"

Summers (famous for *The Vampire, His Kith and Kin* and *The Vampire in Europe*) has been criticized for his inkhorn style, his credulity, and more, but his reporting of the actual case of a German madman, Fritz Haarmann, is choice:

On the morning of 17th April 1925, the London *Daily Express* printed the following incredible story on its front page:

Vampire Brain, Plan to Perserve It for Science

Berlin. Thursday, April 16th. The body of Fritz Haarmann, executed yesterday at Hanover for twenty-seven murders, will not be buried until it has been examined at Gottingen University.

Owing to the exceptional character of the crimes—most of Haarmann's victims were bitten to death—the case aroused tremendous interest among German scientists. It is probable that Haarmann's brain will be removed and preserved by the University authorities.

—Central News.

Fritz Haarmann, who was dubbed "The Hanover Vampire" was born in Hanover, 25th October 1879. His father, 'Olle Haarmann', a locomotive-stoker, was well-known as a rough, cross-grained choleric man, whom Fritz, his youngest son, both hated and feared. As a youth, Fritz Haarmann was educated at a Church

School, and then at a preparatory school for non-commissioned officers at New Breisach. It is significant that he was always dull and stupid, unable to learn; but it appears a good soldier. When released from military service owing to ill-health he returned home, only to be accused in a short while of offences against children. Being considered irresponsible for his actions the Court sent him to an asylum at Hildesheim, whence however he managed to escape and took refuge in Switzerland. Later he returned to Hanover, but the house became unbearable owing to the violent quarrels which were of daily occurrence between him and his father. Accordingly he enlisted and was sent to the crack 10th Jager Battalion, at Colmar in Alsace. Here he won golden opinions, and when released owing to illness, with a pension, his papers were marked 'Recht gut'. When he reached home there were fresh scenes of rancour whilst blows were not infrequently exchanged, and in 1903 he was examined by a medical expert, Dr. Andrae, who considered him morally lacking but yet there were no grounds for sending him to an asylum. Before long he sank to the status of a tramp; a street hawker, at times; a pilferer and a thief. Again and again he was sent to jail, now charged with larceny, now with burglary, now with indecency, now with fraud. In 1918, he was released after a long stretch to find another Germany. He returned to Hanover, and was able to open a small cook shop in the old quarter of the town, where he also hawked meat which was eagerly sought at a time of general hunger and scarcity. He drove yet another trade, that of 'copper's nark', an old lag who had turned spy and informer, and gave secret tips to the police as to the whereabouts of men they wanted. 'Detective Haarmann' he was nick-named by the women who thronged his shop because he always had plenty of fresh meat in store, and he invariably contrived to undersell the other butchers and victuallers of the quarter.

The centre of Hanover was the Great Railway Station, and Hanover was thronged especially at its centre with a vast ever-moving population, fugitives, wanderers and homeless from all parts of dislocated Germany. Runaway lads from towns in every direction made their way here, looking for work, looking for food, idly tramping without any definite object, without any definite goal, because they had nothing else to do. It can well be imagined that the police, a hopelessly inadequate force, kept as sharp a watch as possible on the Station and its purlieus, and Haarmann used to help them in their surveyance. At midnight, or in the early morning, he would walk up and down among the rows of huddled sleeping forms in the third-class waiting halls and suddenly waking up some frightened youngster demand to see his ticket, ask to know whence he had come and where he was going. Some sad story would be sobbed out, and the kindly Haarmann was wont to offer a mattress and a meal in his own place down town.

So far as could be traced the first boy he so charitably took to his rooms was a lad of seventeen named Friedel Rothe, who had run away from home. On 29th September 1918, his mother received a postcard, and it so happened the very same day his father returned from the war. The parents were not going to let their son disappear without a search, and they soon began to hunt for him in real earnest. One of Friedel's pals told them that the missing boy had met a detective who offered him shelter. Other clues were traced and with extraordinary trouble, for the authorities had more pressing matters in hand than tracking truant schoolboys, the family obliged the police to search Cellarstrasse 27, where Haarmann lived. When a sudden entry was made Haarmann was found with another boy in such an unequivocal situation that his friends, the police, were obliged to arrest him there and then, and he received nine months' imprisonment for gross indecency under Section 175 [Homosexuality] of the German Code. Four years later when Haarmann was awaiting trial for twenty-four murders he remarked: 'At the time when the policeman arrested me the head of the boy Friedel Rothe was hidden under a newspaper behind the oven. Later on, I threw it into the canal.'

In September 1919, Haarmann first met Hans Grans, the handsome lad who was to stand beside him in the dock. Grans, the type of abnormal and dangerous decadent which is only too common today, was one of the foulest parasites of society, pilferer and thief, bully, informer, spy, agent provocateur, murderer, renter, prostitute, and what is lower and fouler than all, blackmailer. The influence of this Ganymede over Haarmann was complete. It was he who instigated many of the murders—Adolf Hannappel a lad of seventeen was killed in November 1923, because Grans wanted his pair of trousers; Ernst Spiecker, likewise aged seventeen, was killed on 5th January 1924, because Grans coveted his 'toff [gentleman's] shirt'—it was he who arranged the details, he who very often trapped the prey.

It may be said that in 1918 Hanover, a town of 450,000 inhabitants, was well known as being markedly homosexual. There were inscribed on the police lists no less than 500 'Mannliche Prostitutierten' of whom the comeliest and best-dressed, the mannered and well-behaved elegants, frequented the Café Kropcke in the Georgstrasse, one of the first boulevards of New Hanover; whilst others met their friends at the androgynous balls in the Kalenberger Vorstadt, or in the old Assembly Rooms; and lowest of all there was a tiny dancing-place, 'Zur schwulen Guste', 'Hot-Stuff Guissie's' where poor boys found their clientele. It was here, for example, that Grans picked up young Ernst Spiecker, whose tawdry shirt cost him his life.

With regards to his demeanour at the trial the contemporary newspapers write: 'Throughout the long ordeal Haarmann was utterly impassive and complacent.... The details of the atrocious crimes for which Haarmann will shortly pay with his life were extremely revolting. All his victims were between 12 and 18 years of age, and it was proved that the accused actually sold the flesh for human consumption. He once made sausages in his kitchen, and, together with the purchaser, cooked and ate them.... Some alienists hold that even then the twenty-four murders cannot possibly exhaust the full toll of Haarmann's atrocious crimes, and estimate the total as high as fifty. With the exception of a few counts, the prisoner made minutely detailed confessions and for days the court listened to his grim narrative of how he cut up the bodies of his victims and disposed of the fragments in various ways. He consistently repudiated the imputation of insanity, but at the same time maintained unhesitatingly that all the murders were committed when he was in a state of trance, and unaware of what he was doing. This contention was specifically brushed aside by the Bench, which in its judgment pointed out that according to his own account of what happened, it was necessary for him to hold down his victims by hand in a peculiar way before it was possible for him to inflict a fatal bite on their throats. Such action necessarily involved some degree of deliberation and conscious purpose.'

Another account says with regard to Haarmann: "The killing of altogether twenty-seven young men is laid at his door, the horror of the deeds being magnified by the allegation that he sold to customers for consumption the flesh of those he did not himself eat.... With Haarmann in the dock appeared a younger man, his friend Hans Grans, first accused of assisting in the actual murders but now charged with inciting to commit them and with receiving stolen property. The police are still hunting for a third man, Charles, also a butcher, who is alleged to have completed the monstrous trio...the prosecuting attorney has an array of nearly 200 witnesses to prove that all the missing youths were done to death in the same horrible way.... He would take them to his room, and after a copious meal would praise the looks of his younger guests. Then he would kill them after the fashion of a vampire. Their clothes he would put up on sale in his shop, and the bodies would be cut up and disposed of with the assistance of Charles.'

In open court, however, Haarmann admitted that Grans often used to select his victims for him. More than once, he alleged, Grans beat him for failing to kill the 'game' brought in, and Haarmann would keep the corpses in a cupboard actually in his rooms when there was a body awaiting dismemberment. The back of the place abutted on the river, and the bones and skulls were thrown into the water. Some of them were discovered, but their origin was a mystery until a police inspector paid a surprise visit to the prisoner's home to inquire into a dispute between Haarmann and an intended victim who escaped.

Suspicion had at last fallen upon him principally, owing to the skulls and bones found in the river Leine during May, June, and July 1924. The newspapers said that during 1924, no less than 600 persons had disappeared, for the most part lads between 14 and 18. On the night of 22nd June at the railway station, sometime after midnight, a quarrel broke out between Haarmann and a young fellow named Fromm, who accused him of indecency. Both were taken to the central [police] station, and meanwhile Haarmann's room in the Red Row was thoroughly examined with the result that damning evidence came to light. Before long he accused Grans as his accomplice, since at the moment they happened to be on bad terms. Haarmann was sentenced to be decapitated, a sentence executed with a heavy sword. Grans was condemned to imprisonment for life, afterwards commuted to twelve years' penal servitude. In accordance with the law, Haarmann was put to death on Wednesday, 15th April 1925.

This is probably one of the most extraordinary cases of vampirism known. The violent eroticism, the fatal bite in the throat, are typical of the vampire, and it was perhaps something more than mere coincidence that the mode of execution should be the severing of the head from the body, since this was one of the efficacious methods of destroying a vampire.

Certainly in the extended sense of the word, as it is now so commonly used, Fritz Haarmann was a vampire in every particular.

Additionally, from *The News of the World*, 21 December 1924:

The details of the atrocious crimes for which Haarmann will shortly pay with his life were extremely revolting. All his victims were between 12 and 18 years of age, and it was proved that the accused actually sold the flesh for human consumption. He once made sausages in his kitchen, and, together with the purchaser, cooked and ate them.... Some alienists hold that even then the twenty-four murders cannot possibly exhaust the full toll of Haarmann's atrocious crimes, and estimate the total as high as fifty. With the exception of a few counts, the prisoner made minutely detailed confessions and for days the court listened to his grim narrative of how he cut up the bodies of his victims and disposed of the fragments in various ways. He consistently repudiated the imputation of insanity, but at the same time maintained unhesitatingly that all the murders were committed when he was in a state of trance, and unaware of what he was doing. This contention was specifically brushed aside by the Bench, which in its judgment pointed out that according to his own account of what happened, it was necessary for him to hold down his victims by hand in a peculiar way before

"Gothic & fetish fantasy" in The Midlands of England "presented by The Marquis' Masquerade."

it was possible for him to inflict a fatal bite on their throats. Such action often necessarily involved some degree of deliberation and conscious purpose.

THE VAMPYRE

Lord Byron's secretary and doctor, John Polidori (1795 - 1821), wrote this classic short story, once attributed to Byron himself. It launched the vampire craze in European literature. Polidori committed suicide very young. His tale lives on. If you think the vampire started with Bram Stoker's *Dracula*, you are in for a surprise.

It happened that in the midst of the dissipations attendant upon a London winter, there appeared at the various parties of the leaders of the *ton* a nobleman, more remarkable for his singularities, than his rank. He gazed upon the mirth around him, as if he could not participate therein. Apparently, the light laughter of the fair only attracted his attention, that he might by a look quell it, and throw fear into those breasts where thoughtlessness reigned. Those who felt this sensation of awe, could not explain whence it arose: some attributed it to the dead gray eye, which fixing upon the object's face, did not seem to penetrate, and at one glance to pierce through to the inward workings of the heart; but fell upon the cheek with a leaden ray that weighed upon the skin it could not pass. His peculiarities caused him to be invited to every house; all wished to see him, and those who had been accustomed to violent excitement, and now felt the weight of *ennui*, were pleased at having something in their presence capable of engaging their attention. In spite of the deadly hue of his face, which never gained a warmer tint, either from the blush of modesty, or from the strong emotion of passion, though its form and outline were beautiful, many of the female hunters after notoriety attempted to win his attentions, and gain, at least, some marks of what they might term affection: Lady Mercer, who had been the mockery of every monster shewn in drawing-rooms since her marriage, threw herself in his way, and did all but put on the dress of a mountebank, to attract his notice—though in vain—when she stood before him, though his eyes were apparently fixed upon hers, still it seemed as if they were unperceived–even her unappalled impudence was baffled, and she left the field. But though the common adulteress could not influence even the guidance of his eyes, it was not that the female sex was indifferent to him: yet such was the apparent caution with which he spoke to the virtuous wife and innocent daughter, that few knew he ever addressed himself to females. He had, however, the reputation of a winning tongue; and whether it was that it even overcame the dread of his singular character, or that they were moved by his apparent hatred of vice, he was as often among those females who form the boast of their sex from their domestic virtues, as among those who sully it by their vices.

About the same time, there came to London a young gentleman of the name of Aubrey: he was an orphan left with an only sister in the possession of great wealth, by parents who died while he was yet in childhood. Left also to himself by guardians, who thought it their duty merely to take care of his fortune, while they relinquished the more important charge of his mind to the care of mercenary subalterns, he cultivated more his imagination than his judgment. He had, hence, that high romantic feeling of honour and candour, which daily ruins so many milliners' apprentices. He believed all to sympathise with virtue, and thought that vice was thrown in by Providence merely for the picturesque effect of the scene, as we see in romances: he thought that the misery of a cottage merely consisted in the vesting of clothes, which were warm, but which were better adapted to the painter's eye by their irregular folds and various coloured patches. He thought, in fine, that the dreams of poets were the realities of life. He was handsome, frank, and rich: for these reasons, upon his entering into the gay circles, many mothers surrounded him, striving which should describe with least truth their languishing or romping favourites: the daughters at the same time, by their brightening countenances when he approached, and by their sparkling eyes, when he opened his lips, soon led him into false notions of his talents and his merit. Attached as he was to the romance of his solitary hours, he was startled at finding, that, except in the tallow and wax candles that flickered, not from the presence of a ghost, but from want of snuffing, there was no foundation in real life for any of that congeries of pleasing pictures and descriptions contained in those volumes, from which he had formed his study. Finding, however, some compensation in his gratified vanity, he was about to relinquish his dreams, when the extraordinary being we have above described, crossed him in his career.

He watched him; and the very impossibility of forming an idea of the character of a man entirely absorbed in himself, who gave few other signs of his observation of external objects, than the tacit assent of their existence, implied by the avoidance of their contact: allowing his imagination to picture every thing that flattered its propensity to extravagant ideas, he soon formed this object into the hero of a romance, and determined to observe the offspring of his fancy, rather than the person before him. He became acquainted with him, paid him attentions, and so far advanced upon his notice, that his presence was always recognised. He gradually learnt that Lord Ruthven's affairs were embarrassed, and soon found, from the notes of preparation in —Street, that he was about to travel. Desirous of gaining some information respecting this singular character, who, till now, had only whetted his curiosity, he hinted to his guardians, that it was time for him to perform the tour, which for many generations has been thought necessary to enable the young to take some rapid steps in the career of vice towards putting themselves upon an equality with the aged, and not allowing them to appear as if fallen from the skies, whenever scandalous intrigues are mentioned as the subjects of pleasantry or of praise, according to the degree of skill shewn in carrying them on. They consented: and Aubrey immediately mentioning his intentions to Lord Ruthven, was surprised to receive from him a proposal to join him. Flattered by such a mark of esteem from him, who, apparently, had nothing in common with other men, he gladly accepted it, and in a few days they had passed the circling waters.

Hitherto, Aubrey had had no opportunity of studying Lord Ruthven's character, and now he found, that, though many more of his actions were exposed to his view, the results offered different conclusions from the apparent motives to his conduct. His companion was profuse in his liberality–the idle, the vagabond, and the beggar, received from his hand more than enough to relieve their immediate wants. But Aubrey could not avoid remarking, that it was not upon the virtuous, reduced to indigence by the misfortunes attendant even upon virtue, that he bestowed his alms–these were sent from the door with hardly suppressed sneers; but when the profligate came to ask something, not to relieve his wants, but to allow him to wallow in his lust, or to sink him still deeper in his iniquity, he was sent away with rich charity. This was, however, attributed by him to the greater importunity of the vicious, which generally prevails over the retiring bashfulness of the virtuous indigent. There was one circumstance about the charity of his Lordship, which was still more impressed upon his mind: all those upon whom it was bestowed, inevitably found that there was a curse upon it, for they were all either led to the scaffold, or sunk to the lowest and the most abject misery. At Brussels and other towns through which they passed, Aubrey was surprised at the apparent eagerness with which his companion sought for the centres of all fashionable vice; there he entered into all the spirit of the faro table: he betted, and always gambled with success, except where the known sharper was his antagonist, and then he lost even more than he gained; but it was always with the same unchanging face, with which he generally watched the society around: it was not, however, so when he encountered the rash youthful novice, or the luckless father of a numerous family; then his very wish seemed fortune's law–this apparent abstractedness of mind was laid aside, and his eyes sparkled with more fire than that of the cat whilst dallying with the half-dead mouse. In every town, he left the formerly affluent youth, torn from the circle he adorned, cursing, in the solitude of a dungeon, the fate that had drawn him within the reach of this fiend; whilst many a father sat frantic, amidst the speaking looks of mute hungry children, without a single farthing of his late immense wealth, wherewith to buy even sufficient to satisfy their present craving. Yet he took no money from the gambling table; but immediately lost, to the ruiner of many, the last gilder he had just snatched from the convulsive grasp of the innocent: this might but be the result of a certain degree of knowledge, which was not, however, capable of combating the cunning of the more experienced. Aubrey often wished to represent this to his friend, and beg him to resign that charity and pleasure which proved the ruin of all, and did not tend to his own profit; but he delayed it—for each day he hoped his friend would give him some opportunity of speaking frankly and openly to him; however, this never occurred. Lord Ruthven in his carriage, and amidst the various wild and rich scenes of nature, was always the same: his eye spoke less than his lip; and though Aubrey was near the object of his curiosity, he obtained no greater gratification from it than the constant excitement of vainly wishing to break that mystery, which to his exalted imagination began to assume the appearance of something supernatural.

They soon arrived at Rome, and Aubrey for a time lost sight of his companion; he left him in daily attendance upon the morning circle of an Italian countess, whilst he went in search of the memorials of another almost deserted city. Whilst he was thus engaged, letters arrived from England, which he opened with eager impatience; the first was from his sister, breathing nothing but affection; the others were from his guardians, the latter astonished him; if it had before entered into his imagination that there was an evil power resident in his companion, these seemed to give him almost sufficient reason for the belief. His guardians insisted upon his immediately leaving his friend, and urged, that his character was dreadfully vicious, for that the possession of irresistible powers of seduction, rendered his licentious habits more dangerous to society. It had been discovered, that his contempt for the adulteress had not originated in hatred of her character; but that he had required, to enhance his gratification, that his victim, the partner of his guilt, should be hurled from the pinnacle of unsullied virtue, down to the lowest abyss of infamy and degradation: in fine, that all those females whom he had sought, apparently on account of their virtue, had, since his departure, thrown even the mask aside, and had not scrupled to expose the whole deformity of their vices to the public gaze.

Aubrey determined upon leaving one, whose character had not yet shown a single bright point on which to rest the eye. He resolved to invent some plausible pretext for abandoning him altogether, purposing, in the meanwhile, to watch him more closely, and to let no slight circumstances pass by unnoticed. He entered into the same circle, and soon perceived, that his Lordship was endeavouring to work upon the inexperience of the daughter of the lady whose house he chiefly frequented. In Italy, it is seldom that an unmarried female is met with in society; he was therefore obliged to carry on his plans in secret; but Aubrey's eye followed him in all his windings, and soon discovered that an assignation had been appointed, which would most likely end in the ruin of an innocent, though thoughtless girl. Losing no time, he entered the apartment of Lord Ruthven, and abruptly asked him his intentions with respect to the lady, informing him at the same time that he was aware of his being about to meet her that very night. Lord

Ruthven answered, that his intentions were such as he supposed all would have upon such an occasion; and upon being pressed whether he intended to marry her, merely laughed. Aubrey retired; and, immediately writing a note, to say, that from that moment he must decline accompanying his Lordship in the remainder of their proposed tour, he ordered his servant to seek other apartments, and calling upon the mother of the lady, informed her of all he knew, not only with regard to her daughter, but also concerning the character of his Lordship. The assignation was prevented. Lord Ruthven next day merely sent his servant to notify his complete assent to a separation; but did not hint any suspicion of his plans having been foiled by Aubrey's interposition.

Having left Rome, Aubrey directed his steps towards Greece, and crossing the Peninsula, soon found himself in Athens. He then fixed his residence in the house of a Greek; and soon occupied himself in tracing the faded records of ancient glory upon monuments that apparently, ashamed of chronicling the deeds of freemen only before slaves, had hidden themselves beneath the sheltering soil or many coloured lichen. Under the same roof as himself, existed a being, so beautiful and delicate, that she might have formed the model for a painter, wishing to portray on canvass the promised hope of the faithful in Mahomet's paradise, save that her eyes spoke too much mind of any one to think she could belong to those who had no souls. As she danced upon the plain, or tripped along the mountain's side, one would have thought the gazelle a poor type of her beauties; for who would have exchanged her eye, apparently the eye of animated nature, for that, sleepy luxurious look of the animal suited but to the taste of an epicure. The light step of Ianthe often accompanied Aubrey in his search after antiquities, and often would the unconscious girl, engaged in the pursuit of a Kashmere butterfly, show the whole beauty of her form, floating as it were upon the wind, to the eager gaze of him, who forgot the letters he had just deciphered upon an almost effaced tablet, in the contemplation of her sylph-like figure. Often would her tresses falling, as she flitted around, exhibit in the sun's ray such delicately brilliant and swiftly fading hues, as might well excuse the forgetfulness of the antiquary, who let escape from his mind the very object he had before thought of vital importance to the proper interpretation of a passage in Pausanias. But why attempt to describe charms which all feel, but none can appreciate? It was innocence,

youth, and beauty, unaffected by crowded drawing-rooms and sti-
fling balls. Whilst he drew those remains of which he wished to
preserve a memorial for his future hours, she would stand by, and
watch the magic effects of his pencil, in tracing the scenes of her
native place; she would then describe to him in all the glowing
colours of youthful memory, the marriage pomp she remembered
viewing in her infancy; and then, turning to subjects that had evidently made a greater impression upon her mind, would tell him
all the supernatural tales of her nurse. Her earnestness and apparent belief of what she narrated, excited the interest even of Aubrey;
and often as she told him the tale of the living Vampyre, who had
passed years amidst his friends, and dearest ties, forced every year,
by feeding upon the life of a lovely female to prolong his existence
of the ensuing months, his blood would run cold, whilst he
attempted to laugh her out of such idle and horrible fantasies; but
Ianthe cited to him the names of old men, who had at last detected
one living among themselves, after several of their near relatives
and children had been found marked with the stamp of the fiend's
appetite; and when she found him so incredulous, she begged of
him to believe her, for it had been remarked, that those who had
dared to question their existence, always had some proof given,
which obliged them, with grief and heartbreaking, to confess it was
true. She detailed to him the traditional appearance of these monsters, and his horror was increased, by hearing a pretty accurate
description of Lord Ruthven; he, however, still persisted in per-
suading her, that there could be no truth in her fears, though at
the same time he wondered at the many coincidences which had
all tended to excite a belief in the supernatural power of Lord
Ruthven.

Aubrey began to attach himself more and more to Ianthe; her
innocence, so contrasted with all the affected virtues of the women
among whom he had sought for his vision of romance, won his
heart; and while he ridiculed the idea of a young man of English
habits, marrying an uneducated Greek girl, still he found himself
more and more attached to the almost fairy form before him. He
would tear himself at times from her, and, forming a plan for some
antiquarian research, he would depart, determined not to return
until his object was attained; but he always found it impossible to
fix his attention upon the ruins around him, whilst in his mind he
retained an image that seemed alone the rightful possessor of his

thoughts. Ianthe was unconscious of his love, and was ever the same frank infantile being he had first known. She always seemed to part from him with reluctance; but it was because she had no longer anyone with whom she could visit her favourite haunts, whilst her guardian was occupied in sketching or uncovering some fragment which had yet escaped the destructive hand of time. She had appealed to her parents on the subject of Vampyres, and they both, with several present, affirmed their existence, pale with horror at the very name. Soon after, Aubrey determined to proceed upon one of his excursions, which was to detain him for a few hours; when they heard the name of the place, they all at once begged of him not to return at night, as he must necessarily pass through a wood, where no Greek would ever remain, after the day had closed, upon any consideration. They described it as the resort of the vampyres in their nocturnal orgies, and denounced the most heavy evils as impending upon him who dared to cross their path. Aubrey made light of their representations, and tried to laugh them out of the idea; but when he saw them shudder at his daring thus to mock a superior, infernal power, the very name of which apparently made their blood freeze, he was silent.

Next morning Aubrey set off upon his excursion unattended; he was surprised to observe the melancholy face of his host, and was concerned to find that his words, mocking the belief of those horrible fiends, had inspired them with such terror. When he was about to depart, Ianthe came to the side of his horse, and earnestly begged of him to return, ere night allowed the power of these beings to be put in action—he promised. He was, however, so occupied in his research that he did not perceive that daylight would soon end, and that in the horizon there was one of those specks which, in the warmer climates, so rapidly gather into a tremendous mass, and pour all their rage upon the devoted country. He at last, however, mounted his horse, determined to make up by speed for his delay: but it was too late. Twilight, in these southern climates, is almost unknown; immediately the sun sets, night begins: and ere he had advanced far, the power of the storm was above—its echoing thunders had scarcely an interval of rest—its thick heavy rain forced its way through the canopying foliage, whilst the blue forked lightning seemed to fall and radiate at his very feet. Suddenly his horse took fright, and he was carried with dreadful rapidity through the entangled forest. The animal at last, through fatigue, stopped, and he found, by the glare of lightning, that he was in the neighbourhood of a hovel that hardly lifted itself up from the masses of dead leaves and brushwood which surrounded it. Dismounting, he approached, hoping to find someone to guide him to the town, or at least trusting to obtain shelter from the pelting storm. As he approached, the thunders, for a moment silent, allowed him to hear the dreadful shrieks of a woman mingling with the stifled, exultant mockery of a laugh, continued in one almost unbroken sound–he was startled: but, roused by the thunder which again rolled over his head, he, with a sudden effort, forced open the door of the hut. He found himself in utter darkness: the sound, however, guided him. He was apparently unperceived; for, though he called, still the sounds continued, and no notice was taken of him. He found himself in contact with someone, whom he immediately seized; when a voice cried, 'Again baffled!' to which a loud laugh succeeded; and he felt himself grappled by one whose strength seemed superhuman: determined to sell his life as dearly as he could, he struggled; but it was in vain: he was lifted from his feet and hurled with enormous force against the ground–his enemy threw himself upon him, and kneeling upon his breast, had placed his hands upon his throat-when the glare of many torches penetrating through the hole that gave light in the day, disturbed him–he instantly rose, and, leaving his prey, rushed through the door, and in a moment the crashing of the branches, as he broke through the wood, was no longer heard. The storm was now still; and Aubrey, incapable of moving, was soon heard by those without. They entered; the light of their torches fell upon the mud walls, and the thatch loaded on every individual straw with heavy flakes of soot. At the desire of Aubrey they searched for her who had attracted him by her cries; he was again left in darkness; but what was his horror, when the light of the torches once more burst upon him, to perceive the airy form of his fair conductress brought in a lifeless corpse. He shut his eyes, hoping that it was but a vision arising from his disturbed imagination; but he again saw the same form, when he unclosed them, stretched by his side. There was no colour upon her cheek, not even upon her lip; yet there was a stillness about her face that seemed almost as attaching as the life that once dwelt there–upon her neck and breast was blood, and upon her throat were the marks of teeth having opened the vein–to this the men pointed, crying simultaneously struck with horror, "A

Vampyre! a Vampyre!' A litter was quickly formed, and Aubrey was laid by the side of her who had lately been to him the object of so many bright and fairy visions, now fallen with the flower of life that had died within her. He knew not what his thoughts were–his mind was benumbed and seemed to shun reflection, and take refuge in vacancy–he held almost unconsciously in his hand a naked dagger of a particular construction, which had been found in the hut. They were soon met by different parties who had been engaged in the search of her whom a mother had missed. Their lamentable cries, as they approached the city, forewarned the parents of some dreadful catastrophe. To describe their grief would be impossible; but when they ascertained the cause of their child's death, they looked at Aubrey, and pointed to the corpse. They were inconsolable; both died broken-hearted.

Aubrey being put to bed was seized with a most violent fever, and was often delirious; in these intervals he would call upon Lord Ruthven and upon Ianthe–by some unaccountable combination he seemed to beg of his former companion to spare the being he loved. At other times he would imprecate maledictions upon his head, and curse him as her destroyer. Lord Ruthven chanced at this time to arrive at Athens, and, from whatever motive, upon hearing of the state of Aubrey, immediately placed himself in the same house, and became his constant attendant. When the latter recovered from his delirium, he was horrified and startled at the sight of him whose image he had now combined with that of a Vampyre; but Lord Ruthven, by his kind words, implying almost repentance for the fault that had caused their separation, and still more by the attention, anxiety, and care which he showed, soon reconciled him to his presence. His lordship seemed quite changed; he no longer appeared that apathetic being who had so astonished Aubrey; but as his convalescence began to be rapid, he again gradually retired into the same state of mind, and Aubrey perceived no difference from the former man, except that at times he was surprised to meet his gaze fixed intently upon him, with a smile of malicious exultation playing upon his lips: he knew not why, but this smile haunted him. During the last stage of the invalid's recovery, Lord Ruthven was apparently engaged in watching the tideless waves raised by the cooling breeze, or in marking the progress of those orbs, circling, like our world, the moveless sun–indeed, he appeared to wish to avoid the eyes of all.

Aubrey's mind, by this shock, was much weakened, and that elasticity of spirit which had once so distinguished him now seemed to have fled forever. He was now as much a lover of solitude and silence as Lord Ruthven; but much as he wished for solitude, his mind could not find it in the neighbourhood of Athens; if he sought it amidst the ruins he had formerly frequented, Ianthe's form stood by his side–if he sought it in the woods, her light step would appear wandering amidst the underwood, in quest of the modest violet; then suddenly turning round, would show, to his wild imagination, her pale face and wounded throat, with a meek smile upon her lips. He determined to fly scenes, every feature of which created such bitter associations in his mind. He proposed to Lord Ruthven, to whom he held himself bound by the tender care he had taken of him during his illness, that they should visit those parts of Greece neither had yet seen. They travelled in every direction, and sought every spot to which a recollection could be attached: but though they thus hastened from place to place, yet they seemed not to heed what they gazed upon. They heard much of robbers, but they gradually began to slight these reports, which they imagined were only the invention of individuals, whose interest it was to excite the generosity of those whom they defended from pretended dangers. In consequence of thus neglecting the advice of the inhabitants, on one occasion they travelled with only a few guards, more to serve as guides than as a defence. Upon entering, however, a narrow defile, at the bottom of which was the bed of a torrent, with large masses of rock brought down from the neighbouring precipices, they had reason to repent their negligence; for scarcely were the whole of the party engaged in the narrow pass, when they were startled by the whistling of bullets close to their heads, and by the echoed report of several guns. In an instant their guards had left them, and, placing themselves behind rocks, had begun to fire in the direction whence the report came. Lord Ruthven and Aubrey, imitating their example, retired for a moment behind the sheltering turn of the defile: but ashamed of being thus detained by a foe, who with insulting shouts bade them advance, and being exposed to unresisting slaughter, if any of the robbers should climb above and take them in the rear, they determined at once to rush forward in search of the enemy. Hardly had they lost the shelter of the rock, when Lord Ruthven received a shot in the shoulder, which brought him to the ground. Aubrey hastened to his assistance; and, no longer heeding the contest of his own peril, was soon surprised by seeing the robbers' faces around him—his guards having, upon Lord Ruthven's being wounded, immediately thrown up their arms and surrendered.

By promises of great reward, Aubrey soon induced them to convey his wounded friend to a neighbouring cabin; and having agreed upon a ransom, he was no more disturbed by their presence—they being content merely to guard the entrance till their comrade should return with the promised sum, for which he had an order. Lord Ruthven's strength rapidly decreased; in two days mortification ensued, and death seemed advancing with hasty steps. His conduct and appearance had not changed; he seemed as unconscious of pain as he had been of the objects about him: but towards the close of the last evening, his mind became apparently uneasy, and his eye often fixed upon Aubrey, who was induced to offer his assistance with more than usual earnestness—'Assist me! you may save me—you may do more than that - I mean not my life, I heed the death of my existence as little as that of the passing day; but you may save my honour, your friend's honour.' 'How? tell me how? I would do anything,' replied Aubrey. 'I need but little—my life ebbs apace—I cannot explain the whole—but if you would conceal all you know of me, my honour were free from stain in the world's mouth—and if my death were unknown for some time in England - I - I - but life.' 'It shall not be known.' 'Swear!' cried the dying man, raising himself with exultant violence, 'Swear by all your soul reveres, by all your nature fears, swear that for a year and a day you will not impart your knowledge of my crimes or death to any living being in any way, whatever may happen, or whatever you may see.' His eyes seemed bursting from their sockets: 'I swear' said Aubrey; he sunk laughing upon his pillow, and breathed no more.

Aubrey retired to rest, but did not sleep; the many circumstances attending his acquaintance with this man rose upon his mind, and he knew not why; when he remembered his oath a cold shivering came over him, as if from the presentiment of something horrible awaiting him. Rising early in the morning, he was about to enter the hovel in which he had left the corpse, when a robber met him, and informed him that it was no longer there, having been conveyed by himself and comrades, upon his retiring, to the pinnacle of a neighbouring mount, according to a promise they had given his lordship, that it should be exposed to the first cold ray of the moon that rose after his death. Aubrey was astonished, and taking several of the men, determined to go and bury it upon the spot where it lay. But, when he had mounted to the summit he found no trace of either the corpse or the clothes, though the robbers swore they pointed out the identical rock on which they had laid the body. For a time his mind was bewildered in conjectures, but he at last returned, convinced that they had buried the corpse for the sake of the clothes.

Weary of a country in which he had met with such terrible misfortunes, and in which all apparently conspired to heighten that superstitious melancholy that had seized upon his mind, he resolved to leave it, and soon arrived at Smyrna. While waiting for a vessel to convey him to Otranto, or to Naples, he occupied himself in arranging those effects he had with him belonging to Lord Ruthven. Amongst other things there was a case containing several weapons of offence, more or less adapted to ensure the death of the victim. There were several daggers and ataghans. Whilst turning them over, and examining their curious forms, what was his surprise at finding a sheath apparently ornamented in the same style as the dagger discovered in the fatal hut—he shuddered—hastening to gain further proof, he found the weapon, and his horror may be imagined when he discovered that it fitted, though peculiarly shaped, the sheath he held in his hand. His eyes seemed to need no further certainty–they seemed gazing to be bound to the dagger; yet still he wished to disbelieve; but the particular form, the same varying tints upon the haft and sheath were alike in splendour on both, and left no room for doubt, there were also drops of blood on each.

He left Smyrna, and on his way home, at Rome, his first inquiries were concerning the lady he had attempted to snatch from Lord Ruthven's seductive arts. Her parents were in distress, their fortune ruined, and she had not been heard of since the departure of his lordship. Aubrey's mind became almost broken under so many repeated horrors; he was afraid that this lady had fallen a victim to the destroyer of Ianthe. He became morose and silent; and his only occupation consisted in urging the speed of the postilions, as if he were going to save the life of someone he held dear. he arrived at Calais; a breeze, which seemed obedient to his will, soon wafted him to the English shores; and he hastened to the mansion of his fathers, and there, for a moment, appeared to lose, in the embraces and caresses of his sister, all memory of the past. If she before, by her infantine caresses, had gained his affection, now that the woman began to appear, she was still more attaching as a companion.

Miss Aubrey had not that winning grace which gains the gaze and applause of the drawing-room assemblies. There was none of that light brilliancy which only exists in the heated atmosphere of a crowded apartment. Her blue eye was never lit up by the levity of the mind beneath. There was a melancholy charm about it which did not seem to arise from misfortune, but from some feeling within, that appeared to indicate a soul conscious of a brighter realm. Her step was not that light footing, which strays where'er a butterfly or a colour may attract–it was sedate and pensive. When alone, her face was never brightened by the smile of joy; but when her brother breathed to her his affection, and would in her presence forget those griefs she knew destroyed his rest, who would have exchanged her smile for that of the voluptuary? It seemed as if those eyes, that face were then playing in the light of their own native sphere. She was yet only eighteen, and had not been presented to the world, it having been thought by her guardians more fit that her presentation should be delayed until her brother's return from the continent, when he might be her protector. It was now, therefore, resolved that the next drawing-room, which was fast approaching, should be the epoch of her entry into the 'busy scene'. Aubrey would rather have remained in the mansion of his fathers, and fed upon the melancholy which overpowered him. He could not feel interest about the frivolities of fashionable strangers, when his mind had been so torn by the events he had witnessed; but he determined to sacrifice his own comfort to the protection of his sister. They soon arrived in town, and prepared for the next day, which had been announced as a drawing-room.

The crowd was excessive–a drawing-room had not been held for a long time, and all who were anxious to bask in the smile of royalty, hastened thither. Aubrey was there with his sister. While he was standing in a corner by himself, heedless of all around him, engaged in the remembrance that the first time he had seen Lord Ruthven was in that very place - he felt himself suddenly seized by the arm, and a voice he recognised too well, sounded in his ear–'Remember your oath.' He had hardly courage to turn, fear-

ful of seeing a spectre that would blast him, when he perceived, at
a little distance, the same figure which had attracted his notice on
this spot upon his first entry into society. He gazed till his limbs
almost refusing to bear their weight, he was obliged to take the
arm of a friend, and forcing a passage through the crowd, he threw
himself into his carriage, and was driven home. He paced the room
with hurried steps, and fixed his hands upon his head, as if he were
afraid his thoughts were bursting from his brain. Lord Ruthven
again before him–circumstances started up in a dreadful array–the
dagger–his oath. He roused himself, he could not believe it possible–the dead rise again! He thought his imagination had conjured
up the image his mind was resting upon. It was impossible that it
could be real–he determined, therefore, to go again into society;
for though he attempted to ask concerning Lord Ruthven, the
name hung upon his lips, and he could not succeed in gaining information. He went a few nights after with his sister to the assembly
of a near relation. Leaving her under the protection of a matron,
he retired into a recess, and there gave himself up to his own
devouring thoughts. Perceiving, at last, that many were leaving,
he roused himself, and entering another room, found his sister surrounded by several apparently in earnest conversation; he
attempted to pass and get near her, when one, whom he requested
to move, turned round, and revealed to him those features he most
abhorred. He sprang forward, seized his sister's arm, and, with hurried step, forced her towards the street: at the door he found himself impeded by the crowd of servants who were waiting for their
lords; and while he was engaged in passing them, he again heard
that voice whisper close to him–'Remember your oath!' He did not
dare to turn, but, hurrying his sister, soon reached home.

Aubrey became almost distracted. If before his mind had been
absorbed by one subject, how much more completely was it
engrossed, now that the certainty of the monster's living again
pressed upon his thoughts. His sister's attentions were now
unheeded, and it was in vain that she entreated him to explain to
her what had caused his abrupt conduct. He only uttered a few
words, and those terrified her. The more he thought, the more he
was bewildered. His oath startled him–was he then to allow this
monster to roam, bearing ruin upon his breath, amidst all he held
dear, and not avert its progress? His very sister might have been
touched by him. But even if he were to break his oath, and dis-

close his suspicions, who would believe him? He thought of employing his own hand to free the world from such a wretch; but death, he remembered, had been already mocked. For days he remained in this state; shut up in his room, he saw no one, and ate only when his sister came, who, with eyes streaming with tears, besought him, for her sake, to support nature. At last, no longer capable of bearing stillness and solitude, he left his house, roamed from street to street, anxious to fly that image which haunted him. His dress became neglected, and he wandered, as often exposed to the noon-day sun as to the midnight damps. He was no longer to be recognised; at first he returned with the evening to the house; but at last he laid himself down to rest wherever fatigue overtook him. His sister, anxious for his safety, employed people to follow him; but they were soon distanced by him who fled from a pursuer swifter than any—from thought. His conduct, however, suddenly changed. Struck with the idea that he left by his absence the whole of his friends, with a fiend amongst them, of whose presence they were unconscious, he determined to enter again into society, and watch him closely, anxious to forewarn, in spite of his oath, all whom Lord Ruthven approached with intimacy. But when he entered into a room, his haggard and suspicious looks were so striking, his inward shudderings so visible, that his sister was at last obliged to beg of him to abstain from seeking, for her sake, a society which affected him so strongly. When, however, remonstrance proved unavailing, the guardians thought proper to interpose, and, fearing that his mind was becoming alienated, they thought it high time to resume again that trust which had been before imposed upon them by Aubrey's parents.

Desirous of saving him from the injuries and sufferings he had daily encountered in his wanderings, and of preventing him from exposing to the general eye those marks of what they considered folly, they engaged a physician to reside in the house, and take constant care of him. He hardly appeared to notice, it so completely was his mind absorbed by one terrible subject. His incoherence became at last so great, that he was confined to his chamber. There he would often lie for days, incapable of being roused. He had become emaciated, his eyes had attained a glassy lustre—the only sign of affection and recollection remaining displayed itself upon the entry of his sister; then he would sometimes start, and, seizing her hands, with looks that severely afflicted her, he would desire her not to touch him. 'Oh, do not touch him-if your love for me is aught, do not go near him!' When, however, she enquired to whom he referred, his only answer was, 'True! true!' and again he sank into a state, whence not even she could rouse him. This lasted many months: gradually, however, as the year was passing, his incoherences became less frequent, and his mind threw off a portion of its gloom, whilst his guardians observed, that several times in the day he would count upon his fingers a definite number, and then smile.

The time had nearly elapsed, when, upon the last day of the year, one of his guardians entering his room, began to converse with his physician upon the melancholy circumstance of Aubrey's being in so awful a situation, when his sister was going next day to be married. Instantly Aubrey's attention was attracted; he asked anxiously to whom. Glad of this mark of returning intellect, of which they feared he had been deprived, they mentioned the name of the Earl of Marsden. Thinking this was a young Earl whom he had met with in society, Aubrey seemed pleased, and astonished them still more by his expressing his intention to be present at the nuptials, and desiring to see his sister. They answered not, but in a few minutes his sister was with him. He was apparently again capable of being affected by the influence of her lovely smile; for he pressed her to his breast, and kissed her cheek, wet with tears, flowing at the thought of her brother's being once more alive to the feelings of affection. He began to speak with all his wonted warmth, and to congratulate her upon her marriage with a person so distinguished for rank and every accomplishment; when he suddenly perceived a locket upon her breast; opening it, what was his surprise at beholding the features of the monster who had so long influenced his life. He seized the portrait in a paroxysm of rage, and trampled it under foot. Upon her asking him why he thus destroyed the resemblance of her future husband, he looked as if he did not understand her–then seizing her hands, and gazing on her with a frantic expression of countenance, he bade her swear that she would never wed this monster, for he–But he could not advance–it seemed as if that voice again bade him remember his oath–he turned suddenly round, thinking Lord Ruthven was near him but saw no one. In the meantime the guardians and physician, who had heard the whole, and thought this was but a return of his disorder, entered, and forcing him from Miss Aubrey, desired her to leave him. He fell upon his knees to them, he implored, he begged of them to delay but one day. They, attributing this to the insanity they imagined had taken possession of his mind, endeavoured to pacify him, and retired.

Lord Ruthven had called the morning after the drawing-room, and had been refused with everyone else. When he heard of Aubrey's ill health, he readily understood himself to be the cause of it; but when he learned that he was deemed insane, his exultation and pleasure could hardly be concealed from those among whom he had gained this information. He hastened to the house of his former companion, and, by constant attendance, and the pretence of great affection for the brother and interest in his fate, he gradually won the ear of Miss Aubrey. Who could resist his power? His tongue had dangers and toils to recount–could speak of himself as of an individual having no sympathy with any being on the crowded earth, save with her to whom he addressed himself–could tell how, since he knew her, his existence had begun to seem worthy of preservation, if it were merely that he might listen to her soothing accents–in fine, he knew so well how to use the serpent's art, or such was the will of fate, that he gained her affections. The title of the elder branch falling at length to him, he obtained an important embassy, which served as an excuse for hastening the marriage (in spite of her brother's deranged state), which was to take place the very day before his departure for the continent.

Aubrey, when he was left by the physician and his guardians, attempted to bribe the servants, but in vain. He asked for pen and paper; it was given him; he wrote a letter to his sister, conjuring her, as she valued her own happiness, her own honour, and the honour of those now in the grave, who once held her in their arms as their hope and the hope of their house, to delay but for a few hours that marriage, on which he denounced the most heavy curses. The servants promised they would deliver it; but giving it to the physician, he thought it better not to harass any more the mind of Miss Aubrey by, what he considered, the ravings of a maniac. Night passed on without rest to the busy inmates of the house; and Aubrey heard, with a horror that may more easily be conceived than described, the notes of busy preparation. Morning came, and the sound of carriages broke upon his ear. Aubrey grew almost frantic. The curiosity of the servants at last overcame their vigilance, they gradually stole away, leaving him in the custody of a helpless old woman. He seized the opportunity, with one bound was out of the room, and in a moment found himself in the apartment where all were nearly assembled. Lord Ruthven was the first to perceive him: he immediately approached, and, taking his arm by force, hurried him from the room, speechless with rage. When on the staircase, Lord Ruthven whispered in his ear–'Remember your oath, and know, if not my bride today, your sister is dishonoured. Women are frail!' So saying, he pushed him towards his attendants, who, roused by the old woman, had come in search of him. Aubrey could no longer support himself; his rage not finding vent, had broken a blood-vessel, and he was conveyed to bed. This was not mentioned to his sister, who was not present when he entered, as the physician was afraid of agitating her. The marriage was solemnised, and the bride and bridegroom left London.

Aubrey's weakness increased; the effusion of blood produced symptoms of the near approach of death. He desired his sister's guardians might be called, and when the midnight hour had struck, he related composedly what the reader has perused - he died immediately after.

The guardians hastened to protect Miss Aubrey; but when they arrived, it was too late. Lord Ruthven had disappeared, and Aubrey's sister had glutted the thirst of a VAMPYRE!

Dr. Polidori wrote of his tale of *The Vampyre*:

The superstition upon which this tale is founded is very general in the East.... It did not, however, extend itself to the Greeks until after the establishment of Christianity and it has only assumed its present form since the division of the Latin and Greek churches; at which time, the idea becoming prevalent that a Latin body could not corrupt if buried in their territory, it gradually increased, and formed the subject of many wonderful stories, still extant, of the dead rising from their graves, and feeding upon the blood of the young and beautiful.

In the West it spread, with some slight variation, all over Hungary, Poland, Austria and Lorraine, where the belief existed that vampyres nightly imbibed a certain portion of the blood of their victims, who became emaciated, lost strength, and speedily died of consumptions; whilst these human blood suckers fattened–and their veins became distended to such a state of repletion, as to cause the blood to flow from all passages of their bodies, and even from the very pores of their skins.

In the London Journal, of March, 1732, is a curious, and, of course, *credible* account of a particular case of vampyrism, which it stated to have occurred at Madreyga, in Hungary. It appears, that upon an examination of the commander-in-chief and magistrates of the place, they positively and unanimously affirmed, that, about five years before, a certain Heyduke named Arnold Paul, had been heard to say, that, at Cassovia [Kosice, in Czechoslovakia] on the frontiers of the Turkish Servia, he had been tormented by a vampyre, but had found a way to rid himself of the evil, by eating some of the earth out of the vampyre's grave, and rubbing himself with his blood.

This precaution, however, did not prevent him from becoming a vampyre himself.... For, about twenty or thirty days after his death and burial, many persons complained of having been tormented by him, and a deposition was made, that four persons had been deprived of life by his attacks.

The first issue of a typical fanzine. This one was edited by William G. Obbacy of Cleveland (OH). Others have been published in Los Angeles and elsewhere in the United States; the most consistent probably are those of the Count Dracula Fan Club of New York City. Still others come from organizations in the UK.

3

The Vampire in the Americas

Some of the tradition of vampire-like creatures in pre-Columbia America has presumably been lost with the wanton destruction by Europeans of aboriginal cultures here, but in North, Central, and South America terrible creatures that attacked by night included not only animals such as the jaguar but also supernatural entities. When the vampire bat of the Americas (so-called because it sucked blood, of course) was discovered, the Americas in fact were able to add a touch to the European tradition.

Someone once said that the invention of the electric light was the end of ghosts—naturally it wasn't—and some argue that the modern world has no place for such superstitions as the vampire, but alleged cases of vampirism still are reported and the vampire, as we shall see further in later chapters, is alive and well in popular culture in the Americas. He (or, occasionally, she) turns up on television in series such as *Dark Shadows* and *Buffy the Vampire Slayer* and this is a sure indication—and reinforcement —of the vampire's place in the culture of the Americas.

> But see, amid the human round
> A drawling shape intrude
> A blood-red thing that writhes from out
> The scenic solitude!
> It writhes!—it writhes!—with mortal pangs
> And man becomes its food,

The angels sob at vermin fangs
In human gore imbrued.
—Edgar Allen Poe

WHAT'S GOING TO HAPPEN TO THE TOTS?

The US worries a lot about children—abortions, child abuse, child pornography, what the kiddies may see on television or on the Internet , whether they will get into a good college or collect Social Security, how they are so different from the way we say we were when young. We work and worry. Vampires are well known to children. Should we worry about that? Think of The Count on *Sesame Street*, vampire dolls and various other toys, Count Chocula and other kiddie foods, and Halloween costumes.

Katie Leisman wrote for one of the world's most widely circulated publications, a magazine in perhaps as many homes as The Bible (and consulted far more often), *TV Guide*. There (10 January 1981) she presented a survey, "When Is Television Too Scary for Children?" She began:

> Three-year-old Marcus Clinton curled up with his parents to watch [Stephen King's] *Salem's Lot*, an eerie movie, on television. He squealed over some characters, covering his eyes occasionally, until the first vampire appeared. Then he leaned forward, staring silently at the set. After the show ended, Marcus announced that he wasn't going to bed. That night and the next four nights his parents stayed up with the boy, reassuring him that vampires don't really exist...[and] child psychologist Lee Walk finds Marcus' response a classic one. Parents often assume that the most overtly spooky things, goblins and witches will scare small kids. But nothing may frighten them more than a character that's realistic in every aspect but one—and a vampire looks like everyone else until it opens its mouth.

VAMPIRES IN RHODE ISLAND

Practically the only vampire news from Rhode Island was that reported in the *Norwich Courier* in 1854—some honest citizens digging up a couple of alleged vampires who were preying on the living—until Raymond T. McNally found a newspaper clipping among the papers of Bram Stoker. He believes Stoker was influenced by the story when he wrote *Dracula*. McNally prints the newspaper story (from the *New York World* for 2 February 1896) in *A Clutch of Vampires* (1975) claiming "it has never previously been reprinted in whole or in part by any other vampire devotee." I do not print it "in whole"; I print only the first half of the newspaper article or less, because the rest of it is simply an amateur, potted history of vampirism in Europe (much better covered elsewhere) and not related to life in these United States.

VAMPIRES IN NEW ENGLAND
Dead Bodies Dug Up and Their Hearts
Burned to Prevent Disease

STRANGE SUPERSTITION OF LONG AGO
The Old Belief Was that Ghostly Monsters
Sucked the Blood of Their Living Relatives.

Recent ethnological research has disclosed something very extraordinary in Rhode Island. It appears that the ancient vampire superstition still survives in that State, and within the last few years many people have been digging up dead bodies of relatives for the purpose of burning their hearts.

Near Newport scores of such exhumations have been made, the purpose being to prevent the dead from preying upon the living. The belief entertained is that a person who has died of consumption [modern: tuberculosis] is likely to rise from the grave at night and suck the blood of surviving members of his or her own family, thus dooming them to a similar fate.

The discovery of the survival in highly educated New England of a superstition dating back to the days of Sardanapalus [669-640 *B.C.*] and Nebuchadnezzar [the second king of Babylon of that name, died 562 *B.C.*] has been made by George R. Stetson, an ethnologist of repute. He has found it rampant in the district which includes the towns of Exeter, Foster, Kingstown, East Greenwich, and many scattered hamlets. This region, where abandoned farms are numerous, is the tramping-ground of the book agent, the chromo [picture] peddler and the patent medicine man. The social isolation is as complete as it was two centuries ago.

Two Typical Cases

There is one small village distant fifteen miles from Newport, where within the last few years there have been at least half a dozen resurrections on this account. The most recent was made two years ago [1894] in a family where the mother and four children had already succumbed to consumption. The last of these children was exhumed and the heart burned.

Another instance was noted in a seashore town, not far from Newport, possessing a summer hotel and a few cottages of hot-weather residents. An intelligent man, by trade a mason, informed Mr. Stetson that he had lost two brothers by consumption. On the death of the second brother, his father was advised to take up the body and burn the heart. He refused to do so, and consequently was attacked by the disease. His heart was burned, and in this way the rest of the family escaped.

This frightful superstition is said to prevail in all of the isolated districts of Southern Rhode Island, and it survives to some extent in the large centers of population. Sometimes the body is burned, not merely the heart, and the ashes are scattered....

We may add this: strangely, the heart of those not assumed to be vampires are sometimes saved from burning when the rest of the corpse is cremated. John Trelawney (1792-1881), when the body of his friend Percy Bysshe Shelley, born the same year as Trelawney and drowned in 1822, was burned on the beach, reached into the pyre and snatched the heart of Shelley from the flames! (Tennessee Williams has his character Lord Byron say in *Camino Real* that he witnessed the scene and found it disgusting.)

Has the growing popularity of cremation in America done anything to keep down the vampire population? Americans certainly are afraid of vampires. In New York *botánicas* one can buy balls of bright blue chalk which Puerto Ricans and a few others use to write on their bodies, before they go to sleep for the night, the symbols that ward off vampire attacks. I could not find these for sale anywhere in modern Rhode Island.

VAMPIRE IN CHICAGO

In 1876, a woman who died of tuberculosis was disinterred and her lungs burned so that her relatives would not die of the same disease, a Dr. Dyer reported. Today there is a certain amount of vampiristic play in the sadomasochistic leather bars of Chicago, but the dead do not walk.

VAMPIRE IN BROOKLYN

Professor McNally's paperback anthology quotes William Seabrook's *Witchcraft* about a "vampire in Brooklyn," but admits that the "blood-sucking female presented here is not undead, hence is not a true vampire." Dr. Jeanne Youngson, president of The Count Dracula Fan Club in Manhattan, has introduced me to some real females who say they like to drink actual blood but of course they are not real vampires, any more than are the "vampire landlords" and other "bloodsuckers" we read about in New York City newspapers. I have met as well some psychiatric cases, courtesy of friends working in facilities for the criminally insane, who have drunk the blood of others and even killed to get it, but these are more like the serial killer "Hannibal the Cannibal" in Thomas Harris's well known novel *The Silence of the Lambs* (also an award-winning movie) than The Count. The doctors do assure me, however, that in their own minds these sad cases are vampires and that a few of them actually slept in coffins or, less dramatically, adopted some of the other traditional habits that folklore assigns to predatory creatures of the dark. At least one to my knowledge wanted to sue the state to permit him in custody to practice his "religion" of vampirism. One made the compromise of drinking only the blood of animals which he bought or caught in the streets. That in itself is horrifying to dedicated animal lovers, of whom some cynics might say there may be more than dedicated people lovers in New York City.

VAMPIRE PLACE

There are plenty of US places that are now ghost towns and a number with the word "ghost" in the name (including Ghost Hollow, Ghost Mine, Ghost School, The Ghost Town Capital of Roberts Co. (SD), The Ghost Town in the Glen (PA), and there are even Ghoul Branch, Ghoul Creek, Ghouls Fork, but only one "vampire," Vampire Mine (AZ).

EVIL SISTERS

This (as was noted above) is the title of a scholarly study of women as evil seductresses (1996) by Bram Dijkstra. It is remarkable that in twentieth-century art, fashion, film, and literature the female vampire has so caught on. It

has increasingly introduced into vampire material female sexuality to go along with the increase in violence to be seen in such popular entertainments as *Poltergeist: The Legacy* and *The Hunger* and the runaway success of the fiction of Anne Rice. Vampire stories have become a new kind of pornography.

A VAMPIRE ON THE MISSISSIPPI

George R. Martin's *Fevre Dream* (1982) tells the story of a Mississippi riverboat built operated by Abner Marsh and Joshua York. York is a vampire and dedicated to fighting a group of evil vampires. The riverboat is called the "Fevre Dream" but the old-days action is not supposed to be a fever dream but real.

He had the kind of face that qualified Ernest Thesiger and Peter Cushing to play mad scientists but John Carradine played vampires for about 30 years in a series of second-string movies.

THE IMAGE OF THE VAMPIRE

You won't see it in a mirror (the vampire has no soul) but you will see it in popular US entertainment. There's Morticia in *The Addams Family*. There's Vampira and many another ghoul and boy introducing bad horror films on TV. There's The Count on *Sesame Street*. There is the vampire image in many a pop music group and lots of films about *Lost Boys* and other undead. The silliest, for my money, involves Ken Passariello, a little Connecticut bodybuilder who won big titles though about as wide as he is tall (5'4"). At one point he dubbed himself "The Demon" and began his show by getting out of a coffin.

TRACULA

"Boys' action shows have a hard time falling under the FCC [Federal Communications Commission]-friendly sort of banner," admits producer John Gentile, but he wants to make a buck filling up part of the three hours a week of educational TV for children now demanded by the FCC. One of his pitches is a show whose premise is that a meteor crashes into a junkyard and brings to life some dead vehicles. One is Tracula. The gang sets out to vampirize the world's store of gasoline. The show will have connection, of course, with a line of monster-truck toys.

I suggest *Quackula* (monster ducks), *Vacula* (a vacuum cleaner that goes wild—"It Sucks!"), and *Hackula* (computer hackers steal the time and energy of...fuggeddit). We've already had the musical *Rockula*.

"BLOOD LUST TURNS KIDS INTO HEMO-GOBLINS"

That's just one of the sensational headlines—sometimes aptly called "screamers"—seen as the press works itself up over an imagined widespread threat to America. Tabloids especially exploit public ignorance and fear of young people who, as journalists Jeff Guinn and Andy Grieser's book on blood fanciers put it, have *Something in Blood*. The media cannot fail to

"Theda Bara" (not, as often said, an anagram for the title of a movie called *Arab Death)* was a Vamp.

notice that Anne Rice and other Gothic writers are wildly popular. Count Dracula, as I write, has just come out on an American postage stamp, and that "Gothic" club kids in weirdo drag are seen in the all-night venues.

Many people also know of pop novelists such as Laurell K. Hamilton; she has a detective character called Anita Blake, a vampire hunter though she has a werewolf for a boyfriend, and the sleuth appears in *Guilty Pleasures*, *The Laughing Corpse*, *Circus of the Damned*, *The Lunatic Cafe*, and *Bloody Bones*. Hamilton is but one of hundreds of writers about vampires active today in the United States. There are zines turned out by teenagers of all ages—*Journal of the Dark* out of Stone Mountain, Georgia, is a good one—and on TV, and alternative societies of vampire club kids are everywhere (such as The Undead Poets Society).

The Lost Boys (1987) brought vampires into the age of punk rock. Get out the squirt guns with holy water!

But are there many fangorical young people going around with too much eye makeup and slurping blood in quantity from unwilling people, and killing people?

As a sample of how the press sensationalizes teenage crime, we can cite one example. Indicted for the murder of Richard Wendorf and his wife Ruth in Eustis, Florida, were 5 teenagers. They were Rod Ferrell (16, first-degree murder), Sarah Remington ("Charity Lynn Keesee," 16, accessory), Scott Anderson (17, accessory), Dana Cooper (19, accessory), and the daughter of the couple, Heather Wendorf (15, second-degree murder). The first four, from Murray, Kentucky, met the Wendorf girl, went to her home, and are accused of murdering her parents. The first TV reports mentioned the drinking of the blood of the victims, a detail later denied. The teenagers took the Wendorfs' car, and took off. "Charity Lynn Keesee" telephoned her mother for money. The mother agreed to send money for a hotel room in Baton Rouge, Louisiana. Then she informed authorities, and when the kids got there the police were waiting for them. They were briefly detained and questioned, then taken to Florida and charged.

Hearing that the teenagers may have been members of a large "vampire" gang which in role-playing drank each others' blood, the press went crazy. *America's Most Wanted* and other TV shows, radio shows, magazines, newspapers, all got on the bandwagon under the guise of warning parents about real vampires and telling parents to keep a close watch on wayward teenagers. A psychologist who interviewed Ferrell and others in Baton Rouge said that role-playing and Gothic goofiness were decidedly "not the precipitating factors...they were superficial and inconsequential."

No matter how crazy your kids are—and some from dysfunctional families or with drug or other personal problems are completely whacko—and no matter how they dress or play "vampire" games, they are not likely to be immortal monsters, just immoral or amoral dregs of society.

It's hard to be a teenager in America today. Many kill themselves. Some kill others. None are real vampires, not even the ones who angrily wish they were.

HOMOSEXUALITY AND THE VAMPIRE

There has long been a gay and lesbian strain in vampire literature. It dates back at least as far as LeFanu. We spoke of sex and the vampire in Chapter One. Today the lesbian aspect is strong in the many popular mani-

A piece of the action at the vampire ball in Roman Polanski's 1967 vampire epic.

festations of the fanged in the United States. But we must not forget Lost Boys in various sorts or, for instance, the homosexuality that runs all through the works of Anne Rice. There used to be a joke about how one could kill a Roman Catholic prelate: send him a poisoned choirboy. Anne Rice must, in her Catholic education, have heard that, because in *The Vampire Lestat* Claudia tries to poison Lestat by sending him two boys who have been drugged and whose blood, or blood products, she expects he will consume.

Read James Sheridan Lefanu's "Carmilla" and all its imitators, Eve Kosofsky Sedgwick's *Between Men* and its lesser sociological relatives, Pam Kesey's anthologies entitled *Daughters of Darkness* and *Dark Angels* and follow-ups such as Michael Rowe and Thomas S. Roche's *Sons of Darkness*, Cecilia Tan's "vampire erotica" in *Blood Kiss* and other sexploitation fiction, etc. By singling out these particular much imitated works I mean to hint at the fact that originality may be lacking in much of the homosexual vampire fiction—though some of it goes well beyond a merely *camp* take on the basics or association with sado-masochistic and other extremely transgressive sexuality, including incest and pedophilia—but that an eager public is ready for more and more of it in all the media and with industry if not ingenuity, hacks rush to supply it. For those who cannot or do not read, TV offers *Buffy the Vampire Slayer* and horror flix. *Forever Knight* has run for several seasons. *Kindred* was fading even before its star (Mark Frankel) was killed in 1996 in a motorcycle accident. When the spice of *camp* or uncloseted homosexuality is added, the product is considered just that much more attractive. But, as a public service TV ad warned in 1993, remember *AIDS Bites*.

VAMPIRES ON THE INTERNET

You can subscribe to an *Internet Vampire Tribune Quarterly*, an electronic publication of the Internet Vampire Resources Website, by e-mailing the editor, Benjamin H. Leblanc, at Valmont@lanzen.net and putting "SUBSCRIBE IVTB" on the subject line. It won't take a bite out of your budget. It's free.

On the Internet, if you are at all handy with technology, you can access a lot of vampire material which therefore I do not repeat here. However, a lot of the book reviews are by self-appointed and not always profound fans, and in that particular, as with all other aspects of the Internet, watch out for unreliable information.

THE GOTHS

Club kids, trying hard to be transgressive, have taken to vampire costume and cadaverous makeup. They are in many big and not so big cities, but let us take as our sample the amusingly echo-of-an-echo efforts to be different observed at one of Miami's clubs, Groove. (The very name tells you they are for all their desire to be trendy seriously behind the times). Groove has a weekly "Church" party for guys and ghouls, called *gravers* there. Rick Marin in *New York* (16 February 1998, 41) writes of

> Goth rave kids in flowing black [Vampire] Lestat [from the Anne Rice novel] get ups and Elizabethan collars, exuding deep melancholia. Their enthusiasm, visible under even the most wan and pallid visage [the writing is getting sloppy here, but you get the idea] is catching. The music, which the D.J. tells me is "classic alternative," is Sex Pistols, R.E.M., extremely danceable. If you have a Goth fetish, or even if you don't this may be the most fun you can have without actually being dead.

We shall mention these Goths more than once. They constitute the liveliest "vampire" activity in the United States and Britain today.

FAN CLUBS FOR VAMPIRE LOVERS

I have mentioned before Dr. Jeanne Youngson's eminent *Count Dracula Fan Club* and associated groups (Penthouse North, 29 Washington Square West, New York, NY) and there are fans of The Count gathered in other countries (*The Dracula Society* in Britain was still going when last I looked, there's one in Romania, and so on), but here are some special fan clubs you may not have located (and which may still be Undead):

The Lucy Westerna Society, Christine Raymond, 1141 Tanglewood Drive, Auburn, CA 95003

The Quincy P. Morris Society, Charlotte Simsen, PO Box 381, Ocean Gate, NJ 08740

The Secret Order of the Undead, T.J. Teer, 155 East C Street, Upland, CA 91781

The Forever Knight Fan Club, Lora Haines, PO Box 1108, Boston, MA 02103

Midnight to Midnight, Karen Dove, 11 North Avenue, Mt. Clemens, MI 48043

Check the Internet for current or extra addresses. Things change swiftly these days.

Game playing in New York City, $8 with the ad and $12 without for admission to The Batcave.

DRINK UP

Club kids aping vampires prick their fingers and suck blood but do not quaff blood by the glass. For a substitute drink if you want to play vampire, do not try "stage blood." (It tastes terrible.) I suggest V-8 to DV8 with a little extra salt—served at body temperature, of course. In the Age of AIDS, real blood, even a drop, is playing Russian roulette. Be crazy, but be careful!

By the way, blood fetishists—you know who you are—are not vampires. Such people need fixes rather than crucifixes.

SWEET YOUNG THINGS

Anyone who knows the vampire zine scene will tell you that there is a high proportion of teenage girls gushing over vampires. (We'll get to other manifestations of adolescent sexuality when we speak of poltergeists in the next book in this series.) There are a great many vampire fans who will tell you that Frank Langella was the best Dracula of all time because "he was so cute." A lot of Goth girls are on The Scene just now. Mary Downing Hahn's *Look for Me in the Moonlight* (1997) is not helping romantic girls of today much with its story of a teenager who doesn't realize she is dating a vampire.

To turn to real life, there was a case of teenage girls (Ann and Mary) in Connecticut in 1970-1971 who, playing around with a Ouija board, were sure they had contacted a dashing young Earl of Devonshire who lived in the eighteenth century. They called him Devon. The Ouija board started to explain that he was having a vampiristic affair with Ann, though anyone else hearing the story would be aware how suspiciously close all this was to the plot lines of *Dark Shadows* and *House of Dark Shadows* (the revival of 1991 was years away). In the long run the girls added enough live locals to form a kind of coven, as they called it, and for their part "The Choir" of invisible vampires produced some more "friends."

Today those females are more concerned, presumably, with the menopause than with men. The seventies, however, yields us proof this kind of thing has gone on for years. It also seems quaint and almost innocent compared with the *Vampire Sluts from Sodom* (one entertainment of the eighties) and the blood cults of the nineties.

ANOTHER KIND OF VAMPIRE

In this book when we say *vampire* we mean The Undead. But there are real-life vampires (or rip-offs of various kinds) that are given the name and their existence gives extra meaning to the term. Here is a bit from a short story (*Tricked*, by Robert Rodi) included in David Bergman's anthology *Men on Men 5* (1994). You know about older men vamped by pretty young girls, but here is an unusual case, a gay *femme* who is *fatale*. A middle-aged man is infatuated with a young man half his age and it is considered that it is the older man who is being victimized.

> "He's a vampire," I gasped.... My grandmother from Croatia used to tell me about his kind. They come from nowhere—from the land of the dead.... These vampires, you know what they do? They pick one person, and they attach themselves to you, and they suck you dry.... Granny Zoia always said that back in her village, the old folks would warn the young people not to dress too fancy or make too big a deal of themselves, because that would attract a vampire, and then they'd be doomed. And look at me—big, famous painter. Face all over the media. Of *course* he'd come for me."
>
> She [the speaker's female agent] grabbed my cheeks, "Stop this now or I'll take a cattle prod to you."

"Don't mention cattle prods to Elliot! He'll want to use them during sex."

She got to her feet, "I take it you haven't gotten rid of him."

"How? Granny Zoia used to say try a crucifix, but I haven't got one. Do you?"

"For God's sake, Vance! Besides, Elliot's Jewish. Would a crucifix even work?"

"I suppose not. Nothing will. That's why I have to let him move in."

"*What*? Are you *crazy*?"

"Or maybe he's moved in already. I don't even know if he *has* any stuff of his own. Vampires usually don't."

"If you say 'vampire' one more time, I'm going to drive my cellular phone through your heart"....

VAMPIRES AND COMIC BOOKS

Moderns see no oxymoron in "horror comics." For one aspect of a lively genre, see J. Gordon Melton's *The Vampire and the Comic Book* (1993). It is to be hoped that one or more valuable and extensive collections of horror comics will wind up in some popular culture library in the course of time. Such publications are worthy of study. Meanwhile, they are collectibles, and some of them go for high prices. People even collect baseball cards, of course, but comic books are worth looking into for more than the fools and greater fools syndrome.

INFORMATION AND CHAT SITES

Yahoo! There's a world of fun out there for lovers of vampire lore. Here are a few of the many cyberspace vaults of vampires. There are more than

60,000 places to look on the Internet as I write, so you need some help. See:

Australian Vampire Information
  Society
Darkness of the Edge of Town
Dearth's Grave
Gamelord's Castle
Give Me Myself Again
Impaler Magazine
Internet Vampire Tribune
  Quarterly
Real Vampyres
The Vampire Exchange
The Vampire Society
Vampire White Pages
Vampyre Books

Vampyre Chat
Vampyres 'R Us
Vampyres Film List
Vampires Only
Usenet—alt. vampyres
Catch up with *hhtp://radon.eecs. berkeley.edu/-mudie/vampfic.htm* and David C. Mudie (continuing the work of Travis S. Casey) at *mudie@eecs.berkeley.edu.* There's a FAQ maintained by Barbara Jean Kuehl at *bj@csd.uwm.edu.*

LINES FROM DRACULA PLAYS

Most famous: "I never drink—wine" (various)
Funniest (Jewish vampire confronted with a crucifix): "Hoi, have you got the wrong wampire!" (*The Fearless Vampire Killers* film)
Dumbest: "The place smells horribly of bats" (Deane & Balderston's stage *Dracula*)

SOME SUPER COLLECTIBLE COMIX

Dark Shadows (Gold Key) 1969-1976
Tomb of Dracula (Marvel) 1972-1980
Dracula Lives (Marvel) 1972-1975
Vampire Tales (Marvel) 1972-1975

COMIC BOOKS

The name may convey that they started out as "funny papers" but the comix (as some call this art form) are best known for adventure—and horror. Naturally the vampire looms large in the ghoul and gore department.

Some of you older folks may recall the days, way before bathing trunks that look as if they have been made out the American flag, or even the days of United States flag shirt that some hippie wore to a government hearing to annoy investigators of UnAmericanism. Remember that figure that Joe Simon and Jack Kirby invented? The guy in the flag outfit, called Captain America? He may have been the first to make the vampire prominent in the comics. In 1942, when we were at war with Imperial Japan, Captain America took on the mad scientist Dr. Togu (think Admiral Togo) who had a formula for creating vampires.

Later the vampire stalked in the work of Johnny Craig in the EC Comics series' *Vampirella* and *Tomb of Dracula*, and elsewhere. He turns up now on occasion in *Tales from the Crypt* (and spinoffs), etc. From the comics he made the move to Pop Art, too.

NATIVE-AMERICAN VAMPIRES

There was some blood-drinking among the cannibal tribes of Native Americans and also some vampires in their folklore. The Cherokee believed in witches who ate the livers of the dead. The Ojibwa believed in vampires somewhat like ours: ghosts who drank the blood of the living for their sustenance. The "undead", however, appear to be a European invention.

Native American experts have asked me not to go into pre-Columbian vampire and blood myths of the aboriginals. "The white man already thinks we were savages," one tribal elder explained.

MORTMAIN

Sometimes the dead are said to come back only in part. A speaking head gets the most information across, but a clutching hand is also a standard horror story feature. It might be that of a dead violinist or a dead pianist or even, in this college horror story from *Southern Folklore Quarterly* (1966), the hand of someone whose body was given to science:

> A couple of young med[ical] students finished dissecting a cadaver just before campus vacation. For a joke they cut off one of the cadaver's hands and left it on a door knob in the room of a med student who wasn't going home for the vacation. When this group of med students returned to school, they found the body of the med student with white hair and a cadaver's hand clutching his throat.

Of course superstition has it that anyone who gets a big enough fright has his hair turn white "overnight" or instantly.

AMERICAN SPELLS

In this series you will find an immense variety of spells in *The Complete Book of Spells, Curses, and Magical Recipes*, but (oddly?) there are few if any spells in the wide range of recent books (from C. Nahmad's *Cat Spells* to L. Roseanna's *Supermarket Sorceress*) to call up or drive off vampires. Even A. Saint's *Spells of a Voodoo Doll* and M. Norton's *Spells of Fury* offer nothing—ah—constructive. By the way, all these books are of 1996 vintage, and they represent only the tip of a vast occult iceberg. No wonder ghost and vampire movies, TV shows, comic books, novels, etc., are a booming business. *Tales from the Crypt* has made it from comic books to television to the big screen and the big time. The great American public seems to believe in these things about as much as they believe in God. (That's 94 percent these days.)

Hispanics chant to drive away rain:

> *San Isidro, labrador,*
> *quita el agua*
> *y pon el sol,*

but for driving off vampires they have no incantations.

VAMPIRES IN THE POPULAR PRESS

Although readers of supermarket-checkout sensation sheets are ready to believe that Elvis lives, extraterrestrials have landed, and the world is going to end soon—"momentarily" is the word semiliterates prefer—they are far less likely to be taken in by vampire tales than by ghost or poltergeist stories. Some, however, do appear. Though the flip titles suggest that writers may be a trifle superior to this sort of subject, in familiar magazines and learned periodicals you can find many articles like these recent entries:

Paul Barber, "Staking Claims: The Vampires of Folklore and Fiction," *Skeptical Inquirer* 20 (March-April 1996): 41*ff.*

Candace R. Benefield, "Fangs for the Memories...," *Wilson Library Bulletin* 69 (May 1995): 35*ff.*

Judith E. Johnson, "Women and Vampires...," *Kenyon Review* 15 (Winter 1993): 72*ff.*

Anthony Lane, "Sucking Up" [satire of Anne Rice], *New Yorker,* 17 October 1994, 122.

Toby Manning, "Prime-Time Eroticism," *New Statesman & Society*, 20 January 1995, pp. 31*f.*

John Marks, "Dracula's New Lease on Life: Transylvania Welcomes the Tourist...," *U.S. News & World Report*, 29 May 1995, 45*f.*

TRUE CRIME VAMPIRES

Expectably, some psychopaths think of themselves as—and act like—vampires. Among popular exploitations of this gruesome fact, find:

Lieutenant. R. Biodi & Walt Hecox, *The Dracula Killer* (1992)
John A. Keel, *The Mothman Prophecies* (1975)
Richard Monaco & Bill Burt, *The Dracula Syndrome* (1993)

Among thrill-seekers and bad boys who do not find enough excitement in drugs, body piercing, and punk clothes, there is a small underground of vampire fans who drink their own blood and the blood of others (but mostly just pose). We mentioned them in passing in the first chapter, but they deserve emphasis here because they are chiefly non-European, very American. This foolishness is seldom criminal—though, in the Age of AIDS, always dangerous—because the donors are almost without exception consenting. As ever, the vampire is the ultimate Outsider image. That is the fact that deserves repeating often. Notice, also, that the belief in the vampire tradition is not something confined to the elderly, as is the case with some other Old World superstitions. The young people keep the vampire myth alive today.

POP GOES THE VAMPIRE

A presenter of old horror films on television, "Zacherly," made the vampire even more of a pop icon and even (if I recall correctly) hit the charts with a song called "Dinner with Drac." I know there were a number of vampire-themed pop groups such as *Count Dracula and The Vampires*, *The Vampires*, *The Bloodsuckers*, and *Nosferatu*, not to mention such late, lamented groups as *The Dead Kennedys*. The names were often changed; even in the case of Lou Reed. When he first started out, he played in groups so bad (he says) they had to keep changing the names because no one would book them twice.

Some were real vampire bands and other performers more or less aped the style, in makeup and music, picking it up and dropping it as fashion dictated.

If you want to put together your own CD of old Dractrax—and this would be great for late-night TV ads for commercial salvage "collections" by mail, but pay me a royalty for the idea or I'll sue in the best pop tradition—may I suggest The Theme from *Dark Shadows*, soundtrack selections from vampire movies, and some of the following gems of deepest ray serene from the dark, unfathomed caves of Yesteryear's *Now* Hits? NOT FOR SALE IN ANY STORE, right? Some tracks may be hard to find in a universe in which last year's big success may be a Golden Oldie, and I omit obscure French, German, and other recordings:

Alice Cooper's "Fresh Blood"
Autopsy's "Fiend for Blood"
Bathory's "Woman of Dark Desires"
Bauhaus' "Bela Lugosi's Dead"
Birthday Party's "Release the Bats"
Blue Oyster Cult's "Tattoo Vampire"
Coroner's "Nosferatu"
Dark Theater's "Undead"
Dark Throne's "Transylvania
    Hunger"
Dupont's "Screamin' Ball
    at Dracula Hall"
Entombed's "Blood Song"
Excruciating Pain's "Nosferatu"
J. Geil's Band's "Fright Night"
Grave's "Riboflavin Flavored
    Non-Carbonated
    Polyunsaturated Blood"

Iron Maiden's "Transylvania"
LA Guns' "Hollywood
    Vampires"
Legendary Pink Dots'
    "Casting the Runes"
Mazzy Star's "Taste of Blood"
Mercyful Fake's "Return of
    the Vampire"
Motorhead's "Waltz of the
    Vampires"
Shroud's "Lovers' Bones"
Siouxsie and The Banshees'
    "We Hunger"
Sting's "Moon over Bourbon
    Street"
Warfare's "Screams of the
    Vampire"
Wire's "Feed Me"

INTERVIEW
In the Andy Warhol tradition (or Anne Rice's) pop interviews with wannabe celebrities:

Norine Dresser, *American Vampires: Fans, Victims, Practitioners* (1989)
Isaiah Oke, *Blood Secrets: The True Story of Demon Worship and Ceremonial Murder* (1989)
Carol Page, *Bloodlust: Conversations with Real Vampires* (1981)

SOME RECENT VAMPIRE STORIES IN THE PRESS

Baker, Donald P. "A Tale from the Dark Side," *Washington Post*, 8 May 1996, B 1 [Jon C. Bush, role-playing in Virginia Beach, accused of molesting girls]

Bridis, Ted. "Killings Bring to Light Underground Fascination with Vampire Culture," *Chicago Tribune* 4 December 1996, 2 [role-playing game may have led teenagers to kill people in Florida]

Bruni, Frank. "Count Dracula Never Had His Own Cable TV Show...." *New York Times* 10 August 1996, A25 [but vampires are featured on television now]

Cuthbert, David. "Fangs for the Memories...," *New Orleans Times-Picayune*, 30 October 1996, E 1 [New Orleans, as usual, hails the occult at Halloween, this time Dracula]

Daly, James. "Looking Back on Propaganda, Art and Dracula," *San Francisco Chronicle* 20 October 1996, Rev. 8 [review of books on CD ROM]

Duffy, Maureen. "Something to Sink Her Teeth Into," *New York Times Book Review*, 29 October 1995, 7, 33 [review of Nina Auerbach's *Our Vampires, Ourselves, stretching the vampire myth as metaphor*]

Greene, Bob. "Of 'Teen-Vampires' and Troubled Public Appetites," *Chicago Tribune*, 4 December 1996, 1 [front-page story on the same crimes as in Bridis, above]

James, Caryn. "Happy Birthday, Undead," *New York Times*, 13 March 1997, C13 [celebration of the lasting influence of The Count and his cohorts]

Kozma, Anna-Liza. "Going Batty," *Chicago Tribune*, 6 August 1995, G1 [Elizabeth Miller reports on "The Genesis of Dracula" at a conference in Romania]

Mackie, Bob. "All You Need to Know about Vampire Movies," *The Guardian*, 6 June 1996, 2, 8 [British report does not give you all you need to know]

Murphy, H. Lee. "Hair'evicula' Combines Elvis and Dracula," *Chicago Tribune*, 22 September 1995, 7, 8 [Jonathan Hagloch's musical has Elvis Presley as a vampire]

Pennington, Gail. "Taking the Vamp out of Vampire," *St. Louis Post-Dispatch* 18 April 1996, GO, 39 [A discussion of Fox TV's *Kindred: The Embraced*, about San Francisco vampire clans—which are replicated in some cities around America]

Petersen, Andrea. "What's Chic in Academic Circles?," *Wall Street Journal*, 21 March 1997, B 1 [Leonard Wolf *et al.* at NYU stage a conference on Dracula]

Schmich, Mary. "St. Charles X-Files Reveal a Tale with Bite," *Chicago Tribune*, 30 October 1996, 2C 1 [alleged vampires in St. Charles, IL, are cause for alarm]

See, Carolyn. "Vampire Lore, Bled Dry," *The Washington Post*, 11 November 1995, F2 [Nina Auerbach's book again, this time not altogether praised]

Seller, Andy. "Fall Brings a Blood Bath of Vampire Movies," *USA Today* 19 September 1995, D4 [every season has its vampire movies, some more than others]

Sharp, Deborah. "Vampire Game is Bizarre Twist to Florida Slayings," *USA Today* 9 December 1996, A3 [the case Bridis, above, mentions]

Skal, David J. "Vampire Video," *New Orleans Times-Picayune* 30 October 1996, E1 [top ten vampire videos in the opinion of this researcher, in time for Halloween]

Spolar, Christine. "Marketing Dracula...'," *The Washington Post* 30 May 1995, A 8 [World Dracula Congress held in Bucharest involves many scholars from abroad]

Stein, S. "Vampires and Werewolves and Witches—Oh, My!," *Chicago Tribune* 31 October 1996, 5, 1 [novelist Hamilton's Anita Blake crushes vampires]

Verhoevel, Sam Howe. "Houston Ballet Knows How to Use a Vampire Wisely," *New York Times*, 13 March 1997, C13 [ballet with Dracula in a cape exceeding 22 feet, accompanied by 18 "wives," is spectacular use of the old myth]

Wallace, David. "Punk Gothic," *Denver Post* 7 September 1996, E10 [a vampire clan on The Internet]

This is just a small sampling of the untiring interest in vampires reflected in the popular press, an interest reflected in periodicals (both serious and trivial), television and movie shows (ditto), and hundreds of books (from comic books to reference books) pouring from the presses. In every decade since Bram Stoker's *Dracula* of a century ago, if not before, the vampire character has appeared in one form or another, constantly adapted to the fads and fashions of the period in connection with sex and violence, with parasitism and plagiarism, with the occult, with AIDS, with whatever is fascinating, fearful, frightening. A woman with "iron teeth" bites a boy on a beach in Brazil, an exhibitionist wants some press coverage in Britain, or hick in the American South thinks his pig is a vampire, and the reporters are there. It's a crazy world out there, and *Schlockmeisteren* have it covered!

FEEDING THE DEAD

There are nauseating testimonies to the fact that those unfortunate individuals who underwent premature burial—a fear that particularly haunted Viennese in the eighteenth century and such morbid writers as Edgar Allan Poe in the nineteenth century—often struggled terribly in the coffin and even ate their own flesh.

In the nineteenth century, people worried a great deal about waking up in the coffin. Don't worry about premature burial today. Even if there is no autopsy, embalming is very common, and embalming leaves you with your innards wholly puréed and replaced along with preservative-soaked rags to plump you out. You are not going to wake up from that. Rest assured.

From very ancient times and in all cultures, it appears, there has always been a worry that the dead might not rest. The dead were offered gifts, including food, luxuries such as tobacco—anything to keep them happy wherever they were. No one was anxious to come back. Placing flowers on the grave may be more than a sentiment high in fructose. The perfume of flowers is no longer needed to disguise putrifaction in a world where we embalm even those soon to be cremated. There must be some other reason.

Those relatives who specify that there be no flowers usually ask for donations to be made to the deceased's favorite charity or that some other gift be made. You shouldn't go to a funeral any more than you go to a wedding without a gift.

And you ought to go to funerals, although many Americans shirk the duty. ("I don't go because they depress me," a friend of mine says.) Some people let us off the hook by saying they want no final ceremony, thus avoiding the embarrassment of poor attendance. This modern American tendency is, I think, to be deplored. We need closure, the dead deserve respect, and the grieving need sympathy. Also—if you dis the dead you may live to regret it!

VAMPIRELLA

She was the girl wonder before Buffy the Vampire Slayer came along, and she remains a favorite with many readers of that quintessentially American art form, the Comic. Here is how Vampirella introduced herself in the first such comic ever:

HI, THERE! WELCOME TO THE COOLEST GIRL-MEETS-GHOUL MAG ON THE MARKET! My name's

VAMPIRELLA. I'm the NEWEST thing in comic magazines! And if you take me home with you, YOU can call me . . . VAMP! (That's if I don't call you first!) I've put out the call to all the creepiest eeriest artists in the country (and you know what country: TRAN-SYLVANIA!) . . . and it'll be a BLOODY pity if anyone in the whole wide world doesn't get the word about this way-out mag of fantastic females! My AMAZING ADVENTURES explode here exclusively every issue and in addition you get half a dozen other sock-it-to-you SHOCKERS for gals and guys who're wise to the best in BEWITCHING COMICS! What more do you want—BLOOD? You got it! Get VAMPIRELLA magazine!!

CHECK YOUR HEARTBEAT before reading this magazine and if it hasn't risen 100 beats per minute by the time you lay the issue down (if you CAN lay it down!) you need a transplant and we will give you one free. Just tear off the TOP OF YOUR HEAD and mail it to me, VAMPIRELLA, care of the GHOST OFFICE. If you're my kinda bird or BOYFRIEND, you'll lose your mind over me anyway, so . . . LOOK! READ! GASP! SHIVER! over this FIRST COLLECTOR'S EDITION!!

THE VAMPIRE STALKS CONTEMPORARY CULTURE

I long ago conducted college seminars on this topic, and some are still offered. The best simple survey of the subject lately has been *Blood Read* (1997), edited by Joan Gordon (Nassau Community College, New York) and Veronica Hollander (Trent, Canada). A major new trend is the connection of vampirism with deconstruction and feminist agendas and the involvement of women writers in the field of vampire fiction, both well-known US writers and lesser known but sometimes better foreign ones, such as Mariko Ohara, the prize-winning Japanese author of *Ephemera the Vampire* (1992).

A COMIC BOOK VILLAIN

The first issue of the graphic stories called *Psycho* (January 1971) has an interesting tale of a villain who only pretends to be Count Dracula. In "The Gruesome Faces of Mr. Cliff," an actor, who knows he is dying, goes on a murderous rampage disguised as The Count. After he does a lot of damage he is put out of business by—a spotlight trained on him.

DRACULA ON AND OFF

The Count, would seem to be a natural for the action genre, but after a debut in the fifties Comics Code censorship banned the publication of vampire tales for tots. After *Eerie* (1953), it was almost a decade until *Dracula* appeared in the Fall of 1962. And after one issue it was another four years until the second issue of *Dracula* hit the stands. These comics have become valuable collectors' items. The experts look out for the vampire's appearances under other names such as *Al U. Card* and *Tracula* in the US and a series of other names in the increasingly popular vampire comic books published in Europe and Asia.

Here is one astounding fact about the Dracula icon, famous worldwide: this was a character who came to claim a high and permanent place in popular culture who started in what some would call high culture; Stoker's novel. In this he is not unique—think of Tarzan from the novels of Edgar Rice Burroughs and Sherlock Holmes from the short stories of Sir Arthur Conan Doyle—but it is unusual. Like Superman and Batman and other characters originating in the comic books, Dracula has appeared in every medium, over and over, and you are likely to see him on a T-shirt or in a film, on a greeting card ("Fangs a lot") or TV or video, or as an action figure (which is the term such ingenious ad men created to enable little boys to play with dolls).

HAWTHORNES

Not the bushes whose flowers bring bad luck into your house but Nathaniel Hawthorne and family. Hawthorne himself was haunted by the memory of an ancestor who was a judge in the infamous witchcraft trials in Salem. His equally melancholy son wrote of "the white-shouldered" vampire in a graveyard in Co. Cork, Ireland, not far from "Ballymacheen." If one was not careful one could bring this vampire, a beautiful lady in a white wedding dress, hundreds of years old, back to a sort of life.

DANGEROUS GAMES

Teenagers playing occult games have become a concern of police and public health authorities in various places in the US. In southwest Missouri, for example, the Springfield-Greene Co. officials condemned the game *Masquerade*:

The game starts innocently enough but then in some participants progresses to the actual sucking or licking of blood from a partner... brought to the surface of the skin through a pinprick or cut.

In a country where exaggerated rumors of Satanic child abuse and other, more real and more dangerous horrors abound, even games can greatly worry guardians of law and order and health officials.

An advertisement from the heyday of horror comic books. From Stan Lee's *The Legion of Monsters*, No. 1 (September, 1975).

VAMPIRE JOURNALS

The fanzines are so ephemeral I thought I would not mention them, but I have been talked into giving producers of these things some publicity because they do much to "keep the vampire alive," as one of them put it. Start with these:

Delirium, Sophie Diamantis, 779 Riverside Drive/A-11, New York, (NY) 10032

Journal of the Dark, John Beckett, PO Box 168, Osceola (FL) 46561

Nefarious, Rosey Lettich, 1004 Academy Street, Sumner (WA) 98309

Vampire Information Newsletter, PO Box 290328, Brooklyn (NY) 11229

VAMPIRE TRADING CARDS

This is a lively business, though not as developed as baseball cards. (If you are in middle age, your mother may have thrown out a fortune when she cleared out your collections of cards, comic books, and so on.) Collectors of vampire trading cards are scattered but turn up at conventions and elsewhere. Write to Lee Scott, PO Box 511061, Salt Lake City (UT) 84151 for a list of trading cards.

LAMENT

> Girls seem to be vampires,
> But they won't vampire for me.
> — F. Scott Fitzgerald

FEMALE VAMPIRES

Sex and sensation inform the television epic "Night of the Sorcerers" (starring Jack Taylor, Simon Andreu, Kali Hansa, and Maria Kosti) in an Avco series called *Nightmare Theater*. In Bomba (an imaginary place in Equatorial Africa) poor Agnes is sacrificed to The Great Leopard Devil. Then British soldiers massacre those responsible. Agnes's severed head turns into a busty vampire!

Years later, an expedition of B-Movie types arrives to investigate rumors of The Great Leopard Devil ceremonies continuing. The photographer (Carol) is captured and turned into a vampire Leopard Woman. When the movie ends most of the expedition members are dead meat and Tanica, the naturalist Jonathan's girlfriend, has been bitten by a vampire....

Despite the advertisement, Bela Lugosi did not appear in *Dracula's Daughter* (1936). He was written out of the script before shooting.

This may be among the most unusual vampire productions if not for low quality—that is too close a competition to call—at least for explanations of how vampires are created from decapitated heads. More than twenty years later, nobody else, so far as I know, has used this method of vampire genesis. In another episode in the same series, "Horror Rises from the Tomb", a French knight and his girlfriend who are decapitated for crime reappear as vampires. In most stories, decapitation is the end for a vampire.

A female psychic predator is at the heart of Florence Marryat's notable novel, *The Blood of the Vampire* (1897). It has the same thrust as Charles Wilkins Webber's early *Spiritual Vampirism* (1853), with the woman's touch.

The earliest female vampire of note was Gloria Holden as the Countess Marya Zaleska in *Dracula's Daughter* (Universal, 1936). It is a dreadfully bad film, but it was the first movie I ever saw and I sat entranced through three repetitions of the double bill, which also included the usual newsreel, cartoon, and previews of coming attractions. It holds a special place in my heart, naturally. I intrude this personal detail to underline the fact that many *aficionados* of horror fiction and films owe lifelong obsessions to early childhood experiences. They may become as determined (and defensive) as people who devour western or detective stories. But vampires have more sex!

The silent movie vamp was supposed to be a slinky sexpot. One was dramatically photographed as a spider woman, luring males into her web. (The female black widow spider, as you know, is said to eat the male after sex.) For the movie vamp read biographies of Pola Negri and Nita Naldi and Theda Bara, and articles such as Leslie Fishbein's "The Demise of the

Cult of True Womanhood in Early American Film, 1900-1930...," *Journal of Popular Film and Television* 12:2 (1984): 66-72. Don't miss Charles Lockwood's "Priestess of Sin," *Horizon* 24:1 (1981): 64 - 69.

But sometimes the vamp is no vampire, no flapper, no Betty Boop, no ordinary *femme fatale* but rapacious and gruesome. The sleaziest makeup for any female vampire was probably that sported by Sandra Harrison as Nancy in *Blood of Dracula*. Equally untalented, but striking because only a child, was the female in *Interview with a Vampire*. More recently, female vampires have become more and more seductive. The New Look may date from Carroll Borland and *Mark of the Vampire* and the cult horror films, perked up with sex, of Italy in the sixties. Try *La Maschera del demonio* (1960), or some of the new feminist films.

Feminists will want to read Anne Mellor's *Romanticism and Feminism* (1988) and Nina Auerbach's *Our Vampires, Ourselves* (1995). A specialist study is Andrea Weiss's *Vampires and Violets* (1993); it deals with lesbians in the cinema. I suppose I ought to explain that in the nineteenth century Parma violets were a symbol of lesbianism.

Check out *Pam Keesey's Daughters of Darkness* in cyberspace! And, of course, anything connected with Anne Rice, and authors Nancy Baker, Traci Briery, Poppy Z. Brite, Suzy McKee Charnas, Barbra Hambly, Jeanne Kalogridis, "Marie Kiraly" (Elaine Bergstrom), Kristine Kathryn Rusch, Judy Scott, Chelsea Quinn Yarbro, and the lesbian areas of *Viscera*, the "queer-based vampire webzine."

FEMALE VAMPIRE SLAYER

Young females are usually the victims in horror films. They are often shown cringing in corners, screaming. They are the classic fodder of vampires. However, in at least one celluloid epic the teenage girl is the competent, fearless, sole hope of mankind in the face of the onslaught of the Undead: "one girl in all the world, a chosen one" who can prevent the "old ones," who feed on human blood and threaten to open the gates of Hell and release demons on the world, from exterminating mankind.

In *Buffy the Vampire Slayer*, a sixteen-year-old high-schooler is pitted against The Master and his vampiristic cohorts (all in grotesque, Star Trek monster makeup). "Tonight is the harvest. Unless you can prevent it, The Master walks." Well, he damn near does but doesn't. But you knew that. The latest once-a-century attempted return of the monsters—Madrid in 1843, California in the 1990s—is thwarted by the kickboxing, fence-hurdling wonderwoman. It is all "deeply dangerous" but Buffy meets the challenge; her male companions are just tag-a-longs. There is the expectable male professor with an approximation of a good English accent, but there is no Dr. Helsing. It is Buffy who triumphs. *Buffy* may mark a stage in women's liberation and lead to more females as vampire vanquishers rather than vampire victims.

VAMPIRE RESEARCH CENTER

Dr. Stephen Kaplan set up a Vampire Research Center in Elmhurst, Queens, in the eighties and commented on psychic vampires and such thefts. He was accused by some vampirologists of stealing their ideas! He told columnist Bob Greene "I have drunk human blood, under laboratory conditions.... I have also slept in coffins." He added that vampires do not sleep in coffins. "But this was all a part of my research. I am not a vampire." There seems to be a desperate desire among some vampirologists to get attention. The Rev. Montague Summers drew comment by arriving to do his research in the Reading Room of The British Museum with a larger folder emblazoned VAMPIRES. He did get talked about.

So did Dr. Kaplan, a doctor of what I never discovered. I have not heard of Dr. Kaplan for years. He may be dead, or undead.

VAMPIRES IN ACADEME

Jean Lorrah (Murray State) and myself (Brooklyn CUNY) offered perhaps the first college courses for credit on the vampire as a metaphor in life and literature. For the centenary of *Dracula*, New York University offered a course in "the aesthetics of fear." Many scholars are now writing about the vampire in such trendy fields as feminist, gay and lesbian, and popular culture. My choice of some scholarly works, excluding those I mention elsewhere in this book (and one also might note the great contributions of Devendra P. Varma and other editors who have brought old documents to light):

Leonard R. N. Ashley, *Vampires and the Silver Scream* (1997)
Liahna K. Babener, *Predators of the Spirit: The Vampire Theme in Nineteenth-Century Literature* (UCLA dissertation, 1975)
Alok Bhalla, *The Politics of Atrocity and Lust: The Vampire Tale as a Nightmare History of England in the Nineteenth Century* (1990)

N. Carroll, *The Philosophy of Horror* (1990)

Lynn Chancer, *Sado-Masochism in Everyday Life* (1992)

Basil Copper, *The Vampire in Legend, Fact, and Art* (1973)

Greg Cox, *The Transylvanian Library* (bibliography, 1992)

A. Osborne Eaves, *Modern Vampirism* (1904)

Robert Eighteen-Bisang, *Dracula: An Annotated Bibliography* (1994)

Jacques Fiunné, *La Bibliographie de Dracula* (1986)

Rosemary Ellen Guiley, *The Complete Vampire Companion* (1994)

Peter Haining, *The Dracula Scrapbook* (1976)

——, *The Gentlewomen of Evil* (1967)

Vincent Hillyer, *Vampires* (1988)

Basil F. Kirtley, "*Dracula*, the Monastic Cronicles, and Slavic Folklore," *Midwest Folklore* 6:3 (1956): 133-139

"Konstantinos," *Vampires* (1996)

Marc Lovell, *An Enquiry into the Existence of Vampires* (1974)

Anthony Masters, *The Natural History of the Vampire* (1972)

J. Gordon Melton, *The Vampire Book: The Encyclopedia of the Undead* (1994)

Jan L. Perkowski, *The Darkling: A Treatise on Slavic Vampirism* (1987)

David Punter, *The Literature of Terror* (1980)

Michael Ranft, *De Masticatione mortuorum in tumulis liber* (Book of the Chewing Dead in the Sepulcher, 1728)

Martin V. Riccardo, *Vampires Unearthed* ("multi-media" bibliography, 1983)

Dorothy Scarborough, *The Supernatural in Modern English Fiction* (1917)

David Skal, *V is for Vampire* (1996)

Otto Steiner, *Vampirleichen* (1959)

Rudolf Steiner, *The Occult Significance of Blood* (1912, 1972)

Johann Christian Stock, *Dissertatio physica de cadaveribus sanguissugis* (Dissertation on the Physical Nature of the Blood-Sucking Corpse, 1732)

Montague Summers, *The Vampire, His Kith and Kin* (reprinted *c.* 1961)

——, *The Vampire in Europe* (reprinted *c.* 1961)

Devendra P. Varma, *The Gothic Flame* (1957)

Gregory A. Waller, *The Living and the Undead: From Stoker's Dracula to Romero's Night of the Living Dead* (1986)

Leonard Wolf, *Dracula: A Connoisseur's Guide* (1997)

Johann Heinrich Zopft, *Dissertatio de Vampiris serviensibus* (Dissertation on Enslaved Vampires, 1733)

AMERICAN VAMPIRE NEWSLETTERS AND JOURNALS

These fanzines come and go, but at last check there were many here and abroad. Among US publications in addition to the various items from The Count Dracula Fan Club and information on the Internet, were:

Onyx, PO Box 137, Uniontown OH 44685

Shadows of the Night, PO Box 17006, Rochester NY 14617

Vampire Journal, PO Box 994, Metairie LA 7000

Vampire Junction, 114 NW 13th Street, Gainesville FL 32601

Vamps, PO Box 21067, Seattle WA 98111

Vampire Studies, PO Box 151, Berwyn IL 60402

More such publications will be mentioned elsewhere.

A VAMPIRE RELIGION

In the US there are many advantages to starting your own religion, not the least of which involve favors from the Internal Revenue Service.

Two of the greatest stars of horror films, Lionel Atwill (mad scientist par excellence) and Fay Wray (immortal for *King Kong*), appeared together in *The Vampire Bat* (1933). There are plenty of annoying bats in the little village of Kleinschloss, Edward T. Lowe lets us know in his screenplay based on his own story, but there seems to be a vampire, too! This one has sets from *Frankenstein*, *The Old Dark House*, *The Cat and the Canary* and more. "You shudder in horror!," says the mad scientist, "So did I, the first time; but what are a few lives to be weighed in the balance against the achievements of biological science?" What indeed?

Besides fan groups such as The Secret Order of the Undead (Upland, CA) and vampire covens (there are several in Illinois, more in New York and Los Angeles and New Orleans, etc.) the would-be vampires have their own recognized religion of communication with the dead, a Temple of the Vampire (in Lacey, WA), a Priesthood of Ur, and their own *Vampire Bible* (allegedly based on the *Shurpu Kishpu* or *Book of Sorcery*). The success of such books as *Necronomicon* and the *Satanic Bible* suggests that made-up scriptures and carpentered religions may be good business ventures. Also, the separation of church and state guarantees that religions can get away with some strange practices, such as taking peyote (Native American religions) and mutilating infants (Jewish circumcision of males is an example, although African circumcision of females has roused some recent protests).

THE DEATH OF HALPIN FRASIER

In a short story of this title by Ambrose Bierce—probably best known for "The Occurrence at Owl Creek Bridge"—we meet a society lady of the Napa Valley of California and her son and victim, Halpin Frasier, "a creature of [whose] dreams" she contrives to become. Murdered by her second husband, Catherine Larue Frasier becomes a possessive mother from Hell. With the Oedipus of Sophocles to help him and some atmosphere borrowed from Poe, Bierce deftly creates a terrifying tale which ends with the echoing and "soulless" laugh of a horrifying parent.

The Vampire, United Artists/Gardner–Levy (1957)

AN INTELLECTUAL VAMPIRE

Reginald Clarke in George Sylvester Viereck's *The House of the Vampire* (1907) somewhat recalls the dandified lord, in *The Picture of Dorian Gray* by Wilde, who takes over a rather fey young man's life. In fact, Clarke is based on Oscar Wilde himself and Ernest Fielding not on Wilde's character Earnest but on Wilde's lover, Lord Alfred Douglas, called "Bosie." In real life, Wilde was more the victim of "Bosie" than the other way around, but no matter. Viereck sees plagiarism and homosexuality as varieties of vampirism.

In the story Clarke is a writer who steals ideas from pretty young men. He is an "embezzler of the mind," and he filches the original ideas of Ernest Fielding. Drawing creativity out of the younger man, leaving his victim an empty idiot, Clarke is somewhere between a dirty old man and a demonic vampire. The novel was reprinted in 1976.

American literature has presented us with quite a lot of trashy vampire stories of the bite-night type but also with more stories than you would expect of the psychic or intellectual vampire and stories that link homo-sexuality or lesbianism with vampirism. The vampire-as-plague motif became very popular when the disease first called GRIDS (Gay Immune Deficiency syndrome) and later AIDS (Auto-Immune Deficiency Syndrome) struck. Jeffrey N. Mahan managed to write about gay vampires in the Age of AIDS, however, in *Vampires Anonymous* (1991) without ever mentioning AIDS. Now, a classic tale.

FOR THE BLOOD IS THE LIFE
by F[rancis] Marion Crawford

We had dined at sunset on the broad roof of the old tower, because it was cooler there during the great heat of summer. Besides, the little kitchen was built at one corner of the great square platform, which made it more convenient than if the dishes had to be carried down the steep stone steps broken in places and everywhere worn with age. The tower was one of those built all down the west coast of Calabria by the Emperor Charles V early in the sixteenth century, to keep off the Barbary pirates, when the unbelievers were allied with Francis I against the Emperor and the Church. They have gone to ruin, a few still stand intact, and mine is one of the largest. How it came into my possession ten years ago, and why I spend a part of each year in it, are matters which do not concern this tale. The tower stands in one of the loneliest spots in Southern Italy, at the extremity of a curving, rocky promontory, which forms a small but safe natural harbour at the southern extremity of the Gulf of Policastro, and just north of Cape Scalea, the birthplace of Judas Iscariot, according to the old local legend. The tower stands alone on this hooked spur of the rock, and there is not a house to be seen within three miles of it. When I go there I take a couple of sailors, one of whom is a fair cook, and when I am away it is in charge of a gnome-like little being who was once a miner and who attached himself to me long ago.

My friend, who sometimes visits me in my summer solitude, is an artist by profession, a Scandinavian by birth, and a cosmopolitan by force of circumstances.

We had dined at sunset; the sunset glow had reddened and faded again, and the evening purple steeped the vast chain of the mountains that embrace the deep gulf to eastward and rear themselves higher and higher towards the south. It was hot, and we sat at the landward corner of the platform, waiting for the night breeze to come down from the lower hills. The colour sank out of the air, there was a little interval of deep-grey twilight, and a lamp sent a yellow streak from the open door of the kitchen, where the men were getting their supper.

Then the moon rose suddenly above the crest of the promontory, flooding the platform and lighting up every little spur of rock and knoll of grass below us, down to the edge of the motionless water. My friend lighted his pipe and sat looking at a spot on the hillside. I knew that he was looking at it, and for a long time past I had wondered whether he would ever see anything there that would fix his attention. I knew that spot well. It was clear that he was interested at last, though it was a long time before he spoke. Like most painters, he trusts to his own eyesight, as a lion trusts his strength and a stag his speed, and he is always disturbed when he cannot reconcile what he sees with what he believes that he ought to see.

'It's strange,' he said. 'Do you see that little mound just on this side of the boulder?'

'Yes,' I said, and I guessed what was coming.

'It looks like a grave,' observed Holger.

'Very true. It does look like a grave.'

'Yes,' continued my friend, his eyes still fixed on the spot. 'But the strange thing is that I see the body lying on the top of it. Of course,' continued Holger, turning his head on one side as artists do, 'it must be an effect of light. In the first place, it is not a grave at all. Secondly, if it were, the body would be inside and not outside. Therefore, it's an effect of the moonlight. Don't you see it?'

'Perfectly; I always see it on moonlight nights.'

'It doesn't seem to interest you much,' said Holger.

'On the contrary, it does interest me, though I am used to it. You're not so far wrong, either. The mound is really a grave.'

'Nonsense' cried Holger incredulously. 'I suppose you'll tell me that what I see lying on it is really a corpse!'

'No,' I answered, 'it's not. I know, because I have taken the trouble to go down and see.'

'Then what is it?' asked Holger.

'It's nothing.'

'You mean that it's an effect of light, I suppose?'

'Perhaps it is. But the inexplicable part of the matter is that it makes no difference whether the moon is rising or setting, or waxing or waning. If there's any moonlight at all, from east or west or overhead, so long as it shines on the grave you can see the outline of the body on top.'

Holger stirred up his pipe with the point of his knife, and then used his finger for a stopper. When the tobacco burned well he rose from his chair.

'If you don't mind,' he said, 'I'll go down and take a look at it.'

He left me, crossed the roof, and disappeared down the dark steps. I did not move, but sat looking down until he came out of the tower below. I heard him humming an old Danish song as he crossed the open space in the bright moonlight, going straight to the mysterious mound. When he was ten paces from it, Holger stopped short, made two steps forward, and then three or four backward, and then stopped again. I knew what that meant. He had reached the spot where the Thing ceased to be visible—where, as he would have said, the effect of the light changed.

Then he went on till he reached the mound and stood upon it. I could see the Thing still, but it was no longer lying down; it was on its knees now, winding its white arms round Holger's body and looking up into his face. A cool breeze stirred my hair at that moment, as the night wind began to come down from the hills, but it felt like a breath from another world.

The Thing seemed to be trying to climb to its feet helping itself up by Holger's body while he stood upright, quite unconscious of it and apparently looking towards the tower, which is very picturesque when the moonlight falls upon it on that side.

'Come along!' I shouted. 'Don't stay there all night!'

It seemed to me that he moved reluctantly as he stepped from the mound, or else with difficulty. That was it. The Thing's arms were still round his waist, but its feet could not leave the grave. As he came slowly forward it was drawn and lengthened like a wreath of mist, thin and white, till I saw distinctly that Holger shook himself, as a man does who feels a chill. At the same instant a little wail of pain came to me on the breeze—it might have been the cry of the small owl that lives among the rocks—and the misty presence floated swiftly back from Holger's advancing figure and lay once more at its length upon the mound.

Again I felt the cool breeze in my hair, and this time an icy thrill of dread ran down my spine. I remembered very well that I had once gone down there alone in the moonlight; that presently, being near, I had seen nothing; that, like Holger, I had gone and had stood upon the mound; and I remembered how when I came back, sure that there was nothing there, I had felt the sudden conviction that there was something after all if I would only look behind me. I remembered the strong temptation to look back, a temptation I had resisted as unworthy of a man of sense, until, to get rid of it, I had shaken myself just as Holger did.

And now I knew that those white, misty arms had been round me, too; I knew it in a flash, and I shuddered as I remembered that I had heard the night owl then, too. But it had not been the night owl. It was the cry of the Thing.

I refilled my pipe and poured out a cup of strong southern wine; in less than a minute Holger was seated beside me again.

'Of course there's nothing there,' he said, 'but it's creepy, all the same. Do you know, when I was coming back I was so sure that there was something behind me that I wanted to turn round and look? It was an effort not to.'

He laughed a little, knocked the ashes out of his pipe, and poured himself out some wine. For a while neither of us spoke, and the moon rose higher and we both looked at the Thing that lay on the mound.

'You might make a story about that,' said Holger after a long time.

'There is one,' I answered. 'If you're not sleepy, I'll tell it to you,'

'Go ahead,' said Holger, who likes stories.

Old Alario was dying up there in the village behind the hill. You remember him, I have no doubt. They say that he made his money by selling sham jewelry in South America, and escaped with his gains when he was found out. Like all those fellows, if they bring anything back with them, he at once set to work to enlarge his house, and as there are no masons here, he sent all the way to Paola for two workmen. They were a rough-looking pair of scoundrels— a Neapolitan who had lost one eye and a Sicilian with an old scar half an inch deep across his left cheek. I often saw them, for on Sundays they used to come down here and fish off the rocks. When Alario caught the fever that killed him the masons were still at work. As he had agreed that part of their pay should be their board and lodgings, he made them sleep in the house. His wife was dead, and he had an only son called Angelo, who was a much better sort than himself. Angelo was to marry the daughter of the richest man in the village, and, strange to say, though the marriage was arranged by their parents, the young people were said to be in love with each other.

For that matter, the whole village was in love with Angelo, and among the rest a wild, good-looking creature called Cristina, who was more like a gipsy than any girl I ever saw about here. She had very red lips and very black eyes, she was built like a greyhound, and had the tongue of the devil. But Angelo did not care a straw for her. He was rather a simple-minded fellow, quite different from his old scoundrel of a father, and under what I should call normal circumstances I really believe that he would never have looked at any girl except the nice plump little creature, with a fat dowry, whom his father meant him to marry. But things turned up which were neither normal nor natural.

On the other hand, a very handsome young shepherd from the hills above Maratea was in love with Cristina, who seems to have been quite indifferent to him. Cristina had no regular means of subsistence, but she was a good girl and willing to do any work or go on errands to any distance for the sake of a loaf of bread or a mess of beans, and permission to sleep under cover. She was especially glad when she would get something to do about the house of Angelo's father. There is no doctor in the village, and when the neighbours saw that old Alario was dying they sent Cristina to Scalea to fetch one. That was late in the afternoon, and if they had waited so long it was because the dying miser refused to allow any such extravagance while he was able to speak. But while Cristina was gone matters grew rapidly worse, the priest was brought to the bedside, and when he had done what he could he gave it as his opinion to the by-standers that the old man was dead, and left the house.

You know these people. They have a physical horror of death. Until the priest spoke, the room had been full of people. The words were hardly out of his mouth before it was empty. It was night now. They hurried down the dark steps and out into the street.

Angelo, as I have said, was away. Cristina had not come back— the simple woman-servant who had nursed the sick man fled with the rest, and the body was left alone in the flickering light of the earthen oil lamp.

Five minutes later two men looked in cautiously and crept forward towards the bed. They were the one-eyed Neapolitan mason and his Sicilian companion. They knew what they wanted. In a moment they had dragged from under the bed a small but heavy iron-bound box, and long before anyone thought of coming back to the dead man they had left the house and the village under cover of the darkness. It was easy enough, for Alario's house is the last towards the gorge which leads down here, and the thieves merely went out by the back door, got over the stone wall, and had nothing to risk after that except the possibility of meeting some belated countryman, which was very small indeed, since few of the people use that path. They had a mattock and shovel, and they made their way without accident.

I am telling you this story as it must have happened, for, of course, there were no witnesses to this part of it. The men brought the box down by the gorge, intending to bury it until they should be able to come back and take it away in a boat. They must have been clever enough to guess that some of the money would be in paper notes, for they would otherwise have buried it on the beach in the wet sand, where it would have been much safer. But the paper would have rotted if they had been obliged to leave it there long, so they dug their hole down there, close to that boulder. Yes, just where the mound is now.

Cristina did not find the doctor in Scalea, for he had been sent for from a place up the valley, halfway to San Domenico. If she had found him he would have come on his mule by the upper road, which is smoother but much longer. But Cristina took the short cut by the rocks, which passes about fifty feet above the mound, and goes round that corner. The men were digging when she passed, and she heard them at work. It would not have been like her to go by without finding out what the noise was, for she was never afraid of anything in her life, and, besides, the fishermen sometimes come ashore here at night to get a stone for an anchor or to gather sticks to make a little fire. The night was dark and Cristina probably came close to the men before she could see what they were doing. She knew them, of course, and they knew her, and understood instantly that they were in her power. There was only one thing to be done for their safety, and they did it. They knocked her on the head, they dug the hole deep, and they buried her quickly with the iron-bound chest. They must have understood that their only chance of escaping suspicion lay in getting back to the village before their absence was noticed, for they returned immediately, and were found half an hour later gossiping quietly with the man who was making Alario's coffin. He was a crony of theirs, and had been working at the repairs in the old man's house. So far as I have been able to make out, the only persons who were supposed to know where Alario kept his treasure were Angelo and the one woman-servant I have mentioned. Angelo was away; it was the woman who discovered the theft.

It was easy enough to understand why no one else knew where the money was. The old man kept his door locked and the key in his pocket when he was out, and did not let the women enter to clean the place unless he was there himself. The whole village knew that he had money somewhere, however, and the masons had probably discovered the whereabouts of the chest by climbing in at the window in his absence. If the old man had not been delirious until he lost consciousness he would have been in frightful agony of mind for his riches. The faithful woman-servant forgot their existence only for a few moments when she fled with the rest, overcome by the horror of death. Twenty minutes had not passed before she returned with the two hideous old hags who were always called in to prepare the dead for burial. Even then she had not at first the courage to go near the bed with them, but she made a pretence of dropping something, went down on her knees as if to find it, and looked under the bedstead. The walls of the room were newly white-washed down to the floor, and she saw at a glance that the chest was gone. It had been there in the afternoon, it had therefore been stolen in the short interval since she had left the room.

There are no carabineers stationed in the village; there is not so much as a municipal watchman, for there is no municipality. There never was such a place, I believe. Scalea is supposed to look after it in some mysterious way, and it takes a couple of hours to get anybody from there. As the old woman had lived in the village all her life, it did not even occur to her to apply to any civil authority for help. She simply set up a howl and ran through the village in the dark, screaming out that her dead master's house had been robbed. Many of the people looked out, but at first no one seemed inclined to help her. Most of them, judging her by themselves, whispered to each other that she had probably stolen the money herself. The first man to move was the father of the girl whom Angelo was to marry; having collected his household, all of whom felt a personal interest in the wealth which was to have come into the family, he declared it to be his opinion that the chest had been stolen by the two journeymen masons who lodged in the house. He headed a search for them, which naturally began in Alario's house and ended in the carpenter's workshop, where the thieves were found discussing a measure of wine with the carpenter over the half-finished coffin, by the light of one earthen lamp filled with oil and tallow. The search party at once accused the delinquents of the crime, and threatened to lock them up in the cellar till the carabineers could be fetched from Scalea. The two men looked at each other for one moment, and then without the slightest hesitation they put out the single light, seized the unfinished coffin between them, and using it as a sort of battering ram, dashed upon their assailants in the dark. In a few moments, they were beyond pursuit.

That is the end of the first part of the story. The treasure had disappeared, and as no trace of it could be found the people naturally supposed that the thieves had succeeded in carrying it off. The old man was buried, and when Angelo came back at last he had to borrow money to pay for the miserable funeral, and had some difficulty in doing so. He hardly needed to be told that in losing his inheritance he had lost his bride. In this part of the world marriages are made on strictly business principles, and if the promised cash is not forthcoming on the appointed day, the bride or the bridegroom whose parents have failed to produce it may as well take themselves off, for there will be no wedding. Poor Angelo knew that well enough. His father had been possessed of hardly any land, and now that the hard cash which he had brought from South America was gone, there was nothing left but debts for the building materials that were to have been used for enlarging and improving the old house. Angelo was beggared, and the nice plump little creature who was to have been his, turned up her nose at him in the most approved fashion. As for Cristina, it was several days before she was missed, for no one remembered that she had been sent to Scalea for the doctor, who had never come. She often disappeared in the same way for days together, when she could find a little work here and there at the distant farms among the hills. But when she did not come back at all, people began to wonder, and at last made up their minds that she had connived with the masons and had escaped with them.

I paused and emptied my glass.

'That sort of thing could not happen anywhere else,' observed Holger, filling his everlasting pipe again. 'It is wonderful what a natural charm there is about murder and sudden death in a romantic country like this. Deeds that would be simply brutal and disgusting anywhere else become dramatic and mysterious because this is Italy, and we are living in a genuine tower of Charles V built against genuine Barbary pirates.'

'There's something in that,' I admitted. Holger is the most romantic man in the world inside of himself, but he always thinks it necessary to explain why he feels anything.

'I suppose they found the poor girl's body with the box,' he said presently.

'As it seems to interest you,' I answered, 'I'll tell you the rest of the story.'

The moon had risen high by this time; the outline of the Thing on the mound was clearer to our eyes than before.

The village very soon settled down to its small dull life. No one missed old Alario, who had been away so much on his voyages to South America that he had never been a familiar figure in his native place. Angelo lived in the half-finished house, and because he had no money to pay the old woman-servant, she would not stay with him, but once in a long time she would come and wash a shirt for him for old acquaintance's sake. Besides the house, he had inherited a small patch of ground at some distance from the village; he tried to cultivate it, but he had no heart in the work, for he knew he could never pay the taxes on it and on the house, which would certainly be confiscated by the Government, or seized for the debt of the building material, which the man who had supplied it refused to take back.

Angelo was very unhappy. So long as his father had been alive and rich, every girl in the village had been in love with him; but that was all changed now. It had been pleasant to be admired and courted, and invited to drink wine by fathers who had girls to marry. It was hard to be stared at coldly, and sometimes laughed at because he had been robbed of his inheritance. He cooked his miserable meals for himself, and from being sad became melancholy and morose.

At twilight, when the day's work was done, instead of hanging about in the open space before the church with young fellows of his own age, he took to wandering in lonely places on the outskirts of the village till it was quite dark. Then he slunk home and went to bed to save the expense of a light. But in those lonely twilight hours he began to have strange dreams. He was not always alone, for often when he sat on the stump of a tree, where the narrow path turns down the gorge, he was sure that a woman came up noiselessly over the rough stones, as if her feet were bare; and she stood under a clump of chestnut trees only half a dozen yards down the path, and beckoned to him without speaking. Though she was in the shadow he knew that her lips were red, and that when they parted a little and smiled at him she showed two small sharp teeth. He knew this at first rather than saw it, and he knew that it was Cristina, and that she was dead. Yet he was not afraid; he only wondered whether it was a dream, for he thought that if he had been awake he should have been frightened.

Besides, the dead woman had red lips, and that could only happen in a dream. Whenever he went near the gorge after sunset she was already there waiting for him, or else she very soon appeared, and he began to be sure that she came a little nearer to him every day. At first he had only been sure of her blood-red mouth, but now each feature grew distinct, and the pale face looked at him with deep and hungry eyes.

It was the eyes that grew dim. Little by little he came to know that someday the dream would not end when he turned away to go home, but would lead him down the gorge out of which the vision rose. She was nearer now when she beckoned to him. Her cheeks were not livid like those of the dead, but pale with starvation, with the furious and unappeased physical hunger of her eyes that devoured him. They feasted on his soul and cast a spell over him, and at last they were close to his own and held him. He could not tell whether her breath was as hot as fire, or as cold as ice; he could not tell whether her red lips burned his or froze them, or whether her five fingers on his wrists seared scorching scars or bit his flesh like frost; he could not tell whether he was awake or asleep, whether she was alive or dead, but he knew that she loved him, she alone of all creatures, earthly or unearthly, and her spell had power over him.

When the moon rose high that night the shadow of that Thing was not alone down there upon the mound.

Angelo awoke in the cool dawn, drenched with dew and chilled through flesh, and blood, and bone. He opened his eyes to the faint grey light, and saw the stars still shining overhead. He was very weak, and his heart was beating so slowly that he was almost like a man fainting. Slowly he turned his head on the mound, as on a pillow, but the other face was not there. Fear seized him suddenly, a fear unspeakable and unknown; he sprang to his feet and fled up the gorge, and he never looked behind him until he reached the door of the house on the outskirts of the village. Drearily he went to his work that day, and wearily the hours dragged themselves after the sun, till at last it touched the sea and sank, and the great sharp hills above Maratea turned purple against the dove-coloured eastern sky.

Angelo shouldered his heavy hoe and left the field. He felt less tired now than in the morning when he had begun to work, but he promised himself that he would go home without lingering by the gorge, and eat the best supper he could set himself, and sleep all night in his bed like a Christian man. Not again would he be tempted down the narrow way by a shadow with red lips and icy breath; not again would he dream that dream of terror and delight. He was near the village now; it was half an hour since the sun had set, and the cracked church bell sent little discordant echoes across the rocks and ravines to tell all good people that the day was done. Angelo stood still a moment where the path forked, where it led towards the village on the left, and down to the gorge on the right, where a clump of chestnut trees overhung the narrow way. He stood still a minute, lifting his battered hat from his head and gazing at the fast-fading sea westward, and his lips moved as he silently repeated the familiar evening prayer. His lips moved, but the words that followed them in his brain lost their meaning and turned into others, and ended in a name that he spoke aloud—Cristina! With the name, the tension of his will relaxed suddenly, reality went out and the dream took him again, and bore him on swiftly and surely like a man walking in his sleep, down, down, by the steep path in the gathering darkness. And as she glided beside him, Cristina whispered strange sweet things in his ear, which somehow, if he had been awake, he knew that he could not quite have understood;

but now they were the most wonderful words he had ever heard in his life. And she kissed him also, but not upon his mouth. He felt her sharp kisses upon his white throat, and he knew that her lips were red. So the wild dream sped on through twilight and darkness and moonrise, and all the glory of the summer's night. But in the chilly dawn he lay as one half dead upon the mound down there, recalling and not recalling, drained of his blood, yet strangely longing to give those red lips more. Then came the fear, the awful nameless panic, the mortal horror that guards the confines of the world we see not, neither know of as we know of other things, but which we feel when its icy chill freezes our bones and stirs our hair with the touch of a ghostly hand. Once more Angelo sprang from the mound and fled up the gorge in the breaking day, but his step was less sure this time, and he panted for breath as he ran; and when he came to the bright spring of water that rises halfway up the hillside, he dropped upon his knees and hands and plunged his whole face in and drank as he had never drunk before—for it was the thirst of the wounded man who has lain all night long upon the battlefield.

She had him fast now, and he could not escape her, but would come to her every evening at dusk until she had drained him of his last drop of blood. It was in vain that when the day was done he tried to take another turning and to go home by a path that did not lead near the gorge. It was in vain that he made promises to himself each morning at dawn when he climbed the lonely way up from the shore to the village. It was all in vain, for when the sun sank burning into the sea, and the coolness of the evening stole out as from a hiding-place to delight the weary world, his feet turned towards the old way, and she was waiting for him in the shadow under the chestnut trees; and then all happened as before, and she fell to kissing his white throat even as she flitted lightly down the way, winding one arm about him. And as his blood failed, she grew more hungry and more thirsty every day, and every day when he awoke in the early dawn it was harder to rouse himself to the effort of climbing the steep path to the village; and when he went to his work his feet dragged painfully, and there was hardly strength in his arms to wield the heavy hoe. He scarcely spoke to anyone now, but the people said he was 'consuming himself' for love of the girl he was to have married when he lost his inheritance; and they laughed heartily at the thought, for this is not a very romantic country. At this time Antonio, the man who stays here to look after the tower, returned from a visit to his people, who live near Salerno. He had been away all the time since before Alario's death and knew nothing of what had happened. He has told me that he came back late in the afternoon and shut himself up in the tower to eat and sleep, for he was very tired. It was past midnight when he awoke, and when he looked out the waning moon was rising over the shoulder of the hill. He looked out towards the mound, and he saw something, and he did not sleep again that night. When he went out again in the morning it was broad daylight, and there was nothing to be seen on the mound but loose stones and driven sand. Yet he did not go very near it; he went straight up the path to the village and directly to the house of the old priest.

'I have seen an evil thing this night,' he said; 'I have seen how the dead drink the blood of the living. And the blood is the life.'

'Tell me what you have seen,' said the priest in reply.

Antonio told him everything he had seen.

'You must bring your book and your holy water tonight,' he added. 'I will be here before sunset to go down with you, and if it pleases your reverence to sup with me while we wait, I will make ready.'

'I will come,' the priest answered, 'for I have read in old books of these strange beings which are neither quick nor dead, and which lie ever fresh in their graves, stealing out in the dusk to taste life and blood.'

Antonio cannot read, but he was glad to see that the priest understood the business; for, of course, the books must have instructed him as to the best means of quieting the half-living Thing for ever.

So Antonio went away to his work, which consists largely in sitting on the shady side of the tower, when he is not perched upon a rock with a fishing-line catching nothing. But on that day he went twice to look at the mound in the bright sunlight, and he searched round and round it for some hole through which the being might get in and out; but he found none. When the sun began to sink and the air was cooler in the shadows, he went up to fetch the old priest, carrying a little wicker basket with him; and in this they placed a bottle of holy water, and the basin, and sprinkler, and the stole which the priest would need; and they came down and waited in the door of the tower till it should be dark. But while the light still lingered very grey and faint, they saw something moving, just there, two figures, a man's that walked, and a woman's that flitted beside him, and while her heard lay on his shoulder she kissed his throat. The priest has told me that, too, and that his teeth chattered and he grasped Antonio's arm. The vision passed and disappeared into the shadow. Then Antonio got the leather flask of strong liquor, which he kept for great occasions, and poured such a draught as made the old man feel almost young again; and gave the priest his stole to put on and the holy water to carry, and they went out together towards the spot where the work was to be done. Antonio says that in spite of the rum his own knees shook together, and the priest stumbled over his Latin. For when they were yet a few yards from the mound the flickering light of the lantern fell upon Angelo's white face, unconscious as if in sleep, and on his upturned throat, over which a very thin red line of blood trickled down into his collar; and the flickering light of the lantern played upon another face that looked up from the feast, upon two deep, dead eyes that saw in spite of death—upon parted lips, redder than life itself—upon two gleaming teeth on which glistened a rosy drop. Then the priest, good old man, shut his eyes tight and showered holy water before him, and his cracked voice rose almost to a scream; and then Antonio, who is no coward after all, raised his pick in one hand and the lantern in the other, as he sprang forward, not knowing what the end should be; and then he swears that he heard a woman's cry, and the Thing was gone, and Angelo lay alone on the mound unconscious, with the red line on his throat and the beads of deathly sweat on his cold forehead. They lifted him, half-dead as he was, and laid him on the ground close by; then Antonio went to work, and the priest helped him, though he was old and could not do much; and they dug deep, and at last Antonio, standing in the grave, stooped down with his lantern to see what he might see.

His hair used to be dark brown, with grizzled streaks about the temples; in less than a month from that day he was as grey as a badger. He was a miner when he was young, and most of these fellows have seen ugly sights now and then, when accidents have happened, but he had never seen what he saw that night—that Thing which is neither alive nor dead, that Thing that will abide neither

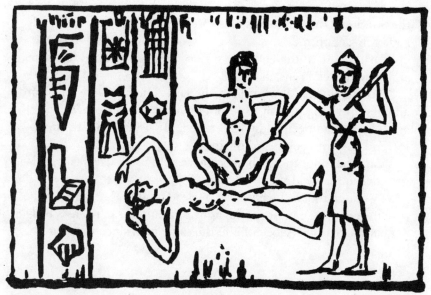

If this Babylonian cylinder seal really depicts a vampire, then it is one of the earliest if not absolutely the earliest pictures of this dreadful creature.

above ground nor in the grave. Antonio had brought something with him which the priest had not noticed. He had made it that afternoon—a sharp stake shaped from a piece of tough old driftwood. He had it with him now, and he had his heavy pick, and he had taken the lantern down into the grave. I don't think any power on earth could make him speak of what happened then, and the old priest was too frightened to look in. He says he heard Antonio breathing like a wild beast, and moving as if he were fighting with something almost as strong as himself; and he heard an evil sound also, with blows, as of something violently driven through flesh and bone; and then, the most awful sound of all—a woman's shriek, the unearthly scream of a woman neither dead nor alive, but buried deep for many days. And he, the poor old priest, could only rock himself as he knelt there in the sand, crying aloud his prayers and exorcisms to drown those dreadful sounds. Then suddenly a small iron-bound chest was thrown up and rolled over against the old man's knee, and in a moment more Antonio was beside him, his face as white as tallow in the flickering light of the lantern, shoveling the sand and pebbles into the grave with furious haste, and looking over the edge till the pit was half full; and the priest said that there was much fresh blood on Antonio's hands and on his clothes.

I had come to the end of my story. Holger finished his wine and leaned back in his chair.

'So Angelo got his own again,' he said. 'Did he marry the prim and plump young person to whom he had been betrothed?'

'No; he had been badly frightened. He went to South America, and has not been heard of since.'

'And that poor thing's body is there still, I suppose," said Holger. 'Is it quite dead yet, I wonder?'

I wonder, too. But whether it be dead or alive, I should hardly care to see it, even in broad daylight. Antonio is as grey as a badger, and he has never been quite the same man since that night.

4

The Vampire in the Rest of the World

THE VAMPIRE AROUND THE WORLD

It has been said, and most people believe, that there is not and never has been a people anywhere in the history of the world who did not or do not believe in the existence of a divine power. With creation, a Creator. With that logically comes a question of purpose and a concept of good and evil; and with that angels, demons. Among the creatures of evil, predators such as the vampire rank high.

This book is designed for readers chiefly in the Americas and Europe and therefore vampires in those traditions take up most of our limited space, but similar compendia of vampire lore could fill whole books devoted to other continents. That devoted to Asia would be a huge tome. In a few pages here I shall attempt to suggest at least a little of the prevalence of the vampire myth in societies less familiar to us.

DR. VAN HELSING ON THE UBIQUITY OF THE VAMPIRE

"Let me tell you," solemnly states the vampire killer in *Dracula*, in Stoker's deliberately awkward style for this character, "he is known everywhere that men have been. In old Greece, in old Rome; he flourish[es] in Germany all over, in France, in India, even in the Chersonese; and in China, so far from us in all ways, there even is he...."

FEED ME!

Vampires are not the only bloodseekers. Ancient peoples in Central America, for instance, believed that they came from the flesh and blood of the gods—and that the gods wanted flesh and blood in return. Especially blood. The people erected vast buildings to resemble mountains and in temples on top of these huge structures they ritually sacrificed adults and children, offering the gods the hearts torn from the bodies, rivers of blood. They sometimes went to war to get captives for sacrifice to their gods, but they sacrificed their own as well. It was even believed that the sun, the source of life, needed to be fed human blood to give it strength to combat the powers of darkness. The rain god was offered blood and the tears of the terrified victims. Even the kings of the people made themselves bleed to please the thirsty deities.

All this may seem strange today, even to Christians who eat the flesh and drink the blood of Christ.

THE SOUL

In the undead there is, superstition says, no soul. The vampire must constantly replenish spirit by drinking the blood (which contains the spirit) of the living.

And what of the souls of the dead? The Catechism has an answer.

In the life after death our spirits will be clothed with a body suited to the new life we shall live with God in heaven. The resurrected body will be a spiritual and not a material body, but it will be like our present body in such a way that our friends will be able to recognize us.

Just one question: Where did they ever get such an idea? How do they *know* that? Our "present body" at the time of death? (In which case, you may be well advised if you want a pretty appearance for eternity to kill yourself while you are young and healthy and look your best.) If our friends will be able to recognize us, will our enemies be able to do so too? One question? There are many. None can really be answered, but every culture tries.

THE DRUNKEN BOY

According to Asian legend, The Drunken Boy is a giant ogre, dressed in scarlet, who feasts on blood like a vampire and is particularly attracted to women, but he may never have been a human being. We may be dealing only with a demon, and certainly his fearful companions are demons.

The story is told in Japan of Raikō or Yorimitsu, a great hero of medieval times. He dressed himself and his stalwart companions as priests and managed to get into The Drunken Boy's lair, where (naturally) a drinking party was in progress. Our hero slipped something into the drinks of the ogres, threw off his disguise, and set upon them. They fought fiercely— The Drunken Boy's head kept battling even after he was decapitated!— but in the end Raiko won. He bore the head back in triumph to Miyako, the imperial capital, bringing along also a bevy of beauties The Drunken Boy had victimized.

Whether The Drunken Boy was an undead human or a demon (they abound in Eastern folklore), Japan does have a lot of ghosts and vampires in its mythology. It has made full use of them in its art, prose, poetry, and drama, which tend to run on repetitive, traditional lines. The most miserable ghosts are the hungry ones (*gaki*), unable to eat and therefore dejected. They occur often in the folk literature of Japan, and are said to be attracted to any large displays of food and drink. Watch out at buffets.

SHURA AND TENGU

The first is the Japanese "furious spirit." "This is a ghost of a dead warrior; he and his forces are full of revenge and continually battle in the skies. They somewhat resemble the *tengu* or "spirit of the air" creatures but are more violent. *Tengu* also are proud and violent dead persons, mostly warriors. Many a mountain peak has its angry *tengu*, a concept borrowed (like so many things Japanese) from the culture of China. Each master *tengu* has a force of bird-headed creatures resembling the *garuda* of Hindu mythology.

One history of mythology says that "in the ages of war, the three centuries that followed the fourteenth, the Japanese were obsessed by superstitious dread of the Tengus and stories about them were manifold."

Ignoring the promising possibilities of a *tengu* flick, the Japanese have perpetrated a string of pedestrian vampire movies. Half a dozen samples:

> *Chi o suu ningyo* (1970)
> *Dakki* (1936)
> *Kuroneko* (1968)
> *Kyuketsu Gokemidoro* (1968)
> *Onna kyuketsuki* (1959)
> The Ugly Vampire (1968)

YUKI-ONNE

This woman (whose name somewhat suggests that of Yoko Ono, and who looks a bit like her) is pale, cold, and dangerous: she marries a man and saps his strength and kills him. She is the Snow Woman. Unwary or exhausted travelers in snowstorms fall into her welcoming arms and perish. She is more of a demon than a vampire, however. Japanese folklore has many a dangerous females. Another is the *Yama-uba* or the Mountain Woman. She haunts the hills and forests. "I am not a human being," she states clearly in the famous old drama concerning her. Therefore, she is not a ghost or a vampire.

CHINESE GHOSTS

In China the ghost story has from time immemorial been a major art form. Chinese ghosts can be good or bad or mixed. Because the Chinese believe in three aspects of the soul (the higher, the lower, and the part that inhabits and is honored at the altar of ancestors) a dead person can appear in several places at once. As is not uncommon in Asia, some Chinese ghosts are ludicrous clowns and others are vengeful and hateful. Some are ridiculously stupid and some infernally clever. The Chinese vampire is less common than the ghost. Charles P. Emmons has written about the vampire in *Chinese Ghosts and ESP* (1982).

It appears now that early Mexican civilization had contact with or was derived from Shang Dynasty civilization in China, and this may go far to explain why Olmec and other Mexican concepts of ghosts and even vampires somewhat resemble Chinese ideas.

One of the interesting aspects of folklore is the way it raises questions of transmission of certain themes in cultural contacts or independent development of basic themes in widely separated cultures. Ghosts, poltergeists, and vampires, like gods and demons, appear to exist in many places and forms; they reflect certain fundamental human speculations and fears. Whether these creatures actually exist or not, in saying that they do we reveal significant aspects of human nature.

Chinese ghosts occasionally are a subject of Chinese films but I have dug up only one Chinese vampire film title, *Xi Xuefu* (The Vampire World), and I don't know if it's really about vampires. Has anyone in the West seen it?

We in the West who are interested in the popular culture of Asia lack adequate language skills to investigate films, comic books, folk tales, and the rest. There is a rich mine of horror stories there to be investigated.

VAMPIRES AMONG THE MUSLIMS

One peculiar source alleges that the crusaders suffered much from vampires among the Muslims from which the Christian knights were trying to wrest back the Holy Land. Various groups of knights hospitaller and others report clashing with vampires of one sort or another and one source suggests that accusations of vampirism were very useful in getting even ecclesiastical authorities out of the way of orders of knights that wished to operate more or less independently, whether Knights Templar, Teutonic Knights, or whatever. It is written: "A powerful vampire masquerading as the Patriarch of Jerusalem was, in 1214, killed by Hashhaskin [Assassin] Assamites—hired by the [Knights] Hospitallers to make it look like a Muslim action."

It is not impossible that the Teutonic Knights brought into their Slavic territories the stories of vampires among the Muslims. The Knights of St. John of Jerusalem, driven off to Rhodes and to Malta, may have spread rumors of their suffering at the hands of vampires. The Knights Templar were frequently accused of picking up various demonic practices from the Muslims, and a belief in vampires may have reached Europe through them, as well.

RAYMOND HERBERT ON TURKISH VAMPIRES

According to the beliefs of the Karachay people, Oburs occur among very old people. The people who become Oburs recognize each other. According to the Oburs themselves, there are Oburism skills and salves. The ones who become Oburs know how to enter into various forms. For example, cats, dogs, and wolves. Oburs, at the time when they become Oburs, strip mother naked in a large house. They smear salve, which they make themselves, on their bodies and wallow in the ashes on the edge of the fire. Afterwards they mount brooms with whips in their hands, and after running around the bottom of the room in circles, they issue from the chimney in the forms of cats. After men's footsteps have ceased, and everyone has gone to bed, they enter by the chimney, drink the children's blood, and leave a black bruise at the place where they have drunk, and then go. If it becomes necessary to go to a place far from the village, they are gathered in twos and threes somewhere, and they enter into the form of wolves. No matter what there is at the summer pastures—cows, oxen, calves, horses, or sheep—they make them lie down,

Sir Richard Burton translated the Arabic tale of *Vikram and the Vampire* (1870).

drink their blood, and sate themselves on blood. The Oburs who will do this do their work at night. With the break of dawn, they leave immediately, enter the house by the place whence they had issued, and enter into their original shapes. In the Karachay, many kinds of stories concerning the Obur are current. If these stories be true, many other stories will become useful.

TURKS, ANTI-SEMITISM, AND VAMPIRES

A report from Percy Bysshe Shelley (at whose house party in The Alps his wife wrote *Frankenstein*, Dr. Polidori wrote *The Vampyre*, and Shelley was too frightened to write anything):

> The Turks have an opinion that men that are buried have a sort of life in their graves. If any man makes an affidavit before a Judge that he heard a noise in a man's grave he is by order dug up and chopped all to pieces. The merchants [of Constantinople], once on horseback, have, as usual, for protection, a Janissary with them. Passing by the burial place of the Jews, it happened that [they saw that] an old Jew sat by a sepulchre. The Janissary rode up to him, and [be]rated him for stinking up the world a second time, and commanded him into his grave again.

VAMPIRES IN INDIA

Some Indian ghosts resemble our vampires in that they are said to "live" on the blood of the living. These are angry creatures who died violently— by suicide or murder—or were not properly buried, Indians say.

THE FOX

In Asia, there are legends of a female spirit called The Fox, which is rapacious, but she may never have been human and might therefore not qualify as a real vampire. Here is a snatch of dialogue between Lien-hsiang, The Fox, and Li, a female ghost, hovering over the bed of a sick young man. The Fox admits there are vampiristic spirits but stoutly maintains she is not one that steals the vitality of young men; she stimulates and enjoys it. This is from P'u Sung-ling (1640-1715):

> *Lien-hsiang*: I've heard that female ghosts rapaciously cause the death of young men so that, after they die, the ghosts may have sex with them. Any truth in that?

Li: Certainly not. Two ghosts having sex can't enjoy it. If they did, there are plenty of young men in the world of the dead anyway.

Lien-hsiang: What a silly girl! If a man had sex with a woman every single night he would soon wear himself out, and ghosts who have been among the dead for awhile are already pretty feeble.

Li: But I've heard that the lusty Fox can cause the death of a young man. How do you manage to have sex with them without debilitating them?

Lien-hsiang: You must be talking about spirits who sap the vitality of their victims to draw strength for themselves. I am not one of that variety. It's true that there are certain fox spirits who damage the young men with whom they have sex, but that comes from their ghostly coldness [not the heat of lust].

As with the *incubi* and *succubæ* of the West, these ghastly, ghostly Asian visitants are not thought to be able to breed, whether the sex is pleasurable (as it seldom is) or not.

DEFENSES OF THE YORUBA

Among the Yoruba in Africa, when one child of newborn twins dies the mother carries around with her a wooden figure designed to represent the dead child. It not only keeps its living brother company but also gives the ghost of the dead child a figure to inhabit so that it will not bother its twin. The dead child otherwise might vampirize the living one.

INSURANCE

There is at least one American insurance company that will write you a policy against immaculate conception—they used to offer insurance against alien abduction or impregnation by aliens but ceased issuing policies after the Heaven's Gate incident happened in early 1997—and against becoming a vampire or a werewolf.

Don't you wonder how you and I could make some money betting that nobody would be able to prove in a court of law that they had become a vampire? For one thing, I doubt that the testimony of someone who claims to be dead (or undead) would be admitted.

PRESERVING THE CORPSE

There are many of the dead still with us, as it were, in person. I have seen a whole museum of mummies in Guanajuato, Mexico, mummies in various Egyptian collections, some saints and movie stars in their long sleep, even Lenin (who looked rather waxy to me) and Jeremy Bentham. Bentham (1748-1832), the Utilitarian philosopher, left his body to University College (London), which he founded. At meetings of the board of governors, I presume, he is wheeled up in his chair (with hat and stick and full suit of clothes and a wax mask, because he started to deteriorate a bit) and recorded as "present but not voting."

The question is whether unburied bodies create restless ghosts, even vampires (who depend upon the preservation of their corpses). Theologians and the merely superstitious argue incessantly about this.

Part cat, part bat, this vampire-like creature is ready to pounce on mice, not humans. The "bug" with a crown and BM to the left is the stamp of The British Museum, which holds the seventeen-century book on China from which this imaginative illustration comes.

I find it hard to imagine Jeremy Bentham as a vampire. Indeed, after years in academia, I would say he is the ideal committee member—and he looks better than some of my former colleagues ever did. He looks benign and content.

MALICIOUS SPIRITS OF MALAYA

An anthropoligist named Fauconnier was but one of the many travelers who visited and quizzed the Malayans, who believe in all sorts of vampires and other malicious spirits. Some were once human and some have always been demons. He was told that all the dead are malicious, and when he objected that he did not think that if he were dead he would return to torment the living, his informant assured him he would. In *The Soul of Malaya*:

> "The Tuan [a title of respect] is not evil, but when dead, he would smell as evil as the rest."
>
> "Then you believe my soul would become a hideous demon flapping around my tomb?"
>
> "Your soul is your soul, Tuan. It will go straight to hell [in the sense of an afterworld, not necessarily a place of punishment]. But there will be perhaps ten thousand demons round your tomb."

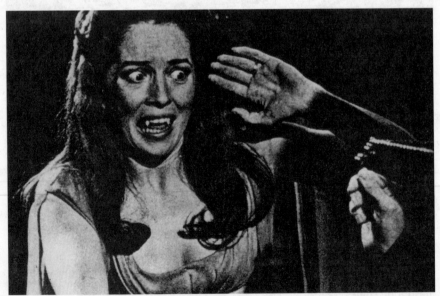

That's a crucifix the lady vampire finds unpleasant. Of course this does not work in non-Christian areas, but then there are defenses in other traditions, too.

"But what are the demons doing there if they are not the souls of the dead?"

"The mouse-deer asks questions of the buffalo," said [I]Smail. "The Tuan is subtle. I do not know."

I, on the contrary, had the impression of being the buffalo.

BORNEO SUBSTITUTES

F. Grabowsky in *International Archiv für Ethnographie* 1 (1888) records that the Oloh Ngadju of Borneo when a person is bothered by a ghost or vampire make poppets of dough or rice flour and throw them under the house of the afflicted person. The idea is to distract the predator's attention from the human victim. Distracting the predator is an old trick. Magic books often suggest you keep witches and other unwanted guests out by putting something laborious to count at the door or window, such as many grains of sand or a handful of flax or other tiny seeds, or even dead animals with many hairs on them.

"I NEVER DRINK—WINE!"

Few actors have ever owned a character the way Dracula was owned by Bela Lugosi (1882–1956). If Clark Gable was The King, Bela Lugosi was The Count. Lugosi lived the part. He was buried in Holy Cross Cemetery in Los Angeles but, at his request, in the costume. The secret of his success was that he was relentlessly malevolent and unstoppable, unalterably opposed to society on screen and in his druggy private life. He fascinated all those who regretted the fact that if you don't follow the rules, they'll kill you.

Lugosi and his Dracula captured the imagination of moviegoers around the world. Whatever language you spoke, however much your society's customs varied from those depicted in the film, the horror was felt—and related to whatever traditions existed in the viewer's society, which was sure to have some hope of life after death, some fear of the dead, some belief that the inhabitants, human and otherwise, of another world could enter ours. There might even be some vicarious pleasure in identifying with the vampire.

The vampire doesn't follow anybody's rules but his own—and you can't kill him, not easily. Even when the picture ended with sunlight turning him to dust, or a stake through the heart doing him in, there was always another picture, right up to the risible, pitiful, and still scary last appearance in a bad movie made by the bad director Ed Wood and the Hollywood fear factories.

Lugosi's acting would have been hammy even in *Mitteleuropa*. His accent has been parodied innumerable times. William Henry Pratt, who called himself "Boris Karloff" and remained basically veddy, veddy English, and spoke British English (though with a lisp) said Lugosi "never took

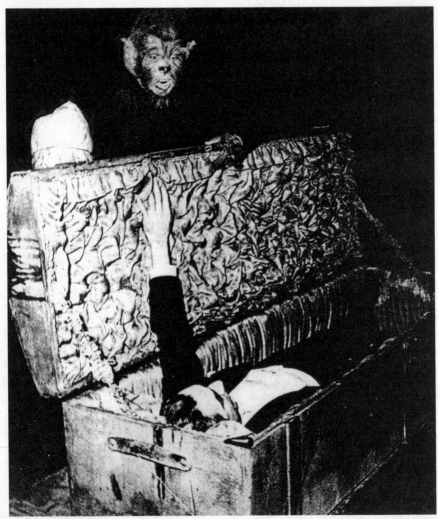

As Dr. Frankenstein had his faithful if unreliable Igor, so vampires find getting good help is difficult. Here Matt Willis in werewolf guise as Andreas helps Béla Lugosi as Armand Tesla, the vampire in *Return of the Vampire* (1944) to make his comeback.

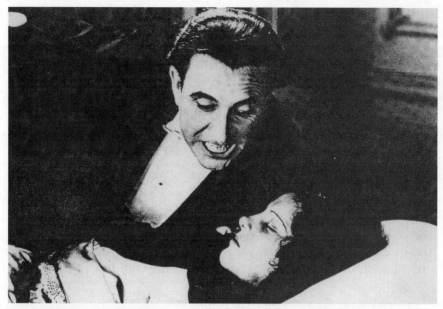

The Spanish-language version of *Dracula* (1931) had Carlos Villarías as The Count and Lupita Továr here as his victim. It was filmed, with an interpreter working for the director, on the sets of the Béla Lugosi *Dracula* and, except for his performance in the title role, exceeded the English-language version in quality. Long thought to be lost, this Villarías version has fairly recently been—unearthed.

the trouble to learn our language." What The Count did learn was something about our most basic terrors, and on them he built his long career. Lugosi had what Carlos Clarens, historian of the fright flick, calls "a kind of corn-ball, demented poetry and total conviction." This worked in any cultural context. In connection with foreign languages and acting styles, in fact, Lugosi's accent and acting may even have looked less hammy!

We hear more of Lugosi elsewhere, but it is fitting to mention him often because he was all the things that the vampire is: driven, solipsistic, ruthless and not in the least aware that he might be not only scary but fundamentally ludicrous (as all evil is). That is understood the wide world over.

A ROYAL PAIN

Today royal families have to worry about the tabloid press, but in Madagascar in olden days the royals were targeted by vampire-like *ramanga*, who not only wanted to drink blue blood but even to eat royal fingernails.

UT

This is the name they give in India to a restless, vampire-like creature who cannot rest in the grave because he was not properly buried—or never sired a son.

ADZE

This is an African vampire that you might think was just a harmless firefly, but if you capture it, it suddenly turns into an undead human being eager to drink the blood of children.

HANNYA

Also dangerous to children are these female bloodsuckers of Japan, vampires or demons. Don't pause to make the distinction. Just run.

OBAYIFU

This was a vampire of West Africa that could assume either sex as desired and when it was not drinking the blood of infants would turn vegetarian and destroy trees and vegetables and fruit by sucking the good out of them.

NEAMMA-PARUSHA

One of many horrors of the Indian subcontinent, this vampire tore off your head and sucked on your skull like a popsicle.

TALAMAUR

This evil creature of Polynesia is really more of a demon than a vampire but it does eat corpses for any shred of vitality it can find. Maybe we should call it a ghoul.

PENANGGALAN

This Malaysian monster is stripped down to essentials, consisting as it does mostly of a human head (intelligence) and a big stomach (to contain the blood it drains, chiefly from children).

MMBYU

I'm not comfortable with the spelling, but my sources assure me this is the correct name of a certain Indian undead creature. He has something in common with the vampire and perhaps more in common with the ghoul. His favorite haunts are places of execution.

RAKSHASAS

More bad news from the Indian subcontinent. The problem is that this one can shape-shift and take any form, many of these forms colorful but terribly grotesque, to get on with its ghoulish business of digging up and eating corpses (like a ghoul), drinking the blood of the living (which it kills in the process and can also bring back to life as a kind of monster), and tearing at everyone with its nails, so long and so garish as to make any American secretary horrified.

HANTPARE

Another doubtful spelling and nasty creature. This Asian predator seeks out people who already are wounded or have open sores. It drinks the blood.

HOUSEHOLD PET VAMPIRES

In Malaysia you can keep a kind of demonic cat—the male is called a *bâjang* and the female is a *langsuir*—and even hand down the pet from one generation to another in the family. You put it in a *tabong* or magical cage—magicians are usually the owners of such pets or familiars—and feed it milk and eggs. If it is not fed regularly it will turn on the family and drink blood. You can sic it on enemies and it will drain their strength until they die.

GHOSTS OF BORNEO

In Borneo it is believed that as long as the flesh has not rotted away completely the spirit will hover near the corpse. (This is the opposite of the Egyptian idea that the body must be preserved so that the *ka* or soul can come back to visit it.) While the spirit is out of the body like this but not free to go on its way, the spirit is nasty and irritable and—here is where this ghost begins to resemble the vampire—can bring disease and death to those still alive. Like vampires, these spirits are said to be particularly dangerous to family members, children most of all.

CHURAIL

A woman who dies ritually "unclean" or pregnant during the Dewali Festival in India may become a vampire. She transforms into a sort of ancient Greek harpy, hideous, with flying hair and pendant breasts and talons for nails, and a black tongue. Some say she is white in front, black behind, which suggests a dual nature the way that the many arms of Indian deities suggest various powers. She attacks relatives, as vampires do, and can be stymied by being buried face down like a vampire, forced then to claw herself deeper.

This creature resembles the European vampire in the way she is burned or buried and in some other particulars. She offers, however, an interesting twist: where European vampires are distracted with mustard seeds or other tiny seeds, rice or other grains, all of which witches and vampires are compelled to count, the *churail* can be kept busy with a ball of twine or wool.

A MUSLIM AMONG THE MAGICIANS

Thelaba is the hero of the poem "Thelaba the Destroyer" (1801) by the English Romantic poet Robert Southey (1774-1843). Thelaba is a destroyer of evil magicians, not a vampire, and while his story has vampire elements it more resembles some sort of magic ring adventure out of *The Arabian* Nights (which also has an occasional vampire-like touch). Here is an excerpt from "Thelaba the Destroyer:"

> A night of darkness and of storms!
> Into the Chamber of the Tomb
> Thalaba led the Old Man,
> To roof him from the rain.
> A night of storms! the wind
> Swept through the moonless sky,
> And moan'd among the pillar'd sepulchres;
> And in the pauses of its sweep
> They heard the heavy rain
> Beat on the monument above.
> In silence on Oneiza's grave
> Her Father and her husband sate.

This is the playbill of the melodrama based on Southey's poem, "Thalaba, The Destroyer."

The Cryer from the Minaret
Proclaim'd the midnight hour.
"Now, now!" cried Thalaba;
And o'er the chamber of the tomb
There spread a lurid gleam,
Like the reflection of a sulphur fire;
And in that hideous light
Oneiza stood before them. It was She...
Her very lineaments,...and such as death
Had changed them, livid cheeks, and lips of blue;
But in her eyes there dwelt
Brightness more terrible
Than all the loathsomeness of death.
"Still art thou living, wretch?"
In hollow tones she cried to Thalaba;
"And must I nightly leave my grave
To tell thee, still in vain,
God hath abandon'd thee?"

"This is not she!" the Old Man exclaim'd;
"A Fiend; a manifest Fiend!"
And to the youth he held his lance;
"Strike and deliver thyself!"
"Strike HER!" cried Thalaba,
And, palsied of all power,
Gazed fixedly upon the dreadful form.
"Yea, strike her!" cried a voice, whose tones
Flow'd with such sudden healing through his soul,
As when the desert shower
From death deliver'd him;
But unobedient to that well-known voice
His eye was seeking it,
When Moath, firm of heart,
Perform'd the bidding; through the vampire corpse
He thrust his lance; it fell,
And howling with the wound,
Its fiendish tenant fled.
A sapphire light fell on them,
And garmented with glory, in their sight
Oneiza's Spirit stood.

"O Thalaba!" she cried,
"Abandon not thyself!
Would'st thou for ever lose me?...O my husband,
Go and fulfil thy quest,
That in the Bowers of Paradise
I may not look for thee
In vain, nor wait thee long."

FEAR OF THE BODY

Our culture, with its mind-body or physical-spiritual dichotomy, distrusts the body while it is alive and fears the body after the soul has departed. Although in the Christian view the body is the Temple of the Holy Ghost, Christians used to mortify it and still do not trust it not to undermine them. The body is subject to degeneration and death and decay.

We shrink from touching corpses; even if starving we certainly are disgusted at the idea of eating the meat. Vampires are dead bodies that walk around and threaten us, and some people believe that zombies are not drugged but reanimated corpses. These horrors deny the ordinary rule that though corpses can be loathsome the dead cannot hurt us. They are fearsome in the same way that werewolves and those possessed of demons are fearsome, because there is in the mortal body an active and perhaps immortal malicious spirit, an enemy of man.

In some cultures foreign to us the possibility of reanimated dead is considered to be much greater. Therefore elaborate defenses are constructed. Those spirits which are thought to be very old are especially feared, for it is imagined that they have had plenty of time to become inhumanely clever and that with one conquest after another have lost all respect for and fear of ordinary mortals. Moreover, it is terrifying to think that one cannot destroy them by destroying a body. If a body they occupy is destroyed, they simply move on to reanimate another. Worst of all, they may resemble ordinary human beings and we may not be able to distinguish between the living and the undead until it is too late to save ourselves.

THE PAINTED SKIN

This is the English title of a striking Chinese vampire story by Pu Sungling. Like most Asian so-called vampire tales, it does not have a bloodsucking vampire of the European type. In this story we do not have an undead human; the human form is merely a disguise for a demon. The skin of the title is a human skin. A hideous green demon with saw-like teeth is observed painting the skin. The startled person who sees this watches as the demon dons the skin in order to appear human.

Poor Wang, the person who observes this, is then seized by the demon, who rips out his heart.

The disconsolate widow calls in a priest. The priest, with a wooden sword, cuts off the demon's head. The priest also throws a gourd vessel at the demon, who is sucked into it. The priest then corks the vessel and departs with the painted skin.

The widow swallows a magic pill and suddenly a lump forms in her throat and she coughs up the heart of Wang. She sews the corpse back together, having inserted its heart, and Wang is brought back to life. A scar is left only as big as a Chinese coin and in time that disappears. Wang is alive and well again.

What the priest did with the painted skin he took from the demon is still unrevealed as this wonderful tale ends.

THE GHOST OF CHANG HÊNG TZU SPEAKS

From a poem by Chang the Teacher (78–139 A.D.):

> The dead man answered me thus:
> "In death I rest. I am at peace.
> In life I worked and streams of Winter
> Better than the melting of Spring.
> All the pride my body knew,
> Was it not lighter than dust I am?...
> I am made of the Primal Spirit.
> I am a wave in the river of Darkness and Light.
> The Creator of All is my father and mother.
> Heaven is my bed, the earth my cushion.
> Thunder and lightning are my drum and fan.
> The sun and moon are my candle and torch.
> The Milky Way is my protective moat, the stars my gems.
> I am now joined with Nature.
> I am void of passion, all desire.
> If you wash me, I shall be no whiter.
> If you foul me, I shall still be clean.
> I do not come, but I am here.
> I do not hasten, but I am swift."
> The voice ceased, and silence followed.

The vampire, produced as a result of something unnatural, in his birth or his life or his death, cannot enjoy this peaceful oneness with Nature. He wanders, restless, alien.

THE DEVILISH CAT
OF NABESHIMA

This is a story the Japanese tell, but whether it is of a demon or a vampire, as we know vampires in the West, is hard to say.

The creature attacked Prince Hizen of the Nabeshima family having killed his mistress, O Toyo, and assumed her shape. When the prince slept with this creature, every morning he awoke weaker. His doctors were unable to put their finger on the cause of his decline, but they did notice that his wasting away was somehow connected to his spending the night with the person they assumed to be O Toyo. They determined to keep a closer watch.

While praying in the temple, Prince Hizen noticed a simple soldier, Ito Soda, and this soldier asked for the privilege of standing guard over the prince's bedroom.

Permission was granted. Soda took up his place. The creature drawing the life out of the prince attempted to put the guard to sleep by a kind of hypnosis, but Soda stabbed himself in the thigh and did not go to sleep. He saw the person he thought to be O Toyo go to the prince's bed.

Convinced that O Toyo was up to no good, Soda went later to O Toyo's chamber and gained entry by saying he was carrying a message. Once inside the room, he attacked O Toyo (as he thought it was) with a dagger, but she put up a battle and when it seemed she might lose she suddenly transformed herself into a cat and escaped.

The prince was informed of this and went hunting for that cat. He found it, slew it, and was free of it thereafter, recovering his strength. However, the vampiristic cat of Nabeshima returns from time to time. It was last seen, it is alleged, in 1929.

AFRICAN CUSTOM

Among the Bantu there is a great fear of vampires but the custom of cutting off the heads of suspected dead appears to keep predations in check. Sometimes the Bantu cut off the arms and legs of corpses, too, for good measure.

THE HUNGRY STONES

Nobel laureate (1913) Sir Rabindranath Tagore (1861-1941) has been practically forgotten, but this Bengali writer's short story of "The Hungry Stones" is aptly quoted here:

My Kinsman and myself were returning to Calcutta from our Puja trip when we met the man in a train. From his dress and bearing we took him at first for an up-country Mahomedan, but we were puzzled as we heard him talk. He discoursed upon all subjects so confidently that you might think the Disposer of All Things consulted him at all times in all that He did. Hitherto we had been perfectly happy, as we did not know that secret and unheard-of forces were at work, that the Russians had advanced close to us, that the English had deep and secret policies, that confusion among the native chiefs had come to a head. But our newly acquired friend said with a sly smile: "There happen more things in heaven and earth, Horatio, than are reported in your newspapers." As we had never stirred out of our homes before, the demeanour of the man struck us dumb with wonder. Be the topic ever so trivial, he would quote science, or comment on the *Vedas*, or repeat quatrains from some Persian poet; and as we had no pretence to a knowledge of science or the *Vedas* or Persian, our admiration for him went on increasing, and my kinsman, a theosophist, was firmly convinced that our fellow-passenger must have been supernaturally inspired by some strange 'magnetism' or 'occult power,' by an 'astral body' or something of that kind. He listened to the tritest saying that fell from the lips of our extraordinary companion with devotional rapture, and secretly took down notes of his conversation. I fancy that the extraordinary man saw this, and was a little pleased with it.

When the train reached the junction, we assembled in the waiting-room for the connection. It was then 10 p.m., and as the train, we heard, was likely to be very late, owing to something wrong in the lines, I spread my bed on the table and was about to lie down for a comfortable doze, when the extraordinary person deliberately set about spinning the following yarn. Of course, I could get no sleep that night.

When, owing to disagreement about some questions of administrative policy, I threw up my post at Junagarh, and entered the service of the Nizam of Hyderabad, they appointed me at once, as a strong young man, collector of cotton duties at Barich.

Barich is a lovely place. The *Susta* 'chatters over stony ways and babbles on the pebbles,' tripping, like a skillful dancing girl, in through the woods below the lonely hills. A flight of 150 steps rises from the river, and above that flight, on the river's brim and at the foot of the hills, there stands a solitary marble palace. Around it there is no habitation of man— the village and the cotton mart of Barich being far off.

About 250 years ago the Emperor Mahmud Shah II had built this lonely palace for his pleasure and luxury. In his days jets of rose-water spurted from its fountains, and on the cold marble floors of its spray-cooled rooms young Persian damsels would sit, their hair dishevelled before bathing, and, splashing their soft naked feet in the clear water of the reservoirs, would sing, to the tune of the guitar, the *ghazals* of their vineyards.

The fountains play no longer; the songs have ceased; no longer do snow-white feet step gracefully on the snowy marble. It is but the vast and solitary quarters of cess-collectors like us, men oppressed with solitude and deprived of the society of women. Now, Karim Khan, the old clerk of my office, warned me repeatedly not to take up my abode there. "Pass the day there, if you like," said he, "but never stay the night." I passed it off with a light laugh. The servants said that they would work till dark, and go away at night. I gave my ready assent. The house had such a bad name that even thieves would not venture near it after dark.

At first the solitude of the deserted palace weighed upon me like a nightmare. I would stay out, and work hard as long as possible, then return home at night jaded and tired, go to bed and fall asleep.

Before a week had passed, the place began to exert a weird fascination upon me. It is difficult to describe or to induce people to believe; but I felt as if the whole house was like a living organism slowly and imperceptibly digesting me by the action of some stupefying gastric juice.

Perhaps the process had begun as soon as I set my foot in the house, but I distinctly remember the day on which I first was conscious of it.

It was the beginning of summer, and the market being dull I had no work to do. A little before sunset I was sitting in an armchair near the water's edge below the steps. The *Susta* had shrunk and sunk low; a broad patch of sand on the other side glowed with the hues of evening; on this side the pebbles at the bottom of the clear shallow waters were glistening. There was not a breath of wind anywhere, and the still air was laden with an oppressive scent from the spicy shrubs growing on the hills close by.

As the sun sank behind the hill-tops a long dark curtain fell upon the stage of day, and the intervening hills cut short the time in which light and shade mingle at sunset. I thought of going out for a ride, and was about to get up when I heard a footfall on the steps behind. I looked back, but there was no one.

As I sat down again, thinking it to be an illusion, I heard many footfalls, as if a larger number of persons were rushing down the steps. A strange thrill of delight, slightly tinged with fear, passed through my frame, and though there was not a figure before my eyes, methought I saw a bevy of joyous maidens coming down the steps to bathe in the *Susta* in that summer evening. Not a sound was in the valley, in the river, or in the palace, to break the silence, but I distinctly heard the maidens' gay and mirthful laugh, like the gurgle of a spring gushing forth in a hundred cascades, as they ran past me, in quick playful pursuit of each other, towards the river, without noticing me at all. As they were invisible to me, so I was, as it were, invisible to them. The river was perfectly calm, but I felt that its still, shallow, and clear waters were stirred suddenly by the splash of many an arm jingling with bracelets, that the girls laughed and dashed and spattered water at one another, that the feet of the fair swimmers tossed the tiny waves up in showers of pearl.

I felt a thrill at my heart—I cannot say whether the excitement was due to fear or delight or curiosity. I had a strong desire to see them more clearly, but naught was visible before me. I thought I could catch all that they said if I only strained my ears; but however hard I strained them, I heard nothing but the chirping of the cicadas in the woods. It seemed as if a dark curtain of 250 years was hanging before me, and I would fain lift a corner of it tremblingly and peer through, though the assembly on the other side was completely enveloped in darkness.

The oppressive closeness of the evening was broken by a sudden gust of wind, and the still surface of the *Susta* rippled and curled like the hair of a nymph, and from the woods wrapt in the evening gloom there came forth a simultaneous murmur, as though they were awakening from a black dream. Call it reality or dream, the momentary glimpse of that invisible mirage reflected from a far-off world,

250 years old, vanished in a flash. The mystic forms that brushed past me with their quick unbodied steps, and loud, voiceless laughter, and threw themselves into the river, did not go back wringing their dripping robes as they went. Like fragrance wafted away by the wind they were dispersed by a single breath of the spring.

Then I was filled with a lively fear that it was the Muse that had taken advantage of my solitude and possessed me—the witch had evidently come to ruin a poor devil like myself making a living by collecting cotton duties. I decided to have a good dinner— it is the empty stomach that all sorts of incurable diseases find an easy prey. I sent for my cook and gave orders for a rich, sumptuous *moghlai* dinner, redolent of spices and *ghee*.

Next morning the whole affair appeared a queer fantasy. With a light heart I put on a *sola* hat like the *sahebs*, and drove out to my work. I was to have written my quarterly report that day, and expected to return late; but before it was dark I was strangely drawn to my house—by what I could not say—I felt they were all waiting, and that I should delay no longer. Leaving my report unfinished I rose, put on my *sola* hat, and startling the dark, shady, desolate path with the rattle of my carriage, I reached the vast silent palace standing on the gloomy skirts of the hills.

On the first floor the stairs led to a very spacious hall, its roof stretching wide over ornamental arches resting on three rows of massive pillars, and groaning day and night under the weight of its own intense solitude. The day had just closed, and the lamps had not yet been lighted. As I pushed the door open a great bustle seemed to follow within, as if a throng of people had broken up in confusion, and rushed out through the doors and windows and corridors and verandas and rooms, to make its hurried escape.

As I saw no one I stood bewildered, my hair on end in a kind of ecstatic delight, and a faint scent of *attar* and unguents almost effaced by age lingered in my nostrils. Standing in the darkness of that vast desolate hall between the rows of those ancient pillars, I could hear the gurgle of fountains splashing on the marble floor, a strange tune on the guitar, the jingle of ornaments and the tinkle of anklets, the clang of bells tolling the hours, the distant note of *nahabat*, the din of the crystal pendants of chandeliers shaken by the breeze, the song of *bulbuls* [nightingales] from the cages in the corridors, the cackle of storks in the gardens, all creating round me a strange unearthly music.

Then I came under such a spell that this intangible, inaccessible, unearthly vision appeared to be the only reality in the world—and all else a mere dream. That I, that is to say, Srijut So-and-so, the eldest son of So-and-so of blessed memory, should be drawing a monthly salary of Rs. 450 by the discharge of my duties as collector of cotton duties, and driving in my dog-cart to my office every day in a short coat and *sola* hat, appeared to me to be such an astonishingly ludicrous illusion that I burst into a horse-laugh, as I stood in the gloom of that vast silent hall.

At that moment my servant entered with a lighted kerosene lamp in his hand. I do not know whether he thought me mad, but it came back to me at once that I was in very deed Srijut So-and-so, son of So-and-so of blessed memory, and that, while our poets, great and small, alone could say whether inside or outside the earth there was a region where unseen fountains perpetually played and fairy guitars, struck by invisible fingers, sent forth an eternal harmony, this at any rate was certain, that I collected duties at the cotton market at Barich, and earned thereby Rs. 450 *per mensem* [per month] as my salary. I laughed in great glee at my curious illusion, as I sat over the newspaper at my camp-table, lighted by the kerosene lamp.

After I had finished my paper and eaten my *moghlai* dinner, I put out the lamp, and lay down on my bed in a small side-room. Through the open window a radiant star, high above the Avalli hills skirted by the darkness of their woods, was gazing intently from millions and millions of miles away in the sky at Mr. Collector lying on a humble camp-bedstead. I wondered and felt amused at the idea, and do not know when I fell asleep or how long I slept; but I suddenly awoke with a start, though I heard no sound and saw no intruder—only the steady bright star on the hilltop had set, and the dim light of the new moon was stealthily entering the room through the open window, as if ashamed of its intrusion.

I saw nobody, but felt as if some one was gently pushing me. As I awoke she said not a word, but beckoned me with her five fingers bedecked with rings to follow her cautiously. I got up noiselessly, and, though not a soul save myself was there in the countless apartments of that deserted palace with its slumbering sounds and waking echoes, I feared at every step lest any one should wake up. Most of the rooms of the palace were always kept closed, and I had never entered them.

I followed breathless and with silent steps my invisible guide—
I cannot now say where. What endless dark and narrow passages,
what long corridors, what silent and solemn audience-chambers
and close secret cells I crossed!

Though I could not see my fair guide, her form was not invisible to my mind's eye—an Arab girl, her arms, hard and smooth
as marble, visible through her loose sleeves, a thin veil falling on
her face from the fringe of her cap, and a curved dagger at her
waist! Methought that one of the thousand and one Arabian Nights
had been wafted to me from the world of romance, and that at the
dead of night I was wending my way through the dark narrow alleys
of slumbering Baghdad to a trysting-place fraught with peril.

At last my fair guide stopped abruptly before a deep blue
screen, and seemed to point to something below. There was nothing there, but a sudden dread froze the blood in my heart—
methought I saw there on the floor at the foot of the screen a
terrible negro eunuch dressed in rich brocade, sitting and dozing
with outstretched legs, with a naked sword on his lap. My fair guide
lightly tripped over his legs and held up a fringe of the screen. I
could catch a glimpse of a part of the room spread with a Persian
carpet—some one was sitting inside on a bed—I could not see her,
but only caught a glimpse of two exquisite feet in gold-embroidered slippers, hanging out from loose saffron-coloured *paijamas*
and placed idly on the orange-coloured velvet carpet. On one side
there was a bluish crystal tray on which a few apples, pears, oranges,
and bunches of grapes in plenty, two small cups, and a gold-tinted
decanter were evidently awaiting the guest. A fragrant intoxicat-
ing vapour, issuing from a strange sort of incense that burned
within, almost overpowered my senses.

As with trembling heart I made an attempt to step across the
outstretched legs of the eunuch, he woke up suddenly with a start,
and the sword fell from his lap with a sharp clang on the marble
floor.

A terrific scream made me jump, and I saw I was sitting on that
camp-bedstead of mine sweating heavily; and the crescent moon
looked pale in the morning light like a weary sleepless patient at
dawn; and our crazy Meher Ali was crying out, as is his daily custom, "Stand back! Stand back!!" while he went along the lonely road.

Such was the abrupt close of one of my Arabian Nights; but
there were yet a thousand nights left.

Then followed a great discord between my days and nights. During the day I would go to my work worn and tired, cursing the bewitching night and her empty dreams, but as night came my daily life with its bonds and shackles of work would appear a petty, false, ludicrous vanity.

After nightfall I was caught and overwhelmed in the snare of a strange intoxication. I would then be transformed into some unknown personage of a bygone age, playing my part in unwritten history, and my short English coat and tight breeches did not suit me in the least. With a red velvet cap on my head, loose *paijamas*, an embroidered vest, a long flowing silk gown, and coloured handkerchiefs scented with *attar*, I would complete my elaborate toilet, sit on a high-cushioned chair, and replace my cigarette with a many-coiled *narghileh* [water pipe] filled with rose-water, as if in eager expectation of a strange meeting with the beloved one.

I have no power to describe the marvellous incidents that unfolded themselves as the gloom of the night deepened. I felt as if in the curious apartments of that vast edifice the fragments of a beautiful story, which I could follow for some distance, but of which I could never see the end, flew about in a sudden gust of the vernal breeze. And all the same I would wander from room to room in pursuit of them the whole night long.

Amid the eddy of these dream-fragments, amid the smell of *henna* and the twanging of the guitar, amid the waves of air charged with fragrant spray, I would catch like a flash of lightning the momentary glimpse of a fair damsel. She it was who had saffron-coloured *paijamas*, white ruddy soft feet in gold-embroidered slippers with curved toes, a close-fitting bodice wrought with gold, a red cap, from which a golden frill fell on her snowy brow and cheeks.

She had maddened me. In pursuit of her I wandered from room to room, from path to path among the bewildering maze of alleys in the enchanted dreamland of the nether world of sleep.

Sometimes in the evening, while arraying myself carefully as a prince of the blood-royal before a large mirror, with a candle burning on either side, I would see a sudden reflection of the Persian beauty by the side of my own. A swift turn of her neck, a quick eager glance of intense passion and pain glowing in her large dark eyes, just a suspicion of speech on her dainty red lips, her figure, fair and slim, crowned with youth like a blossoming creeper, quickly uplifted in her graceful tilting gait, a dazzling flash of pain and craving and ecstasy, a smile and a glance and a blaze of jewels and silk, and she melted away. A wild gust of wind, laden with all the fragrance of hills and woods, would put out my light, and I would fling aside my dress and lie down on my bed, my eyes closed and my body thrilling with delight, and there around me in the breeze, amid all the perfume of the woods and hills, floated through the silent gloom many a caress and many a kiss and many a tender touch of hands, and gentle murmurs in my ears, and fragrant breaths on my brow; or a sweetly-perfumed kerchief was wafted again and again on my cheeks. Then slowly a mysterious serpent would twist her stupefying coils about me; and heaving a heavy sigh, I would lapse into insensibility, and then into a profound slumber.

One evening I decided to go out on my horse—I do not know who implored me to stay—but I would listen to no entreaties that day. My English hat and coat were resting on a rack, and I was about to take them down when a sudden whirlwind, crested with the sands of the *Susta* and the dead leaves of the Avalli hills, caught them up, and whirled them round and round, while a loud peal of merry laughter rose higher and higher striking all the chords of mirth till it died away in the land of sunset.

I could not go out for my ride, and the next day I gave up my queer English coat and hat for good.

That day again at dead of night I heard the stifled heart-breaking sobs of some one—as if below the bed, below the floor, below the stony foundation of that gigantic palace, from the depths of a dark damp grave, a voice piteously cried and implored me: "Oh, rescue me! Break through these doors of hard illusion, deathlike slumber and fruitless dreams, place me by your side on the saddle, press me to your heart, and, riding through hills and woods and across the river, take me to the warm radiance of your sunny rooms above!"

Who am I? Oh, how can I rescue thee? What drowning beauty, what incarnate passion shall I drag to the shore from this wild eddy of dreams? O lovely ethereal apparition! Where didst thou flourish and when? By what cool spring, under the shade of what date-groves, wast thou born—in the lap of what homeless wanderer in the desert? What Bedouin snatched thee from thy mother's arms, an opening bud plucked from a wild creeper, placed thee on a horse swift as lightning, crossed the burning sands, and took thee to the slave-market of what royal city? And there, what officer of the Badshah, seeing the glory of thy bashful blossoming youth, paid for thee in gold, placed thee in a golden palanquin, and offered thee as a present for the seraglio of his master? And O, the history of that place! The music of the *sareng*, the jingle of anklets, the occasional flash of daggers and the glowing wine of Shiraz poison, and the piercing flashing glance! What infinite grandeur, what endless servitude! The slave-girls to thy right and left waved the *chamar*, as diamonds flashed from their bracelets; the Badshah, the king of kings, fell on his knees at thy snowy feet in bejeweled shoes, and outside the terrible Abyssinian eunuch, looking like a messenger of death, but clothed like an angel, stood with a naked sword in his hand! Then, O, thou flower of the desert, swept away by the blood-stained dazzling ocean of grandeur, with its foam of jealousy, its rocks and shoals of intrigue, on what shore of cruel death wast thou cast, or in what other land more splendid and more cruel?

Suddenly at this moment that crazy Meher Ali screamed out: "Stand back! Stand back!! All if false! All is false!!" I opened my eyes and saw that it was already light. My *chaprasi* [servant] came and handed me my letters, and the cook waited with a *salam* [bow] for my orders.

I said: "No, I can stay here no longer." That very day I packed up, and moved to my office. Old Karim Khan smiled a little as he saw me. I felt nettled, but said nothing, and fell to my work.

As evening approached I grew absent-minded; I felt as if I had an appointment to keep; and the work of examining the cotton accounts seemed wholly useless; even the *Nizamat* of the Nizam did not appear to be of much worth. Whatever belonged to the present, whatever was moving and acting and working for bread seemed trivial, meaningless, and contemptible.

I threw my pen down, closed my ledgers, got into my dog-cart, and drove away. I noticed that it stopped of itself at the gate of the marble palace just at the hour of twilight. With quick steps I climbed the stairs, and entered the room.

A heavy silence was reigning within. The dark rooms were looking sullen as if they had taken offence. My heart was full of contrition, but there was no one to whom I could lay it bare, or of whom I could ask forgiveness. I wandered about the dark rooms with a vacant mind. I wished I had a guitar to which I could sing to the unknown: "O fire, the poor moth that made a vain effort to fly away has come back to thee! Forgive it but this once, burn its wings and consume it in thy flame!"

Suddenly two tear-drops fell from overhead on my brow. Dark masses of clouds overcast the top of the Avalli hills that day. The gloomy woods and the sooty waters of the *Susta* were waiting in terrible suspense and in an ominous calm. Suddenly land, water, and sky shivered, and a wild tempest-blast rushed howling through the distant pathless woods, showing its lightning-teeth like a raving maniac who had broken his chains. The desolate halls of the palace banged their doors, and moaned in the bitterness of anguish.

The servants were all in the office, and there was no one to light the lamps. The night was cloudy and moonless. In the dense gloom within I could distinctly feel that a woman was lying on her face on the carpet below the bed—clasping and tearing her long dishevelled hair with desperate fingers. Blood was trickling down her fair brow, and she was now laughing a hard, harsh, mirthless laugh, now bursting into violent wringing sobs, now rending her bodice and striking at her bare bosom, as the wind roared in through the open window, and the rain poured in torrents and soaked her through and through.

All night there was no cessation of the storm or of the passionate cry. I wandered from room to room in the dark, with unavailing sorrow. Whom could I console when no one was by? Whose was this intense agony of sorrow? Whence arose this inconsolable grief?

And the mad man cried out: "Stand back! Stand back!! All is false! All is false!!"

I saw that the day had dawned, and Meher Ali was going round and round the palace with his usual cry in that dreadful weather. Suddenly it came to me that perhaps he also had once lived in that house, and that, though he had gone mad, he came there every day, and went round and round, fascinated by the weird spell cast by the marble demon.

Despite the storm and rain I ran to him and asked: "Ho, Meher Ali, what is false?"

The man answered nothing, but pushing me aside went round and round with his frantic cry, like a bird flying fascinated about the jaws of a snake, and made a desperate effort to warn himself by repeating: "Stand back! Stand back!! All is false! All is false!!"

I ran like a mad man through the pelting rain to my office, and asked Karim Khan: "Tell me the meaning of all this!"

What I gathered from that old man was this: That one time countless unrequited passions and unsatisfied longings and lurid flames of wild blazing pleasure raged within that palace, and that the curse of all the heart-aches and blasted hopes had made its every stone thirsty and hungry, eager to swallow up like a famished ogress any living man who might chance to approach. Not one of those who lived there for three consecutive nights could escape these cruel jaws, save Meher Ali, who had escaped at the cost of his reason.

I asked: "Is there no means whatever of my release?" The old man said: "There is only one means, and that is very difficult. I will tell you what it is, but first you must hear the history of a young Persian girl who once lived in that pleasure-dome. A stranger or a more bitterly heart-rending tragedy was never enacted on this earth."

Just at this moment the coolies announced that the train was coming. So soon? We hurriedly packed up our luggage, as the train steamed in. An English gentleman, apparently just aroused from slumber, was looking out of a first-class carriage endeavouring to read the name of the station. As soon as he caught sight of our fellow-passenger, he cried, "Hallo," and took him into his own compartment. As we got into a second-class carriage, we had no chance of finding out who the man was nor what was the end of his story.

I said: "The man evidently took us for fools and imposed upon us out of fun. The story is pure fabrication from start to finish." The discussion that followed ended in a lifelong rupture between my theosophist kinsman and myself.

Jack Beale disposes of evidence in *The Vampire*, a Gramercy film of 1957.

INTERNATIONAL DRACULA

Bram Stoker's novel has been translated into French (Eve and Lucie Paul-Marguerite, 1946, and Lucienne Molitor—which may be a pseudonym based on Ulrich Molitor—1968), Spanish (anonymous, published by Molino, Madrid, in 1966), Italian (Adriana Pelligrini, 1966), German (Stasi Kull, 1967), even Gaelic (Seán Ó Currín, 1933). The worldwide fame of Stoker's creation, however, is chiefly attributable to the universal language of the motion picture, silent or made in various languages and occasionally dubbed or with subtitles.

A TOUCH OF VAMPIRISM MAKES THE WHOLE WORLD KIN

Later we shall devote a whole chapter to vampire films but to stress international appeal, here is one film from each of 30 different countries to underline the point that the subject was universal appeal, and over the decades, too. English titles when available.

Argentina: *Il Vampiro negro* (1953)
Australia: *Thirst* (1979)
Austria: *Lilith* (1919)
Belgium: *La Fée sanguinaire* (1968)
Britain: *Brides of Dracula* (1960)
Canada: *Dracula* (1973)
Czechoslovakia: *Valerie a Tyden Divu* (1969)
Denmark: *Vampyrdanserinden* (1912)
France: *Tendre Dracula, ou Les Confessions d'un buveur de sang* (1973)
Germany: *Jonathan, Vampire sterben nicht* (1970)
Hong Kong: *The Legend of the Seven Golden Vampires* (1975)
Hungary: *Drakula* (1921)
India: *Shikari* (1964)
Italy: *Black Sunday* (1961)
Japan: *The Evil of Dracula* (1975)
Korea: *Dracula Rises from the Coffin* (1982)
Malaya: *Pontianak kembali* (1963)
Mexico: *La Invasión de los vampiros* (1962)
The Netherlands: *Bloedverwanten* (date?)
New Zealand: *Moonrise* (1992)
The Philippines: *Drakulita* (1969)
Poland: *Wampyry Warszawy* (1925)
Romania: *Subspecies* (1991)

Singapore: *Pontianak* (1957)
Spain: *Parque de juegos* (1963)
Sweden: *Vampyrn* (1912)
Switzerland: *Draculas lusterne Vampire* (1970)
Turkey: *Hannah, Queen of the Vampires* (1972)
United States: *The Hunger* (1983)
USSR: *Viy* (based on a short story by Nicolai Gogol, 1967)
Yugoslavia: *A Vampire's Nostalgia* (1968)

CONDEMNED TO LIVE (1935)

Universal City lent its extant stock for this vampire story: the bell tower from *The Hunchback of Notre Dame*, scenery from *Frankenstein*, period costumes from *The Bride of Frankenstein* and a couple of Charles Dickens classics (*Great Expectations* and *The Mystery of Edwin Drood*), etc. In fact, the same music and the same director went into Majestic's *The Vampire Bat* (1933).

Despite all this borrowing, *Condemned to Live* stands pretty high among the few independent vampire movies of the Hollywood thirties, according to the experts. Much of this is due to the clever use of limited facilities available—including nearby real locations which were in Boston Canyon but were passed off as near the sea in Europe—and especially the fact that at the center of it all is Ralph Morgan as a vampire who was unfortunately born that way. His mother—the mother who holds the baby version of him

In *Condemned to Live* (1935), directed by veteran horror master Frank R. Strayer, screenplay by Karen DeWolf, Prof. Paul Kristan (Ralph Morgan) doesn't even know that he is the vampire when terror first comes to a small Eastern European village.

is silent-screen star Barbara Bedford—was bitten by a vampire bat, in Africa. He is a very sympathetic character and people sacrifice to save him but of course he must perish in the long run.

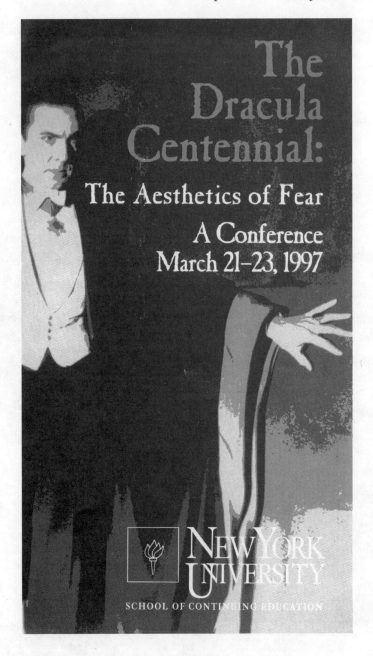

In *Nosferatu* (1922) the hideous vampire is Max Schreck (presumably for "Maximum Fright").

5

The Vampire on the Screen

THE VAMPIRE AT THE MOVIES AND ON TV

People love to be thrilled. Horror films, a significant percentage of which deal with the vampires and similar threats to us, are popular entertainment. To some extent they offer experience comparable to rollercoaster rides, not only in their breath-taking surprises but in the fact that we can have a taste of danger and at the same time feel perfectly safe. After all, the vampire cannot come off the silver screen and attack us. There is a sheet of glass that stands between the vampire on television and the couch potato.

However, the vampire, and every other icon of popular entertainment, does get into our heads and so into our lives. The influence of horror and violence in popular entertainment, including vampire stories, is unquestioningly felt in our society.

"He was obsessed with the occult," says a character in *Raiders of the Lost Ark*, and the remark can be made of many people connected to cinema art, either as creators or consumers.

This chapter could have been a book, given the topic, but such books already exist. The movies, in connection with everything from molding the popular imagination to contributing to the science of signs, will get just a nod here. Look elsewhere for vast filmographies, *auteur* studies, and lists of what is available on videotape.

I thought of expanding this chapter with the full shooting script of a famous Dracula film, but reading a shooting script requires the same sort of expertise that reading a blueprint does. Filmmakers and architects enjoy those things; the rest of us would gain more from seeing the film or walking through the building.

BÉLA LUGOSI, THE MOST FAMOUS DRACULA

Blasco Béla (in Hungarian the surname comes first) was born in Lugos in 1882 and later took the name Béla Lugosi. By 1903 he was in the theater, by 1911 onstage in Bucharest, by 1913 a member of the National Theatre of Hungary. After service in World War I, he made his first film; the Hungarian title translates as *The Leopard*, and he the stage name Arisztid Olt. The Hungarian revolution drove him out of Hungary, first to Austria and later to Germany. In Germany he made several films and then left for America. It was 1921. His American stage debut (he promised on being cast that he would be able to speak English by opening night) was in *The Red Poppy* (1922). His first film in the United States was *The Silent Command* (1923). He played Dracula on Broadway (1927) and in the film version from Universal Studios (1931) and the rest is history. His best pictures were *Dracula* and perhaps *Mark of the Vampire* (for MGM, 1935), after

Three female vampires take an interest in Jonathan Harker's body in *Dracula* (1931).

which his career declined. His worst pictures are now cult classics of kitsch: *Plan 9 from Outer Space* (1959) and *Glen or Glenda?* (1953). At the end he was reduced to appearing in Ed Wood movies, Ed Wood being most film buffs' candidate for the worst director of all time.

Lugosi was offered the part of the monster in *Frankenstein*. He turned it down because he would not be recognized through the heavy makeup and, worse, there were no lines. It was taken by an English actor whose pronounced lisp wouldn't matter. His name was Clarence Pratt but, in the monster-movie tradition Lugosi had done so much to establish, he changed it to something foreign: Boris Karloff. Lugosi and Karloff appeared in several films together, trying hard to upstage each other. When Lugosi turned to hard drugs and went downhill, he dropped out of movies pretty much and his TV series *Dr. Alucard* never got made. But he died with a B-movie script in his hand. Karloff became the king of the genre. Later he had to defer to Vincent Price, Peter Cushing, Christopher Lee, and other actors.

FRANK LANGELLA, THE BEST DRACULA

Everyone has a favorite Dracula. Mine is Frank Langella, who created a Dracula for the stage and for a movie version (script from Hamilton Deane & John L. Balderson's stage play of 1927, with the Hollywood touch of W. D. Richter, who perpetrated *Invasion of the Body Snatchers*). No, he's not Dracula quite as Bram Stoker saw him; he's more late twentieth century. I think Douglas Edwards ("A Round-Up of Summer Releases," *The Advocate*, 23 August 1979) hit on it: Langella brings out the sex in The Count. Edwards wrote:

> Effete, infinitely cultured, witty, passionate, fierce, tender, alternately seductive and repellent, and, for the most part, sexy as hell, Langella recreates the role with which he captivated Broadway. There is something chillingly mesmeric about Langella's Count Dracula which taps into the primal appeal of the character. A promise of dangerous, potentially self-destructive, ecstatic oblivion blazes in his eyes—an only partially veiled reference to sado-

masochistic urges longing to burst the constraints of Victorian (and twentieth century post-Victorian) morality.

Langella does not look like a skeleton *nosferatu* nor like a stiff, painted corpse rising from a tufted coffin lining, nor does he sport a hideous hairdo and clothes that seem to be the mad dreams of some Japanese drag queen. I think people are already giggling about Lugosi and his ilk and even Brad Pitt and the Pitt-ifuls, but that Langella's motion picture performance (directed by John Badham and with a John Williams score that helped a great deal) will still have power generations from now. Seeing Langella in

Frank Langella as Dracula on television.

1996 as a fey narcissist in Coward's *Present Laughter*, I noticed qualities that were there in the Dracula performance but which somehow did not register at that time on my conscious mind.

Looking back, we see that we have had teenage vampires and Filipino vampires (bloodsuckers are a main subject of B-minus movies from the Philippines as well as from Italy and France, etc.), outright gay and lesbian vampires, blaxploitation vampires (from *Blacula* to *Vampire in Brooklyn*), vampires from outer space, and theater as opportunity for huge special effects. True, *Frankenstein*—one version in the eighties set the record for the most expensive nonmusical staging to that date—offers even more scope, whether onstage or in an Andy Warhol or other cinema version, than *Dracula*. Commercial packagers have found myriad uses of the undying appeal of the vampire. Even Andy Warhol's factory worked over the original by Stoker. The Count appears in ever-new versions or non-Stoker characters, as in *Dead Men Walk*, *Mark of the Vampire*, and the strangely titled *The Vampire's Ghost*.

Langella's count, however, captures best the erotic side of the monster. Horror has been used to discuss forbidden sex ever since lesbian "Carmilla." Heterosexual *Varney the Vampire* opens with a scene of a female victim sprawled on a bed, her hair (to the Victorians as to many others a potent sexual stimulus) flowing in all directions, her breast heaving. Anne Rice's *Interview with the Vampire* brought to the screen a doomed gay love story. Feminists see in vampires a perfect symbol for sexual exploitation, but not all of them would go so far as Andrea Dworkin and denounce all sex as rape and blame men for stealing the very souls of women (and gays).

The advertisements announcing the Langella *Dracula* (which premiered Friday, 13 July 1979) shouted: "Throughout history he has filled the hearts of men with *terror*, and the hearts of women with *desire*." Today's films have become an almost immeasurable distance from the mere hints of sex in Alice Eis and Bert French's "vampire dance" in the three-reeler *The Vampire* (1913). On stage it has grown increasingly explicit, and now it would be intolerable to the suburban London audiences who first saw a version in a theater in Wimbeldon in 1925.

VAMPIRE CIRCUS

This can stand for all the vampire films that feature a count other than Dracula. Here it is Count Mittergouse of the village of Schtettel (a word that means "village"). This British film, made on the set of *Twins of Evil* and on a shoestring budget in 1972, has vampires, murder, incest, plague, sex, sadism, and suspense, and of course a circus, where a leopard turns into a man. Ingredients for a large-popcorn horror movie! Moray Grant wrote the screenplay. Probably fast.

A SELECTION OF THE OLD AND CLASSIC VAMPIRE FILMS

Le Manoir du diable (The Devil's Castle). France, 1897. Directed by Georges Méliès.

The Vampire's Trail. USA, 1910. No further details available.

The Vampire. USA, 1911, Selig.

Danse vampiresque (Vampire Dance). Denmark, 1912, Nordisk.

Drakula, Hungary, 1921. Directed by Karoly Lajthay.

Nosferatu, eine Symphonies des Grauens (Nosferatu, A Symphony of Horrors). Germany, 1922, Prana. Directed by Friedrich Wilhelm Murnau. Nosferatu: "Max Schreck."

Dracula. Universal, USA, 1931. Directed by Tod Browning. Dracula: Bela Lugosi. Made also in Spanish on the same set, directed by Georges Melford, with Carlos Villarías as Dracula.

Son of Dracula. Universal, 1943, USA. Robert Siodmak. Count Alucard: Lon Chaney, Jr.

Dime comic books such as the one (1954) from which this page is taken are now valuable collectors' items.

House of Dracula. Universal, 1945, USA. Erle C. Kenton. Dracula: John
   Carradine.
Drakula İnstanbulu (Dracula in Istanbul). Turkey, 1952. Directed by
   Mehmet Muhtar, with Atif Kaptan as Dracula.
Blood of Dracula. American-International, 1957, USA. Herbert L. Strock.
Dracula. NBC TV, 1957. With John Carradine.
The Return of Dracula. United Artists, 1958, USA. Paul Landres. Bellac:
   Francis Lederer.
Horror of Dracula. Hammer, 1958, UK. Terence Fisher. Dracula: Christo-
   pher Lee.
The Brides of Dracula. Hammer, 1960, UK. Terence Fisher. Baron Mein-
   ster: David Peel.
Blacula. USA, 1972. William Marshall as an African-American Dracula.
Andy Warhol's Dracula. Italy, 1974. Written and directed by Paul Morrisey.
   With Udo Kier, Joe D'Allessandro.
Martin. USA, 1977. Directed by George A. Romero. John Amplas, Lin-
   coln Maazel.
Bram Stoker's Original Dracula. Meta-Philm, 1978, UK. Directed by Ken
   Russell.
Dracula. France, 1978. Directed by Roger Vadim.
Salem's Lot. USA, 1979. Directed by Tobe Hooper. David Soul, James
   Mason.
Pale Blood. USA, 1990. Directed by W. D. Hsu. George Chakiris, Pamela
   Ludwig.

In passing, we might note that really bad vampire movies often appear
under more than one title. Some examples, in no particular order of merit,
are *The Terror from Beyond Space/The Vampire from Outer Space* (US, 1958),
L'Amante del vampiro/The Vampire and the Ballerina (Italy, 1960), *The Blood
Beast Terror/The Vampire Beast Craves Blood* (UK, 1967), *Le Frisson des vam-
pires/Sex and the Vampire* (France, 1970), *Crypt of the Living Dead/Vampire
Woman* (US, 1972), *I Bought a Vampire Motorcycle/I Bought a Vampire Motor-
bike* (UK, 1990), *Grampire/Moonrise* (New Zealand, 1992), etc. For a survey, consult one or more of the many books on horror literature. For a
quick overview see T. Lindvall's "The Vampire Film from *Nosferatu* to *Bram
Stoker's Dracula*," *Choice* 31 (March 1994): 1141. See also Donald A. Reed's
The Vampire on the Screen (1965), David J. Skal's *Hollywood Gothic* (1990),
and James Craig Holte's *Dracula in the Dark: Dracula Film Adaptations*
(1997).

DRACULA OUT OF THE BOX AND ON THE BOX

The occult rivets the attention of couch potatoes. So the ghost and the vampire have joined abductions by extraterrestrials in series that leave "the unexplained" still unexplained. It is standard boob-tube fare. There have been many unsuccessful attempts to improve upon *In Search of Dracula* (1971, also in Swedish) as a slick survey. There have naturally been as well many fright-night reruns of *Kiss of the Vampire* (UK, 1962), *Lust for a Vampire* (UK, 1970), *Count Yorga, Vampire* (US, 1970), *Grave of the Vampire* (US, 1972), *I Married a Vampire* (US, 1986), and the very violent slasher films of the nineties, with lesbian or some other spice. Some few are better than most made-for-TV or cobbled-for-cable vampire and other horror films. A "vampire," male or female, as presenter of second-rate horror films on TV has not been uncommon. Who else would bring you material the life has long gone out of?

Designed for TV was the Dracula reanimation with Louis Jourdain, in advanced age still sexy but more sinister than as the handsome suitor of *Gigi*. He starred in an opulent, multi-part adaptation of Bram Stoker's novel. The best TV vampire experience is non-Dracula. It is Stephen King's *Salem's Lot* for CBS-TV, with David Soul and James Mason. This has been often rerun, but some people say not nearly enough. It was directed by Tobe Hooper, of *Texas Chainsaw Massacre* fame. Brace yourself.

But, really, you could always leave a light on as you watch the box. Cheap thrills! There is that sheet of glass between Them and Us; they can't get us! It's not nearly so dangerous as going out into the streets of the big city. You can stay home and be safe but scared. And you don't have to go to the trouble of reading—which is work for most Americans these days—those huge trilogies by Anne Rice or the many collections of short stories about vampires such as Richard Pasco's *Classic Vampire Short Stories* and Molly Cooper's *Classic Vampire Stories* (both 1996), among many other titles available at the library or bookstore.

Commercials break the television experience and shatter the mood of horror stories. They might be death to the most terrifyingly onrushing vampire tale of all, *Varney the Vampire*.

HERZOG'S COUNT DOESN'T COUNT

In 1979 Werner Herzog (famous for *Blow-Up* and *Last Tango in Paris*) did a remake of F. W. Murnau's vampire classic, *Nosferatu*. It did all right in European release but when it reached the United States, in an English dubbing, lines such as "Count Dracula has written from Transylvania" sent Los Angeles sneak preview audiences into paroxysms of laughter. Worse, that year it was up against Steve Dragoti's comic *Love at First Bite* (George Hamilton *acts!*) and John Badham's *Dracula* (Frank Langella fresh from the stage and the grave, with Lord Olivier as Dr. Van Helsing). Paul Monette, who knocked off the novelization of Werner Herzog's movie, complained that Avon Books had told him that "Fox was hoping for another *Star Wars*." No. Down the drain.

Thomas G. Aylesworth's *Monsters from the Movies* and many other surveys will acquaint the interested film student with the titles of a host of vampire pictures, but many of these have perished; in a lot of cases neither the old celluloid nor the shooting scripts have come down to us.

HOUSE OF FRANKENSTEIN

Seen on television in October 1997, this effort combined monsters, vampires, and werewolves in one over-the-top presentation. Werewolves are increasingly unusual, while vampires are now considered "cool"—if not clammy.

VAMPIRISM CURED

It is the folklore tradition that once you are bitten by a vampire you are doomed, although in some stories it takes more than one contact and those who have not lost blood too often may recuperate, especially if the vampire who bit them is killed.

In the film *Near Dark* young Caleb has fallen in with the vampires but his father (Loy) loyally tracks him down, takes him back home, and by giving him a transfusion of his own untainted blood saves him from vampirism. Later Caleb is able to cure another victim of the vampire clan, Mae, by giving her a transfusion of his now clean blood.

In Chinese folklore the *chiang-shih* can be driven out, if it takes possession of its victim, by fire. There are a few other ways of rescuing the victim of a vampire suggested in various other traditions, but on the whole once you have communed with a vampire and the vital fluid has been exchanged, you have had it.

This made the comparison of vampires and the carriers of AIDS possible, much to the disgust of gays and lesbians and all those who wish disease to be considered apart from morality and treated, not condemned or seen as punishment from God.

IN THE DARKNESS

The vampire has been one of the standbys of horror movies. In the limited space we have here only a brief mention is possible, but you can consult, among many other books on the vampire in the cinema, Stephen Jones' *The Illustrated Vampire Movie Guide* (1995) as well as references such as Rosemary Ellen Guiley's *The Complete Vampire Companion* (1994) and Matthew Bunson's *The Vampire Encyclopedia* (1993). As you can see, there's a book of this type out about every year. Some are schlock, but on the whole they are labors of love.

DRACULA MEETS FRANKENSTEIN

The movies have often put more than one monster in a film on the Hollywood principle that more is better, but Dracula is a human being who is "undead," while Frankenstein's monster is simply made of bits of dead human beings given life. Neither the nameless "Modern Prometheus" of Mary Shelley's great novel nor the Golem of Jewish folklore (also manufactured from bits of corpses) is anything like a vampire in essence, though you wouldn't want to meet any of them on a dark night.

In the movies, poor old Dracula has "met" everyone from Mickey Mouse and Abbot & Costello to Frankenstein and The Wolf Man. Cameo parts in B movies did much to tarnish The Count's reputation.

DEAD MEN WALKING

George Romero created the classic "Horror in New Jersey" movie *in Night of the Living Dead* (1968). He followed it up with morbid mayhem, a mall mauling, that is vastly superior (I think) in *Dawn of the Dead* (1979). That is a real nail-biter and gross-out champion.

His reanimated corpses, however, have more in common with science-fiction movies in which some nuclear nonsense unleashes mutants, than with vampire movies, because his monsters are ghoulish, not vampiristic. In his movies, Romero's corpses on the loose are easily (and gorily) disposed of; vampires are much harder to dispatch. An entire film can be devoted to eliminating even one of the bloodsuckers. Romero's influence led to many imitations, among them Umberto Lenzi's Italian extravaganza known in English as *City of the Walking Dead* (1983). Its all in the same vein as *Invasion of the Body Snatchers* and *The Thing* as well as *Dracula*.

THE VAMPIRE'S KISS

Robert Bierman directed this 1988 movie in such a way as to make the question of whether the sleazy leading male, significantly surnamed Low, becomes a vampire—or not—after he has sex with Rachel, whom he picks up in a louche singles' bar and who is undoubtedly a vampire. The Low character (played by Nicholas Cage) certainly has sex with her—his first name is significantly Peter—but whether their sharing bodily fluids (including his blood) qualifies him to be a vampire is less certain. In any case, he never develops fangs (he buys a plastic set) and he just gets to be dead, not undead. He is murdered by the brother of a woman he rapes, and the murderer puts a stake through his heart in the process of killing him.

Low is actually made to seem a far worse person than Rachel the vampire. This is one example of a recent trend in which the victims of the vampire may be nastier than the vampire himself, or herself. Moreover, in the past only male vampires were able to generate new vampires, while now females are being credited with being able to do so, with men or with women. The vampire increasingly moves in a world of steamy sexuality, straight or not, the kinky being stressed more than the supernatural. The thinly veiled message seems to be that the vampire's victims now are not only willing (as they usually have been) but perverse, and the victims of VTD (Vampire-Transmitted Doom) are often equated more or less with the allegedly culpable victims of STD (Sexually-Transmitted Diseases). They are punished for promiscuity under some strange law of rough justice.

This questionable morality apparently appeals to modern audiences. We have come far from Mina and Lucy to "serves 'em right". If you kiss a vampire, don't come crying to me. If you are lonely or lusty, stay out of make-out bars or you will wind up alienated and worse.

EIGHTIES MOVIE TRASH

There are a great many really bad vampire movies—and those many vampire encyclopedias today that will list them for you—but here are the titles of half a dozen of the truly awful productions of the late eighties. That was a time when, some experts think, a new low was achieved:

> *Mr. Vampire* (1985)
> *Fright Night* (1985)
> *Life Force* (1985)
> *Graveyard Shift* (1986)

Geek Maggot Bingo (1987)
Beverly Hills Vampire (1988)

Mr. Vampire, out of the busy Hong Kong studios, was the first of a series.

EARLY VAMPIRE MOVIES

A great deal of old film has perished, even productions of the big studios after the invention of talking pictures, but I have already noted that vampires appeared on the silent screen very early. Before a lost *Dracula* of the twenties which preceded the famous Bela Lugosi movie, there were others. Here are some that followed the Swedish short *Vampyre* of 1912: *The Vampire* (1913), *Le Vampire* (1914), *In the Grip of the Vampire* (1914), *The Vampire's Tower* (1914), *The Vampire's Trail* (1914), *Vampires of Warsaw* (1914), *Saved from the Vampire* (1914), *Vampires of the Night* (1914), *Was She a Vampire?* (1915), *A Night of Horror* (1916), *A Village Vampire* (1916), *Mr. Vampire* (1916), *A Vampire Out of Work* (1916), *Ceneri e Vampe* (1916), *The Beloved Vampire* (1917), *Magia* (1917), *Alraune* (1918), *Lilith* (1919).

A *Village Vampire* was made by the famous Edison Company, but no one seems to have been able to find a copy. A great pity. For all we know, Edison may have filmed not only the first kiss on the screen but the first vampire bite. I do not think the great Tod Browning—he was the weird director who made *Freaks*—vampire film survives. I have seen a still of Lon Chaney in it. It was called *London after Midnight*. If any film historian can locate these films and restore them, many fans will be grateful. Who knows when or if they will turn up. Someone bought Buster Keaton's house and discovered a trove of his old comic films behind a door locked for many years. There may be vampire films awaiting discovery.

Les Vampires was a French serial of 1915—without any vampires in it.

CHINESE VAMPIRE FILMS

Ghosts are a standby of Chinese films but the Chinese also have made a number of vampire films known to experts. I have never seen the following (English titles). They were made by a single director in the seventies: *The Night of the Vampire* (1970), *Lake of Dracula* (1971), and *The Evil of Dracula* (1975).

Lists of films are given by many vampire encyclopedists, as you know, but we need a Chinese film historian to supply the titles and as much detail as possible about the very many relevant movies, whatever their quality, of which Westerners are ignorant.

GERMAN VAMPIRE FILMS

Here are some cinema titles from the country that gave us *Nosferatu* (1922) and a remake by Werner Herzog (1979) with Klaus Kinski as Nosferatu. It should be noted that were we not, to use an awkward term, so western-oriented, we would find vampire materials in the popular entertainments and serious art of many countries all around the world. Some of these, naturally, have picked up western superstition and subjects and translated them into their own terms, but others have authentic native traditions. The German productions are notable, along with the better-known American ones, for exerting an international influence. Some of the following films were made with Italian, French, Yugoslavian, or other participation. As films, they were capable of appealing to a large international market and were shown in countries where their language was foreign but their message was understood well. I give some English titles where available:

Der Fluch der Grünen Augen (1963)
Beiss mich, liebling (Bite Me, Darling, 1970)
Jonathan (1970)
The Bloody Countess (Countess Báthory, 1973)
Blut on den Lippen (Blood on the Lips, 1971)
Happening der Vampire (1971)
Der Schlangengruber und das Pendel (The Blood Demon, 1967)
The Little Vampire (1969)
Mutanto, The Horrible (1961)
Nacht des Grauens (Night of Horrors, 1916)
Nosferatu (remake 1979)

The German interest in the gothic, not to say the startling museums of torture devices to be found in Germany, may explain some of their fascination with horror films. That and the usefulness in such films of the exaggerations of the Expressionist style to which Germany contributed so much in the art of cinematography. When movies began to be in color, Germany seems to have lost some of its command of the medium, but it still made horror films there and with international companies.

THE VAMP

It was in a film called *Vampirish Dance* (1911) from Denmark that the character of the vamp (as in Theda Bara's *A Fool there Was*, 1914) came to the screen, unless it was even earlier in the American film *A Vampire of the Coast* (1909). In real life, the vamp was much affected by the French *femme fatale* and the real life dancer who called herself Mata Hari. She was shot as a spy in World War I. Theda Bara (Theodosia Goodman)'s character in the movies was based on Kipling's poem "The Vampire". You'll find that poem later in this book.

DANCE OF DEATH

A regrettable still of Gloria Holden in *Dracula's Daughter*. Vampires do not cast a shadow!

The vampire has been the subject of many ballets. Nicolle Platt, in "Nosferatutu: Dracula Returns," *Dance Magazine* 67 (October 1993): 35*ff.*, has an entertaining introduction to Dracula and other vampires in dance in America and elsewhere. There is a Soviet film (directed by D. Tikhomirov, 1962) whose title translates *Star of the Morning*. I have not seen it but it reportedly shows the ballet of a nobleman seduced by a female vampire.

BLOOD OF DRACULA

The Hammer films made in Britain were especially bloody versions of *Dracula* and other monster mashes. It is interesting to note that they were often made in more than one version. The tamest version was for British consumption, the goriest always for the Japanese market. All versions were sexy.

I VAMPIRI

In addition to Dracula films produced in foreign countries and languages, there have been many English-language vampire flicks dubbed into foreign languages. For example, in Italian you could see *Dracula il vampiro*

(The Horror of Dracula, 1958), *Vampiri amanti* (The Vampire Lovers, 1970), and *Intervista con vampiro* (Interview with the Vampire, 1994).

These were all shown in Milan in April and May 1998 at the Cinema Mexico, Milan, in connection with the "greatest vampire exhibition" at the *Musei di Porta Romana*, 5 March - 31 May, sponsored by the city, the province, and the Lombardy region. There was a huge assemblage of vampire literature in various European languages, vampire movie stills and posters from all over, vampires on film and on video and in popular music, vampire cartoons, toys, games, and Dracula memorabilia of all sorts. The nearby McDonald's and pizza parlors offered special vampire promotions and the Moldova restaurant a "vampire meal," with a free cup of a blood-red cocktail.

SOME SPANISH LANGUAGE VAMPIRE FILMS

Spanish soundtracks have been in evidence in vampire movies (not to count dubbing) ever since the *Dracula* (1931) of Tod Browning was also made on the same sets, in Spanish. In addition to films made in Spain, The Philippines, Mexico, and elsewhere in other languages, consider this list of more than 50 flicks, still very incomplete.

El Baul macabro (1936)
El Castillo de los monstruous (1958)
El Ataud del vampiro (1958)
El Vampiro (1959)
La Sangre de Nostradamus (1960)
La Maldición de Nostradamus (1960)
Nostradamus y el genio de las tinebras (1960)
Frankenstein, el vampiro y CIA (that's "and Co.," not the CIA, 1961)
Nostradamus y el destructor de monstruos (1961)
El Vampiro sangriento (1961)
Capurcita y pulgarcito (1962)
El Mundo de los vampiros (1962)
La Invasión de los vampiros (1962)
Enchenme al vampiro (1963)
La Huella macabre (1963)
La Maldición de los Karnsteins (1963)
Un Vampiro para dos (1966)
Charro de las calaveras (1967)
El Imperio de Dracula (1967)

La Sangre de vírgenes (1968)
Las Vampiras (1969)
Vampir-Cuadecuc (1969)
Vino de Ummo (1969)
Malenka la vampira (1969)
La Marca del hombre lobo (1969)
La Noche de Walpurgis (1970)
El Conde Dracula (1970)
Vampiros Lesbos (1970)
Dugong vampira (1970)
El Vampiro del autopista (1970)
Chantoc contra el tigre y el vampiro (1971)
La Invasión de los muertos (1972)
Angeles y querubines (1972)
Dracula contra el Dr. Frankenstein (1972)
La Llamada del vampiro (1972)
Capulina contra los vampiros (1972)
La Hija de Dracula (1972)
La Novia ensangrentada (1972)
Pastel de sangre (1972)
El gran Amór del Conde Dracula (1973)
El Attaque de los muertos (1973)
Ceremonia sangrienta (1973)
Orgia nocturna de los vampiros (1973)
La Noche de terrór ciego (1973)
El Retorno de Walpurgis (1973)
La Saga de los Draculos (1973)

This still leaves the last quarter century unaccounted for, and I do not know what one good filmographer meant by a "Santos Cycle" (a bunch of Mexican films 1962-1973, I believe), or why Nostradamus so appeals to the Mexicans grinding out vampire movies, or why it is *vampiros* and not *vampiras* on Lesbos. Obviously, this needs a lot of work. Hispanicists, to your researches!

FOR THE FILM BUFFS

It is always daunting to make choices or even bibliographies in fields where the fans truly recall the origin of that word, which is *fanatic*. I cannot mention every vampire movie you may know about. Let me try to give a list of Top 10 old movies with a vampire twist you very likely have not seen or even heard of.

Attack of the Giant Leeches (US, 1959)
The Bowery Boys Meet the Monsters (US, 1954)
Count Downe (UK, 1973)
Leech Woman (US, 1960)
Not of this Earth (US, 1957)
O Macabro Dr. Scivano (Brazil, 1971)
Red-Blooded American Girl (Canada, 1989)
Sperula (France, 1976)
L'ultima Preda del vampiri (Italy, 1960)
Valerie a Tyden Divu (Czechoslovakia, 1969)

SCARED IN THE DARK

Butler, I. *The Horror Film* (1967)
Clarens, C. *An Illustrated History of the Horror Film* (1967)
Jarratt, V. *The Italian Cinema* (1952)
Kracauer, S. *From Caligari to Hitler* (German movies, 1947)
Lanclos, M. *Le Fantastique au cinéma* (The Fantastic in the Cinema, 1966)
Sadoul, G. *French Film* (1954)

VAMPIRES IN FOREIGN HORROR FILMS

Since George Méliès' *La Manoir du diable*, at the very start of commercial films, the vampire has been a feature of the foreign cinema. There have been over fifty films of interest. In addition to worthless Filipino and Asian vampire films in profusion and the Romanian life of *Vlad Țepeș* (Vlad the Impaler, 1978) consider this select list of ten:

Un Revenant (A Ghost, 1946)
La Demoiselle et son revenant (The Girl and Her Ghost, 1952)
El Tesoro de Dracula (Dracula's Treasure, 1968)
Nacht der Vampire (Night of the Vampire, 1970)
Vampyros lesbos (Lesbian Vampires, 1971)
El gran Amór del Conde Dracula (Count Dracula's Great Love, 1973)
Dracula, père et fils (Dracula, Father and Son, 1976)
Graf Dracula in Öberbayern (Count Dracula in Upper Bavaria, 1979)
Mama Dracula (Mother Dracula, 1980)
Der Aten (The Spirit, 1989)

It should be added that as late as 1960 Hollywood was producing over 100 horror films a year and that as the century ends the supernatural is still a major cinema draw in the United States and in many—if not most—foreign countries. Where would B-movies be without it?

PRESAGES OF THE VAMPIRE

This production by *Il Carrozzone* is analyzed in the special issue "Italian Theatre" of *Drama Review* 22 (March 1978).

WILLING VICTIMS

It is a well established truth, in vampire myth, that the predator cannot hurt a victim without being invited. Superstition holds that a vampire cannot enter a house without permission. He does not attack those whose piety protects them. When Dracula bit Mina, she confesses she did not "wish to hinder him."

It is comforting to believe that unless we succumb to evil it cannot harm us, and also that there are actions one can take, such as wearing amulets, using garlic and crucifixes, and so on, to protect against vampires or to destroy them. As horror stories have developed in our age of waning faith, mankind is portrayed as ever more defenseless in the face of evil. In vampire films now the cross no longer wards off attack.

THE THREE MOST IMPORTANT VAMPIRE FILMS OF ALL TIME

Easy! *Nosferatu* (1922) from Germany, *Dracula* (1931) from the US, and *The Nightmare of Dracula* (1958) from the UK. Don't agree with that last, Terence Fisher, title? Hear Christopher Lee, seen in *Il Castello dei morti* (1965), *El Conde Dracula* (1970), *Devils of Darkness* (1965), *Dr. Terror's House of Horror* (1964), *Dracula Has Risen from the Grave* (1968), *Dracula père et fils* (1976), *Dracula, Prince of Darkness* (1965), *Ercole al centro della terra* (1962), *The Horror of Dracula* (1958), *In Search of Dracula* (1971), *The Magic Christian* (1969), *La Maldición de Karnsteins* (1963), *The Oblong Box* (1969), *One More Time* (1969), *The Satanic Rites of Dracula* (1974), *The Scars of Dracula* (1970), *Die Schlangengruber und das Pendel* (1968), *Scream and Scream Again* (1970), *Taste the Blood of Dracula* (1969), *Tempi duri per i vampiri* (1962), *The Theatre of Death* (1966)—did I miss any?—when he says of *The Nightmare of Dracula*:

It's the only one that I've ever done that's ever been any good, in my opinion. It's the only one that remotely resembles the original book.

There have, of course, been early and late examples trying to "resemble the original book," but none of those except *The Nightmare of Dracula* ever had Christopher Lee in the cast!

JOURNALISM ABOUT VAMPIRES AND THE CINEMA

Vampire movies are naturally a common subject of commentary in film journals: see Richard Dyer's "Dracula and Desire" in *Sight & Sound* 3 (January 1993, 8–12) and Amy Taubin's "Bloody Tales" in *Sight & Sound* 5 (January 1995, 8–11), for example. They are also noted for special effects and costumes, for odd casting (Tom Cruise and Gary Oldman), and other aspects of showbiz. Vampire flicks if classic enough pop up in literary journals, as in Gilberto Pérez's "*Nosferatu*" in *Raritan* 13 (Summer 1993): 1–29, and if "with-it" enough in periodicals with articles such as Tom Matthews' "Fangs for Nothing" in *Newsweek* 30 November 1992, 74-75. Particularly noted are the recent connections with the AIDS plague, Anne Rice novels, and women on the prowl in films such as *Innocent Blood, The Vampire's Kiss, Near Dark, Vamp, Transylvania 6-5000,* and *The Hunger* (a trend surveyed in Eugenia Bone's "Bella Donnas," *Premier* 6, January 1993, 32 and in her "If Looks Could Kill," *Harper's Bazaar*, October 1992, 173). Vampires are chic at Sundance and other competitions. Think of *The Addiction* and *Nadja*; they inevitably attract critics, reporters, and interviewers. Much of the journalism plays down any artistic elements. It regards vampire material as either occasion for satire or for sociology. See, for example, Anthony Lane's "Sucking Up" in the *New Yorker*, 17 October 1994, 122; Katherine M. Ramsland's "Hunger for the Marvelous: The Vampire Craze in the Computer Age" in *Psychology Today* (November 1989), 31-35; and Mary Gaitskill's "Unearthing Dracula" in *Vogue* (November 1992), 298-303.

SOME TRULY FOREIGN VAMPIRE MOVIES

Un Vampire au paradis (A Vampire in Paradise, 1992) doesn't actually have a vampire, just a madman who runs around thinking he is one, and biting people. There is, however, a bit of demonic possession of a young girl.

Nightlife (1990) is a made-for-oblivion or at least made-for-TV movie set in Mexico. Angelique gets blood out of people without killing them, which annoys Vlad, a regular vampire.

Le Manoir du diable (English title *The Haunted Castle*, 1896) is only 2 minutes long. George Méliès is one of the fathers of cinema.

Magia (Magic, 1917). The great director later to be known as Sir Alexander Korda made this feature in Hungary. The hero looks into Baron Merlin's magic mirror and discovers that the baron is really a vampire, kept alive by drinking the blood of a young man every one-thousandth full moon.

Watch out for foreign films, whose titles mislead people into thinking they are going to get a real vampire. We do this in the US as well. For example, *The Vampire* (1928, seen in France also) is about a vamp, not a vampire.

MORE ODD VAMPIRE FILMS

William Edwards' *Dracula—The Dirty Old Man* (1960)
David Niven as "Vladimir Dracula" in *Old Dracula* (1974)
Roger Corman's two-vampire film (one good, one bad) *Dracula Rising* (1992)

BLACULA

William Marshall played Prince Manuwalde ("Bloodsucker! Deadlier than Dracula!") and Charles Macaulay played The Count ("Warm young bodies will feed his hunger and hot, fresh blood his awful thirst") in the blaxploitation film, *Blacula* (1972). This film had cast members rather unknown (names like Thalmus Rasulala, Gordon Pinsent, Vonetta McGee, Denise Nichols). More recently more famous actors have appeared, such as Eddie Murphy as *A Vampire in Brooklyn*.

THE DEATH'S HEAD MOTH

It may interest some to note that the Death's Head Moth figures both in *Dracula* and in *Silence of the Lambs*, though there is a world of difference between Count Dracula and Dr. Hannibal Lecter as bloodthirsty terrors.

VAMPIRE EVIL AT THE MOVIES

Paul Oppenheimer's *Evil and the Demonic* (1997) offers "a new theory of monstrous behavior," and among its serial killers, terrorists, sex offenders, and other figures of evil in the movies "significant reservoir of the mod-

ern mass-soul" he identifies the many vampires that people flock to see in gruesome action. Besides the comforting aspects of the promise of a supernatural reality (and the prospect of some kind of life after death) there is also the comforting thought that rescue is possible and that evil may be destroyed, that we are not all doomed to be helpless victims. When confronted with rampant evil we have, as you might say, a stake in the matter.

BIGGEST HOWL
IN A VAMPIRE MOVIE

House of Frankenstein warmed up a sweeps week of 1997 TV. J. B. White's script had the vampire say, "I am not a man to be crossed."

The first illustration of Dracula. Cover of the sixpenny paperback (abridged) edition of 1901.

There is a host of European publications on the vampire. This is a German advertisement of the seventies for *Vampir*.

6

A Clutch of Vampire Tales

THE VAMPIRE IN FICTION

Throughout this book I have included vampire stories, but here I want to offer a select anthology of vampire fiction. I cannot undertake to print very long stories or novellas, or even to excerpt exciting passages from the spate of vampire novels that have come out recently. I give you elsewhere lists of a great many novels you can find for yourself if you are interested. There are so many that the average reader could fill all the time available with nothing but vampire fiction. Indeed some people seem to do this, for they are great experts in the subject and debate with enthusiasm the merits of writers in the genre both living and dead.

I hope that they as well as you will agree that the clutch of vampire tales here presents an interesting variety and some good reading. I cannot borrow much from works under copyright and this certainly cannot be a fully representative selection, but I trust it is an interesting one. It may not include your personal favorites. However, you may find a new favorite. If nothing else, you will now read, as we begin this chapter the missing opening of Bram Stoker's famous novel!

DRACULA'S GUEST

Here is a short story from *Dracula's Guest and Other Weird Stories* (published posthumously, 1914) by Bram Stoker, author of *Dracula* (as everyone knows). Not everyone knows this story. It was the original first chapter of *Dracula*. It was cut because the publishers thought the book was too long and did not want to bother going through it carefully making the minor cuts from which it certainly could have benefited.

When we started for our drive the sun was shining brightly on Munich, and the air was full of the joyousness of early summer. Just as we were about to depart, Herr Delbrück (the maître d'hôtel of the Quatre Saisons, where I was staying) came down, bareheaded, to the carriage and, after wishing me a pleasant drive, said to the coachman, still holding his hand on the handle of the carriage door:

"Remember you are back by nightfall. The sky looks bright but there is a shiver in the north wind that says there may be a sudden storm. But I am sure you will not be late." Here he smiled, and added, "for you know what night it is."

Johann answered with an emphatic, "Ja, mein Herr," and, touching his hat, drove off quickly. When we had cleared the town, I said, after signaling to him to stop:

"Tell me, Johann, what is to-night?"

He crossed himself, as he answered laconically:

"*Walpurgis Nacht.*" Then he took out his watch, a great, old-fashioned German silver thing as big as a turnip, and looked at it, with his eyebrows gathered together and a little impatient shrug of his shoulders. I realised that this was his way of respectfully protesting against the unnecessary delay, and sank back in the carriage, merely motioning him to proceed. He started off rapidly, as if to make up for lost time. Every now and then the horses seemed to throw up their heads and sniff the air suspiciously. On such occasions I often looked round in alarm. The road was pretty bleak, for we were traversing a sort of high, wind-swept plateau. As we drove, I saw a road that looked but little used, and which seemed to dip through a little, winding valley. It looked so inviting that, even at the risk of offending him, I called Johann to stop—and when he had pulled up, I told him I would like to drive down that road. He made all sorts of excuses, and frequently crossed himself as he spoke. This somewhat piqued my curiosity, so I asked him various questions. He answered fencingly, and repeatedly looked at his watch in protest. Finally I said:

"Well, Johann, I want to go down this road. I shall not ask you to come unless you like; but tell me why you do not like to go, that is all I ask." For answer he seemed to throw himself off the box, so quickly did he reach the ground. Then he stretched out his hands appealingly to me, and implored me not to go. There was just enough of English mixed with the German for me to understand the drift of his talk. He seemed always just about to tell me something—the very idea of which evidently frightened him—but each time he pulled himself up, saying, as he crossed himself:

"*Walpurgis Nacht!*"

I tried to argue with him, but it was difficult to argue with a man when I did not know his language. The advantage certainly rested with him, for although he began to speak in English, of a very crude and broken kind, he always got excited and broke into his native tongue—and every time he did so, he looked at his watch. Then the horses became restless and sniffed the air. At this he grew very pale, and, looking around in a frightened way, he suddenly jumped forward, took them by the bridles and led them on some twenty feet. I followed, and asked why he had done this. For answer he crossed himself, pointed to the spot we had left and drew his carriage in the direction of the other road, indicating a cross, and said, first in German, then in English: "Buried him—him what killed themselves."

I remembered the old custom of burying suicides at crossroads: "Ah! I see, a suicide. How interesting!" But for the life of me I could not make out why the horses were frightened.

Whilst we were talking, we heard a sort of sound between a yelp and a bark. It was far away; but the horses got very restless, and it took Johann all his time to quiet them. He was pale, and said; "It sounds like a wolf—but yet there are no wolves here now."

"No?" I said, questioning him; "isn't it long since the wolves were so near the city?"

"Long, long," he answered, "in the spring and summer; but with the snow the wolves have been here not so long."

Whilst he was petting the horses and trying to quiet them, dark clouds drifted rapidly across the sky. The sunshine passed away, and a breath of cold wind seemed to drift past us. It was only a breath, however, and more in the nature of a warning than a fact, for the sun came out brightly again. Johann looked under his lifted hand at the horizon and said:

"The storm of snow, he comes before long time."

Then he looked at his watch again, and, straightway holding his reins firmly—for the horses were still pawing the ground restlessly and shaking their heads—he climbed to his box as though the time had come for proceeding on our journey.

I felt a little obstinate and did not at once get into the carriage.

"Tell me," I said, "about this place where the road leads," and I pointed down.

Again he crossed himself and mumbled a prayer, before he answered: "It is unholy."

"What is unholy?" I enquired.

"The village."

"Then there is a village?"

"No, no. No one lives there hundreds of years."

My curiosity was piqued: "But you said there was a village."

"There was."

"Where is it now?"

Whereupon he burst out into a long story in German and English, so mixed up that I could not quite understand exactly what he said, but roughly I gathered that long ago, hundreds of years, men had died there and been buried in their graves; and sounds were heard under the clay, and when the graves were opened, men and women were found rosy with life, and their mouths red with blood. And so, in haste to save their lives (aye, and their souls!—and here he crossed himself) those who were left fled away to other places, where the living lived, and the dead were dead and not—not something. He was evidently afraid to speak the last words. As he proceeded with his narration, he grew more and more excited. It seemed as if his imagination had got hold of him, and he ended in a perfect paroxysm of fear—white-faced, perspiring, trembling and looking round him, as if expecting that some dreadful presence would manifest itself there in the bright sunshine on the open plain. Finally, in an agony of desperation, he cried:

"*Walpurgis Nacht!*" and pointed to the carriage for me to get in. All my English blood rose at this, and, standing back, I said:

"You are afraid, Johann—you are afraid. Go home; I shall return alone; the walk will do me good." The carriage door was open. I took from the seat my oak walking-stick—which I always carry on my holiday excursions—and closed the door, pointing back to Munich, and said, "Go home, Johann—*Walpurgis Nacht* doesn't concern Englishmen."

The horses were now more restive than ever, and Johann was trying to hold them in, while excitedly imploring me not to do anything so foolish. I pitied the poor fellow, he was so deeply in earnest; but all the same I could not help laughing. His English was quite gone now. In his anxiety he had forgotten that his only means of making me understand was to talk my language, so he jabbered away in his native German. It began to be a little tedious. After giving the direction "Home!" I turned to go down the crossroad into the valley.

With a despairing gesture, Johann turned his horses towards Munich. I leaned on my stick and looked after him. He went slowly along the road for a while then there came over the crest of the hill a man tall and thin. I could see so much in the distance. When he drew near the horses, they began to jump and kick about, then to scream with terror. Johann could not hold them in; they bolted down the road, running away madly. I watched them out of sight, then looked for the stranger, but I found that he, too, was gone.

With a light heart I turned down the side road through the depending valley to which Johann had objected. There was not the slightest reason, that I could see, for his objection; and I dare say I tramped for a couple of hours without thinking of time or distance, and certainly without seeing a person or a house. So far as the place was concerned, it was desolation itself. But I did not notice this particularly till, on turning a bend in the road, I came upon a scattered fringe of wood; then I recognised that I had been impressed unconsciously by the desolation of the region through which I had passed.

I sat down to rest myself, and began to look around. It struck me that it was considerably colder than it had been at the commencement of my walk—a sort of sighing sound seemed to be around me, with, now and then, high overhead, a sort of muffled roar. Looking upwards I noticed that great thick clouds were drifting rapidly across the sky from North to South at a great height. There were signs of coming storm in some lofty stratum of the air. I was a little chilly, and, thinking that it was the sitting still after the exercise of walking, I resumed my journey.

The ground I passed over was now much more picturesque. There were no striking objects that the eye might single out but in all there was a charm of beauty. I took little heed of time and it was only when the depending twilight forced itself upon me that

Bram Stoker in 1884

I began to think of how I should find my way home. The brightness of the day had gone. The air was cold, and the drifting of
clouds high overhead was more marked. They were accompanied
by a sort of far-away rushing sound, through which seemed to come
at intervals that mysterious cry which the driver had said came from
a wolf. For a while I hesitated. I had said I would see the deserted
village, so on I went, and presently came on a wide stretch of open
country, shut in by hills all around. Their sides were covered with
trees which spread down to the plain, dotting, in clumps, the gen-
tler slopes and hollows which showed here and there. I followed
with my eye the winding of the road, and saw that it curved close
to one of the densest of these clumps and was lost behind it.

As I looked there came a cold shiver in the air, and the snow
began to fall. I thought of the miles and miles of bleak country I
had passed, and then hurried on to seek the shelter of the wood
in front. Darker and darker grew the sky, and faster and heavier
fell the snow, till the earth before and around me was a glistening
white carpet the further edge of which was lost in misty vagueness.
The road was here but crude, and when on the level its bound-
aries were not so marked as when it passed through the cuttings,
and in a little while I found that I must have strayed from it, for I
missed underfoot the hard surface, and my feet sank deeper in the
grass and moss. Then the wind grew stronger and blew with ever-
increasing force, till I was fain to run before it. The air became
icy cold, and in spite of my exercise I began to suffer. The snow
was now falling so thickly and whirling around me in such rapid
eddies that I could hardly keep my eyes open. Every now and then
the heavens were torn asunder by vivid lightning, and in the flashes
I could see ahead of me a great mass of trees, chiefly yew and
cypress and heavily coated with snow.

I was soon amongst the shelter of the trees, and there, in comparative silence, I could hear the rush of the wind high overhead.
Presently the blackness of the storm had become merged in the
darkness of the night. By-and-by the storm seemed to be passing
away: it now only came in fierce puffs or blasts. At such moments
the weird sound of the wolf appeared to be echoed by many similar sounds around me.

Now and again, through the black mass of drifting cloud, came
a straggling ray of moonlight, which lit up the expanse, and showed
me that I was at the end of a dense mass of cypress and yew trees.

As the snow had ceased to fall, I walked out from the shelter and began to investigate more closely. It appeared to me that, amongst so many old foundations as I had passed, there might be still standing a house in which, though in ruins, I could find some sort of shelter for a while. As I skirted the edge of the copse, I found that a low wall encircled it and following this I presently found an opening. Here the cypresses formed an alley leading up to a square mass of some kind of building. Just as I caught sight of this, however, the drifting clouds obscured the moon, and I passed up the path in darkness. The wind must have grown colder, for I felt myself shiver as I walked; but there was hope of shelter, and I groped my way blindly on.

I stopped, for there was a sudden stillness. The storm had passed; and in sympathy with nature's silence, my heart seemed to cease to beat. But this was only momentarily; for suddenly the moonlight broke through the clouds, showing me that I was in a graveyard, and that the square object before me was a great massive tomb of marble, as white as the snow that lay on and all around it. With the moonlight there came a fierce sigh of the storm, which appeared to resume its course with a long, low howl, as of many dogs or wolves. I was awed and shocked, and felt the cold perceptibly grow upon me till it seemed to grip me by the heart. Then while the flood of moonlight still fell on the marble tomb, the storm gave further evidence of renewing, as though it was returning on its track. Impelled by some sort of fascination, I approached the sepulcher to see what it was, and why such a thing stood alone in such a place. I walked around it, and read, over the Doric door, in German—

COUNTESS DOLINGEN OF GRATZ

IN SYRIA

SOUGHT AND FOUND DEATH

1801

On the top of the tomb, seemingly driven through the solid marble—for the structure was composed of a few vast blocks of stone—was a great iron spike or stake. On going to the back I saw, graven in great Russian letters:

"The dead travel fast."

There was something so weird and uncanny about the whole thing that it gave me a turn and made me feel quite faint. I began to wish, for the first time, that I had taken Johann's advice. Here a thought struck me, which came under almost mysterious circumstances and with a terrible shock. This was *Walpurgis Night!*

Walpurgis Night, when, according to the belief of millions of people, the devil was abroad—when the graves were opened and the dead came forth and walked. When all evil things of earth and air and water held revel. This very place the driver had specially shunned. This was the depopulated village of centuries ago. This was where the suicide lay; and this was the place where I was alone—unmanned, shivering with cold in a shroud of snow with a wild storm gathering again upon me! It took all my philosophy, all the religion I had been taught, all my courage, not to collapse in a paroxysm of fright.

And now a perfect tornado burst upon me. The ground shook as though thousands of horses thundered across it; and this time the storm bore on its icy wings, not snow, but great hailstones which drove with such violence that they might have come from the thongs of Balearic slingers—hailstones that beat down leaf and branch and made the shelter of the cypresses of no more avail than though their stems were standing corn. At the first I had rushed to the nearest tree; but I was soon fain to leave it and seek the only spot that seemed to afford refuge, the deep Doric doorway of the marble tomb. There, crouching against the massive bronze door, I gained a certain amount of protection from the beating of the hailstones, for now they only drove against me as they ricocheted from the ground and the side of the marble.

As I leaned against the door, it moved slightly and opened inwards. The shelter of even a tomb was welcome in that pitiless tempest, and I was about to enter it when there came a flash of forked lightning that lit up the whole expanse of the heavens. In the instant, as I am a living man, I saw, as my eyes were turned into the darkness of the tomb, a beautiful woman, with rounded cheeks and red lips, seemingly sleeping on a bier. As the thunder broke overhead, I was grasped as by the hand of a giant and hurled out into the storm. The whole thing was so sudden that, before I could realise the shock, moral as well as physical, I found the hailstones beating me down. At the same time I had a strange dominating feeling that I was not alone. I looked towards the tomb. Just then there came another blinding flash which seemed to strike the iron stake that surmounted the tomb and to pour through to the earth, blasting and crumbling the marble, as in a burst of flame. The dead woman rose for a moment of agony, while she was lapped in the flame, and her bitter scream of pain was drowned in the thunder-crash. The last thing I heard was this mingling of dreadful sound, as again I was seized in the giant grasp and dragged away, while the hailstones beat on me, and the air around seemed reverberant with the howling of wolves. The last sight that I remembered was a vague, white, moving mass, as if all the grave around me had sent out the phantoms of their sheeted dead, and that they were closing in on me through the white cloudiness of the driving hail.

Gradually there came a sort of vague beginning of consciousness; then a sense of weariness that was dreadful. For a time I remembered nothing; but slowly my senses returned. My feet seemed positively racked with pain, yet I could not move them. They seemed to be numbed. There was an icy feeling at the back of my neck and all down my spine, and my ears, like my feet, were dead, yet in torment; but there was in my breast a sense of warmth which was, by comparison, delicious. It was as a nightmare—a physical nightmare, if one may use such an expression; for some heavy weight on my chest made it difficult for me to breathe.

This period of semi-lethargy seemed to remain a long time, and as it faded away I must have slept or swooned. Then came a sort of loathing, like the first stage of sea-sickness, and a wild desire to be free from something—I knew not what. A vast stillness enveloped me, as though all the world were asleep or dead—only broken by the low panting as of some animal close to me. I felt a warm rasping at my throat, then came a consciousness of the awful truth, which chilled me to the heart and sent the blood surging up through my brain. Some great animal was lying on me and now licking my throat. I feared to stir, for some instinct of prudence bade me lie still; but the brute seemed to realize that there was now some changes in me, for it raised its head. Through my eyelashes I saw above me the two great flaming eyes of a gigantic wolf. Its sharp white teeth gleamed in the gaping red mouth, and I could feel its hot breath fierce and acrid upon me.

For another spell of time I remembered no more. Then I became conscious of a low growl, followed by a yelp, renewed again and again. Then seemingly very far away, I heard a "Holloa! holloa!" as of many voices calling in unison. Cautiously I raised my head and looked in the direction whence the sound came; but the cemetery blocked my view. The wolf still continued to yelp in a strange way, and a red glare began to move round the grove of cypresses, as though following the sound. As the voices drew closer, the wolf yelped faster and louder. I feared to make either sound or motion. Nearer came the red glow, over the white pall which stretched into the darkness around me. Then all at once from beyond the trees there came at a trot a troop of horsemen bearing torches. The wolf rose from my breast and made for the cemetery. I saw one of the horsemen (soldiers by their caps and their long military cloaks) raise his carbine and take aim. A companion knocked up his arm, and I heard the ball whizz over my head. He had evidently taken my body for that of the wolf. Another sighted the animal as it slunk away, and a shot followed. Then, at a gallop, the troop rode forward—some towards me, others following the wolf as it disappeared amongst he snow-clad cypresses.

As they drove nearer I tried to move, but was powerless, although I could see and hear all that went on around me. Two or three of the soldiers jumped from their horses and knelt beside me. One of them raised my head, and placed his hand over my heart.

"Good news, comrades!" he cried. "His heart still beats!"

Then some brandy was poured down my throat; it put vigour into me, and I was able to open my eyes fully and look around. Lights and shadows were moving among the trees, and I heard men call to one another. They drew together, uttering frightened exclamations; and the lights flashed as the others came pouring out of the cemetery pell-mell, like men possessed. When the further ones came close to us, those who were around me asked them eagerly:

"Well, have you found him?"

The reply rang out hurriedly:

"No! no! Come away quick—quick! This is no place to stay, and on this of all nights!"

"What was it?" was the question, asked in all manner of keys. The answer came variously and all indefinitely as though the men were moved by some common impulse to speak, yet were restrained by some common fear from giving their thoughts.

"It—it—indeed!" gibbered one, whose wits had plainly given out for the moment.

"A wolf—and yet not a wolf!" another put in shudderingly.

"No use trying for him without the sacred bullet," a third remarked in a more ordinary manner.

"Serve us right for coming out on this night! Truly we have earned our thousand marks!" were the ejaculations of a fourth.

"There was blood on the broken marble," another said after a pause—"the lightning never brought that there. And for him— is he safe? Look at his throat! See, comrades, the wolf has been lying on him and keeping his blood warm."

The officer looked at my throat and replied:

"He is all right; the skin is not pierced. What does it all mean? We should never have found him but for the yelping of the wolf."

"What became of it?" asked the man who was holding up my head, and who seemed the least panic-stricken of the party, for his hands were steady and without tremor, on his sleeve was the chevron of a petty officer.

"It went to its home," answered the man, whose long face was pallid, and who actually shook with terror as he glanced around him fearfully. "There are graves enough there in which it may lie. Come, comrades—come quickly! Let us leave this cursed spot."

The officer raised me to a sitting posture, as he uttered a word of command; then several men placed me upon a horse. He sprang to the saddle behind me, took me in his arms, gave the word to advance; and, turning our faces away from the cypresses, we rode away in swift, military order.

As yet my tongue refused its office, and I was perforce silent. I must have fallen asleep; for the next thing I remembered was find- ing myself standing up, supported by a soldier on each side of me. It was almost broad daylight, and to the north a red streak of sun- light was reflected, like a path of blood, over the waste of snow. The officer was telling the men to say nothing of what they had seen, except that they found an English stranger, guarded by a large dog.

"Dog! that was no dog," cut in the man who had exhibited such fear. "I think I know a wolf when I seen one."

The young officer answered calmly: "I said a dog."

"Dog!" reiterated the other ironically. It was evident that his courage was rising with the sun; and, pointing to me, he said, "Look at his throat. Is that the work of a dog, master?"

Instinctively I raised my hand to my throat, and as I touched it I cried out in pain. The men crowded round to look, some stooping down from their saddles; and again there came the calm voice of the young officer:

"A dog, as I said. If aught else were said we should only be laughed at."

I was then mounted behind a trooper, and we rode on into the suburbs of Munich. Here we came across a stray carriage, into which I was lifted, and it was driven off to the Quatre Saisons—the young officer accompanying me, whilst a trooper followed with his horse, and the others rode off to their barracks.

When we arrived, Herr Delbrück rushed so quickly down the steps to meet me, that it was apparent he had been watching within. Taking me by both hands he solicitously led me in. The officer saluted me and was turning to withdraw, when I recognized his purpose, and insisted that he should come to my rooms. Over a glass of wine I warmly thanked him and his brave comrades for saving me. He replied simply that he was more than glad, and that Herr Delbrück had at the first taken steps to make all the searching party pleased; at which ambiguous utterance the maître d'hôtel smiled, while the officer pleaded duty and withdrew.

"But Herr Delbrück," I enquired, "how and why was it that the soldiers searched for me?"

He shrugged his shoulders, as if in depreciation of his own deed, as he replied:

"I was so fortunate as to obtain leave from the commander of the regiment in which I served, to ask for volunteers."

"But how did you know I was lost?" I asked.

"The driver came hither with the remains of his carriage, which had been upset when the horses ran away."

"But surely you would not send a search-party of soldiers merely on this account?"

"Oh, no!" he answered; "but even before the coachman arrived, I had this telegram from the Boyar whose guest you are," and he took from his pocket a telegram which he handed to me, and I read:

BISTRITZ

"Be careful of my guest—his safety is most precious to me. Should aught happen to him, or if he be missed, spare nothing to find him and ensure his safety. He is English and therefore adventurous. There are often dangers from snow and wolves at night. Lose not a moment if you suspect harm to him. I answer your zeal with my fortune. —Dracula."

As I held the telegram in my hand, the room seemed to whirl around me; and, if the attentive maître d'hôtel had not caught me, I think I should have fallen. There was something so strange in all this, something so weird and impossible to imagine, that there grew on me a sense of my being in some way the sport of opposite forces—the mere vague idea of which seemed in a way to paralyse me. I was certainly under some form of mysterious protection. From a distant country had come, in the very nick of time, a message that took me out of the danger of the snow-sleep and the jaws of the wolf.

VAMPIRE FICTION

In an article on leaving money to colleges and universities, *Forbes* (20 April 1998, 470) says that if you don't take care the money may go to teaching courses in—"Vampire Fiction" or "Soap Opera."

Actually, higher education does offer such courses already. I taught one of the former myself, years ago, at Brooklyn College of The City University of New York. The seminar had many sound educational advantages: it attracted students from majors as different as literature and music and film; it produced students eager to attend and enjoy a course in which they had a genuine interest; it started them reading carefully and discussing with passion a wide range of comparative literature; it made them consider the importance of popular culture; it taught them to the joys of collecting information and even of collecting items, from movie stills to breakfast food boxes, with a theme. They learned to be intellectuals, experts of a sort on a topic in which everyone has at least a passing interest. They met with each other outside of class and rented movies to see and talk about together! They "lived" the subject, at least for a semester, and discovered what it is like to be possessed by ideas.

Some day I may get around to publishing an anthology of vampire stories, probably to be titled with a bit of *Hamlet* in his "Now I could drink hot blood" mood. What do you think of *Churchyards Yawn*? Meanwhile, we continue with our small sampling of Vampire Fiction.

THAT GIRL

Phlegon the Lydian, historian in the reign of the Emperor Hadrian, admixed stories of the supernatural which he regarded as true. One involved an "undead" girl, *The Bride of Amphipolis*:

Demostratus and Charito's daughter Philinnion has died, but a visitor named Machates doesn't realize that the young girl who comes to his bed at night is anything more unusual than the daughter of the house in the usual traveling salesman stories. Philinnion's nurse sees the couple in bed and tells Charito, the dead girl's mother. The next morning, Charito questions Machates about what happened the previous night. Machates admits he slept with the girl. He shows a gold ring she gave him and a ribbon from her nightdress which she left behind. He is informed that these belong to a dead girl. Machates is particularly distressed to think he has been sleeping with a ghost, but he doesn't go away. In fact, he promises to let the household know if and when the girl returns. In his masculine pride, he rather thinks she will come back for more.

In *Night Fright* (1985), Stephen Geoffreys played a young vampire (Evil Ed) whose brow had been seared with a cross.

The girl returns. Machates alerts the household and the girl is caught. She complains to her mother that she can't have sex in the house without interference from her parents even now that she is dead. Then she falls down lifeless.

The whole town is thrown into disorder and debate. The tomb of Philinnion is opened and the body is not there. The amazed townspeople, however, do find a ring which Machates says he gave to Philinnion the night of her first visit. (This is reminiscent of Greek plays whose plots often hinge on some token for recognition.) A local seer suggests that the body of Philinnion must be burned and various sacrifices made to the gods. This is done. The girl ghost is laid, one might say.

Machates commits suicide, perhaps in the hope of being with his beloved in death. As a suicide, he may wind up tortured by giant birds with the faces of women, the notorious Harpies of Greek mythology, but love laughs at ornithology. Suicide, by the way, was considered to be one of the ways of condemning oneself to being a vampire, and suicides were not buried in consecrated ground. They were often buried, like criminals, at crossroads.

This tale is frequently presented as a vampire story because of the "undead" aspect but there is no blood involved—unless Philinnion was a virgin.

The story has been told and retold. Undoubtedly the most famous version is Goethe's *Die Braut von Corinth* (The Bride of Corinth), a favorite with English Romantics of the nineteenth century. There is, however, more of a connection with the Christian demonology of *incubus* and *succuba*, an attempt to explain erotic dreams, than with the vampire. Victims of the vampire are involved with blood, not other body fluids such as semen. This is properly a ghost story. I put it here among vampire stories only because this is where people who know of it will probably seek it.

Throughout this book the problem is, of course, what to put in and what to leave out. I attempt to strike a happy balance between the essential—which is expected by the experts and must appear for those who do not know these details—and the entertainingly unusual, which I have sought far and wide. Every reader will get the fundamentals here, and in a way that makes learning fun. Even the most knowledgable reader will, I trust, learn new things. For many, the bride of Amphipolis may be a fresh feature. I wish someone would make an opera or a nice romantic ballet of it!

THE MARQUISE OF O.

M. Greenburg translated from the German *The Marquise of O. and Other Stories* (1963). The stories are by Kleist, whom the old joke identifies as "the Chinese Messiah." Bernd Heinrich Wilhelm von Kleist (1777-1811) was a major German writer and *The Marquise of O.* is a little masterpiece. In this story the marquise of O. encounters and becomes pregnant by a Russian identified as Count F. This handsome if very pale lover goes away, there are rumors that he is dead, and he returns. Love and death are concerns of the story and there is some confusion as to whether we are dealing with an incubus (demon), vampire, or human. Ernest Jones highly praised this as an essential vampire story. There is an undoubted vampire in Kleist's play *Penthe-silea* (1808) but this short story is a *locus classicus* of the Romantic vampire.

Another classic of the Romantics is from the pen of Jonathan Ludwig Tieck (1773-1853). His interest in folk tales much influenced his work—he made a play of the familiar story of "Puss in Boots"—but in *Wake Not the Dead*, which follows, he is dealing in darker material. The old fashioned English translation may strike the modern reader as more clumsy than quaint; it does, nonetheless, capture the style the Romantics liked, and it was greatly influential. "Words such as men do use," the ideal of Wordsworth and Coleridge, were not regarded as sufficiently literary by the Germans—or those who translated their masters in the nineteenth century. The piece is also long—but where else would you find it if we do not give it place here? It is not tedious if you will discern in it important elements of the vampire ledgend.

WAKE NOT THE DEAD
by Johann Ludwig Tieck

"Wilt thou forever sleep? Wilt thou never more awake, my beloved, but henceforth repose for eternity from thy short pilgrimage on earth? Doth the play shroud become thee better than the bridal veil? Is the chamber of the grave a warmer bed than the couch of love? Is the spectre Death more welcome to thy arms than thy enamored consort?" Such were the lamentations which Walter poured forth for his Brunhilda, the partner of his youthful, passionate love; thus did he bewail over her grave at the midnight hour, which time legions of shadows flit beneath the moon and across the earth to transmit wild and agitating thoughts over the sinner's bosom; thus did he lament under the tall linden trees by her grave, while his head reclined on the cold stone.

Walter was a powerful lord in Burgundy, who, in his earliest youth, had been smitten with the charms of the fair Brunhilda, a beauty far surpassing in loveliness all her rivals, for her tresses—dark as the raven face of night, streaming over her shoulders—set off to the utmost advantage the beaming lustre of her slender form. The rich dye of a cheek was tinted deep and brilliant as that of the western heaven. Her eyes did not resemble those burning orbs whose pale glow gem the vault of night and whose immeasurable distance fills the soul with deep thoughts of eternity, but were rather as the sober beams which cheer this nether world, and which, while they enlighten, kindle the sons of earth to joy and love.

Brunhilda became the wife of Walter, and, both equally enamored and devoted, they abandoned themselves to the enjoyment of a passion that rendered them reckless of aught besides, while it lulled them in a fascinating dream. Their sole apprehension was less aught should awaken them from a delirium which they prayed might continue forever. Yet how vain is the wish that would arrest the decrees of destiny!—as well might it seek to divert the circling planets from their eternal course. Short was the duration of this frenzied passion; not that it gradually decayed and subsided into apathy, but death snatched away his blooming victim and left Walter to a widowed couch. Impetuous, however, as was his first burst of grief, he was not inconsolable, for ere long another bride became the partner of the youth.

Swanhilda also was beautiful—although nature had formed her charms on a very different model from those of Brunhilda. Her golden locks waved bright as the beams of morn. Only when excited by some emotion of her soul did a rosy hue tinge the lily paleness of her cheek. Her limbs were proportioned in the nicest symmetry, yet did they not possess that luxuriant fullness of animal life. Her eye beamed eloquently, but it was with the milder radiance of a star tranquillizing to tenderness rather than exciting to warmth. Thus formed, it was not possible that she should steep him in his former delirium, although she rendered happy his waking hours. Tranquil and serious, studying in all things her husband's pleasure, she restored order and comfort in his family. Her mild benevolence tended to restrain the fiery, impetuous disposition of Walter, while at the same time her prudence recalled him in some degree from his vain, turbulent wishes and his aspirings after unattainable enjoyments to the duties and pleasures of actual life.

Swanhilda bore her husband two children, a son and a daughter. The latter was mild and patient as her mother—well contented with her solitary sports. The boy possessed his father's fiery, restless disposition, tempered, however, with the solidity of his mother. Attached by his offspring more tenderly towards their mother, Walter now lived for several years very happily. His thoughts would frequently, indeed, recur to Brunhilda, but without their former violence, merely as we dwell upon the memory of a friend of our earlier days borne from us on the rapid current of time to a region where we know that he is happy.

But clouds dissolve into air, flowers fade, the sand of the hourglass runs imperceptibly away, and even so do human feelings dissolve, fade, and pass away, and with them too, human happiness. Walter's inconstant breast again sighed for the ecstatic dreams of those days which he had spent with his equally romantic Brunhilda. Again did she present herself to his ardent fancy in all the glow of her bridal charms, and he began to draw a parallel between the past and the present. Nor did imagination, as it is wont, fail to array the former in the brightest hues, while it proportionately obscured the latter, so that he pictured to himself the one much richer in enjoyment, and the other much less so than what actually was.

This change in her husband did not escape Swanhilda, whereupon, redoubling her attentions towards him and her cares towards their children, she expected by this means to reunite the knot that was slackened. Yet the more she endeavored to regain his affections the colder did he grow, the more intolerable did her caresses seem, and the more continually did the image of Brunhilda haunt his thoughts. The children, whose endearments had now become indispensable to him, alone stood between the parents as genii eager to effect a reconciliation; and, beloved by them both, formed a uniting link between them. Yet, as evil can be plucked from the heart of man only ere its root remains fixed deep within—too firmly set to be wholly eradicated—so was Walter's diseased fancy too far affected to have its disorder stopped; and, in a short time, completely tyrannized him. Frequently of a night, instead of retiring to his consort's chamber he repaired to Brunhilda's grave where he murmured forth his discontent saying: "Wilt thou sleep forever?"

One night as he was thus reclining on the turf indulging in his wonted sorrow, a sorcerer from the neighboring mountains entered into this field of death for the purpose of gathering for his mystic spells such herbs as grew only from the earth wherein the dead repose, and which, as if the last production of mortality, are gifted with a powerful and supernatural influence. The sorcerer perceived the mourner, and approached the spot where he was lying.

"Wherefore, fond wretch, dost thou grieve thus for what is now a hideous mass of mortality—mere bones, and nerves, and veins? Nations have fallen unlamented. Even worlds themselves, long ere this globe of ours was created, have mouldered into nothing, nor hath anyone wept over them. Why then should thou indulge this vain affliction for a child of the dust—a being as frail as thyself, and, like thee, the creature but of a moment?"

Walter raised himself up. "Let yon worlds that shine in the firmament," replied he, "lament for each other as they perish. It is true, that I who am myself clay lament for my fellow-clay. Yet is this clay impregnated with a fire—with an essence that none of the elements of creation possess—with love. This divine passion I felt for her who now sleepeth beneath this sod."

"Will thy complaints awaken her; or could they do so, would she not soon upbraid thee for having disturbed that repose in which she now is hushed?"

"Avaunt, cold-hearted being: thou knowest not what is love. Oh! that my tears could wash away the earthly covering that conceals her from these eyes—that my groan of anguish could rouse her from her slumber of death! No, she would not again seek her earthy couch."

"Insensate that thou art, and couldst thou endure to gaze without shuddering on one disgorged from the jaws of the grave? Art thou too thyself the same from whom she parted; or hath time passed o'er thy brow and left no traces there? Would not thy love rather be converted into hate and disgust?"

"Say rather that the stars would leave yon firmament, that the sun will henceforth refuse to shed his beams through the heavens. Oh! that she stood once more before me; that once again she reposed on this bosom! How quickly should we then forget that death or time had ever stepped between us."

"Delusion! Mere delusion of the brain from heated blood, like to that which arises from the fumes of wine. It is not my wish to tempt thee—to restore to thee thy dead—else wouldst thou soon feel that I have spoken sooth."

"How! Restore her to me," exclaimed Walter. "Oh, if thou art indeed able to effect that, grant it to my earnest supplication; if one throb of human feeling vibrates in thy bosom, let my tears prevail with thee. Restore me my beloved; so shalt thou hereafter bless the deed, and see that it was a good work."

"A good work! A blessed deed!" returned the sorcerer with a smile of scorn. "For me there exists no good, nor evil—since my will is always the same. Ye alone know evil, who will that which ye should not. It is indeed in my power to restore her to thee. Yet bethink thee well whether it will prove thy weal. Consider too, how deep the abyss between life and death. Across this my power can build a bridge, but it can never fill up the frightful chasm."

Walter would have spoken, and have sought to prevail on this powerful being my fresh entreaties, but the latter prevented him, saying: "Peace! Bethink thee well, and return hither to me tomorrow at midnight. Yet once more do I warn thee: wake not the dead."

Having uttered these words, the mysterious being disappeared. Intoxicated with fresh hope, Walter found no sleep on his couch, for fancy—prodigal of her richest stores—expanded before him the glittering web of futurity; and his eyes, moistened with the dew of rapture, glanced from one vision of happiness to another.

During the next day he wandered through the woods, lest wonted objects, by recalling the memory of later and less happier times, might disturb the blissful idea that he should again behold her—again fold her in his arms, gaze on her beaming brow by day, repose on her bosom at night; and, as this sole idea filled his imagination, how was it possible that the least doubt should arise, or that the warning of the mysterious old man should recur to his thoughts.

No sooner did the midnight hour approach, than he hastened towards the grave-field where the sorcerer was already standing by that of Brunhilda. "Hast thou maturely considered?" inquired he.

"Oh, restore to me the object of my ardent passion," exclaimed Walter with impetuous eagerness. "Delay not thy generous action, lest I die even this night, consumed with disappointed desire, and behold her face no more."

"Well then," answered the old man, "return hither again tomorrow at the same hour. But once more do I give thee this friendly warning: wake not the dead."

In all the despair of impatience, Walter would have prostrated himself at his feet and supplicated him to fulfill at once a desire now increased to agony; but the sorcerer had already vanished into the night. Pouring forth his lamentations more wildly and impetuously than ever, he lay upon the grave of his adored one until the grey dawn streaked the east.

During the day, which seemed to him longer than any he had ever experienced, he wandered to and fro, restless and impatient, seemingly without any object, and deeply buried in his own reflections, inquiet as the murderer who mediates his first deed of blood. The stars of evening found him once more at the appointed spot. At midnight the sorcerer returned also.

"Hast thou yet maturely deliberated?" inquired he, "as on the preceding night?"

"Oh what should I deliberate?" returned Walter impatiently. "I need not to deliberate. What I demand of thee, is that which thou hast promised me—that which will prove my bliss. Or dost thou but mock me? If so, hence from my sight, lest I be tempted to lay my hand on thee."

"Once more do I warn thee," answered the old man with undisturbed composure, "wake not the dead—let her rest."

"Aye, but not in the cold grave. She shall rather rest on this bosom which burns with eagerness to clasp her."

"Reflect, thou may'st not quit her until death, even though aversion and horror should seize thy heart. There would then remain only one horrible means."

"Dotard!" cried Walter, interrupting him, "how may I hate that which I love with such intensity of passion? How should I abhor that for which my every drop of blood is burning?"

"Then be it even as thou wishest," answered the sorcerer; "Step back."

The old man now drew a circle round the grave, all the while muttering words of enchantment. Immediately the storm began to howl among the tops of the trees; owls flapped their wings and uttered their low voice of omen; the stars hid their mild, beaming aspect, that they might not behold so unholy and impious a spectacle. The stone then rolled from the grave with a hollow sound, leaving a free passage for the inhabitant of that dreadful tenement. The sorcerer scattered into the yawning earth roots and herbs of most magic power, and of most penetrating odor so that the worms crawling forth from the earth congregated together, and raised themselves in a writhing column over the grave, while rushing wind burst from the earth, scattering the mould before it until at length the coffin lay uncovered. The moon-beams fell on it, and the lid burst open with a tremendous sound. Into the opening the sorcerer poured some blood from out of a human skull, exclaiming at the same time: "Drink, sleeper, drink of this warm stream, that thy heart may again beat within thy bosom." And after a short pause, shed on her some other mystic liquid. Then he cried aloud with the voice of one inspired: "Yes, thy heart beats once more with the flood of life. Thine eye is again opened to sight. Arise, therefore, from thy tomb."

As an island suddenly springs forth from the dark waves of the ocean, raised upwards from the deep by the force of subterraneous fires, so did Brunhilda start from her earthy couch, borne forward by some invisible power. Taking her by the hand, the sorcerer led her towards Walter, who stood at some little distance rooted to the ground with amazement.

"Receive again," said he, "the object of thy passionate sighs. Mayest thou never more require my aid; should that however happen, so wilt thou find me during the full of the moon, upon the mountains in that spot where the three roads meet."

Instantly did Walter recognize in the form that stood before him her whom he so ardently loved; and a sudden glow shot through his frame at finding her thus restored to him: yet the night-frost had chilled his limbs and palsied his tongue. For a while he gazed upon her without either motion or speech, and during this pause all again became hushed and serene; and the stars shone brightly in the clear heavens.

"Walter!" exclaimed the figure; and at once the well-known sound, thrilling to his heart, broke the spell by which he was bound.

"Is it reality? Is it truth," cried he, "or a cheating delusion?"

"No, it is no imposture. I am really living. Conduct me quickly to thy castle in the mountains."

Walter looked around. The old man had disappeared, but he perceived close by his side a coal-black steed of fiery eye, ready equipped to conduct him thence. On his back lay all proper attire for Brunhilda who lost no time in arraying herself. This being done, she cried: "Haste, let us away ere the drawn breaks, for my eye is yet too weak to endure the light of day."

Fully recovered from his stupor, Walter leaped into his saddle, and spurred on across the wild, towards the mountains as furiously as if pursued by the shadows of the dead hastening to recover from him their sister.

The castle to which Walter conducted his Brunhilda was situated on a rock between other rocks rising up above it. Here they arrived unseen by any save one aged domestic, on whom Walter imposed secrecy by the severest threats.

"Here will we tarry," said Brunhilda, "until I can endure the light, and until thou canst look upon me without trembling as if struck with a cold chill."

They accordingly continued to make that place their abode, yet no one knew that Brunhilda existed save only that aged attendant who provided their meals. During seven entire days they had no light except that of tapers; during the next seven, the light was admitted through the lofty casements only while the rising or setting sun faintly illumined the mountain tops—the valleys being still enveloped in shade.

Seldom did Walter quit Brunhilda's side. A nameless spell seemed to attach him to her—even the shudder which he felt in her presence, and which would not permit him to touch her, was not unmixed with pleasure like that thrilling, awesome emotion felt when strains of sacred music float under the vault of some temple. He rather sought, therefore, than avoided this feeling. Never till now had her voice sounded with such tones of sweetness; never before did her language possess such eloquence as it now did when she conversed with him on the subject of the past. And this was the magic fairy-land towards which her words constantly conducted him. Ever did she dwell upon the days of their first love, those hours of delight in which they had participated together when the one derived all enjoyment from the other; and so rapturous, so enchanting, so full of life did she recall to his imagination that blissful season, that he never doubted whether he had ever experienced with her so much felicity, or had been so truly happy. And, while she thus vividly portrayed their hours of past delight, she delineated in still more glowing, more enchanting colors, those hours of approaching bliss which now awaited them—richer in enjoyment than any preceding ones. In this manner did she charm her attentive auditor with enrapturing hopes for the future, and lull him in dreams of more than mortal ecstasy; so that while he listened to her siren strain he entirely forgot how little blissful was the latter period of their union when he had often sighed at her imperiousness, and at her harshness both to himself and to his household. Yet even had he recalled this to mind would it have disturbed him in his present delirious trance? Had she not now left behind in the grave all the frailty of mortality? Was she not cheerful as the morning hour in spring—affectionate and mild as the last beams of an autumnal sun?

In this manner had twice seven days elapsed, and, for the first time, Walter beheld the being now dearer to him than ever in the full light of day. Every trace of the grave had disappeared from her countenance; a roseate tinge like the ruddy streaks of dawn again beamed on her pallid cheek; the faint, mouldering taint of the grave was changed into a delightful violet scent—the only sign of earth that never disappeared. He no longer felt either apprehension or awe as he gazed upon her in the sunny light of day. It was not until now that he seemed to have recovered her completely; and, glowing with all his former passion towards her, he would have pressed her to his bosom, but she gently repulsed him, saying: "Not yet. Spare your caresses until the moon has again filled her horn."

Despite his impatience, Walter was obliged to await the lapse of another period of seven days; but on the night when the moon was arrived at the full he hastened to Brunhilda, whom he found more lovely than she had ever appeared before. Fearing no obstacles to his transports, he embraced her with all the fervor of a deeply enamored and successful lover. Brunhilda, however, still refused to yield to his passion. "What!" exclaimed she, "is it fitting that I who have been purified by death from the frailty of mortality should become thy concubine, while a mere daughter of the earth bears the title of thy wife? Never shall it be. No, it must be within the walls of thy palace, within that chamber where I once reigned as queen, that thou obtainest the end of thy wishes—and of mine also," she added, imprinting a glowing kiss on his lips, and immediately withdrew.

Heated with passion, and determined to sacrifice everything to the accomplishment of his desires, Walter hastily quitted the apartment, and, shortly after, the castle itself. He travelled over mountain and across heath with the rapidity of a storm, so that the turf was flung up by his horse's hoofs; nor once stopped until he arrived home.

Here, however, neither the affectionate caresses of Swanhilda or those of his children could touch his heart, or induce him to restrain his furious desires. Alas, is the impetuous torrent to be checked in its devastating course by the beauteous flowers over which it rushes? The stream sweeps over them unregarding, and in a single moment annihilates the pride of a white summer.

Shortly afterwards did Walter begin to hint to Swanhilda that they were ill-suited to each other—that he was anxious to taste that wild, tumultuous life so well according with the spirit of his sex, while she, on the contrary, was satisfied with the monotonous cycle of household routine—that he was eager for whatever promised novelty, while she felt most attached to what was familiarized to her by habit—and lastly, that her cold disposition, bordering upon indifference, ill assorted with his ardent temperament. It was therefore more prudent that they should seek apart from each other that happiness which they could not realize together.

A sigh and a brief acquiescence to his wishes was all the reply that Swanhilda made. On the following morning he presented her with a paper of separation, informing her that she was at liberty to return home to her father. She received it most submissively; yet, ere she departed, she gave him the following warning: "Too well do I conjecture to whom I am indebted for this our separation. Often have I seen thee at Brunhilda's grave, and beheld thee there even on that night when the face of the heavens was suddenly enveloped in a veil of clouds. Hast thou rashly dared to tear aside the awful veil that separates the mortality that dreams from that which dreameth not, O, then woe to thee, thou wretched man, for thou hast attached to thyself that which will prove thy destruction." She ceased; nor did Walter attempt any reply, for the similar admonition uttered by the sorcerer flashed upon his mind, all obscured as it was by passion, just as the lightning glares momentarily through the gloom of night without dispersing the obscurity.

Swanhilda then departed, first pronouncing to her children a tearful farewell, for they—according to the custom of the nation—belonged to the father, quitted her husband's residence, and returned to the home of her father.

Thus was the kind and benevolent Swanhilda driven an exile from those halls where she had presided with such grace—from halls which were now newly decorated to receive another mistress.

The day at length arrived on which Walter, for the second time, conducted Brunhilda home as a newly made bride. And he caused it to be reported among the domestics that his new consort had gained his affections by her extraordinary likeness to Brunhilda, their former mistress. How ineffably happy did he deem himself as he conducted his beloved once more into the chamber which had often witnessed their former joys, and which was now newly gilded and adorned in a most costly style. Figures of angels scattering roses decorated the purple draperies whose ample folds o'ershadowed the nuptial couch. With what impatience did he await the hour that was to put him in possession of those joys for which he had already paid so high a price, but whose consummation was to cost him most dearly yet.

Happy however, as Walter now was, his household were far from being equally so. The strange resemblance between their new lady and the deceased Brunhilda filled them with a secret dismay—an undefinable horror; for there was not a single difference of feature, tone of voice, or gesture. To add too to these mysterious circumstances, her female attendants discovered a particular mark on her back exactly like one which Brunhilda had. A report was now circulated that their lady was no other than Brunhilda herself, who had been recalled to life by the power of necromancy. How truly horrible was the idea of living under the same roof with one who had been an inhabitant of the tomb, and of being obliged to attend upon her, and acknowledge her as mistress! There was also in Brunhilda much to increase this aversion and favor their superstition. No ornaments of gold ever decked her person. All that others were wont to wear of this metal, she had formed of silver. No richly colored and sparkling jewels glittered upon her; pearls alone lent their pale luster to adorn her bosom. Most carefully did she always avoid the cheerful light of the sun, and was wont to spend the brightest days in the most retired and gloomy apartments. Only during the twilight of the commencing or declining day did she ever walk abroad. But her favorite hour was when the phantom light of the moon bestowed on all objects a shadowy appearance, and a sombre hue. Always too at the crowing of the cock an involuntary shudder was observed to seize her limbs.

Imperious as before her death, she quickly imposed her iron yoke on everyone around her, while she seemed even far more terrible than ever, since a dread of some supernatural power attached to her appalled all who approached her. A malignant withering glance seemed to shoot from her eye on the unhappy object of her wrath, as if it would annihilate its victim. In short, those halls which, in the time of Swanhilda were the residence of cheerfulness and mirth, now resembled an extensive desert tomb. With fear imprinted on their pale countenances, the domestics glided through the partments of the castle; and in this abode of terror there was no one save Walter who but shuddered at meeting her in a lonely place in the dusk of evening, or by the light of the moon. So great was the apprehension of her female attendants that they pined in continual disquietude, and, by degrees, all quitted her. In the course of time even others of the domestics fled, for an insupportable horror had seized them.

The art of the sorcerer had indeed bestowed upon Brunhilda an artificial life, and due nourishment had continued to support the restored body; yet, this body was not able of itself to keep up the genial glow of vitality, and to nourish the flame whence springs all the affections and passions— whether of love or hate—for death had forever destroyed and withered it: all that Brunhilda now possessed was a chilled existence, colder than that of the snake. It was nevertheless necessary that she should love, and return with equal ardor the warm caresses of her spell-enthralled husband, to whose passion alone she was indebted for her renewed existence. It was necessary that a magic draught should animate the dull current in her veins, and awaken her to the glow of life and the flame of love; a potion of abomination—one not even to be named without a curse—human blood imbibed whilst yet warm from the veins of youth. This was the hellish drink for which she thirsted.

Possessing no sympathy with the purer feelings of humanity, deriving no enjoyment from aught that interests in life and occupies its varied hours, her existence was a mere blank unless when in the arms of her paramour husband, and therefore was it that she craved incessantly after the horrible draught. It was with the utmost effort that she could forbear sucking even the blood of Walter himself as he reclined beside her. Whenever she beheld some innocent child whose lovely face denoted the exuberance of infantile health and vigor, she would entice it by soothing words and fond caresses into her most secret apartment, where lulling it to sleep in her arms, she would suck from its bosom the warm, purple tide of life. Nor were youths of either sex safe from her horrid attack. Having first breathed upon her unhappy victim, who never failed to sink immediately into a lengthened sleep, she would then in a similar manner drain his veins of the vital juice. Thus children, youths, and maidens quickly faded away, as flowers gnawed by the cankering worm: the fullness of their limbs disappeared; a sallow hue succeeded to the rosy freshness of their cheeks; the liquid luster of the eye was deadened; and their locks became thin and grey, as if already ravaged by the storm of life. The grave swallowed up one after the other or did the miserable victim survive, he became cadaverous and wrinkled even in the very morn of existence. Parents observed with horror this devastating pestilence snatch away their offspring—a pestilence which no herb however potent, nor charm, nor holy taper, nor exorcism could avert. They either beheld their children sink one after the other into the grave, or their youthful forms, withered by the unholy vampire embrace of Brunhilda, assume the decrepitude of sudden age.

At length strange surmises and reports began to prevail. It was whispered that Brunhilda herself was the cause of all these horrors, although no one could pretend to tell in what manner she destroyed her victims, since no marks of violence were discernible. Yet when young children confessed that she had frequently lulled them asleep in her arms, and elder ones said that a sudden slumber had come upon them whenever she began to converse with them, suspicion became converted into certainty; and those whose offspring had hitherto escaped unharmed, quitted their hearths and home in order to rescue from so horrible a fate those who were dearer to their simple affections than aught else the world could give.

Thus did the castle daily assume a more desolate appearance; daily did its environs become more deserted. None but a few aged, decrepit old women and grey-headed menials were to be seen remaining of the once numerous retinue. Such will, in the latter days of the earth, be the last generation of mortals, when child-bearing shall have ceased, when youth shall no more be seen, nor any arise to replace those who shall await their fate in silence.

Walter alone noticed not, or heeded not, the desolation around him. He apprehended not death, lapped as he was in a glowing elysium of love. Far more happy than formerly did he now seem in the possession of Brunhilda. All those caprices and frowns which had been wont to overcloud their former union had now entirely disappeared. She even seemed to dote on him with a warmth of passion that she had never exhibited even during the happy season of bridal love; for the flame of that youthful blood—of which she drained the veins of others—rioted in her own. At night, as soon as he closed his eyes, she would breathe on him till he sank into delicious dreams from which he awoke only to experience more rapturous enjoyments. By day she would continually discourse with him on the bliss experienced by happy spirits beyond the grave, assuring him that, as his affection had recalled her from the tomb, they were now irrevocably united. Thus fascinated by a continual spell, it was not possible that he could perceive what was taking place around him. Brunhilda, however, foresaw with savage grief that the source of her youthful ardour was daily decreasing, for, in a short time, there remained nothing gifted with youth save Walter and his children, and these later she resolved should be her next victims.

On her first return to the castle, she had felt an aversion towards the offspring of another, and therefore abandoned them entirely to the attendants appointed by Swanhilda. Now, however, she began to pay considerable attention to them, and caused them to be frequently admitted into her presence. The aged nurses were filled with dread at perceiving these marks of regard from her towards their young charges, yet dared they not to oppose the will of their terrible and imperious mistress. Soon did Brunhilda gain the affection of the children, who were too unsuspecting of all guile to apprehend any danger from her; on the contrary, her caresses won them completely to her. Instead of ever checking their mirthful gambols, she would rather instruct them in new sports. Often too did she recite to them tales of such strange and wild interest as to exceed all the stories of their nurses. Were they wearied either with play or with listening to her narratives, she would take them on her knees and lull them to slumber. Then did visions of the most surpassing magnificence attend their dreams. So delightful did these dreams in short time become to the children, that they longed for nothing so eagerly as to slumber on Brunhilda's lap, for never did they else enjoy such visions of heavenly forms. Thus were they most anxious for that which was to prove their destruction.

These innocents stretched out their arms to approaching death, for while they were lapped in these ecstatic slumbers, Brunhilda sucked the life-stream from their bosoms. On waking, indeed, they felt themselves faint and exhausted, yet did no pain nor take any mark betray the cause. Shortly, however, did their strength entirely fail, even as the summer brook is gradually dried up. Their sports became less and less noisy; their loud, frolicksome laughter was converted into a faint smile; the full tones of their voices died away into a mere whisper. Their attendants were filled with horror and despair. Too well did they conjecture the dreadful truth, yet dared not to impart their suspicions to Walter, who was so devotedly attached to his horrible partner. Death had already smote his prey: the children were but the mere shadows of their former selves, and even this shadow quickly disappeared.

The anguished father deeply bemoaned their loss, for, notwithstanding his apparent neglect, he was strongly attached to them, nor until he had experienced their loss was he aware that his love was so great. His affliction could not fail to excite the displeasure of Brunhilda: "Why dost thou lament so fondly," said she, "for these little ones? What satisfaction could such unformed beings yield to thee, unless thou wert still attached to their mother? Thy heart then is still hers? Say is thy spirit so lumpish, or thy love so weak, or thy faith so hollow, that the hope of being mine forever is unable to touch thee?" Thus did Brunhilda express her indignation at her consort's grief, and forbade him her presence. The fear of offending her beyond forgiveness and his anxiety to appease her soon dried up his tears; and he again abandoned himself to his fatal passion until approaching destruction at length awakened him from his delusion.

Neither maiden, nor youth, was any longer to be seen either within the dreary walls of the castle or the adjoining territory. All had disappeared, for those whom the grave had not swallowed up had fled from the region of death. Who, therefore, now remained to quench the horrible thirst of the female vampire, save Walter himself? And his death she dared to contemplate unmoved; for that divine sentiment that unites two beings in one joy and one sorrow was unknown to her bosom. Was he in his tomb, so would she be free to search out other victims, and glut herself with destruction until she herself should, at the last day, be consumed with the earth itself.

She now began to fix her blood-thirsty lips on Walter's breast when, cast into a profound sleep by the odor of her violet breath, he reclined beside her quite unconscious of his impending fate. Soon did his vital powers begin to decay, and many a grey hair peeped through his raven locks. With his strength, his passion also declined; and he now frequently left her in order to pass the whole day in the sports of the chase, hoping thereby to regain his wonted vigor.

As he was reposing one day in a wood beneath the shade of an oak, he perceived on the summit of a tree a bird of strange appearance, and quite unknown to him; but before he could take aim at it with his bow it flew away into the clouds, at the same time letting fall a rose-colored root which dropped at Walter's feet. He immediately took it up, and, although he was well acquainted with almost every plant, he could not remember to have seen any at all resembling this. Its delightfully odoriferous scent induced him to try its flavor; but ten times more bitter than wormwood, it was as gall in his mouth. Impatient of the disappointment, he flung it away with violence. Had he, however, been aware of its miraculous quality, and that it acted as a countercharm against the opiate perfume of Brunhilda's breath, he would have blessed it in spite of its bitterness. Thus do mortals often blindly cast away in displeasure the unsavory remedy that would otherwise work their weal.

When Walter returned home in the evening, and laid him down to repose as usual by Brunhilda's side, the magic power of her breath produced no effect upon him; and, for the first time during many months did he close his eyes in a natural slumber. Yet hardly had he fallen asleep, ere a pungent, smarting pain disturbed him from his dreams; and, opening his eyes, he discerned by the gloomy rays of a lamp that glimmered in the apartment, what for some moments transfixed him quite aghast: for it was Brunhilda, drawing with her lips the warm blood from his bosom. The wild cry of horror which at length escaped him terrified Brunhilda, whose mouth was besmeared with the warm blood. "Monster!" exclaimed he, springing from the couch, "is it thus that you love me?"

"Aye, even as the dead love," replied she with a malignant coldness.

"Creature of blood," continued Walter, "the delusion which has so long blinded me is at an end: thou art the fiend who has destroyed my children— who has murdered the offspring of my vassals."

Raising herself upwards, and, at the same time, casting on him a glance that froze him to the spot with dread, she replied: "It is not I who have murdered them—I was obliged to pamper myself with warm youthful blood in order that I might satisfy thy furious desires—thou art the murderer!" These dreadful words summoned before Walter's terrified conscience the threatening shades of all those who had thus perished; while despair choked his voice. "Why," continued she in a tone that increased his horror, "why doest thou make mouths at me like a puppet? Thou who hadst the courage to love the dead—to take into thy bed one who had been sleeping in the grave, the bedfellow of the worm—who hast clasped in thy lustful arms the corruption of the tomb. Dost thou, unhallowed as thou art, now raise this hideous cry for the sacrifice of a few lives? They are but leaves swept from their branches by a storm. Come, chase these idiot fancies, and taste the bliss thou has so dearly purchased." So saying, she extended her arms towards him; but this motion served only to increase his terror, and exclaiming: "Accursed being," he rushed out of the apartment.

All the horrors of a guilty, upbraiding conscience became his companions now that he was awakened from the delirium of his unholy pleasures. Frequently did he curse his own obstinate blindness for having given no heed to the hints and admonitions of his children's nurses, but treating them as vile calumnies. But his sorrow was now too late, for, although repentance may gain pardon for the sinner, it cannot alter the immutable decrees of fate—it cannot recall the murdered from the tomb. No sooner did the first break of dawn appear, than he set out for his lonely castle in the mountains, determined no longer to abide under the same roof with so loathsome a being. Yet vain was his flight, for, on waking the following morning, he perceived himself in Brunhilda's arms, and quite entangled in her long raven tresses which seemed to involve him and bind him in the fetters of his fate; the powerful fascination of her breath held him still more captivated so that, forgetting all that had passed, he returned her caresses until awakening as if from a dream, he recoiled in unmixed horror from her embrace. During the day he wandered through the solitary wilds of the mountains, as a culprit seeking an asylum from his pursuers; and, at night, retired to the shelter of a cave, fearing less to couch himself within such a dreary place than to expose himself to the horror of again meeting Brunhilda. But, alas, it was in vain that he endeavored to flee her. Again, when he awoke, he found her the partner of his miserable bed. Nay, had he sought the center of the earth as his hiding place; had he even imbedded himself beneath rocks, or formed his chamber in the recesses of the ocean, still had he found her his constant companion; for, by calling her again into existence, he had rendered himself inseparably hers— so fatal were the links that united them.

Struggling with the madness that was beginning to seize him, and brooding incessantly on the ghastly visions that presented themselves to his horror-stricken mind, he lay motionless in the gloomiest recesses of the woods from the rise of sun till the shade of eve. But, no sooner was the light of day extinguished in the west and the woods buried in impenetrable darkness, than the apprehension of resigning himself to sleep drove him forth among the open mountains. The storm played wildly with the fantastic clouds. It roared among the summits of the oaks as if uttering a voice of fury, while its hollow sound, rebounding among the distant hills, seemed as the moans of a departing sinner, or as the faint cry of some wretch expiring under the murderer's hand. Walter's hair flew disorderly in the wind like black snakes wreathing around his temples and shoulders, while each sense was awake to catch fresh horror. In the clouds he seemed to behold the forms of the murdered; in the howling wind to hear their laments and groans; in the chilling blast itself he felt the dire kiss of Brunhilda; in the cry of the screeching bird he heard her voice; in the mouldering leaves he scented the charnelbed out of which he had awakened her. "Murderer of thy own offspring," exclaimed he in a voice making night and the conflict of the elements still more hideous, "paramour of a bloodthirsty vampire, reveler with the corruption of the tomb!" while in his despair he rent the wild locks from his head. Just then the full moon darted from beneath the bursting clouds; and this sight recalled to his mind the advice of the sorcerer when he trembled at the first apparition of Brunhilda rising from her sleep of death—namely, to seek him at the season of the full moon in the mountains where three roads met. Scarcely had this gleam of hope broke in on his bewildered mind than he flew to the appointed spot.

On his arrival, Walter found the old man seated there upon a stone as calmly as though it had been a bright, sunny day, and completely oblivious of the uproar around. "Art thou come then?" exclaimed he to the breathless wretch who, flinging himself at his feet, cried in a tone of anguish: "Oh save me—succor me—rescue me from the monster that scattereth death and desolation around her."

"I am acquainted with all," returned the sorcerer; "Thou now perceivest how wholesome was the advice—WAKE NOT THE DEAD."

"And wherefore a mere mysterious warning? Why didst thou not rather disclose to me at once all the horrors that awaited my sacrilegious profanation of the grave?"

"Wert thou able to listen to any other voice than that of thy impetuous passions? Did not thy eager impatience shut my mouth at the very moment I would have cautioned thee?"

"True, true: thy reproof is just. But what does it avail now—I need the promptest aid."

"Well," replied the old man, "there remains even yet a means of rescuing thyself, but it is fraught with horror, and demands all thy resolution."

"Utter it then, utter it; for what can be more appalling, more hideous than the misery I now endure?"

"Know then," continued the sorcerer, "that only on the night of the new moon does she sleep the sleep of mortals; and then all the supernatural power which she inherits from the grave totally fails her. 'Tis then that thou must murder her."

"How? Murder her!" echoed Walter.

"Aye," returned the old man calmly, "pierce her bosom with a sharpened dagger which I will furnish thee with; at the same time renounce her memory forever, swearing never to think of her intentionally, and that, if thou dost involuntarily, thou wilt repeat the curse."

"Most horrible! Yet what can be more horrible than what she herself is? I'll do it."

"Keep then this resolution until the next new moon."

"What, must I wait until then?" cried Walter. "Alas, ere then either her savage thirst for blood will have forced me into the night of the tomb, or horror will have driven me into the night of madness."

"Nay," replied the sorcerer, "that I can prevent"; and, so saying, he conducted him to a cavern further among the mountains. "Abide here twice seven days," said he, "so long can I protect thee against her deadly caresses. Here wilt thou find all due provision for thy wants; but take heed that nothing tempt thee to quit this place. Farewell. When the moon renews itself, then do I repair hither again." The sorcerer then drew a magic circle around the cave, and disappeared into the darkness beyond.

Twice seven days did Walter continue in this solitude where his companions were his own terrifying thoughts and his bitter repentance. The present was all desolate and dead; the future presented the image of a horrible deed which he must perforce commit, while the past was empoisoned by the memory of his guilt. Did he think on his former happy union with Brunhilda, her horrible image presented itself to his imagination with her lips defiled with dropping blood; or, did he call to mind the peaceful days he had passed with Swanhilda, he beheld her sorrowful spirit in the shadows of her murdered children. Such were the horrors that attended him by day. Those of night were still more dreadful, for then he beheld Brunhilda herself, who, wandering round the magic circle which she could not pass, called upon his name till the cavern re-echoed the horrible sound. "Walter, my beloved," cried she, "wherefore dost thou avoid me? Art thou not mine forever—mine here, and mine hereafter? And doest thou seek to murder me? Ah! commit not a deed which hurls us both to perdition— thyself as well as me." In this manner did the horrible visitant torment him each night, and, even when she departed, robbed him of all repose.

The night of the new moon at length arrived, dark as the deed it was doomed to bring forth. The sorcerer entered the cavern; "Come," said he to Walter, "let us depart hence, the hour is now arrived." And he forthwith conducted him in silence to a coal-black steed, the sight of which recalled to Walter's remembrance the fatal night. He then related to the old man Brunhilda's nocturnal visits, and anxiously inquired whether her apprehensions of eternal perdition would be fulfilled or not. "Mortal eye," exclaimed the sorcerer, "may not pierce the dark secrets of another world, or penetrate the deep abyss that separates earth from heaven." Walter hesitated to mount the steed. "Be resolute," exclaimed his companion, "but this once is it granted to thee to make the trial, and, should thou fail now, nought can rescue thee from her power."

"What can be more than the abominations she inflicted I am determined." And he leaped on the horse; the sorcerer mounting also behind him.

Carried with a rapidity equal to that of the storm that sweeps across the plain, they in brief space arrived at Walter's castle. All the doors flew open at the bidding of his companion, and they speedily reached Brunhilda's chamber, and stood beside her couch. Reclining in a tranquil slumber, she reposed in all her native loveliness. Every trace of horror had disappeared from her countenance. She looked so pure, meek and innocent that all the sweet hours of their endearments rushed to Walter's memory like interceding angels pleading in her behalf. His unnerved hand could not take the dagger which the sorcerer presented to him. "The blow must be struck now," said the latter, "shouldst thou delay but an hour, she will die at day-break on thy bosom, sucking the warm life-drops from thy heart."

"Horrible! Most horrible!" faltered the trembling Walter, and turning away his face, he thrust the dagger into her bosom, exclaiming: "I curse thee forever!" and the cold blood gushed upon his hand. Opening her eyes once more she cast a look of ghastly horror on her husband, and in a hollow dying accent said: "Thou too art doomed to perdition."

"Lay now thy hand upon her corpse," said the sorcerer, "and swear the oath."

Walter did as he commanded, saying: "Never will I think of her with love, never recall her to mind intentionally, and, should her image recur to my mind involuntarily, so will I exclaim to it: be thou accursed."

"Thou hast now done everything," returned the sorcerer, "restore her therefore to the earth from which thou so foolishly recalled her; and be sure to recollect thy oath, for, shouldst thou forget it but once, she would return and thou wouldst be inevitably lost. Adieu: we see each other no more." Having uttered these words he quitted the apartment and Walter also fled from this abode of horror, having first given directions that the corpse should be speedily interred.

Again did Brunhilda repose within her grave; but her image continually haunted Walter's imagination, so that his existence was one continued martyrdom in which he incessantly struggled to dismiss from his recollection the hideous phantoms of the past. Yet, the stronger his effort to banish them, so much the more frequently and the more vividly did they return, as the night-wanderer, who is enticed by a fire-wisp into quagmire or bog, sinks the deeper into his damp grave the more he struggles to escape. His imagination seemed incapable of admitting any other image than that of Brunhilda. Now he fancied he beheld her expiring, the blood streaming from her beautiful bosom; at other times he saw the lovely bride of his youth, reproaching him with having disturbed the slumbers of her tomb; and to both he was compelled to utter the dreadful words, "I curse thee forever." The terrible imprecation was constantly passing his lips, yet he was in constant terror lest he should forget it, or dream of her without being able to repeat it, and then, on awaking, find himself in her arms. Else would he recall her expiring words, and, appalled at their terrific import, imagine that the doom of his perdition was irrecoverably passed. Whence should he fly from himself, or how erase from his brain these images and forms of horror?

At length, after many a weary and fruitless wandering he returned to his castle. Here all was deserted and silent, as if the sword or a still more deadly pestilence had laid everything to waste, for the few inhabitants that still remained, and even those servants who had once shown themselves the most attached, now fled from him as though he had been branded with the mark of Cain. With horror he perceived that, by uniting himself as he had with the dead, he had cut himself off from the living. Stripped of all earthly hope, bereft of every consolation, he was rendered as poor as mortal can possibly be on this side of the grave.

Riding through the forest in the neighborhood of his castle, absorbed in his gloomy meditations, the sudden sound of a horn roused him from his reverie. Shortly after he saw appear a female figure clad in black, and mounted on a steed of the same color. Her attire was like that of a huntress, but, instead of a falcon, she bore a raven on her hand; and she was attended by a gay troop of cavaliers and dames. The first salutations being passed, he found that she was proceeding on the same road as himself; and, when she found that Walter's castle was close at hand, she requested that he would lodge her for that night, the evening being far advanced. Most willingly did he comply with this request since the appearance of the beautiful stranger had struck him greatly—so wonderfully did she resemble Swanhilda, except that her locks were brown, and her eye dark and full of fire. With a sumptuous banquet did he entertain his guests, whose mirth and songs enlivened the lately silent halls.

Three days did revelry continue, and so exhilarating did it prove to Walter that he seemed to have forgotten his sorrows and his fears; nor could be prevail upon himself to dismiss his visitors, dreading lest on their departure the castle would seem a hundred times more desolate than before, and his grief be proportionately increased. At his earnest request, the stranger consented to stay seven days, and again another seven days. Without being requested, she took upon herself the superintendence of the household, which she regulated as discreetly and cheerfully as Swanhilda had been wont to do, so that the castle, which had so lately been the abode of melancholy and horror, became the residence of pleasure and festivity, while Walter's grief disappeared altogether in the midst of so much gaiety.

Daily did his attachment to the fair unknown increase; he even made her his confidante; and, one evening as they were walking together apart from any of her train, he related to her his melancholy and frightful history.

"My dear friend," returned she, as soon as he had finished his tale, "it ill beseems a man of thy discretion to afflict thyself on account of all this. Thou hast awakened the dead from the sleep of the grave, and afterwards found what might have been anticipated—that the dead possess no sympathy with life. What then? Thou wilt not commit this error a second time. Thou hast however murdered the being thou had thus recalled again into existence—but it was only in appearance, for thou couldst not deprive that of life which properly had none. Thou hast too lost a wife and two children; but, at your years, such a loss is most easily repaired. There are beauties who will gladly share your couch, and make you a father again. But you dread the reckoning of hereafter. Go open the graves and ask the sleepers there whether that hereafter disturbs them." In such manner would she frequently exhort and cheer Walter, and so successful were her efforts, that in a short time his melancholy entirely disappeared.

He now ventured to declare to the unknown the passion with which she had inspired him, nor did she refuse him her hand. Within seven days afterwards the nuptials were celebrated with the utmost magnificence.

With the first dawn of day commenced the labors of those who were busied in preparing the festival; ad, if the walls of the castle had often echoed before to the sounds of mirth and revelry, the very foundations now seemed to rock from the wild tumultuous uproar of unrestrained riot. The wine streamed in abundance; the goblets circled incessantly; intemperance reached its utmost bounds, while shouts of laughter almost resembling madness burst from the numerous train belonging to the unknown.

At length Walter, heated with wine and love, conducted his bride into the nuptial chamber. But scarcely had he clasped her in his arms, ere she transformed herself into a monstrous serpent, which, entwining him in its horrid folds, crushed him to death. Flames crackled on every side of the apartment. In a few minutes after the whole castle was enveloped in a blaze that consumed it entirely; while, as the walls fell in with a horrid crash, a voice exclaimed aloud— "WAKE NOT THE DEAD."

THE FATE OF MADAME CABANEL

The unfortunate lady was an Englishwoman and therefore an outsider among the superstitious peasants of Brittany. Eliza Lynn Linton (1822-1898) in her story here, first published in 1880, shows how the vampire superstition and the provinciality of some people can lead to mob violence against anyone who is thought to be strange. In our own time the vampire has been linked to many kinds of outsiders and many alienated people have turned to this myth for self-identification and the outraging of the Establishment.

Progress had not invaded, science had not enlightened, the little hamlet of Pieuvrot, in Brittany. They were a simple, ignorant, superstitious set who lived there, and the luxuries of civilization were known to them as little as its learning. They toiled hard all the week on the ungrateful soil that yielded them but a bare subsistence in return; they went regularly to mass in the little rock-set chapel on Sundays and saints' days; believed implicitly all that *Monsieur le curé* said to them, and many things which he did not say; and they took all the unknown, not as magnificent, but as diabolical.

The sole link between them and the outside world of mind and progress was Monsieur Jules Cabanel, the proprietor, par excellence, of the place; *maire* [mayor], *juge de paix* [justice of the peace], and all the public functionaries rolled into one. And he sometimes went to Paris whence he returned with a cargo of novelties that excited envy, admiration, or fear, according to the degree of intelligence in those who beheld them.

Monsieur Jules Cabanel was not the most charming man of his class in appearance, but he was generally held to be a good fellow at bottom. A short, thickset, low-browed man, with blue-black hair cropped close like a mat, as was his blue-black beard, inclined to obesity and fond of good living, he had need have some virtues behind the bush to compensate for his want of personal charms. He was not bad, however; he was only common and unlovely.

Up to fifty years of age he had remained the unmarried prize of the surrounding country; but hitherto he had resisted all the overtures made by maternal fowlers, and had kept his liberty and his bachelorhood intact. Perhaps his handsome housekeeper, Adèle, had something to do with his persistent celibacy. They said she had, under their breath as it were, down at *la Veuve Prieur's* [the Widow Prieur's]; but no one dared to so much as hint the like to herself. She was a proud, reserved kind of woman; and had strange notions of her own dignity which no one cared to disturb. So, whatever the underhand gossip of the place might be, neither she nor her master got wind of it.

Presently and quite suddenly, Jules Cabanel, who had been for a longer time than usual in Paris, came home with a wife. Adèle had only twenty-four hours' notice to prepare for this strange home-coming; and the task seemed heavy. But she got through it in her old way of silent determination; arranged the rooms as she knew her master would wish them to be arranged; and even supplemented the usual nice adornments by a voluntary bunch of flowers on the salon table.

"Strange flowers for a bride," said to herself little Jeannette, the goose-girl who was sometimes brought into the house to work, as she noticed heliotrope—called in France *la fleur des veuves* [the flower of widows]—scarlet poppies, a bunch of belladonna, another of aconite—scarcely, as even ignorant little Jeannette said, flowers of bridal welcome or bridal significance. Nevertheless, they stood where Adèle had placed them; and if Monsieur Cabanel meant anything by the passionate expression of disgust with which he ordered them out of his sight, madame seemed to understand nothing, as she smiled with that vague, half-deprecating look of a person who is assisting at a scene of which the true bearing is not understood.

Madame Cabanel was a foreigner, and an Englishwoman; young, pretty and fair as an angel.

"*La beauté du diable*," [the beauty of The Devil] said the Pieuvrotines, with something between a sneer and a shudder; for the words meant with them more than they mean in ordinary use. Swarthy, ill-nourished, low of stature and meagre in frame as they were themselves, they could not understand the plump form, tall figure and fresh complexion of the Englishwoman. Unlike their own experience, it was therefore more likely to be evil than good. The feeling which had sprung up against her at first sight deepened when it was observed that, although she went to mass with praiseworthy punctuality, she did not know her missal and signed herself *à travers* [in reverse]. *La beauté du diable*, in faith!

"*Pouf!*" said Martin Briolic, the old gravedigger of the little cemetery; "with those red lips of hers, her rose cheeks and her plump shoulders, she looks like a vampire and as if she lived on blood."

He said this one evening down at *la Veuve Prieur's*; and he said it with an air of conviction that had its weight. For Martin Briolic was reputed the wisest man of the district; not even excepting *Monsieur le curé* who was wise in his own way, which was not Martin's—nor Monsieur Cabanel who was wise in his, which was neither Martin's nor the *curé's*. He knew all about the weather and the stars, the wild herbs that grew on the plains and the wild shy beasts that eat them; and he had the power of divination and could find where the hidden springs of water lay far down in the earth when he held the *baguette* [dowsing rod] in his hand. He knew too, where treasures could be had on Christmas Eve if only you were quick and brave enough to enter the cleft in the rock at the right moment and come out again before too late; and he had seen with his own eyes the White Ladies dancing in the moonlight; and the little imps, the Infins, playing their prankish gambols by the pit at the edge of the wood. And he had a shrewd suspicion as to who, among those black-hearted men of La Crèche-en-bois—the rival hamlet—was a *loupgarou* [werewolf], if ever there was one on the face of the earth and no one had doubted that! He had other powers of a yet more mystic kind; so that Martin Briolic's bad word went for something, if, with the illogical injustice of ill-nature, his good went for nothing.

Fanny Campbell, or, as she was now, Madame Cabanel, would have excited no special attention in England, or indeed anywhere but at such a dead-alive, ignorant, and consequently gossiping place as Pieuvrot. She had no romantic secret as her background; and what history she had was commonplace enough, if sorrowful too in its own way. She was simply an orphan and a governess; very young and very poor; whose employers had quarrelled with her and left her stranded in Paris, alone and almost moneyless; and who had married Monsieur Jules Cabanel as the best thing she could do for herself. Loving no one else, she was not difficult to be won by the first man who showed her kindness in her hour of trouble and destitution; and she accepted her middle-aged suitor, who was fitter to be her father than her husband, with a clear conscience and a determination to do her duty cheerfully and faithfully—all without considering herself as a martyr or an interesting victim sacrificed to the cruelty of circumstances. She did not know, however, of the handsome housekeeper Adèle, nor of the housekeeper's little nephew—to whom the master was so kind that he allowed him to live at the Maison Cabanel and had him well taught by the *curé*. Perhaps if she had she would have thought twice before she put herself under the same roof with a woman who for a bridal bouquet offered her poppies, heliotrope and poison-flowers.

If one had to name the predominant characteristic of Madame Cabanel it would be easiness of temper. You saw it in the round, soft, indolent lines of her face and figure; in her mild blue eyes and placid, unvarying smile; which irritated the more petulant French temperament and especially disgusted Adèle. It seemed impossible to make madame angry or even to make her understand when she was insulted, the housekeeper used to say with profound disdain; and, to do the woman justice, she did not spare her endeavours to enlighten her. But madame accepted all Adèle's haughty reticence and defiant continuance of mistresshood with unwearied sweetness; indeed, she expressed herself gratified that so much trouble was taken off her hands, and that Adèle so kindly took her duties on herself.

The consequences of this placid lazy life, where all her faculties were in a manner asleep, and where she was enjoying the reaction from her late years of privation and anxiety, was, as might be expected, an increase in physical beauty that made her freshness and good condition still more remarkable. Her lips were redder, her cheeks rosier, her shoulders plumper than ever; but as she waxed, the health of the little hamlet waned, and not the oldest inhabitant remembered so sickly a season, or so many deaths. The master too suffered slightly; the little Adolphe desperately.

This failure of general health in undrained hamlets is not uncommon in France or in England; neither is the steady and pitiable decline of French children; but Adèle treated it as something out of all the liens of normal experience; and, breaking her habits of reticence spoke to every one quite fiercely of the strange sickliness that had fallen on Pieuvrot and the Maison Cabanel; and how she believed it was something more than common; while as to her little nephew, she could give neither a name nor find a remedy for the mysterious disease that had attacked him. There were strange things among them, she used to say; and Pieuvrot had never done well since the old times were changed. Jeannette used to notice how she would sit gazing at the English lady, with such a deadly look on her handsome face when she turned from the foreigner's fresh complexion and grand physique to the pale face of the stunted, meagre, fading child. It was a look, she said afterwards, that used to make her flesh get like ice and creep like worms.

One night Adèle, as if she could bear it no longer, dashed down to where old Martin Briolic lived, to ask him to tell her how it had all come about—and the remedy.

"Hold, Ma'am Adèle," said Martin, as he shuffled his greasy tarot cards and laid them out in triplets on the table; "there is more in this than one sees. One sees only a poor little child become suddenly sick; that may be, is it not so? and no harm done by man? God sends sickness to us all and makes my trade profitable to me. But the little Adolphe has not been touched by the Good God. I see the will of a wicked woman in this. *Hein!*" Here he shuffled the cards and laid them out with a kind of eager distraction of manner, his withered hands trembling and his mouth uttering words that Adèle could not catch. "Saint Joseph and all the saints protect us!" he cried; "the foreigner—the Englishwoman—she whom they call Madame Cabanel—no rightful madame she!—Ah, misery!"

"Speak, Father Martin! What do you mean!" cried Adèle, grasping his arm. Her black eyes were wild; her arched nostrils dilated; her lips, thin, sinuous, flexible, were pressed tight over her small square teeth.

"Tell me in plain words what you would say!"

"*Broucolaque!*" [Vampire] said Martin in a low voice.

"It is what I believed!" cried Adèle. "It is what I knew. Ah, my Adolphe! woe on the day when the master brought that fair-skinned devil home!"

"Those red lips don't come by nothing, Ma'am Adèle," cried Martin nodding his head. "Look at them—they glisten with blood! I said so from the beginning; and the cards, they said so too. I drew 'blood' and a 'bad fair woman' on the evening when the master brought her home, and I said to myself, 'Ha, ha, Martin! you are on the track, my boy— on the track. Martin!'—and, Ma'am Adèle, I have never left it! *Broucolaque*! that's what the cards say, Ma'am Adèle. Vampire. Watch and see; watch and see; and you'll find that the cards have spoken true."

"And when we have found, Martin?" said Adèle in a hoarse whisper.

The old man shuffled his cards again. "When we have found, Ma'am Adèle?" he said slowly. "You know the old pit out there by the forest?— the old pit where the lutins [spirits] run in and out, and where the White Ladies wring the necks of those who come upon them in the moonlight? Perhaps the White Ladies [monsters] will do as much for the English wife of Monsieur Cabanel; who knows?"

"They may," said Adèle, gloomily.

"Courage, brave woman!" said Martin. "They will."

The only really pretty place about Pieuvrot was the cemetery. To be sure there was the dark gloomy forest which was grand in its own mysterious way; and there was the broad wide plain where you might wander for a long summer's day and not come to the end of it; but these were scarcely places where a young woman would care to go by herself; and for the rest, the miserable little patches of cultivated ground, which the peasants had snatched from the surrounding waste and where they had raised poor crops, were not very lovely. So Madame Cabanel, who, for all the soft indolence that had invaded her, had the Englishwoman's inborn love for walking and fresh air, haunted the pretty little graveyard a good deal. She had no sentiment connected with it. Of all the dead who laid there in their narrow coffins, she knew none and cared for none; but she liked to see the pretty little flower-beds and the wreaths of immortelles, and the like; the distance too, from her own home was just enough for her; and the view over the plain to the dark belt of forest and the mountains beyond, was fine.

The Pieuvrotines did not understand this. It was inexplicable to them that any one, not out of her mind, should go continually to the cemetery—not on the day of the dead and not to adorn the grave of one she loved—only to sit there and wander among the tombs, looking out on to the plain and the mountains beyond when she was tired.

"It was just like—" The speaker, one Lesouëf, had got so far as this, when he stopped for a word.

He said this down at *la Veuve Prieur's* where the hamlet collected nightly to discuss the day's small doings, and where the main theme, ever since she had come among them, three months ago now, had been Madame Cabanel and her foreign ways and her wicked ignorance of her mass-book and her wrong-doings of a mysterious kind generally, interspersed with jesting queries, banded from one to the other, of how Ma'am Adèle liked it?—and what would become of *le petit* [little] Adolphe when the rightful heir appeared?—some adding that *monsieur* was a brave man to shut up two wild cats under the same roof together; and what would become of it in the end? Mischief of a surety.

"Wander about the tombs just like what, Jean Lesouëf?" said Martin Briolic. Rising, he added in a low but distinct voice, every word falling clear and clean: "I will tell you like what, Lesouëf—like a vampire! *La femme* [the woman] Cabanel has red lips and red cheeks; and Ma'am Adèle's little nephew is perishing before your eyes. *La femme* Cabanel has red lips and red cheeks; and she sits for hours among the tombs. Can you read the riddle, my friends? For me it is as clear as the blessed sun."

"Ha, Father Martin, you have found the word—like a vampire!" said Lesouëf with a shudder.

"Like a vampire!" they all echoed with a groan.

"And I said vampire the first," said Martin Briolic. "Call to mind I said it from the first."

"Faith! and you did," they answered; "and you said true."

So now the unfriendly feeling that had met and accompanied the young Englishwoman ever since she came to Pieuvrot had drawn to a focus. The seed which Martin and Adèle had dropped so sedulously had at last taken root; and the Pieuvrotines would have been ready to accuse of atheism and immorality any one who had doubted their decision, and had declared that pretty Madame Cabanel was only a young woman with nothing special to do, a naturally fair complexion, superb health—and no vampire at all, sucking the blood of a living child or living among the tombs to make the newly buried her prey.

The little Adolphe grew paler and paler, thinner and thinner; the fierce summer sun told on the half-starved dwellers within those foul mud-huts surrounded by undrained marshes; and Monsieur Jules Cabanel's former solid health followed the law of the rest. The doctor, who lived at Crèche-en-bois, shook his head at the look of things; and said it was grave. When Adèle pressed him to tell her what was the matter with the child and with *monsieur*, he evaded the question; or gave her a word which she neither understood nor could pronounce. The truth was, he was a credulous and intensely suspicious man; a viewy man who made theories and then gave himself to the task of finding them true. He had made the theory that Fanny was secretly poisoning both her husband and the child; and though he would not give Adèle a hint of this, he would not set her mind at rest by a definite answer that went on any other line.

As for Monsieur Cabanel, he was a man without imagination and without suspicion; a man to take life easily and not distress himself too much for the fear of wounding others; a selfish man but not a cruel one; a man whose own pleasure was his supreme law and who could not imagine, still less brook, opposition or the want of love and respect for himself. Still, he loved his wife as he had never loved a woman before. Coarsely moulded, common-natured as he was, he loved her with what strength and passion of poetry nature had given him; and if the quantity was small, the quality was sincere. But that quality was sorely tried when—now Adèle, now the doctor—hinted mysteriously, the one at diabolical influences, the other at underhand proceedings of which it behoved him to be careful, especially careful what he eat and drank and how it was prepared and by whom; Adèle adding hints about the perfidiousness of English women and the share which the devil had in fair hair and brilliant complexions. Love his young wife as he might, this constant dropping of poison was not without some effect. It told much for his steadfastness and loyalty that it should have had only so small effect.

One evening, however, when Adèle, in an agony, was kneeling at his feet—madame had gone out for her usual walk—crying: "Why did you leave me for such as she is?—I, who loved you, who was faithful to you and she who walks among the graves, who sucks your blood and our child's—she who has only the devil's beauty for her portion and who loves you not?"—something seemed suddenly to touch him with electric force.

"Miserable fool that I was!" he said, resting his head on Adèle's shoulders and weeping. Her heart leapt with joy. Was her reign to be renewed? Was her rival to be dispossessed?

From that evening Monsieur Cabanel's manner changed to his young wife but she was too easy-tempered and unsuspicious to notice anything, or if she did, there was too little depth in her own love for him—it was so much a matter of untroubled friendliness only—that she did not fret but accepted the coldness and brusqueness that had crept into his manner as good-naturedly as she accepted all things. It would have been wiser if she had cried and made a scene and come to an open fracas with Monsieur Cabanel. They would have understood each other better; and Frenchmen like the excitement of a quarrel and a reconciliation.

Naturally kind hearted, Madame Cabanel went much about the village, offering help of various kinds to the sick. But no one among them all, not the very poorest—indeed, the very poorest the least—received her civilly or accepted her aid. If she attempted to touch one of the dying children, the mother, shuddering, withdrew it hastily to her own arms; if she spoke to the adult sick, the wan eyes would look at her with a strange horror and the feeble voice would mutter words in a patois she could not understand. But always came the same word, "*broucolaque!*"

"How these people hate the English!" she used to think as she turned away, perhaps just a little depressed, but too phlegmatic to let herself be uncomfortable or troubled deeply.

It was the same at home. If she wanted to do any little act of kindness to the child, Adèle passionately refused her. Once she snatched him rudely from her arms, saying as she did so: "Infamous *broucolaque*! before my very eyes?" And once, when Fanny was troubled about her husband and proposed to make him a cup of beef-tea *à l'Anglaise*, the doctor looked at her as if he would have looked through her; and Adèle upset the saucepan; saying insolently—but yet hot tears were in her eyes—"Is it not fast enough for you, madame? Not faster, unless you kill me first!"

To all of which Fanny replied nothing; thinking only that the doctor was very rude to stare so fixedly at her and that Adèle was horribly cross; and what an ill-tempered creature she was; and how unlike an English housekeeper!

But Monsieur Cabanel, when he was told of the little scene, called Fanny to him and said in a more caressing voice than he had used to her of late: "Thou wouldst not hurt me, little wife? It was love and kindness, not wrong, that thou wouldst do?"

"Wrong? What wrong could I do?" answered Fanny, opening her blue eyes wide. "What wrong should I do to my best and only friend?"

"And I am thy friend? thy lover? thy husband? Thou lovest me dear?" said Monsier Cabanel.

"Dear Jules, who is so dear; who so near?" she said kissing him, while he said fervently:

"God bless thee!"

The next day Monsieur Cabanel was called away on urgent business. He might be absent for two days, he said, but he would try to lessen the time; and the young wife was left alone in the midst of her enemies, without even such slight guard as his presence might prove.

Adèle was out. It was a dark, hot summer's night, and the little Adolphe had been more feverish and restless than usual all the day. Towards evening he grew worse; and though Jeannette, the goose-girl, had strict commands not to allow madame to touch him, she grew frightened at the condition of the boy, and when madame came into the small parlour to offer her assistance, Jeannette gladly abandoned a charge that was too heavy for her and let the lady take him from her arms.

Sitting there with the child in her lap, cooing to him, soothing him by a low, soft nursery song, the paroxysm of his pain seemed to her to pass and it was as if he slept. But in that paroxysm he had bitten both his lip and tongue; and the blood was now oozing from his mouth. He was a pretty boy; and his mortal sickness made him at this moment pathetically lovely. Fanny bent her head and kissed the pale still face—and the blood that was on his lips was transferred to hers.

While she still bent over him—her woman's heart touched with a mysterious force and prevision of her own future motherhood—Adèle, followed by old Martin and some others of the village, rushed into the room.

"Behold her!" she cried, seizing Fanny by the arm and forcing her face upwards by the chin—behold her in the act! Friends, look at my child—dead, dead in her arms; and she with his blood on her lips! Do you want more proofs? Vampire that she is, can you deny the evidence of your own senses?"

"No! no!" roared the crowd hoarsely. "She is a vampire—a creature cursed by God and the enemy of man; away with her to the pit. She must die as she has made others to die!"

"Die, as she has made my boy to die!" said Adèle; and more than one who had lost a relative or child during the epidemic echoed her words, "Die, as she has made mine to die!"

"What is the meaning of all this?" said Madame Cabanel, rising and facing the crowd with the true courage of an Englishwoman. "What harm have I done to any of you that you should come about me, in the absence of my husband, with these angry looks and insolent words?"

"What harm has thou done?" cried old Martin, coming close to her. "Sorceress as thou hast bewitched our good master; and vampire as thou art, thou nourishest thyself on our blood! Have we not proof of that at this very moment? Look at thy mouth—cursed *broucolaque;* and here lies thy victim, who accuses thee in his death!"

Fanny laughed scornfully, "I cannot condescend to answer such folly," she said lifting her head. "Are you men or children?"

"We are men, madame," said Legros the miller; "and being men we must protect our weak ones. We have all had our doubts—and who more cause that I, with three little ones taken to heaven before their time—and now we are convinced."

"Because I have nursed a dying child and done my best to soothe him!" said Madame Cabanel with unconscious pathos.

"No more words!" cried Adèle, dragging her by the arm from which she had never loosed her hold. "To the pit with her, my friends, if you would not see all your children die as mine has died—as our good Legros's have died!"

A kind of shudder shook the crowd; and a groan that sounded in itself a curse burst from them.

"To the pit!" they cried. "Let the demons take their own!"

Quick as though Adèle pinioned the strong white arms whose shape and beauty had so often maddened her with jealous pain; and before the poor girl could utter more than one cry Legros had placed his brawny hand over her mouth. Though this destruction of a monster was not the murder of a human being in his mind, or in the mind of any there, still they did not care to have their nerves disturbed by cries that sounded so human as Madame Cabanel's. Silent then, and gloomy, that dreadful cortège took its way to the forest, carrying its living load; gagged and helpless as if it had been a corpse among them. Save with Adèle and old Martin, it was not so much personal animosity as the instinctive self-defence of fear that animated them. They were executioners, not enemies; and the executioners of a more righteous law than that allowed by the national code. But one by one they all dropped off till their numbers were reduced to six; of whom Legros was one, and Lesouëf, who had lost his only sister, was also one.

The pit was not more than an English mile from the Maison Cabanel. It was a dark and lonesome spot, where not the gravest man of all that assembly would have dared to go alone after nightfall, not even if the *curé* had been with him; but a multitude gives courage, said old Martin Briolic; and half a dozen stalwart men, led by such a woman as Adèle, were not afraid of even lutins or the White Ladies.

As swiftly as they could for the burden they bore, and all in utter silence, the cortège strode over the moor; one or two of them carrying rude torches; for the night was black and the way was not without its physical dangers. Nearer and nearer they came to the fatal bourn; and heavier grew the weight of their victim. She had long ceased to struggle; and now lay as if dead in the hands of her bearers. But no one spoke of this or of aught else. Not a word was exchanged between them; and more than one, even of those left, began to doubt whether they had done wisely, and whether they had not better have trusted to the law. Adèle and Martin alone remained firm to the task they had undertaken; and Legros too was sure; but he was weakly and humanly sorrowful for the thing he felt obliged to do. As for Adèle, the woman's jealousy, the mother's anguish and the terror of superstition, had all wrought in her so that she would not have raised a finger to have lightened her victim of one of her pains, or have found her a woman like herself and no vampire after all.

The way got darker; the distance between them and their place of execution shorter; and at last they reached the border of the pit where this fearful monster, this vampire—poor innocent Fanny Cabanel—was to be thrown. As they lowered her, the light of their torches fell on her face.

"*Grand Dieu*! [Great God!]" cried Legros, taking off his cap; "she is dead!"

"A vampire cannot die," said Adèle, "it is only an appearance. Ask Father Martin."

"A vampire cannot die unless the evil spirits take her, or she is buried with a stake thrust through her body," said Martin Briolic sententiously.

"I don't like the look of it," said Legros; and so said some others.

They had taken the bandage from the mouth of the poor girl; and as she lay in the flickering light, her blue eyes half open; and her pale face white with the whiteness of death, a little return of human feeling among them shook them as if the wind had passed over them.

Suddenly they heard the sound of horses' hoofs thundering across the plain. They counted two, four, six; and they were now only four unarmed men, with Martin and Adèle to make up the number. Between the vengeance of man and the power and malice of the wood-demons, their courage faced and their presence of mind deserted them. Legros rushed frantically into the vague darkness of the forest; Lesouëf followed him; the other two fled over the plain while the horsemen came nearer and nearer. Only Adèle held the torch high above her head, to show more clearly both herself in her swarthy passion and revenge and the dead body of her victim. She wanted no concealment; she had done her work, and she gloried in it. Then the horsemen came plunging to them—Jules Cabanel the first, followed by the doctor and four *gardes champêtres* [forest guards].

"Wretches! murderers!" was all he said, as he flung himself form his horse and raised the pale face to his lips.

"Master," said Adèle, "she deserved to die. She is a vampire and she has killed our child."

"Fool!" cried Jules Cabanel, flinging off her hand. "Oh, my loved wife! thou who did no harm to man or beast, to be murdered now by men who are worse than beasts!"

"She was killing thee," said Adèle. "Ask *Monsieur le docteur*. What ailed the master, *monsieur*?"

"Do not bring me into this infamy," said the doctor looking up from the dead. "Whatever ailed *monsieur*, she ought not to be here. You have made yourself her judge and executioner, Adèle, and you must answer for it to the law."

"You say this too, master?" said Adèle.

"I say so too," returned Monsieur Cabanel. "To the law you must answer for the innocent life you have so cruelly taken—you and all the fools and murderers you have joined to you."

"And is there to be no vengeance for our child?"

"Would you revenge yourself on God, woman?" said Monsieur Cabanel sternly.

"And our past years of love, master?"

"Are memories of hate, Adèle," said Monsieur Cabanel, as he turned again to the pale face of his dead wife.

"Then my place is vacant," said Adèle, with a bitter cry. "Ah, my little Adolphe, it is well you went before!"

'Hold, Ma'am Adèle!" cried Martin.

But before a hand could be stretched out, with one bound, one shriek, she had flung herself into the pit where she had hoped to bury Madame Cabanel; and they heard her body strike the water at the bottom with a dull splash, as of something falling from a great distance.

"They can prove nothing against me, Jean," said old Martin to the *garde* who held him. "I neither bandaged her mouth nor carried her on my shoulders. I am the gravedigger of Pieuvrot, and, *ma foi* [my faith], you would all do badly, you poor creatures, when you die, without me! I shall have the honour of digging madame's grave, never doubt it; and, Jean," he whispered, "they may talk as they like, those rich aristos who know nothing.

She is a vampire, and she shall have a stake through her body yet! Who knows better than I? If we do not tie her down like this, she will come out of her grave and suck our blood; it is a way these vampires have."

"Silence there!" said the *garde*, commanding the little escort. "To prison with the assassins; and keep their tongues from wagging."

"To prison with martyrs and the public benefactors," retorted old Martin. "So the world rewards its best!"

And in this faith he lived and died, as a *forçat* [prisoner] at Toulon, maintaining to the last that he had done the world a good service by ridding it of a monster who else would not have left one man in Pieuvrot to perpetuate his name and race. But Legros and also Lesouëf, his companion, doubted gravely of the righteousness of that act of theirs on that dark summer's night in the forest; and though they always maintained that they should not have been punished, because of their good motives, yet they grew in time to disbelieve old Martin Briolic and his wisdom, and to wish that they had let the law take its own course unhelped by them—reserving their strength for the grinding of the hamlet's flour and the mending of the hamlet's *sabots* [shoes]—and the leading of a good life according to the teaching of *Monsieur le curé* and the exhortations of their own wives.

THE COFFIN LID

There is an old Russian folk tale that illustrates the belief in vampires in czarist times.

A peasant, stopping by a graveyard to rest his horse, let the horse loose to graze and himself lay down on a grave for a nap. Suddenly the grave beneath him began to move. He jumped up and hid himself and saw that out of the grave came a corpse, wrapped in a white shroud and carrying his coffin's lid. The corpse placed the coffin lid at the church door and went away.

The peasant took and hid the coffin lid and awaited the return of the corpse, who after a while came back.

"Give me my coffin lid or I shall tear you to pieces!"

"Look at my ax," replied the peasant. "I can cut you to pieces!"

"Please give me back my coffin lid," pleaded the corpse, now less arrogant.

"Tell me first where you have been and what you have been doing out of your grave."

"I have been in the village and have killed a couple of children," the corpse confessed.

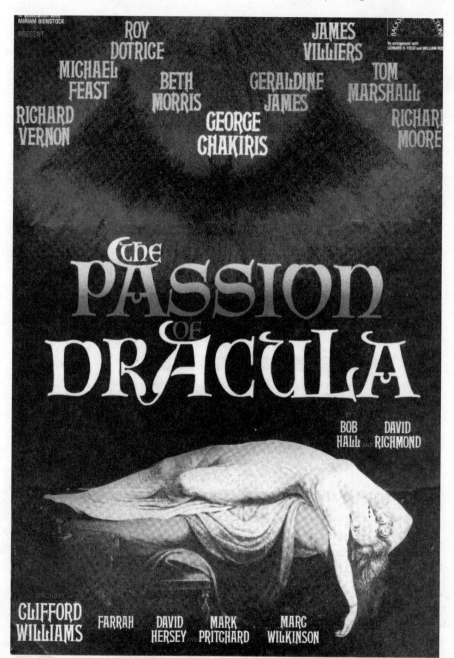

QUEENS THEATRE
SHAFTESBURY AVE. LONDON W1

"If you will tell me how they can be brought back to life and your evil deeds undone," said the peasant, "you can have your coffin lid back."

"Very well," said the corpse. "Cut off the left skirt of my shroud and take it to the house in the village where the dead children are. Put in the room with them a brazier of live coals, place the shroud on it to burn, and shut the door. The smoke will bring them back to life. Now give me back my coffin lid so I can go back into my grave."

The peasant cut a piece off the shroud, took it to the village, and did as he had been instructed. The children came back to life. But instead of thanking him the villagers said, "If you are able to bring them back to life, you may be the one who killed them!" And they were ready to turn him over to the authorities as a murderer.

So he told them the story and they went with him to the graveyard, opened the grave of the corpse in question, found him to be a vampire, and drove a stake into his heart.

Then the peasant was paid great honor and all the villagers rejoiced.

CHILD OF THE NIGHT

Remember *Rosemary's Baby*? Nancy Kilpatrick did. The author of the vampire novel *Near Death* must have thought its central idea too good not to copy and wrote *Child of the Night* (1996). Imitation is, they say, the sincerest form of flattery.

Carol Robin is an American on vacation in Bordeaux when she falls into the clutches of a vampire, who gets her pregnant. When the baby is born she is let go (her mind washed clean of memory) because she does not want to become a vampire. Nine years later, Carol sees a bottle of Bordeaux and the memories flood back. She tracks down the son she has lived without up until then. His name is Michel. (One might have guessed Bordeaux, because Margaux Hemingway was named for a bottle her parents enjoyed the night of her conception.)

Will her son be a vampire? Will Carol? Do you care? I mention this book only to suggest that in the UK (where the book was first printed) and in the US (where it was reprinted), both times by very minor presses, vampire books are constantly being ground out.

FROM *LA GUZLA* BY PROSPER MÉRIMÉE

One night, the two women of the house having left us alone about an hour since, and to avoid drinking, I was singing for my host a few songs of his native country when we were interrupted by horrible shrieks from the bedroom; normally there is only one in a house and everyone uses it.

We ran, armed, there and saw a frightful sight. The mother, pale and disheveled, was holding up her even paler daughter, who had fainted and was stretched out now on a pile of straw that was used as a bed. She cried, "A vampire! A vampire! My poor child is dead!"

The two of us managed to bring back [to consciousness] her poor [daughter] Kava. She had seen, she told us, the window open and a man, pale and swathed in cerements, [came in and] threw himself on her and bit her and tried to strangle her. When she managed to scream, the specter fled and she fainted.

Now, she had recognized as the vampire a man of the vicinity, dead over a fortnight and named Wieczany. She had a small red mark on her neck, but I cannot testify that if this was a natural mark or if some insect might have bitten her during her nightmare....

At dawn the entire village stirred. Men had armed themselves with guns and axes. Women carried red-hot irons. Children had sticks and stones. They went to the cemetery execrating the dead for injuries. I found it difficult to make my way through this enraged mob and to find a place near the grave [of Wieczany]....

Just as the shroud covering the body was lifted a terrifyingly piercing shriek made my hair stand on end. It came from a woman standing beside me: "He's a vampire! He has not been eaten by worms!" A hundred mouths took up the cry at once.

At the same moment twenty gunshots all fired together blew the head of the corpse to pieces, and the father and whole family of Kava struck at the body repeatedly with their long knives. The women mopped up with linen the red liquid that oozed from the mangled corpse so that they could apply it to the neck of the victim.

Then several young men dragged the body out of the grave and, despite the fact that it was riddled with wounds, took the precaution of tying it securely to the trunk of a pine; then they dragged it, all the children trailing after it, to a small orchard across from the house [of Kava]. There a pyre of faggots and straw had been built. They set it on fire and threw the corpse onto it and danced around and shouted each other down....

The neck of the victim was wrapped with the rags stained with the red and odorous liquid which they took for blood and which made a vivid contrast with the half bare throat and shoulders of the poor Kava.

La Guzla was inspired by Serbian poetry that Merimée knew. However, he actually created what he pretended was Serbian literature in this collection, which he said was discovered by an Italian and originally composed by Hyacinth Maglanovitch—a completely fictitious writer. The sensational pieces (all but one "translated" by Mérimée were so powerful that people were quite willing to accept this imposture and add *La Guzla* to Balkan folklore. This qualifies Mérimée to rank with important literary forgers such as Thomas Chatterton (who faked medieval poetry), "Ossian" (who faked old epics), William Ireland (who faked a passable "Shakespeare" play), and others nearer our day who had best be left unidentified.

LE MAGNOLIA

Rémy de Gourmont (1858-1915) was not only a leading critic who defended the decadence of Huysmans but the author who wrote a tale (in *Histoires magiques*, 1894) that dealt in decadent fancies. The heroine (Arabelle) marries an old man and the two are compared to a dying and a flourishing magnolia on a tree. He dies, and when Arabelle is supernaturally drawn to the tree the old man appears as terrible ghost: "the shadow extended its arms, arms which were fluid and sepentine, then let them fall, like two vipers from hell, onto her shoulders, where they writhed and hissed." Arabella, drained of her vital fluids, drops dead at the foot of the magnolia tree.

THÉOPHILE GAUTIER

Théophile Gautier (1811-1872) is much more famous than Gourmont. Gautier was hailed for *Mademoiselle de Maupin* (1835) but soon after he published a vampire tale, *La Morte amoureuse*, which deserves to be better known. It is the story of Clarimonde, who seduces and has an affair with a priest, but the priest's superiors discover this and also the fact that Clarimonde is a vampire.

This French master of the macabre also wrote "*Spirite*," in which Guy de Malivert has as his lover a woman who died for love of him and who communicates with him by means of automatic writing, all the rage at the time. Eventually Malivert is killed, in Greece, and is joined with his love. In *"Omphale"* a man falls in love with a woman, long dead, whose portrait he sees in an old tapestry. In *"Le Pied de momie"* a young man buys a mummy's foot as a curio, to use as a paperweight. There may be a touch of foot fetishism here. Anyway, the woman whose foot it is comes from the grave to claim it. In all of these stories the supernatural is eerily handled and the striking details of settings owe much to Gautier's first love, painting.

While American imitators of the nineteenth-century French writers, our heavyweights such as Poe and "O. Henry," tend to rely on ratiocination (leading to the detective story) and plot twists, Gautier and other masters of macabre moods and dark colors were not so taken up here. In the twentieth century, however, American Gothic in all media has captured a worldwide audience. Our modern horror writers are read worldwide. They offer even more *frissons* than did Gautier in his *"La Morte amoreuse."* Here's a bit from F. C. de Sumichrast's translation (1903) which gives the narrator, he says afterward, "strange doubts about Clarimonde":

> One day I was seated by her bed breakfasting at a small table, in order not to leave her a minute. As I pared the fruit I happened to cut a finger rather deeply. The blood immediately flowed in a purple stream, and a few drops fell on Clairimonda. Her eyes lighted up, her face assumed an expression of fierce and savage joy which I had never before beheld. She sprang from her bed with the agility of an animal...and sprang to my wound, which she began to suck with an air of inexpressible delight.... "I shall not die!" she said, half mad with joy.... I shall be able to love you a long time yet. My life is in yours, and all that I am comes from you. A few drops of your rich, noble blood, more precious and efficacious than all the elixirs in the world, have restored my life."

CHRISTINA ROSSETTI

Christina (1830-1894), sister of Dante Gabriel Rossetti, leading light of the Pre-Raphaelite movement in England, in "Goblin Market" (1862) gave proof of her fascination with the supernatural and she wrote poems such as "The House and the Ghost", "The Poor Ghost", and "The Ghost's Pension." She was consciously exploiting tried and true themes of German Romanticism. She did that with consummate skill. In America, German themes of the supernatural were also popular throughout the nineteenth century, but they tended here to be handled with less lightness of touch than Christina Rossetti could manage. Reading her, one thinks of speaking German and quaffing May wine. Reading the American authors who came under German influence, one thinks of guttural noises over a big meal of pork, potato pancakes, and red cabbage.

SYDNEY HORLER

Horler was an extremely prolific and often bestselling author of the first part of the twentieth century. A short extract from the middle of his book *The Vampire* (1935) will illustrate the sort of thing his reading public loved. Ziska is more demon than vampire.

The devil-worshipper, after looking round, advanced to two large standard lamps standing one on each side of the other end of the room, which he lit after a reverential obeisance to the altar. Then, crossing to the fireplace, which was surrounded by a handsome and massively carved mantelpiece, he pressed hard on one of the protuberances in the carving. Going now to one of the scarlet hangings, he pushed it aside, revealing a handleless door, also blood-red in colour, which opened to his touch, swinging to with a quiet click as he passed through into a second apartment.

This was even stranger in appearance than the one he had just left. It was a slightly smaller chamber, circular in shape, and opposite the door was a large window, heavily curtained in black. The whole of this second room, ceiling and walls, was draped in black, but in the centre was a large, low altar, and this was covered with blood-red material, around which the bare, uncarpeted floor was marked with dark, horrible-looking stains which could have been made only by one means—the shedding of blood. From the centre of the domed black roof hung a magnificently jewelled bronze lamp, which burned with a bluish flame and shed a dim, sulphurous light around.

Between the altar and the window, painted red on the floor, was a large five-pointed star with a small bronze lamp at each point. Within the star were several curiously shaped phials.

Apart from these, the only other article in this second room was a long, low, carved oak chest, obviously very old. Stepping over to this, Ziska drew from it a scarlet robe closely resembling the cope of a priest. Donning this garment, he stepped, after a low obeisance to the altar, inside the space formed by the star. Around himself he drew, with a finger moistened with the contents of one of the phials, a pentagon. He then lit the lamps at the points of the stars, and these burned with a tiny blue flame. Sprinkling the floor at his feet with the contents of the second phial, he began to mutter a monotonous incantation, the while making strange signs with his hands. Almost immediately the flames from the lamps leapt up and burned brightly, gradually forming a complete circle of bluish flame, whilst the flare from the hanging lamp grew dimmer and dimmer. Over the altar a tiny cloud appeared, which by degrees at last assumed a monstrous, unearthly, and yet half-human shape.

Ziska fell to his knees as the shape continued to materialize, worshipping it with wild and abominable words.

The Thing approached close to the devil-worshipper. From it came a half-whisper.

"What has *thou* brought me here for, Ziska? What wouldst thou?"

"O great and mighty one, I beg thy help. I wish thee to aid me."

"Say thy desire, Ziska."

"My desire is to compel a man named Martin Kent to come to this house, where he can be held prisoner, and so I may get my vengeance. I promise to sacrifice him here in this room on the great festival of the New Moon."

"Is that all thy desire?"

"That is all my desire."

The shape emitted a low, evil chuckle.

"So be it, Ziska! Farewell."

In the unearthly silence that followed, the dreadful thing slowly began to disappear.

A deep sigh escaped from Ziska's lips. After making one more obeisance to the altar, he stepped out of the pentagon and stars, the lamps of which had gone out as the shape disappeared, and, laying the red cope reverently on the altar, he knelt before it.

Taking a third phial, he sprinkled his head with the contents, once more muttering an incantation.

Horror—ghastly and unbelievable to the uninitiated—followed: from the Baron's shoulders there emerged a hump which grew and grew until it revealed itself as a pair of huge, bat-like wings. Standing up, Ziska fluttered these once or twice, and then crossed to the window, which opened at his touch. He looked intently at the moon and the flickering lights of London.

"Martin Kent, I come for thee," he whispered—and then, his face convulsed, he stepped out on to the sill.

The next moment Ziska the Vampire had flown out into the darkness of the night.

A LIBRARY OF OCCULT FICTION

This is, of course, a challenging judgment call but I venture to recommend above all others this list in which you will recognize a lot of famous names. I do not separate ghost stories and vampire tales here nor short stories from longer ones. I want you to see the vampire tale in the context of the genre of occult fiction. I even include Stephen Leacock's sharp send-up of the genre and all types of tales.

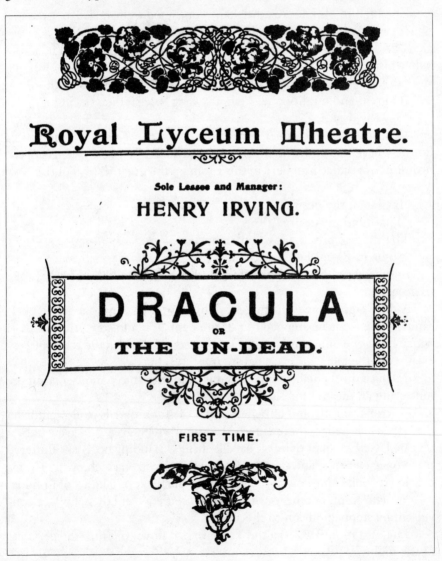

Robert Aikman, "Ringing the Changes"
Peter Allan, "Domdaniel"
Woody Allen, "Count Dracula"
Michael Arlen, "The Ghoul of Golder's Green"
M. R. S. Andrews, "Dundonald's Destroyer"
Enid Bagnold, "The Amorous Ghost"
J. Kendrick Bangs, "The Water Ghost of Harrowby Hall"
Sabine Baring-Gould, "A Dead Finger"
_____, "The Room in the Tower"
E. F. Benson, "Mrs. Amworth"
Ambrose Bierce, "Cold Greeting"
Algernon Blackwood, "The Empty House"
Robert Bloch, "The Hungry House"
Elizabeth Bowen, "The Cheery Soul"
Ray Bradbury, "The Man Upstairs"
Mary Elizabeth Braddon, "Good Lady Ducayne"
Elizabeth Bowen, "Green Holly"
"M. Bowen," "The Avenging of Ann Leete"
Charlotte Brontë, "Napoleon and the Spectre"
William Cullen Bryant, "Indian Spring"
Donn Byrne, "Mrs. Dutton Intervenes"
Sir A. Caldecott, "Authorship Disputed"
G. K. Chesterton, "Vampire of the Village"
Irving S. Cobb, "The Second Coming of a First Husband"
Wilkie Collins, "The Ghost's Touch"
A. E. Coppard, "Adam and Eve and Pinch Me"
F. Marion Crawford, "The Blood is the Life"
"Clemence Dane," "Spinster's Rest"
M. P. Dare, "Unholy Relics"
Walter de la Mare, "Seaton's Aunt"
August W. Derleth, "Just a Song at Twilight"
Charles Dickens, "The Signal-Man"
C. C. Dobie, "Elder Brother"
Sir Arthur Conan Doyle, "Lot No. 249"
Edward, Lord Dunsany, "The Haunting of Halahanstown"
Lawrence Durrell, "Carnival"
Mary E. Wilkins Freeman, "The Gentle Ghost"
R. A. Freeman, "The Apparition of Burling Court"
Jane Gardam, "The Meeting House"
Elizabeth Gaskell, "The Old Nurse's Story"

Théophile Gautier, "*La Morte amoreuse*"
J. Gloag, "Lady without Appetite"
"Maxim Gorki," "The Story of a Novel"
C. I. M. Graves, "The Cost of Wings"
Sir H. Rider Haggard, "Only a Dream"
Knut Hamsun, "An Apparition"
Thomas Hardy, "Withered Arm"
Bret Harte, "A Child's Ghost Story"
L. P. Hartley, "Travelling Grave"
Nathaniel Hawthorne, "The Gray Champion"
Lafcadio Hearn, "Shriyō"
James Hogg, "The Mysterious Bridge"
Elizabeth Jane Howard, "Three Miles Up"
Robert E. Howard, "The Horror from the Mound"
William Dean Howells, "His Apparition"
Robert Thurston Hopkins, "The Vampire of Woolpit Grange"
L. L. Hynd, "A Vampire"
W. E. Ingersoll, "The Centenarian"
Washington Irving, "The Adventure of the German Student"
C. Jacobi, "Revelations in Black"
Henry James, "The Turn of the Screw"
Montague Rhodes James, "The Thin Ghost"
W. W. Jacobs, "The Monkey's Paw"
Rudyard Kipling, "They"
Heinrich v. Kleist, "The Beggar Woman of Locarno"
Owen Lattimore, "Ghosts of Wulakai"
Stephen Leacock, "Buggam Grange"
"Vernon Lee," "Oke of Okehurst"
Joseph Sheridan LeFanu, "The Ghost and the Bone-Setter"
_____, "Schalken the Painter"
Penelope Lively, "Revenant as Typewriter"
F. B. Long, "It Will Come to You"
H. P. Lovecraft and August W. Derleth, "The Survivor"
Alison Lurie, "The Highboy"
Edward, Lord Lytton, "The Haunted and the Haunters"
Arthur Machan, "Munitions of War"
John Mansfield, "Ghosts"

Don Marquis, "Too American"
Richard Matheson, "The Funeral"
Guy de Maupassant, "*La Horla*"
André Maurois, "The House"
R. H. Middleton, "On the Brighton Road"
Kálmán Mikszáth, "Fiddlers Three"
P. Morand, "Chinese Phantoms"
William Morris, "The Lovers"
Arthur Morrison, "Chamber of Light"
Jan Neruda, "The Vampire"
Charles Nodier, "*Inès de las Sierras*"
F. J. O'Brien, "What Was It?"
Margaret Wilson Oliphant, "The Open Door"
R. C. O'Neill, "The Lady and the Ghost"
Oliver Onions, "The Beckoning Fair One"
Thomas Nelson Page, "No Haid Pawn"
Barry Pain, "Not on the Passenger List"
Elia Wilkinson Peattie, "From the Loom of the Dead"
E. Peirce, "The Doom of the House of Duryea"
Eden Phillpotts, "Grimm's Ghost"
Luigi Pirandello, "The Haunted House"

Pliny, "The Haunted House"
Edgar Allan Poe, "Berenice"
T. F. Powys, "I Came as a Bride"
Sir Arthur Quiller-Couch, "The Haunted Yacht"
Simon Raven, "Chriseis"
Victor Roman, "Four Wooden Stakes"
A. L. Rowse, "All Souls' Night"
Alan Ryan, "Baby's Blood"
"Saki," "Laura"
Sir Walter Scott, "The Tapestried Chamber"
Mary Shelley, "The Transformation"
William Gilmore Simms, "Carl Werner"
Lady Eleanor Furneaux Smith, "Satan's Circus"
Evelyn E. Smith, "Softly, While You're Sleeping"
Eric, Count Stenbock, "The True Story of a Vampire"
Robert Louis Stevenson, "Thrawn Janet"
Frank R. Stockton, "The Transferred Ghost"
Bram Stoker, "The Judge's House"
Harriet Beecher Stowe, "Tom Toothacher's Ghost Story"
Sir Rabindrinath Tagore, "The Hungry Stones"
James Thurber, "The Night the Ghost Got In"
Johann Ludwig v. Tieck, "Wake Not the Dead"
J. R. R. Tolkein, "Riddles in the Dark"
Ivan Turgenev, "Apparitions"
"Mark Twain," "Ghost Story"
Peter Underwood, "The Italian Count"
A. E. Van Vogt, "Asylum"
H. Russell Wakefield, "The Seventeenth Hole at Duncaster"
Sir Hugh Walpole, "Mrs. Lunt"
H. G. Wells, "The Inexperienced Ghost"
Eudora Welty, "The Purple Hat"
Edith Wharton, "Afterward"
Oscar Wilde, "The Canterville Ghost"
Virginia Woolf, "The Haunted House"
Alexander Woolcott, "Full Fathom Five"
P. C. Wren, "Fear"
"S, Ex-Private," "Smee"
Israel Zangwill, "The Double-Barrelled Ghost"
Arnold Zweig, "An Apparition"

Paper cover of the first French translation of *Dracula* ("The Man of the Night"). Paris 1920.

and

Anon., *Ghost Stories. Collected with a Particular View to Counteract the Vulgar Belief in Ghosts and Apparitions* (1823, reprinted 1865)

H. Addington Bruce, *Historic Ghosts and Ghost Hunters* (1908)

John Canning, *Fifty Great Ghost Stories* (1966)

Michael Cox, *The Oxford Book of Twentieth-Century Ghost Stories* (1996)

Christopher Frayling, *The Vampire: A Bedside Companion* (1978)

Joseph Lewis French, *Great Ghost Stories* (1918)

Peter Haining, *Great Tales of Terror from Europe and America* (1973)

————, *Vampire: Chilling Tales of the Undead* (1985)

Sharon Jarvis, *True Tales of the Uninvited* (1989)

Alexander Lang, *Great Ghost Stories of the World* (1939)

Geoffrey Palmer and Noël Lloyd, *Ghost Stories Round the World* (1965)

"Leslie Shepard," *The Dracula Book of Great Vampire Stories* (1977)

Richard "Red" Skelton, *A Red Skeleton in Your Closet* (1965)

Andrew Tackaberry, *Famous Ghosts, Phantoms, and Poltergeists for the Millions* (1966)

Devendra P. Varma, *Voices from the Vaults* (1987)

Ornella Volta & Valeria Riva, *The Vampire: An Anthology* (1963)

Here are some more classic ghost-story collections (and the number of stories in each) by Cynthia Asquith (*Ghost Book*, 16), John Kendrick Bangs (*Ghosts I Have Met*, 7), Sabine Baring-Gould (*White Flag*, 21), Algernon Blackwood (*The Empty House*, 10), V. H. Collins (*Ghosts and Marvels*, 15, and *More Ghosts and Marvels*, 20), R. A. Cram (*Black Spirits and White*, 6), H. Dale (*Great Ghost Stories*, 15), W. D. Howells and H. M. Alden (*Shapes that Haunt the Dusk*, 10), Montague Rhodes James (*Collected Ghost Stories*, 31), Boris Karloff (*And the Darkness Falls*, 59), J. G. B. Lynch (*Best Ghost*

Stories, 10), Elia W. Peattie (*The Shape of Fear*, 13), E. H. Sechrist (*Thirteen Ghostly Yarns*), M. Sinclair (*Uncanny Stories*, 7), Edward Charles Wagenknecht (*The Fireside Book of Ghost Stories*, 41), etc. Don't miss regional collections such as those from August House in Arkansas (W. K. McNeil's *Ghost Stories from the American South*, 1985, and Richard Alan Young and Judy Dockery Young's *Ghost Stories from the American Southwest*, 1991), collections about your town or county (such as Gail White's *Haunted San Diego*, 1992), and the collections devoted to various ethnic groups (such as Donald M. Hynes's *Ghost Voices*, 1992, which deals with the Yakima Indian traditions).

Frank Simon of the San José Public Library compiled a useful *Ghost Story Index* of thousands of stories in nearly 200 books (1967). Thirty years later, as I write, it is time for that list to be brought up to date on the Internet.

The pop media of a much earlier day were the broadside and the chapbook sold in the streets. This is a very specialized source now of the ghost, poltergeist, and vampire literature—the haunt of scholars, you might say. Items would include the likes of the typically anonymous and sensational *Ghosts! Spectres! Apparitions!* This is, as you surely realize, exactly the same kind of pap you see peddled on television in the 1990s by entertainers who claim to have "X files" or "hard copy" or the inside poop on the "strange universe."

MORE UNDEAD

No dates this time, because you probably won't be able to find old books like these. Harvey's, for instance, is unclear as to date anyway; I'd guess the mid-forties. But if you do manage to find one of these, congratulations:

Rosemary Ellen Guiley, *Vampires Among Us*
Peter Haining, *The Midnight People*
Gerald Harvey, *Vampires and Grave-Robbers*
Eric Held, *Vampire Information Exchange Bibliography*
Carol Page, *Bloodlust: Conversations with Real Vampires*
Paul Monette, *Nosferatu, The Vampire*
Henry Steel Olcott, *The Vampire*
Gabriel Ronay, *The Dracula Myth*
"Leslie Shepard," *The Dracula Book of Great Vampire Stories*
Ted Tiller, *Count Dracula*
Leonard Wolf, *The Essential Dracula*
Jeanne Youngson, *The Further Perils of Dracula*

LITTLE THEATRE

JOHN STREET, ADELPHI, STRAND

Licensed by the Lord Chamberlain to JOSÉ G. LEVY   Lessee: JOSÉ G. LEVY

MONDAY, FEBRUARY 14th, at 8.30

By arrangement with JOSÉ G. LEVY and HENRY MILLAR

HAMILTON DEANE and H. L. WARBURTON

PRESENT

THE VAMPIRE PLAY

"DRACULA"

By

HAMILTON DEANE

Adapted from BRAM STOKER'S Famous Novel

PROGRAMME

A London theatre program, 14 February 1927.

SOME VAMPIRE FICTION OF THE SEVENTIES, EIGHTIES, AND NINETIES

This is a select list (not all items are select in the sense of good quality, though it begins, alphabetically, with the first-rate science-fiction writer Brian W. Aldiss). It will give you some inkling of the vampire industry today. This clutch demonstrates great variety. You do not need, I trust, to be introduced to Anne Rice, creator of *The Vampire Lestat*, Stephen King of *Salem's Lot*, or "The Canadian Anne Rice" Nancy Baker of *The Night Inside*.

Brian W. Aldiss, *Dracula Unbound* (1991)
Amanda Ashley, *Empire of the Night* (1995)
"Stephen Brett," *The Vampire Chase* (1979)
Poppy Z. Brite, *Lost Souls* (1992)
Kurt Brokaw, *A Night in Transylvania* (1976)
Virginia Coffman, *The Vampire of Moura* (1970)
Larry Cohen, *A Return to Salem's Lot* (1987)
Dark Shadows Book of Vampires and Werewolves (1970)
Jewelle Gomez, *The Gilda Stories* (1991)
Laurell K. Hamilton, *Guilty Pleasures* (1993)
Jeanne Kalogridis, *Covenant with a Vampire* (1994)
Lee Killough, *Blood Hunt* (1987)
Briam Lumley, *Bloodwars* (1994)
George R. R. Martin, *Fevre Dream* (1982)
Robert R. McCammon, *They Thirst* (1986)
Christopher Moore, *Bloodsucking Fiends* (1995)
Kim Newman, *Anno Dracula* (1993)
Michael Romkey, *I, Vampire* (1984)
Lucius Shepard, *The Golden* (1993)
Dan Simmons, *Carrion Comfort* (1989)
Whitley Streiber, *The Hunger* (1981)
Michael Talbot, *The Delicate Dependency* (1982)
F. Paul Wilson, *The Keep* (1981)
Chelsea Quinn Yarbro, *Hotel Transylvania* (1977)

THE ROOM IN THE TOWER

E[dward]. F[rederic] Benson (1867-1940) wrote more than 90 books, most notably humor. His Lucia has created a cult, and there are numerous admirers of his Dodo, who preceded the inimitable Lucia. Here is Benson's most famous vampire story. It is no laughing matter.

It is probable that everybody who is at all a constant dreamer has had at least one experience of an event or a sequence of circumstances which have come to his mind in sleep being subsequently realized in the material world. But, in my opinion, so far from this being a strange thing, it would be far odder if this fulfillment did not occasionally happen, since our dreams are, as a rule, concerned with people whom we know and places with which we are familiar, such as might very naturally occur in the awake and daylit world. True, these dreams are often broken into by some absurd and fantastic incident, which puts them out of course in regard to their subsequent fulfillment, but on the mere calculation of chances, it does not appear in the least unlikely that a dream imagined by anyone who dreams constantly should occasionally come true. Not long ago, for instance, I experienced such a fulfillment of a dream which seems to me in no way remarkable and to have no kind of physical significance. The manner of it was as follows.

A certain friend of mine, living abroad, is amiable enough to write to me about once in a fortnight. Thus, when fourteen days or thereabouts have elapsed since I last heard from him, my mind, probably, either consciously or subconsciously, is expectant of a letter from him. One night last week I dreamed that as I was going upstairs to dress for dinner I heard, as I often heard, the sound of the postman's knock on my front door, and diverted my direction downstairs instead. There, among other correspondence, was a letter from him. Thereafter the fantastic entered, for on opening it I found inside the ace of diamonds, and scribbled across it in his well-known handwriting, "I am sending you this for safe custody, as you know it is running an unreasonable risk to keep aces in Italy." The next evening I was just preparing to go upstairs to dress when I heard the postman's knock, and did precisely as I had done in my dream. There, among other letters, was one from my friend. Only it did not contain the ace of diamonds. Had it done so, I should have attached more weight to the matter, which, as it stands, seems to me a perfectly ordinary coincidence. No doubt I consciously or subconsciously expected a letter from him, and this suggested to me my dream. Similarly, the fact that my friend had not written to me for a fortnight suggested to him that he should do so. But occasionally it is not so easy to find such an explanation, and for the following story I can find no explanation at all. It came out of the dark, and into the dark it has gone again.

All my life I have been a habitual dreamer: the nights are few, that is to say, when I do not find on awaking in the morning that some mental experience has been mine, and sometimes, all night long, apparently, a series of the most dazzling adventures befall me. Almost without exception these adventures are pleasant, though often merely trivial. It is of an exception that I am going to speak.

It was when I was about sixteen that a certain dream first came to me, and this is how it befell. It opened with my being set down at the door of a big red-brick house, where, I understood, I was going to stay. The servant who opened the door told me that tea was going on in the garden, and led me through a low dark-panelled hall, with a large open fireplace, on to a cheerful green lawn set round with flower beds. There were grouped about the tea-table a small party of people, but they were all strangers to me except one, who was a school-fellow called Jack Stone, clearly the son of the house, and he introduced me to his mother and father and a couple of sisters. I was, I remember, somewhat astonished to find myself here, for the boy in question was scarcely known to me, and I rather disliked what I knew of him; moreover, he had left school nearly a year before. The afternoon was very hot, and an intolerable oppression reigned. On the far side of the lawn ran a red-brick wall, with an iron gate in its centre, outside which stood a walnut tree. We sat in the shadow of the house opposite a row of long windows inside which I could see a table with cloth laid, glimmering with glass and silver. This garden front of the house was very long, and at one end of it stood a tower of three storeys, which looked to me much older than the rest of the building.

Before long, Mrs. Stone, who, like the rest of the party, had sat in absolute silence, said to me, "Jack will show you your room: I have given you the room in the tower."

Quite inexplicably my heart sank at her words. I felt as if I had known that I should have the room in the tower, and that it contained something dreadful and significant. Jack instantly got up, and I understood that I had to follow him. In silence we passed through the hall, and mounted a great oak staircase with many corners, and arrived at a small landing with two doors set in it. He pushed one of these open for me to enter, and without coming in himself, closed it behind me. Then I knew that my conjecture had been right: there was something awful in the room, and with the terror of nightmare growing swiftly and enveloping me, I awoke in a spasm of terror.

Now that dream or variations on it occurred to me intermittently for fifteen years. Most often it came in exactly this form, the arrival, the tea laid out on the lawn, the deadly silence succeeded by that one deadly sentence, the mounting with Jack Stone up to the room in the tower where horror dwelt, and it always came to a close in the nightmare of terror at that which was in the room, though I never saw what it was. At other times I experienced variations on this same theme. Occasionally, for instance, we would be sitting at dinner in the dining-room, into the windows of which I had looked on the first night when the dream of this house visited me, but wherever we were, there was the same silence, the same sense of dreadful oppression and foreboding. And the silence I knew would always be broken by Mrs. Stone saying to me, "Jack will show you your room: I have given you the room in the tower." Upon which (this was invariable) I had to follow him up the oak staircase with many corners, and enter the place that I dreaded more and more each time that I visited it in sleep. Or, again, I would find myself playing cards still in silence in a drawing-room lit with immense chandeliers, that gave a blinding illumination. What the game was I have no idea; what I remember, with a sense of miserable anticipation, was that soon Mrs. Stone would get up and say to me, "Jack will show you your room: I have given you the room in the tower." This drawing-room where we played cards was next to the dining-room, and, as I have said, was always brilliantly illuminated, whereas the rest of the house was full of dusk and shadows. And yet, how often, in spite of those bouquets of lights, have I not pored over the cards that were dealt me, scarcely able for some reason to see them. Their designs, too, were strange: there were no red suits, but all were black, and among them there were certain cards which were black all over. I hated and dreaded those.

As this dream continued to recur, I got to know the greater part of the house. There was a smoking-room beyond the drawing-room, at the end of a passage with a green baize door. It was always very dark there, and as often as I went there I passed somebody whom I could not see in the door-way coming out. Curious developments, too, took place in the characters that peopled the dream as might happen to living persons. Mrs. Stone, for instance, who, when I first saw her, had been black haired, became grey, and instead of rising briskly, as she had done when she said, "Jack will show you your room: I have given you the room in the tower," got up very feebly, as if the strength was leaving her limbs. Jack also grew up, and became a rather ill-looking young man, with a brown moustache, while one of the sisters ceased to appear, and I understood she was married.

Then it so happened that I was not visited by this dream for six months or more, and I began to hope, in such inexplicable dread did I hold it, that it had passed away for good. But one night after this interval I again found myself being shown out on to the lawn for tea, and Mrs. Stone was not there, while the others were all dressed in black. At once I guessed the reason, and my heart leaped at the thought that perhaps this time I should not have to sleep in the room in the tower, and though we usually all sat in silence, on this occasion the sense of relief made me talk and laugh as I had never yet done. But even then matters were not altogether comfortable, for no one else spoke, but they all looked secretly at each other. And soon the foolish stream of my talk ran dry, and gradually an apprehension worse than anything I had previously known gained on me as the light slowly faded.

Suddenly a voice which I knew well broke the stillness, the voice of Mrs. Stone, saying, "Jack will show you your room: I have given you the room in the tower." It seemed to come from near the gate in the red-brick wall that bounded the lawn, and looking up, I saw that the grass outside was sown thick with gravestones. A curious greyish light shone from them, and I could read the lettering on the grave nearest me, and it was, 'IN EVIL MEMORY OF JULIA STONE.' And as usual Jack got up, and again I followed him through the hall and up the staircase with many corners. On this occasion it was darker than usual, and when I passed into the room in the tower I could only just see the furniture, the position of which was already familiar to me. Also there was a dreadful odour of decay in the room, and I woke screaming.

The dream, with such variations and developments as I have mentioned, went on at intervals for fifteen years. Sometimes I would dream it two or three nights in succession; once, as I have said, there was an intermission of six months, but taking a reasonable average, I should say that I dreamed it quite as often as once in a month. It had, as is plain, something of nightmare about it, since it always ended in the same appalling terror, which so far from getting less, seemed to me to gather fresh fear every time that I experienced it. There was, too, a strange and dreadful consistency about it. The characters in it, as I have mentioned, got regularly older, death and marriage visited this silent family, and I never in the dream, after Mrs. Stone had died, set eyes on her again. But it was always her voice that told me that the room in the tower was prepared for me, and whether we had tea out on the lawn, or the scene was laid in one of the rooms overlooking it, I could always see her gravestone standing just outside the iron gate. It was the same, too, with the married daughter; usually she was not present, but once or twice she returned again, in company with a man, whom I took to be her husband. He, too, like the rest of them, was always silent. But, owing to the constant repetition of the dream, I had ceased to attach, in my waking hours, any significance to it. I never met Jack Stone again during all those years, nor did I ever see a house that resembled this dark house of my dream. And then something happened.

I had been in London in this year, up till the end of July, and during the first week in August went down to stay with a friend in a house he had taken for the summer months, in the Ashdown Forest district of Sussex. I left London early, for John Clinton was to meet me at Forest Row Station, and we were going to spend the day golfing, and go to his house in the evening. He had his motor with him, and we set off, about five of the afternoon, after a thoroughly delightful day, for the drive, the distance being some ten miles. As it was still so early we did not have tea at the club house, but waited till we should get home. As we drove, the weather, which up till then had been, though hot, deliciously fresh, seemed to me to alter in quality, and become very stagnant and oppressive, and I felt that indefinable sense of ominous apprehension that I am accustomed to before thunder. John, however, did not share my views, attributing my loss of lightness to the fact that I had lost both my matches. Events proved, however, that I was right, though I do not think that the thunderstorm that broke that night was the sole cause of my depression.

Our way lay through deep high-banked lanes, and before we had gone very far I fell asleep, and was only awakened by the stopping of the motor. And with a sudden thrill, partly of fear but chiefly of curiosity, I found myself standing in the doorway of my house of dream. We went, I half wondering whether or not I was dreaming still, through a low oak-panelled hall, and out on to the lawn, where tea was laid in the shadow of the house. It was set in flower-beds, a red-brick wall, with a gate in it, bounded one side, and out beyond that was a space of rough grass with a walnut tree. The facade of the house was very long, and at one end stood a three-storeyed tower, markedly older than the rest.

Here for the moment all resemblance to the repeated dream ceased. There was no silent and somehow terrible family, but a large assembly of exceedingly cheerful persons, all of whom were known to me. And in spite of the horror with which the dream itself had always filled me, I felt nothing of it now that the scene of it was thus reproduced before me. But I felt the intensest curiosity as to what was going to happen.

Tea pursued its cheerful course, and before long Mrs. Clinton got up. And at that moment I think I knew what she was going to say. She spoke to me, and what she said was:

"Jack will show you your room: I have given you the room in the tower."

At that, for half a second, the horror of the dream took hold of me again. But it quickly passed, and again I felt nothing more than the most intense curiosity. It was not very long before it was amply satisfied.

John turned to me.

"Right up at the top of the house," he said, "but I think you'll be comfortable. We're absolutely full up. Would you like to go and see it now? By Jove, I believe that you are right, and that we are going to have a thunderstorm. How dark it has become."

I got up and followed him. We passed through the hall, and up the perfectly familiar staircase. Then he opened the door, and I went in. And at that moment sheer unreasoning terror again possessed me. I did not know for certain what I feared: I simply feared. Then like a sudden recollection, when one remembers as name which has long escaped the memory, I knew what I feared. I feared Mrs. Stone, whose grave with the sinister inscription, 'IN EVIL MEMORY', I had so often seen in my dream, just beyond the lawn which lay below my window. And then once more the fear passed so completely that I wondered what there was to fear, and I found myself, sober and quiet and sane, in the room in the tower, the name of which I had so often heard in my dreams, and the scene of which was so familiar.

I looked round it with a certain sense of proprietorship, and found that nothing had been changed from the dreaming nights in which I knew it so well. Just to the left of the door was the bed, lengthways along the wall, with the head of it in the angle. In a line with it was the fireplace and a small bookcase; opposite the door the outer wall was pierced by two lattice-paned windows, between which stood the dressing-table, while ranged along the fourth wall was the washing-stand and a big cupboard. My luggage had already been unpacked, for the furniture of dressing and undressing lay orderly on the wash-stand and toilet-table, while my dinner clothes were spread out on the coverlet of the bed. And then, with a sudden start of unexplained dismay, I saw that there were two rather conspicuous objects which I had not seen before in my dreams: one a life-sized oil painting of Mrs. Stone, the other a black-and-white sketch of Jack Stone, representing him as he had appeared to me only a week before in the last of the series of these repeated dreams, a rather secret and evil-looking man of about thirty. His picture hung between the windows, looking straight across the room to the other portrait, which hung at the side of the bed. At that I looked next, and as I looked I felt once more the horror of nightmare seize me.

It represented Mrs. Stone as I had seen her last in my dreams: old and withered and white haired. But in spite of the evident feebleness of body, a dreadful exuberance and vitality shone through the envelope of flesh, an exuberance wholly malign, a vitality that foamed and frothed with unimaginable evil. Evil beamed from the narrow, leering eyes; it laughed in the demon-like mouth. The whole face was instinct with some secret and appalling mirth; the hands, clasped together on the knee, seemed shaking with suppressed and nameless glee. Then I saw also that it was signed in the left-hand bottom corner, and wondering who the artist could be, I looked more closely, and read the inscription, "Julia Stone by Julia Stone".

There came a tap at the door, and John Clinton entered.

"Got everything you want?" he asked.

"Rather more than I want," said I, pointing to the picture.

He laughed.

"Hard-featured old lady," he said. "By herself, too, I remember. Anyhow, she can't have flattered herself much."

"But don't you see?" said I. "It's scarcely a human face at all. It's the face of some witch, of some devil."

He looked at it more closely.

"Yes; it isn't very pleasant," he said. "Scarcely a bedside manner, eh? Yes; I can imagine getting the nightmare if I went to sleep with that close by my bed. I'll have it taken down if you like."

"I really wish you would," I said.

He rang the bell, and with the help of a servant we detached the picture and carried it out on to the landing, and put it with its face to the wall.

"By Jove, the old lady is a weight," said John, mopping his forehead. "I wonder if she had something on her mind."

The extraordinary weight of the picture had struck me too. I was about to reply when I caught sight of my own hand. There was blood on it, in considerable quantities, covering the whole palm.

"I've cut myself somehow," said I.

John gave a little startled exclamation.

"Why, I have too," he said.

Simultaneously the footman took out his handkerchief and wiped his hand with it. I saw that there was blood also on his handkerchief.

John and I went back into the tower room and washed the blood off; but neither on his hand nor on mine was there the slightest trace of a scratch or cut. It seemed to me that, having ascertained this, we both, by a sort of tacit consent, did not allude to it again. Something in my case had dimly occurred to me that I did not wish to think about. It was but a conjecture, but I fancied that I knew the same thing had occurred to him.

The heat and the oppression of the air, for the storm we had expected was still undischarged, increased very much after dinner, and for some time most of the party, among whom were John Clinton and myself, sat outside on the path bounding the lawn, where we had had tea. The night was absolutely dark, and no twinkle of star or moon ray could penetrate the pall of cloud that overset the sky. By degrees our assembly thinned, the women went up to bed, men dispersed to the smoking or billiard room, and by eleven o'clock my host and I were the only two left. All the evening I thought that he had something on his mind, and as soon as we were alone he spoke.

"The man who helped us with the picture had blood on his hand, too, did you notice?" he asked. "I asked him just now if he had cut himself, and he said he supposed he had, but that he could find no mark of it. Now where did that blood come from?"

By dint of telling myself that I was not going to think about it, I had succeeded in not doing so, and I did not want, especially just at bedtime, to be reminded of it.

"I don't know," said I, "and I don't really care so long as the picture of Mrs. Julia Stone is not by my bed."

He got up.

"But it's odd," he said. "Ha! Now you'll see another odd thing."

A dog of his, an Irish terrier by breed, had come out of the house as we talked. The door behind us into the hall was open, and a bright oblong of light shone across the lawn to the iron gate which led on to the rough grass outside, where the walnut tree stood. I saw that the dog had all his hackles up, bristling with rage and fright; his lips were curled back from his teeth, as if he were ready to spring at something, and he was growling to himself. He took not the slightest notice of his master or me, but stiffly and tensely walked across the grass to the iron gate. There he stood for a moment, looking through the bars and still growling. Then all of a sudden his courage seemed to desert him: he gave one long howl, and scuttled back to the house with a curious crouching sort of movement.

"He does that half-a-dozen times a day," said John. "He sees something which he both hates and fears."

I walked to the gate and looked over it. Something was moving on the grass outside, and soon a sound which I could not instantly identify came to my ears. Then I remembered what it was: it was the purring of a cat. I lit a match, and saw the purrer, a big blue Persian, walking round and round in a little circle just outside the gate, stepping high and ecstatically, with tail carried aloft like a banner. Its eyes were bright and shining, and every now and then it put its head down and sniffed at the grass.

I laughed.

"The end of that mystery, I am afraid," I said. "Here's a large cat having Walpurgis night all alone."

"Yes, that's Darius," said John. "He spends half the day and all night there. But that's not the end of the dog mystery, for Toby and he are best of friends, but the beginning of the cat mystery. What's the cat doing there? And why is Darius pleased, while Toby is terror-stricken?"

At the moment I remembered the rather horrible detail of my dreams when I saw through the gate, just where the cat was now, the white tombstone with the sinister inscription. But before I could answer the rain began, as suddenly and heavily as if a tap had been turned on, and simultaneously the big cat squeezed through the bars of the gate, and came leaping across the lawn to the house for shelter. Then it sat in the doorway, looking out eagerly into the dark. It spat and struck at John with its paw, as he pushed it in, in order to close the door.

Somehow, with the portrait of Julia Stone in the passage outside, the room in the tower had absolutely no alarm for me, and as I went to bed, feeling very sleepy and heavy, I had nothing more than interest for the curious incident about our bleeding hands, and the conduct of the cat and dog. The last thing I looked at before I put out my light was the square empty space by my bed where the portrait had been. Here the paper was of its original full tint of dark red: over the rest of the walls it had faded. Then I blew out my candle and instantly fell asleep.

My awaking was equally instantaneous, and I sat bolt upright in bed under the impression that some bright light had been flashed in my face, though it was now absolutely pitch dark. I knew exactly where I was, in the room which I had dreamed in dreams, but no horror that I ever felt when asleep approached the fear that now invaded and froze my brain. Immediately after a peal of thunder crackled just above the house, but the probability that it was only a flash of lightning which awoke me gave no reassurance to my galloping heart. Something I knew was in the room with me, and instinctively I put out my right hand, which was nearest the wall, to keep it away. And my hand touched the edge of a picture frame hanging close to me.

I sprang out of bed, upsetting the small table that stood by it, and I heard my watch, candle, and matches clatter on to the floor. But for the moment there was no need of light, for a blinding flash leaped out of the clouds, and showed me that by my bed again hung the picture of Mrs. Stone. And instantly the room went into blackness again. But in that flash I saw another thing also, namely a figure that leaned over the end of my bed, watching me. It was dressed in some close-clinging white garment, spotted and stained with mould, and the face was that of the portrait.

Overhead the thunder cracked and roared, and when it ceased and the deathly stillness succeeded, I heard the rustle of movement coming nearer me, and, more horrible yet, perceived an odour of corruption and decay. And then a hand was laid on the side of my neck, and close beside my ear I heard quick-taken eager breathing. Yet I knew that this thing, though it could be perceived by touch, by smell, by eye and by ear, was still not of this earth, but something that had passed out of the body and had power to make itself manifest. Then a voice, already familiar to me, spoke.

"I knew you would come to the room in the tower," it said. "I have been long waiting for you. At last you have come. Tonight I shall feast; before long we will feast together."

And the quick breathing came closer to me; I could feel it on my neck.

At that the terror, which I think had paralysed me for the moment, gave way to the wild instinct of self-preservation. I hit wildly with both arms, kicking out at the same moment, and heard a little animal-squeal, and something soft dropped with a thud beside me. I took a couple of steps forward, nearly tripping up over whatever it was that lay there, and by the merest good luck found the handle of the door. In another second I ran out on the landing, and had banged the door behind me. Almost at the same moment I heard a door open somewhere below, and John Clinton, candle in hand, came running upstairs.

"What is it?" he said. "I slept just below you, and heard a noise as if— Good heavens, there's blood on your shoulder."

I stood there, so he told me afterwards, swaying from side to side, white as a sheet, with the mark on my shoulder as if a hand covered with blood had been laid there.

"It's in there," I said, pointing. "She, you know. The portrait is in there too, hanging up on the place we took it from."

At that he laughed.

"My dear fellow, this is a mere nightmare," he said.

He pushed by me, and opened the door, I standing there simply inert with terror, unable to stop him, unable to move.

"Phew! What an awful smell!" he said.

Then there was silence; he had passed out of my sight behind the open door. Next moment he came out again, as white as myself, and instantly shut it.

"Yes, the portrait's there," he said, "and on the floor is a thing—a thing spotted with earth, like what they bury people in. Come away, quick, come away."

How I got downstairs I hardly know. An awful shuddering and nausea of the spirit rather than of the flesh had seized me, and more than once he had to place my feet upon the steps, while every now and then he cast glances of terror and apprehension up the stairs. But in time we came to his dressing-room on the floor below, and there I told him what I have here described.

The sequel can be made short; indeed, some of my readers have perhaps already guessed what it was, if they remember that inexplicable affair of the churchyard at West Fawley, some eight years ago, when an attempt was made three times to bury the body of a certain woman who had committed suicide. On each occasion the coffin was found in the course of a few days again protruding from the ground. After the third attempt in order that the thing should not be talked about, the body was buried elsewhere in unconsecrated ground. Where it was buried was just outside the iron gate of the garden belonging to the house where this woman had lived. She had committed suicide in a room at the top of the tower in that house. Her name was Julia Stone.

Subsequently the body was again secretly dug up, and the coffin was found to be full of blood.

FOR THE CHILDREN

If you have children of appropriate ages you will be familiar with Bunnicula and Count Chocula, as well as plastic fangs, but you may not know of the many juvenile books. Here are half a dozen titles:

Nancy Garden, *Vampires* (1973)
Edward Gorey, *Dracula: A Toy Theater* (1979)
Glen A. Larson & Michael Sloan, *The Hardy Boys and Nancy Drew Meet Dracula* (1978)
Jan Wahl, *Dracula's Cat* (1978)
R. C. Welch, illus. Steve Feldman, *Vampire Almanac* (1995)
Jeanne Youngson, *A Child's Garden of Vampires* (1980)

THE DEATH OF THE VAMPIRE

This is, if you will excuse the pun, always at stake in a vampire story. The stake is a common way to nail down closure. Sunlight (reminding us that once the sun was worshipped as god) works well; Dracula crumbles to dust.

Elsewhere we note an imitation Dracula, played by a mad actor, who dies as a result of a spotlight. You could try drowning a vampire—they are notoriously adverse to water—or burn the body. Of all the ways out, my candidate for the most spectacular is in Angus Hall's novel *The Scars of Dracula* (1971). The vampire is "set alight like a human firework" and the effect is cinematic in the extreme.

Seabury Quinn's Mongolian elemental (created by witchcraft but resembling a vampire) appears in *Mortmain* (1940). This one is almost impossible to slay.

The gypsy *mollo* is hard to get rid of because it may take animal shape and not be recognized for what it is or, worse, become invisible.

As vampire tales proliferate new "ancient traditions" of the vampire have to be created all the time, just to add novelty to oft-told tales. Ending the story and ending the vampire—sometimes in such a way as to permit of resuscitation for a sequel or series—presents a real challenge to the bending author. If you are an avid reader of these tales, make a list of the best and worst exits. Notice that lately, in the works of Anne Rice, for instance, a vampire doesn't have to die, like a homosexual in a gay novel of the fifties, at the end of the story.

Count Dracula (his face painted green for dramatic effect under the lights of the stage, is introduced to the Broadway theater.

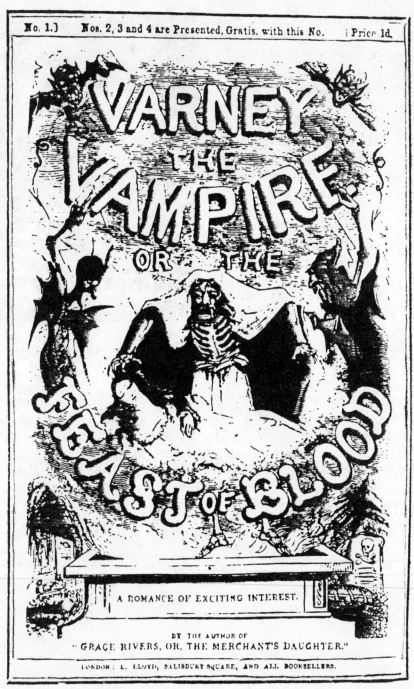

Varney the Vampire; or, *The Feast of Blood*. Part 1 for a penny, with Parts 2, 3, and 4 free!

7

The Vampire in Literature and Folklore

THE VAMPIRE IN THE LIBRARY AND THE ORAL TRADITION

In this last chapter the vampire will be further discussed in terms of fiction and other genres of literature will be touched on, poetry and prose, drama and melodrama, etc. We shall also consider the vampire as a figure of superstition very important in the oral tradition. There will be a little space to suggest the importance of the vampire in music and other arts as well, though a whole large book could be devoted to the vampire in the visual arts.

DRACULA AS A NOVEL

Perhaps literary critics have been off the mark to describe Bram Stoker's *Dracula* as a clumsy novel. Perhaps Stoker was writing in the tradition of the romance, not the epistolatory or any other kind of novel.

The Canadian critic Northrup Frye in *The Anatomy of Criticism* (1957) wrote this about the genre of romance:

> The romancer does not attempt to create "real people" so much as stylized figures which expand into psychological archetypes. It

is in the romance that we find [Swiss psychologist Carl] Jung's libido, anima, and shadow reflected in the hero, heroine, and villain respectively. That is why the romance so often radiates a glow of subjective intensity that the novel lacks, and why a suggestion of allegory is constantly creeping in around its fringes.

Try reading *Dracula* in the light of that statement. Does the power of the book not lie in the intense grip of the horror story and does that story not appeal most because it is an allegory of threatened good and predatory evil in the real world? Does not this thriller, like science fiction, derive its importance from the fact that underneath it all the fantasy is commenting on real life?

As to the use of *clumsy*, permit another quotation. This is from W. J. McCormack, University of Leeds, in *Great Writers of the English Language: Novelists* (1979):

In *Dracula* Stoker adapted the device more subtly employed by Wilkie Collins of attributing various strands of the narrative to various narrators; in Collins it contributes to a psychological mystery; in Stoker it heightens a fearful ignorance. The incorporation of telegrams, extracts from letters and diaries, even the use of broken English and transliterated shorthand, helps the author to disguise the appalling lack of coherent style which marks his other work. The result is an ever-shifting, discontinuous chronicle of fascination and pursuit, where sexual, religious, racial, and historical obsessions are intermittently undulged in and deplored.

To repeat: Though this harsh criticism is basically justified, the novel, romance, chronicle—call it what you will—has become a cult object despite being politically incorrect today (it introduces Roman Catholic superstition, the jingoism more evident in Stoker's *The Lair of the White Worm*, and presents women as pretty sappy) and badly written (even if the missing opening chapter is restored). However, it flourishes in all our media simply because it touches on everlasting questions of sexual and spiritual predation and plays with humanity's constant questions about good and evil and how these are rewarded or punished in the afterlife. It appeals mightily as well to our pleasure in being scared.

Some academics at work are collected by Elizabeth Miller in *Reflections on Dracula: Ten Essays* (1997). Wolf and Leatherdale are the real experts.

AN EARLIER SUGGESTION OF THE DRACULA STORY

Nobody knows who wrote in German the very thrilling tale of Count Azzo that was translated into English and appeared in one of the numerous Victorian magazines, *Odds and Ends*, in 1860. It was called by a title that will look familiar to readers of "Mark Twain," *The Mysterious Stranger*. The plot will look a great deal more familiar to readers of Bram Stoker's *Dracula*. Moreover, the anonymous German writer has a directness of effect that Stoker could only have envied. Witness this brief sample:

> Now listen! I had walked up and down my room for a long time; I was excited—out of spirits—I do not know exactly what. It was almost midnight ere I lay down, but I could not sleep. I tossed about, and at length it was only from sheer exhaustion that I dropped off. But what a sleep it was! An inward fear ran through me perpetually. I saw a number of pictures before me, as I used to do in childish sickness. I do not know whether I was asleep or half awake. Then I dreamed, but as clearly as if I had been wide awake, that a sort of mist filled the room, and out of it stepped the knight Azzo. He gazed at me for a time, and then letting himself slowly down on one knee, imprinted a kiss on my throat. Long did his lips rest there, and I felt a slight pain, which always increased, until I could bear it no more. With all my strength I tried to force the vision from me, but succeeded only after a long struggle. No doubt I uttered a scream, for that awoke me from my trance. When I came a little to my senses I felt a sort of superstitious fear creeping over me—how great you may imagine when I tell you that, with my eyes open and awake, it appeared to me as if Azzo's figure were still by my bed, and then disappearing gradually into the mist, vanished at the door!
>
> "You must have dreamed very heavily, my poor friend," began Bertha, but suddenly paused. She gazed with surprise at Franziska's throat. "Why, what is that?" she cried. "Just look: how extraordinary—a red streak on your throat!"

SOURCES OF *DRACULA*

Some of the sources of Stoker's novel are clear, but names give unusual clues as to Stoker's reading before he launched on this hastily constructed and in some ways derivative novel. For instance, Arthur Holmwood, who lives at Ring, and is Lucy Westerna's fiancé, recalls one Ringwood, fiancé of Clara Crofton, a victim of the vampire in *Varney the Vampire*. At one point, Stoker slips and calls Holmwood, Hopwood—but the -wood is consistent.

DRACULA'S SOLUTION TO WELFARE PROBLEMS

The historical Dracula (Little Dragon) has had something of a bad rap ever since he came to prominence in the fifteenth century. His history was not that of an undead creature nor could he have become one at his death (because his head was cut off). Still he is *the* vampire.

He is, however, notorious for a number of actual occurrences. It is reported that when emissaries from the Ottoman sultan came to his court they did not remove their turbans. The uncovered head was an expected gesture of respect. He told them the custom was that princes such as himself should be greeted bareheaded. They replied that was not the custom of their country. He had their turbans nailed to their heads "with small iron nails" and told them to go back and tell the Sultan that Turkish customs were not welcome in Vlad's territories. As a matter of fact, Vlad was a Christian hero. He put up admirable defenses against Turkish intrusion into Christian Europe.

Nailing the turbans on did not kill the emissaries (as is falsely reported in some documents); that would not have got his message delivered. As for Vlad's act as a barbarous attack on innocent heads, when Vlad was eventually killed his head was cut off and delivered to the sultan as proof of his death.

No, he did not eat his lunch where people were being put to death on stakes. Public execution was to impress his seriousness on the populace, not to entertain himself.

But let us get to Vlad's solution to welfare problems, a drastic one that some people today might nevertheless secretly envy for its effectiveness.

Vlad made it known that the poor and sick and old and others who could not get by without charity should all come to his capital. They arrived in droves, expecting handouts. He gathered the crowds in a vast hall and set them down to a huge banquet. They ate and drank merrily and then began to dance and sing and perhaps engage in less conventional public behaviors. At this point Vlad asked them if they had enjoyed the party. They shouted that they had. What did they now want him to do for them? Oh, anything he wished, they said, expecting more benefits. Vlad had all the doors locked as he left the building. Then he gave orders that the building be burned down with all the vagabonds and gypsies, beggars and destitute persons, inside.

"Know that I did this," he told his nobles, "that I did this first of all that they might no longer impose a burden on others and secondly so that there should no longer be any poor people in my lands, so that everyone might be rich."

Rather than drink the blood of others as a vampire, in fact Vlad put an end to those who would parasitically drain the blood of society. His governmental policies were, admittedly, barbaric, as were most in his time and (of course!) none are in ours.

All the political aspects of the historical Dracula are missing from Bram Stoker's *Dracula*. There everything is concentrated on the bloodlust of the central character. This, and similar books about vampires, however, have been read in modern times as political texts by critics who see politics in everything.

POLIDORI AND WHAT CAME AFTER HIM

For once, I'll reprint here something I wrote for another publication, just to bring to readers' attention still once more to the existence of the leading vampire group (though there are others in the US, the UK, etc.) and to the anthology of which this snippet is a book review. Here is one of my articles from Dr. J. Youngson's lively bulletin of The Count Dracula Fan Club. It appeared in the March/April 1992 *Bites & Pieces*.

John William Polidori (1795-1821) took his medical degree at Edinburgh and soon, and briefly, thereafter he was physician, secretary, and companion to Lord Byron. In 1819 he published *The Vampyre*, attributing it to Byron. In fact, though Goethe said it was by far the best work Byron had ever done, Polidori had written the vampire tale himself. [I now believe Byron may have given Polidori some draft or ideas, though I have seen a letter, donated to the CDFC by Robert A. Ashley in 1983, in Byron's handwriting in which he tells the editor of a periodical he was not the author of *The Vampyre* and had never heard of the work in question until it was mentioned in Gaglianani's *Journal*.] Before he died, as his own hand and as a result of depression over a gambling debt, Polidori published some fiction under his own name, but nothing achieved the fame of *The Vampyre*. It became the first English classic in a vigorous genre.

A good selection of vampire literature of the nineteenth century...is collected by Christopher Frayling in *Vampyres: Lord Byron to Count Dracula* (Faber, 1992, £17.50)....

Varney the Vampire has been republished in modern times, all three long volumes of it. The selection from it in this anthology will very likely be as much as any modern reader will want....

It was in the nineteenth century that the vampire tales spread from Transylvania to the rest of Europe and age-old superstitions were given, as it were, a new lease on life....

A DISTURBING THOUGHT FROM
A DOCTOR OF THE CHURCH

From the writings of Tertullian (*AD c.* 160-*c.* 225): *Certum est quia impossibile est.* "It is certain because it is impossible."

THE SPECTRE BRIDEGROOM AND OTHER HORRORS

Alexa's "terrific and interesting tale" of *The Spectre Bridegroom* (early nineteenth century) appeared in an anthology of this title, put together by R. Reginald and D. Menville in 1976. With it was included some other rarities such as Smyth Upton's *The Last of the Vampires* (Weston-*super*-Mare, 1845), in which the mysterious Baron von Oberfels is a vampire who has to kill a young girl every ten years to maintain his youth. In modern America, some men marry a different young girl every ten years for a somewhat similar purpose.

THOMAS PRESKETT PREST

He is often said to be the author of *Varney the Vampire*, though there has been some argument among scholars that the attribution of this typical "penny dreadful" is, as often happens, incorrect. In any case, Prest was incontrovertibly a leader among the prolific writers of these popular novels. In early Victorian times he produced, it is reported, 200 or more three-volume novels. The titles give you a fair idea of his interests and those of his readers: *The Maniac Father; or, The Victim of Seduction* and *Sawney Bean, The Man-Eater of Midlothian* (supposedly based on a real-life Scot who lived in a cave and was a cannibal and was put to death in the most horrible way, in the fifteenth century, with his cannibal wife and fourteen cannibal children) and *The Skeleton Clutch; or, The Goblet of Gore* (with sensational events typical of the melodrama then so popular) and *The Death Grasp; or, A Father's Curse,* etc. His best-known work has attracted Stephen Sondheim's major talents: it is *Sweeney Todd; or, The Demon Barber of Fleet Street.* (It featured shepherds' pies with real shepherds in them).

Edward Lloyd published *Varney the Vampire; or, The Feast of Blood* in London in 1847 to great acclaim. It was widely distributed in penny parts in 1853. It is a long tale of some 220 chapters, 869 pages, but every word was greedily soaked up by the public, which adored "shockers." The work was reprinted often in Victorian England and in the United States in the latter part of the twentieth century. In Colin Wilson's *The Sex Diary of Gerard Sorme* (1963) a character is said to be writing a fantastic opera based on *Varney*, but, as far as I can ascertain, this excellent idea is entirely fictional, and *Varney* still has to burst onto the stage and the big and smaller screens. If anyone wants to write music for my script or libretto, let me know!

Varney is set in the early eighteenth century, in the reign of Queen Anne. There are attempts to suggest that, like the Sweeney Todd story, behind the fiction there are some terrible actual events. The Gothic, like all fantastic literature, is a way of discussing aspects of reality. When successful, it touches places deep down within us all.

George Gordon, Lord Byron (1788–1824), though he did not contribute really important writings to the literature of vampires, set a style for the dandy outsider. He did publish a "Bride of Corinth" (1815) but his chief contribution was the Byronic Hero, alienated, mysterious, weighed down with secret sorrow and sin. Byron's physician, John Polidori, wrote *The Vampyre*, once attributed to his romantic employer.

UPYR'

Count Tolstoy's nephew, Aleksej, combined the family's interests in literature with his own special interest, the occult. He was a great admirer of Horace Walpole and other English Gothic novelists, of Charles Nodier and other dramatists of Paris melodrama stages, Eugène Sue of *The Wandering Jew*, and similar writers. His story of sixty-eight pages is crammed with "borrowed material" and my late friend and colleague Charles Passage well summed it all up as an amateur effort, first read at the house of a noble friend and submitted to the censor under a pen name (Krasnorogskij), and no more than "a belated Gothic novel, overburdened with plot and carrying little psychological conviction, [which] has little to recommend it." Aleksej's literary fame, greater than his uncle's in his time, reveals more about Russians' superstitions than their taste.

Upyr' spawned also *La Famille du Vourdalak*, a tale of a Slavonic vampire, written in French, not published in the author's lifetime, finally printed in Russian translation in 1884. It is set in the eighteenth century (1769) and has a hairsbreadth escape of the hero from a clan of vampires. A more famous Russian writer, Ivan Turgenev, published a thrilling *Clara Milich* (1882). It is much better.

Russian folklore is full of demons and vampires and werewolves. I suppose we tend to forget now what a threat wolves were to people in olden days. I grew up thinking about it because on the wall of my room as a child there was a dramatic old engraving that showed a peasant in a sleigh carrying the coffin of some loved one through the storm—pursued by wolves. At least there was not an engraving of a vampire.

A TALE OF HOFFMANN

E. T. A. Hoffmann has a brief vampire tale in his *Serapionsbrüder* collection. It's one of those scraps that dedicated vampire fans seek out in major authors from Ovid and Philostratus down to our day. It's the prose equivalent of hunting down minor stuff in Robert Southey (*Thelaba, The Destroyer*), and not so minor stuff (Samuel Taylor Coleridge's *Christabel*, fine work—look it up), etc. The rise of folklore in Germany with the rise of national fervor in the nineteenth century produced a great many minor short stories and pale imitations of *Die Braut von Corinth*. Hoffmann's ghost stories include *The Deserted House* and *The Entail*.

WHAT TO READ ABOUT VAMPIRES

To all the lists of books I have included in this book, I have to add one *caveat*, and that is, as my former Brooklyn College CUNY colleague John Ashbery said, "We must begin at the beginning, that is, the present." Even if you have never yet read *Dracula* or any of the other so-called classics that I mention— this is unlikely, but possible—you may wish to go to the bookstore and read the very latest vampire books, books that came out yesterday, books published after I finished writing this little encyclopedia of vampires.

Despite the titles of my series, no book can ever be truly *Complete*. The most important thing about vampire literature—and by that I mean all media, for film and video and television are very much alive for people who hardly read a book a year—is that it is very much alive, contemporary and copious. It is being added to all the time. It is a vigorous genre today, and that gives it its special importance in modern American life. Perhaps some of the most recent books are careless of the tradition, intended only to get on the band-wagon of a popular trend. Some may be trash. But their very existence proves that the subject of the vampire continues to be of interest.

If you are a real vampire buff, don't worry about a canon or a course of reading. In the long run you will find that you have read most of the available vampire books, seen a lot of the vampire movies, and are always ready for something new as well as something old. Once bitten, you will be addicted. I hope that this one book will give you some idea of how inter-esting the subject can be and how, after all, it connects to the larger and serious issues of (among other things) sex and power, faith and supersti-tion, fact and fiction, life and death. Use your fascination with The Count and his crew to amuse yourself and also to tempt yourself into collecting information and *thinking* about your whole culture and yourself. Consider everything you can get your hands on and, as Sir Francis Bacon suggested, distinguish between books that are to be tasted and others that are wor-thy of being inwardly digested.

MORE BOOKS ABOUT VAMPIRES

Most of the recent publications about vampires are to be found in the schol-arly journals here and abroad (*Contemporary Legend, Discourse, Journal of the History of Ideas, Journal of Popular Culture* and also *Littératures* in French, *Chasqui* in Spanish, *Literatutoe Obozrenie* in Russian, *Polska Sztuka Lodowa* in Polish, etc.) but of course there are anthologies and book-length stud-ies. Samples from Bari, New Delhi, Paris, London, etc.:

Beahm, George, ed. *The Unauthorized Anne Rice Companion* (1996)
Bhalla, Alok. *The Politics of Atrocity and Lust: The Vampire Tale as a Night-mare History of England in the Nineteenth Century* (1990)
Gelder, Ken. *Reading the Vampire* (1994)
Giovanni, Fabio. *Il libro dei vampiri* (The Book of the Vampire, 1985)
Olivier, Jean-Michel. *Lautréamont: La text du* Vampire (1982)
Pucat-Guinoisseau, Ginette, ed. *Le Vampire et Le Delateur* (Charles Nodier, 1990)
Senf, Carol A. *The Vampire in Nineteenth-Century English Literature* (1988)
Waller, Gregory A. *The Living and the Undead* (1985)

UND SO WEITER

Varied examples from Germany, whose writers, booksellers and readers are addicted to vampire lore, some fans allege:

Hamburger, Klaus. *Über Vampirismus* (On Vampirism, 1992)

Hellwig, Albert. *Ritualmord und Blutaberglaube* (Ritual Murder and Blood Magic, 1913)

Klaniczay, Gábor. *Heilige, Hexen, Vampire: Vom Nutzen des Übernatürlichen Wagenbach* (Spirits, Witches, Vampires..., 1991, useful bibliography)

Pirie, David. *Vampir Filmkult* (Vampire Film Cult, 1977)

Schroeder, Albert. *Vampirismus* (Vampirism, 1973)

Spindler, C. *Der Vampyr und seine Braut* (The Vampire and His Bride, 1832)

Strack, Hermann L. *Der Blutaberglaube...* (Blood Magic, 1892)

Sturmm David & Klaus Völker, *Von der Vampiren oder Menschensaugern...* (Of Vampires &c., 1968)

EN FRANÇAIS

Bérnard, Syprien. *Lord Ruthven; ou, Les Vampires* (Lord Ruthven; or, The Vampires, 1820)

Histoire des vampires et des spectres malfaisans (History of Vampires and Malevolent Specters, 1825)

Hugo, Victor. *Han d'Island* (Jan of Iceland, 1823)

Villeneuve, Roland & Jean-Louis Degaudenzi, *Le Musée des vampires* (Vampire Museum, 1976)

Volta, Ornella, *Le Vampire* (The Vampire, 1952, available in translation)

SUPERSTITION

"Superstition is the religion of feeble minds."
—Edmund Burke (1729-1797)

"Superstition is the poetry of life."—Johann von Goethe (1749-1832)

"The greatest American superstition is the belief in facts."
—Hermann Keyserling (1880-1946)

How then are we to account for the taste which maintained for so long the works of terror and blood? Most easily. It is the privilege of the ignorant and the weak to love superstition. The only strong mental sensation they are capable of is fear.... There are millions of minds that have no resource between vapid sentimentality, and the ridiculous spectra of the nursery.

—James Malcolm Rymer, *Popular Writing* (1842)

THE VAMPIRE'S PLIGHT

"You see," says one of Anne Rice's undead in *Interview with the Vampire*, "someone must die every night that I walk, until I have the courage to end it...."

Traditional vampires can't kick the habit. They have to be destroyed by others.

Female Vampire by Max Kahn (*c.*1895). In the tradition came the vamps of the silent films. "Kiss me, you fool!" Theda Bara said in *A Fool There Was* (1914).

The modern excuse from *West Side Story*, "We're depraved because we're deprived," plus *Sympathy for the Devil*, combine to excuse contemporary vampires, poor babies. They have such a hard life as minority people.

THE RECEPTION OF DRACULA, 1897

The Athenaeum: "'Dracula' is highly sensational, but it is wanting in the constructive art as well as in the higher literary sense. It reads at times like a mere series of grotesquely incredible events; but there are better moments that show more power, though even these are never productive of the tremor such subjects evoke under the hand of a master. At times Mr. Stoker almost succeeds in creating the sense of possibility in impossibility; at others he merely commands an array of crude statements of incredible actions.... Still, Mr. Stoker has got together a number of horrid details, and his object, assuming it is to be ghastliness, is fairly well fulfilled."

The Bookman: "Since Wilkie Collins left us we have had no tale of mystery so liberal in manner and so closely woven. But with the intricate plot, and the methods of the narrative, the resemblance to the stories of the author of 'The Woman in White' ceases; for the audacity and horror of 'Dracula' are Mr. Stoker's own.... A summary of the book would shock and disgust; but we must own that, though here and there in the course of the tale we hurried over things with repulsion, we read nearly the whole with rapt attention. It is something of a triumph for the writer that neither the improbability, nor the necessary number of hideous incidents recounted of the man-vampire are long foremost in the reader's mind, but that the interest of the danger, of the complications, of the pursuit of the villain, of human skill and courage pitted against inhuman wrong and superhuman strength, rises always to the top."

Daily Mail: "In seeking a parallel to this weird, powerful and horrible story, our minds revert to such tales as 'The Mysteries of Udolpho,' 'Frankenstein,' 'Wuthering Heights,' 'The Fall of the House of Usher,' and 'Marjery of Quelher.' But 'Dracula' is even more appalling in its gloomy fascination than any of these."

Pall Mall Gazette: "It is horrid and creepy to the last degree. It is also excellent, and one of the best things in the supernatural line that we have been lucky enough to hit upon."

Punch: "The story is told in diaries and journals, a rather tantalising and somewhat wearisome form of narration, whereof Wilkie Collins was a past-master.... This weird tale is about vampires, not a single, quiet, creeping vampire, but a whole band of them, governed by a vampire monarch who is apparently a first cousin to Mephistopheles. It is a pity that Mr. Bram Stoker was not content to employ such supernatural anti-vampire receipts as his wildest imagination might have invented without venturing on a domain where angels fear to tread. But for this we could have reservedly recommended so ingenious a romance to all those who enjoy the weirdest of weird tales."

AN ADAPTATION OF DRACULA

From the start, when Bram Stoker's widow saw the property getting away from her and found someone to put together an authorized version of *Dracula* for the stage, theatrical adaptations have abounded. Dracfans have not always applauded them. I cite as one example that can stand for many destined "to please the brain dead rather than the undead." This one I did not see—it played the Hackney Empire in London in February 1998—but

I heard about it thanks to a British friend who knows I collect really nasty theater reviews. (Ellis Raab as Hamlet, the Eugene Field review in which the critic said someone played the King in *Hamlet* all evening "as if he were afraid someone was about to play the ace," Dorothy Parker's cheap but cheery shots, John Simon on Liza Minelli—that sort of thing.)

James Christopher in the London *Times* briefly savaged this adaptation by James Gill, saying the script seemed "as if he sat down and stitched this from a thousand drunken hours of bleary, late-night Hammer [movie] horrors."

Point One, fans do not welcome departures from the traditional script and each and every new Count has to bear comparison with a wide variety of earlier actors, with or without fangs and pointed ears (which these days is too reminiscent of Dr. Spock on *Star Trek*).

Point Two, ever since Lugosi, The Count has on occasion been played with a ludicrous accent. In the Hackney-ed production, Padraig Casey's accent marked him, says the critic, as someone "tutored by a failed British Rail announcer." Frankly, I do not understand why someone as clever as Count Dracula does not speak perfect, unaccented English. After all, he has had centuries to study it.

Point Three, these dramas of the supernatural need atmospheric and special effects. Lavish movies have encouraged us to expect both convincing scenery and extraordinary sets. Fringe theater productions on a budget are asking for trouble:

> Drapes with heads poking through gallop across the stage pretending to be railway carriages. Toffee-nosed ladies and gents ignore each other in parks. And a large chest successfully upstages several performers by impersonating a carriage, a ship and a bed when all the while we know it is stuffed full of the vampires.

We could go on about a lot more points, but what's the use? The principal point to be made is that while the story has a tremendous appeal, and has often been presented in various media, by the time it reaches a stage production these days it has a great deal going against its success. The Count's tale can descend into farce if awkwardly handled and the show can be unfortunately stolen by "Renfield, Dracula's fly-eating stooge, who delivers a brilliant piece of head-rolling, twitching lunacy" as played by Anthony Burroughs in this regrettable production at a once-fashionable old London music hall.

There have been whole books devoted to the theatrical history of *Hamlet*. Now, while *Dracula* is not in the same league as a work of art there are those who love it. Perhaps someone will write a thorough history of stage productions and film and television versions (including presentations with Count Alucard, Count Downe, Count Yorga, and Blacula), quoting the original critical reactions.

THÉÂTRE DES VAMPIRES

DANCING

tuesday nites
9pm · 2am
dj shane **AND**
eric showing
vampire films

GRANDIA ROOM
5657 MELROSE
HOLLYWOOD
$3.00

A WORD ABOUT WEREWOLVES

The werewolf is a living human being (suffering from lycanthropy). He turns into a wolf, or he gets a lot of body hair to the delight of movie makeup men. The vampire is likewise voracious, but the vampire is an "undead" human being, which is not the same thing as being alive. The vampire if any change occurs most likely changes into evening clothes or a slinky gown. The werewolf changes into an animal or a beastly human. Despite the movies in which the vampire turns into a bat, the vampire has to retain his human shape at all times. Indeed he cannot cast off the dead body and let it rot to free his tortured spirit.

The werewolf is a metaphor for the good and evil in man and the fearful alteration that madness can bring. Like Dr. Jekyll turning into Mr. Hyde, the werewolf's outer transformation is supposed to symbolize his inner transformation, from good to bad. The werewolf is a lunatic in the strictest sense: the full moon brings on his mad attacks.

The vampire is a way of speaking not so much about good and evil sides of the living but about life and death and how a bad life is punished in the afterlife. The werewolf is a loner; he (a female werewolf is virtually unheard of) destroys his victims. The vampire suffers loneliness, too; but he recruits company.

Both the werewolf and the vampire are classic examples of the monsters that fear conjures up. Both offer ample evidence of the widespread fascination with such creatures that imagination constructs and folklore renders enduring.

GHOULS JUST WANNA HAVE FUN

We should distinguish between vampires, who rise from their graves to drink the blood of the living, and ghouls, who desecrate the graves of others and feast on corpses. Ghouls are not frequent in recent literature, but see Michael Slade's devastating horror novel, *Ghoul* (1987). Don't read it if you are alone in the house.

GRAVESITE

Along with instructions about whether or not you wish to be resuscitated or have what are oddly called heroic measures expended to keep you alive at the last, why not take the trouble to specify whether you want your organs harvested and that you want to be buried facing east or west?

Ancient superstition says that burial in the northern part of a cemetery is a mark of shame and that old graves in which the bodies lie facing north or south may indicate that the corpses were suicides. Remember, suicides can become vampires, old belief tells us. Better not take any chances.

SILVER

Iron (as I say elsewhere in this series of books) was long supposed to scare off or dispatch evil creatures. We must not, however, forget that silver was also thought powerful against evil. There are stories of the vampire, and especially the *loup-garou* or werewolf, being killed with a silver bullet. Folklore also records that a silver knife put under a pillow would guarantee you a good night's sleep free of the fear of vampires.

Folklore can reveal marvelous things about the way ordinary people have viewed the world.

HOW TO MAKE SOMEONE LOVE YOU

I knew this would catch your attention, and why not? In a previous book in this series (*The Complete Book of Spells, Curses, and Magical Recipes*) you will find a number of suggestions, including one involving a dead cat, about which some animal-lovers wrote to me reprovingly. (I respond that I record, not recommend, these things.) Here, in connection with vampires, there is something to be said about an aphrodisiac that is a blood product and related to the idea of tampering with the soul of another.

How to put this delicately? Simply, superstition holds that if a male wants a female to fall in love with him he should sneak some of his semen into her food. Presumably this works for gays, too, but lesbians are out of luck.

In some vampire stories the vampire not only sucks the blood of the victim but the infatuated victim sucks blood (often from the chest) of the vampire.

PSYCHIC VAMPIRES

"Dion Fortune" (Violet Mary Firth) wrote convincingly about psychic attacks by energy-draining "vampires." Her *Psychic Self Defense* (1930) is a classic in its field. It shows that the folklore vampire has equivalents in real life.

DARK SHADOWS

There are so many avid fans of this vampire television series and of the Barnaby Collins books that I cannot undertake to tell even part of the *DS* story here; there have been whole books on the subject. Dr. Jeanne Youngson, who attends a great many conferences,has told me that at a recent meeting of vampire buffs *The Dark Shadows Cookbook* was offered for sale at $750.00. That will give you some idea of the hold *DS* has on its fans. I can only suggest that if you are seriously interested in this well-documented and almost cult-like topic you

Barnabas Collins (Jonathan Frid), the reluctant vampire of *Dark Shadows*

investigate *DS* for yourself. Barnaby Collins may have been a reluctant vampire but none of his numerous and devoted fans will be the least reluctant to tell you all about him.

FOR FANS OF DARK SHADOWS

Fan clubs and their publications come and go. Fans grow tired, or grow up. However, some or all of the following may be around to help if you want information on the much cherished *Dark Shadows* books, television series, memorabilia, etc., and there are always the search engines of cyber-world to put you in touch if "snail mail" is too slow for you.

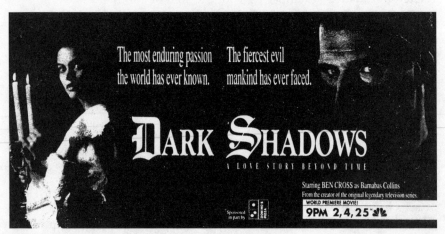

A television series spawns a television movie.

Dark Shadows Fan Club, Louis Wendruck, PO Box 69A04, West Hollywood, CA 90069

Dark Shadows Official Fan Club, Anne Wilson, PO Box 92, Maplewood, NJ 07040

The World of *Dark Shadows*, Kathleen Resch, PO Box 1766, Temple City, CA 91780

Dark Shadows Collectibles, Sue-Ellen Wilson, 6173 Roquois Terrace, Mentor, OH 44060

The Secret Room, PO Box 1872, Azle, TX 76098

There are *DS* organizations all over the US. For instance, there are the New England *Dark Shadows* Society (PO Box 6023, Boston, MA 02101) and the New Orleans/Louisiana *Dark Shadows* Group (PO Box 922, Belle Chase, LA 70037).

VAMPIRE MELODRAMA

Roxanna Stuart in *Stage Blood* (1994) discusses, among other plays, W. T. Moncrieff's *The Vampire* (Royal Coburg 1820, Mr. Kemble as the vampire), James Robinson Planché's *Giovanni the Vampire!!!* (Adelphi, 1821, the hero a woman in a "britches part"), Edward Fitzball's staging of Robert Southey's poem *Thelaba, The Destroyer* (Royal Coburg, 1823, with Mr. Stanley in the title role), George Blick's *The Vampire Bridge; or, The Tenant of the Tomb* (1838), etc. Alexandre Dumas *père's Le Vampire* (Ambigù-Comique, Paris, 1851, starring M. Arnault as Lord Ruthven) and Harris's *Ruthven* (Royal Strand, 1872) were both drawn from Maturin. Dion Boucicault's *The Vampire* played both London (Princess, 1852) and New York (Wallach's Lyceum, 1857). One of the last of the type in Victorian London was Richard Henry's *The Vampire's Victim* (Gaiety, 1887).

A Taste for Friends & Lovers

Vampire Vineyards

SPECIAL EFFECTS IN VAMPIRE MELODRAMAS

The vampire craze was a big boost to special effects on the Victorian stage. Thomas Leonard Colwin has a dissertation on *Magic, Trick-Work, and Illusion in the Vampire Plays* (1988). Generations of stage magicians learned from those who used "smoke and mirrors" and clever contraptions. Plays were actually written around devices that were invented. Oddly, I have never seen a production of *Hamlet* where The Ghost uses a vampire trapdoor to appear and disappear. I'd like to see The Ghost as a hologram that The Gloomy Dane could walk right through.

50 PSEUDONYMOUS VAMPIRE AUTHORS

There are a number of good reasons for not signing your real name to a book about vampires. Among these, in no particular order, are the following: a lot of the vampire novels are trash no one would want to claim; some are produced under "house names" belonging to a paperback or other publisher; some are produced by teams of writers; some writers are trying to assume or hide ethnicity or gender; and some people just want a fancier name on their books or a name to distinguish their vampire fiction from their other productions. Some men take female pseudonyms (such as "Amarantha Knight") but women authors pretending to be men (such as "Dion Fortune") are more common. I include one example of a person with more than a single pseudonym: "Clarissa Ross" and "Marilyn Ross" are the same prolific male.

The following list is by no means complete. Who can keep up with pulp fiction? Also I omit the gay and lesbian and heterosexual pornography notable in this genre—but these 50 titles may be illustrative.

I give a sample book title in each case (sometimes the author has only one vampire book I know of, sometimes there are others) and there may be other dates for other editions (foreign, paperback, revised, retitled, etc.). I don't bother to give the writers' real names. They obviously wanted to hide them and in many cases I well appreciate why. You will not find the real names of most of these people in ordinary dictionaries of pseudonyms; most of them are too unimportant for anyone but absolutely fanatic Drac-fans to care about. A few, however, are fine and famous under pseudonyms. Some pseudonyms are obvious ("The Spectre" wrote *Ye Vampyres* in 1897, which no one I know has ever read) and some are never suspected of being disguises at all.

Armstrong, F.W. *The Devouring* (1987)
Ascher, Eugene. *To Kill a Corpse* (19654)
Bainbridge, Sharon. *Blood and Roses* (1993)
Blacque, Dovya. *South of Heaven* (1991)
Bok. *Vampires of the China Coast* (1932)
Brett, Stephen. *The Vampire Chase* (1979)
Drake, Asa. *I Am Dracula* (1993)
Dreadstone, Carl. *Dracula's Daughter* (1977)
Eccarius, H. G. *The Last Days...the Vampire* (1988)
Enfield, Hugh. *Kronos* (1972)
Finney, Jack. *Invasion of the Body Snatchers* (reprinted 1990)
Fortune, Dion. *The Demon Lover* (1927)
Giles, Raymond. *Night of the Vampire* (1969)
Girdon, Julien. *Vampires* (1891)
Halidom, M. Y. *The Woman in Black* (1906)
Hawke, Simon. *The Dracula Caper* (1988)
Ketchum, Jack. *She Wakes* (1989)
Kiraly, Marie. *Mina* (1994)
Knight, Amarantha. *Darker Passions: Dracula* (1993)
Lecale, Errol. *Castledoom* (1974)
Leinster, Murray. *The Brain-Stealers* (1954)
Lovell, Mark. *Vampire in the Shadows* (1976)
Manheim, Karl. *Vampires of Venus* (1950)
Morrow. H. H. *The Black Madonna* (1990)
Murdoch, Mordecai. *The Wroclaw Dracula* (1985)
Ohnet, Georges. *Peter's Soul* (translation *c.* 1895)
Paul, D. W. *The Orgy at Madam Dracula's* (1968)
Randolph, Arabella. *The Vampire Tapes* (1977)
Raven, Simon. *Doctors Wear Scarlet* (1960)
Robeson, Kenneth. *The Blood Countess* (1975)
Rohmer, Sax. *Grey Face* (1924)
Ross, Clarissa. *The Secret of the Pale Lover* (1969)
Ross, Marilyn. *Barnabas Collins* (1968)
Salem, Richard. *New Blood* (1981)
Samuels, Victor. *The Vampire Women* (1973)
Saxon, Peter. *The Torturer* (1966)
Selby, Curt. *Blood County* (1981)
Shayne, Maggie. *Twilight Phantasies* (1993)
Sherman, J. *Vampire* (1981)

Somtow, S. P. *Valentine* (1992)
Stanwood, Brook. *The Glow* (1980)
Stockbridge, Grant. *The Dark Reign of the Vampire King* (1975)
Sturgeon, Theodore. *Some of Your Blood* (1961)
Swanson, Logan. *Earthbound* (1982)
Tremayne, Peter. *Dracula Unborn* (1977)
Wallace, Robert. *The Vampire Murders* (1965)
Williamson, J. N. *Death Coach* (1982)
Winston, D. *The Vampire Curse* (1971)
Worth, Margaret. *Red Wine of Rapture* (1973)
Yeovil, Jack. *Warhammer: Drachenfeis* (1989)

On the whole, the average reader would be well advised to skip any paperback with an unknown's name on it and stick to the likes of Brian Aldis (*Dracula Unbound*, 1991), Nancy Baker (*The Night Inside*, 1993), and Elaine Bergstrom (*Blood Rites*, 1994), these being three very different kinds of popular books but all good of their type—or read all of the works of Chelsea Yarbro or some other grind-'em-out writer if they like the first one they pick up by that author. A few way-out fans read the complete series of Barnabas Collins annually the way Janeites read Miss Austen.

LIVE VAMPIRES

According to some authorities, you don't have to be dead (well, *undead*) to be a vampire; you can be a live human being.

In Africa they have witches and witchdoctors who are sometimes described as vampires because they are credited with being able to drain the vital force out of a person. They don't, however, go around biting people and drinking blood. Instead, they cook up a magical potion in a pot—it is more like water than blood—and which is said to contain the strength, even the life force, of the victims. The nasties consume this. If they drink too much of it, the victim dies.

In my view, these mumbo-jumbo bozos are not vampires at all, any more than the drugged "walking dead" we call zombies are vampires. In 1928

One of the great names of folklore study in America, Alan Dundes, has published a casebook on the most feared of all folklore monsters, bringing together experts in psychology and sociology, literature and folklore, indeed all aspects of vampires old and new. The book was published by the University of Wisconsin Press, 1998.

someone under the pseudonym "Gertrude C. Dunn" perpetrated a novel called *Vampires Living and Dead*, but vampires by definition are not living.

THE LIVING DEAD

The vampire myth was tailor-made for the Romantic Period, with Keats' knight haunted by "*La Belle Dame sans Merci*," Shelley's rebels, Coleridge's fascination with the "fearful fiend" and the artist himself as a kind of vampire ("The Rime of The Ancient Mariner"), Maturin's *Melmoth the Wanderer*, Byron's melancholy misfit standing on the cliff with his long hair blowing in the breeze.

In fact, it is as a study of Romanticism that James B. Twitchell produced the best organized study of the vampire archetype to date when he published in 1981 *The Living Dead*. That is a book you must read.

The vampire myth is also tailormade for the melodrama, whether on artfully trapped stages or FX-laden film. Sir Noël Coward some years ago jotted down a note on the theater that went like this: "The most important ingredients of a play are life, death, food, sex, and money—but not necessarily in that order." The vampire myth measures up extremely well by these standards. It also lends itself to popular trends such as sex, violence, teenage angst, feminism, demonizing of people, serial murder, and visitors from outer space.

An African-American vampire (*Blacula*) is unusual, but fear of the cross is conventional. A more unusual black vampire occurs in *Vampira* (1973): Dracula's wife is revived with blood from a black woman and becomes black.

LAMIA

In classical myth, the goddess Hera turned a beautiful woman into a horrid creature, half serpent and (upper half) woman, called the lamia. It lured passersby to their deaths. The lamia sometimes gets confused with the vampire or the vamp.

John Keats (1795-1821) wrote these familiar lines:

> Do not all charms fly
> At the mere touch of cold philosophy?
> There was an awful rainbow once in heaven;
> We know her woof, her texture; she is given
> In the dull catalogue of common things.
> Philosophy will clip an angel's wings,
> Conquer all mysteries by rule and line,
> Empty the haunted air and gnomèd mine—
> Unweave a rainbow, as it erewhile made
> The tender-person'd Lamia melt into a shade.

In mixing classical and Christian elements in his story, and beauty and ugliness in Lamia herself, Keats is right on the track of the Romantic. The Romantic must have (as Coleridge insisted) something of strangeness in it. "Lamia" (begun early in 1819 and interrupted by Keats' drama of *Ortho*) argues that feeling is more than intellect and that illusion can be more valuable than reason. Most of all, in Keats' "fine excess" as he treats myths of vampiric and enchanting women, deep truths are touched upon that plodding realism cannot examine.

SOME VAMPIRE MOVIES OF THE SEVENTIES

It is impossible, you understand, to describe here or even list all the vampire films ever made, by independent amateurs like Don Glut or by professionals here and abroad. But here are a few relevant films of the seventies, a lively decade for kitsch and one in which a few notable vampire films were made. These can hint at the great variety of vampire cinema available. The thirties saw the emergence of the vampire as a popular theme, with growing attention given to younger audiences. The seventies did not usually offer the big budgets available to features that fill the 'plexes of the nineties, nor do the seventies represent (in the opinion of most Dracfans) the acme of vampire cinema, but I believe this decade is interesting and I offer a sample from each year of it. These are films from far enough back to play on nostalgia and yet acceptable, on one level or another, today. If there were a Dracula Seventies Festival, I think it would have to include these films:

The Vampire Lovers (1970). James Sheridan LeFanu's *Carmilla* done well with Ingrid Pitt, Peter Cushing, Dawn Addams, directed by Roy Ward. Women, regarded more as objects than people in the vampire melodramas of old, began to take center stage more and more often and by the nineties there would be much more explicit manipulation of the underlying sexuality of vampirism, and more lesbianism on screen as well. We've had Dracula's daughter, a forties version and with The Count in London in 1973, and even Dracula's widow (in a Mexican film). What next?

Vampire Circus (1971). It's the early nineteenth century and a circus of vampire animals comes to town already hard hit by the plague. Sometimes nothing goes right. This is a good example of how vampire cinema gained from costume drama, antique trappings, the horror genre equivalent of Merchant-Ivory productions in which anachronistically modern people move about in quaint, picturesque period settings. If you do not change the locale, you could change the names (Count Orlock was in the 1922 film, Count Yorga was in a 1970 film) or other details.

Dracula A.D. 1972 (1972). Swinging Chelsea—the London one—and a group of young Satanists. Peter Cushing, Christopher Lee, Stephanie Beacham, directed by Alan Gibson. The teenage market for horror films having proved profitable, this was another approach. Adults were thinking that young people, Beautiful People, were going the way of The Devil anyway. Christopher Lee is the standard UK vampire as Béla Lugosi is the US one, but The Count has been played by many, from John Carradine and George Hamilton and David Niven to Zandor Virkov (Swiss) and Atif Kaptan (Turkish).

Satanic Rites of Dracula (1973). In the US this Brit Bit was called *Count Dracula and his Vampire Bride*. The Count as a real estate speculator. The Satanic abuse scare in the US was gaining momentum and this fit right in. Where some other monsters declined into comedy, the vampire often remained "serious" by attaching himself to some issue of the day.

Vampyres (1974). Two gal pals are murdered and the lesbian lovers come back from the dead as vampires to kill men. This film starred Marianne Morris, Anulka, and others but, as critic David Pirie attested, "the budget and [shooting] schedule were insignificant even by British exploitation standards." The vampire obviously is sexier than any other monster (such as the werewolf or the mummy) and, though this was too early to connect blood with AIDS, homosexuality always goes straight to the emotions of regular audiences.

Deafula (1975). Written and directed by and starring Peter Wechsburg (himself hearing inpaired), is a most unusual black-and-white vampire drama in Signscope (closed-caption signing for the deaf). In Portland (OR), Steve Adams discovers that he is a vampire; he has inherited the curse from his father, Dracula (played by the producer, Gary Holmstrom).

Nightmare in Blood (1976). This was somehow not a big year for unusual vampire films so we were stuck with this one from Independent Producers. It followed up the comparative success of their *Bloodsucking Freaks* (1975, produced, written, and directed by Joel Reed). The 1976 production starred Barrie Youngfellow, Hy Pyke, Ray Gorman, Drew Estelmann, and Guy Pion. There names are not often seen, so I undertook to place them here.

Dracula's Dog (1978). Known in Britain as *Zoltan, Hound of Dracula*. The Count's faithful servant (played by Reggie Nalder, later to be a vampire himself in *Salem's Lot*, here identified as a "fractional lamia!") is lost now that Dracula is gone. However, hope, like the vampire, springs eternal. Could it be that the dog could help him find a new master? How about Dracula's last living descendant, one Michael Drake, residing in the US?

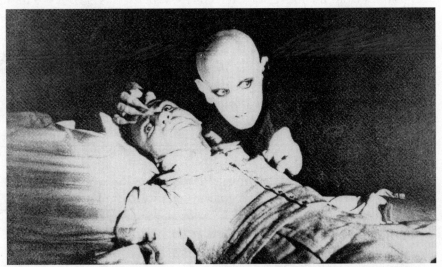

Klaus Kinski bites Bruno Ganz in Werner Herzog's *Nosferatu, The Vampire* (1979).

Starring Jose Ferrer. Directed by Albert Band, whose son, Charles Band, produced it. Not such a dog of a movie as you might expect. Meanwhile, in Belgium, they were releasing *Bloedverwanten* (Blood Relations) with everyone loose in that area, including Eddie Constantine, an ex-American. Wim Linder directed that one.

Dracula (1979). Frank Langella in a handsome production of (basically) the original Hamilton Deane & John L. Balderstone stage script adapted for the first important movie in the genre, *Dracula* (1931). This is big-budget and not as kooky as the Gary Oldman film to come later, or the Andy Warhol extravaganza. Like Stephen King's *Salem's Lot*, it reached a mass audience through television as well. Langella thus pulled off what Britons would call the hat trick and Americans the triple crown of stage, screen, and television. The same year, I cannot help adding, John Holmes, Annette Haven, and others produced a hard-core pornographic *Dracula Sucks*. Later a toned-down version was released, but purists (if we can call them that) will want to view the original.

"I NEVER QUOTE—LINES!":
DEATHLESS LINES FROM VAMPIRE MOVIES

Thanks to McFarland's *Fantastic Cinema Subject Guide* (Brian Senn & John Johnson, 1992, an absolutely indispensible reference book) here are some famous lines from the movies. Fasten your seat belts, this is going to be a bloody ride. If you have friends who are trivia buffs and think they know *all* about vampire movies, instead of asking them to place in the correct flicks *Belac, Count Alucard, Dr. Lahos, Lucard, Count Orlock, Count Yorga, Vlad Teppes*, and so on—not to mention *Mircalla Karnstein. Dr. Callistratus*, and *Baron Meinster*—let them give you the source of each of these "deathless lines." A perfect score would be astonishing, and proof positive of a wasted youth....

"According to a recent survey, one in three people is a vampire." *Dracula and Son* (1979)

"Are you gay?" "I'm not even human." *Dance of the Damned* (1988)

"A monstrous bat had fastened to your mother's throat. They beat it off, but the harm was already done." *Condemned to Live* (1935)

"Children of the night—shut up!" *Love at First Bite* (1979)

"Enough of your science! I know what I have to do." *Nosferatu, The Vampire* (1970)

"Even the power of evil cannot stand against the power of faith." *Return of the Vampire* (1944)

"For reasons of his own, von Husen claims to be an earthly reproduction of his notorious ancestor, owing his continual existence to the consumption of human blood." *My Son, The Vampire* (1988)

"I am Count Dracula, and Dracula sucks." *Dracula Sucks* (1978)

"I don't think I have ever met anyone so completely strange." *The Curse of Nostradamus* (1960)

"I'll drain them drop by drop." *Vampire* (1979)

"I mean I don't mind bein' a vampire and all that shit, but this really ain't hip." *Scream, Blacula, Scream* (1973)

"I must confess I prefer human blood...I have a drinking problem." *Return to Salem's Lot* (1987)

"In Europe the vampire walks in dread of the crucifix, but here it would be the image of the Lord Buddha." *The Legend of the Seven Golden Vampires* (1974)

"It only remains for me to await the daylight hour, when, with God's help, I will forever end this man's reign of terror. *House of Dracula* (1958)

"Listen to them, the children of the night. What music they make!" *Count Dracula* (BBC-TV, 1977)

"Once a man sets foot in this place he never leaves." *Blood of the Vampire* (1958)

"Please kill me, before the night is over, before dawn." *Dinner with a Vampire* (1988)

"There are as many species of vampire as there are beasts of prey." *Captain Kronos, Vampire Hunter* (1973)

"There exist certain beings whose very lives seem bound by invisible chains to the supernatural...." *Vampyr* (1931)

"The worst thing about this is the fact that my son is the vampire." *Lake of Dracula* (1972)

"They only drink the blood of those they love the best." *Black Sabbath* (1964)

"They prey on young virgins, put a spell on them." *Lust for a Vampire* (1971)

"To be really dead. That must be glorious!" *Dracula* (1931)

"Vampirism exists. It's not just a myth, its an actual virus." *Red-Blooded American Girl* (1990)

"What a beautiful neck!" *Nosferatu* (1922)

"What we need today is young blood and brains." *Abbott & Costello Meet Frankenstein* (1948)

"When the hunger hurts so much it knows no reason, *then* you'll have to
feed." *The Hunger* (1983)

"You'll see that I get lives...small ones, with blood in them?" *Dracula* (1931)

"You must have the blood of a virgin or in a few weeks you will be dead."
Andy Warhol's Dracula (1974)

JUVENALIA

People who heard that I was writing this book offered me a number of
poems, mostly by themselves, most of which could not by any stretch of
the imagination be called verse (even in these days when prose scattered
over the page with no reason for line endings passes as poetry), let alone
literature. For my example of bad verse about vampires—and there is a
plethora of it, new and old—I have chosen to embarrass no one alive and
I turn to some *juvenalia* of a minor Victorian. This is "The Vampyre," an
imitation Scottish ballad by James Clerk-Maxwell (1831-1879). Be kind;
he wrote it when he was only fourteen years old. The antique Scottish
dialect gives it an added flavor.

> Thair is a knichte rydis through the wood,
>   And a douchty knichte is hee.
> And sure hee is on a message sent,
>   He rydis sae hastilie.
> Hee passit the aik, and hee passit the birk,
>   And hee passit monie a tre,
> Bot plesant to him was the saugh sae slim,
>   For beneath it hee did see
> The boniest ladye that ever hee saw,
>   Scho was sae schyn and fair.
> And thair scho sat, beneateh the saugh,
>   Kaiming hir gowden hair.
> And then the knichte—"Oh ladye brichte,
>   What chance has broucht you here?
> But say the word, and ye schall gang
>   Back to your kindred dear."
> Then up and spok the ladye fair—
>   "I have nae friends or kin,
> Bot in a little boat I live,
>   Amidst the waves' loud din."
> Then answered thus the douchty knichte—

"I'll follow you through all,
For gin ye bee in a littel boat,
The world to it seemis small."
They goed through the wood, and through the wood,
To the end of the wood they came :
And when they came to the end of the wood
They saw the salt sea faem.
And then they saw the wee, wee boat,
That daunced on the top of the wave,
And first got in the ladye fair,
And then the knichte sae brave.
They got into the wee, wee boat,
And rowed wi' a' their micht;
When the knichte sae brave, he turnit about,
And lookit at the ladye bricht;
He lookit at her bonnie cheik,
And hee lookit at hir twa bricht eyne,
Bot hir rosie cheik growe ghaistly pale,
And schoe seymit as scho deid had been.
The fause, fause knichte growe pale wi' frichte.
And his hair rose up on end,
For gane—by days cam to his mynde,
And his former luve he kenned.
Then spake the ladye-"Thou, fause knichte,
Hast done to me much ill,
Thou didst forsake me long ago,
Bot I am constant still;
For though I ligg in the woods sae cald,
At rest I canna bee
Until I sucks the gude lyfe blude
Of the man that gart me dee."
Hee saw hir lipps were wet wi' blude,
And hee saw hir lufelessee eyne,
And loud hee cry'd, "Get frae my syde,
Thou vampyr corps encleane!"
Bot no, hee is in hir magic boat,
And on the wyde, wyde sea;
And the vampyr suckis his gude lyfe blude,
Sho suckis hyum till hee dee.

So now beware, whoe'er you are,
That walkis in this lone wood:
Beware of that deceitfull spright,
The ghaist that suckis the blude.

DION BOUCICAULT

Despite his French surname, this actor and playwright was born in Dublin (1822) and died in New York (1890). He was never the one to miss an opportunity to put something popular on the stage in either Britain or America, and one of his successes was an imitation of a French vogue. It was a thrilling melodrama called *The Phantom*, which is not about a ghost but a vampire. In the melodrama, anyone who was foolish enough to wander among the ruins of Raby Castle at night wound up wounded—on the right side of the neck, by the bite of a vampire. The victim was always found the next morning—no blood on the scene—dead! deathly pale!! and with a hideously fixed expression of inexpressible horror!!!

VETALA

This is one of many spellings of the name of a green and white Indian horror (sometimes mounted on a green horse) that goes around sucking the blood of crazy old women, an unusual pastime because vampires are generally supposed to prefer young and more vital blood. Sir Richard Burton has one of these ghouls of the geriatric in his version of the folktales supposedly recited to entertain an Indian king. Burton shortens the king's name to Vikram and calls his tales *Vikram and the Vampire* (1870). Presumably Bram Stoker knew this book.

STRANGE STORIES FROM THE LODGE OF LEISURES

These are folktales (translated by Soulie in 1913) from the Chinese. Very exciting is the story of a vampire whose burial has been delayed for months, thus preventing the spirit from leaving the corpse. Such spirits, folklore says, lust for blood in an effort to revive their bodies. The Chinese vampire is quite a different creature than the Western one (though both have fierce eyes and terrible teeth and often sharp talons) and is simply after blood as sustenance; the Chinese vampire does not pass on vampire characteristics to those it bites. It just kills them for nourishment.

A STORY FROM A POLISH LADY IN WESTBOURNE PARK

Eric, Count Stenbock was a Charlus-like character in London in the Gay Nineties. He left us in *A True Story of a Vampire* (1894) a tale that this lady I mention in the heading tells of her long-dead brother. The brother was a rather fey vegetarian, just the kind of "gazelle-like" young fellow that the vampire, tall, handsome, and rather effeminate also, liked. The count himself was homosexual and had about him something of the air of the vampire he describes: "His figure had something serpentine about it." Presumably he spent time standing around in stained-glass attitudes.

The tale is not very well written but has often appeared as an example of gay as well as of vampire literature. It departs notably from the figure of the vampire of folklore.

Those who run vampire societies often complain that they are beseiged by people who confuse vampirism with a blood fetish. Count Stenbock's vampire seems to comingle vampirism with pederasty. The story is an early example from The Decadence of a theme that turns up in literature still, even in science fiction and pornography. By

A film was made of the notorious Peter Kürten

the twenties in England (when Kenneth Grant wrote *Cults of The Shadow*, 1926) there was discussion not of folklore vampires but elementals with vampiristic intent who could invade the dreams of people, fill them with wild sexuality, and drive them to suicide. The elemental vampire weakened victims by feeding on energy he needed to keep himself going. Some such creatures wish they were human and do not wish to be vampires. Consider M. T. Anderson's *Thirsty* (1997): the bloodsucker struggles to remain human.

NINETEENTH-CENTURY BALLETS

Among now-obscure entertainments of the nineteenth century were ballets such as *Morgano* (Taglioni & Hertzel, 1857) and *Il Vampiro* (Rotta & Giorza, 1861). These reflected the vampire appeals of the melodramas.

DANCING DRACULA

In Paris, where Aaron Copland was one of the Lost Generation (as Gertrude Stein called them) of exiles after World War I, this American composer tried his hand at ballet music based on the film, *Nosferatu*. He worked on the score some more after returning to the US in 1924, but the vampire ballet never was finished or, if finished, was not worthy of attention. Some bits of the music Copland used in a later composition for the dance. I believe had the vampire ballet appeared it would have had the title *Grogh*.

PORTRAITS

These figure in a number of stories about the occult such as Poe's *The Oval Portrait* and Wilde's *The Portrait of Dorian Gray*. Vampires appear in portraits in Nisbet's *The Old Portrait* and M. R. James' *Count Magus*. It is interesting to see how the appearance, in portrait or in person, of the vampire changes over time and also how literary themes and tricks are adopted and adapted. The modern writer of vampire tales is limited by the "that's been done" argument and either helped or hindered by the large number of so-called characteristics of the vampire that writers have made up over the years. Must a vampire sleep in a coffin? Must she or he have some native earth in that coffin? Is the vampire able to walk in sunlight? Will a magic circle or a crucifix or bits of a consecrated Host work against the vampire? Do vampires have eyes that show red, as in bad flash photography?

BRIAN LUMLEY

This is an author enjoying great popularity for his paperback novels featuring one Harry Keogh and his twin sons battling the forces of the Undead. His Necroscope stories include *The Last Aerie* and *Bloodwars* and reach their peak in *Blood Brothers* (1992). Lumley's other works are numerous and range from *Vamphyri* to *Demogorgon* and the troubling short stories of *Fruiting Bodies and Other Fungi*. Even readers of Stephen King and Anne Rice may be quite unaware of the reputations of authors like Lumley, but fans are not.

VAMPIRE GAMES

Vampires crept into role-playing games such as *Dungeons and Dragons* and evidenced their popularity among the young in a number of other ways.

Since the early nineties vampires have been featured in electronic games, ingeniously created by computer whizzes. Very addictive. Early in the field were (among others) the following far from famous persons and in certain circles quite famous games:

L. Lee Cerney & Bradley K. Devit's *Nightlife* (1990)
Elvira, Mistress of the Dark (1990) and its sequel, *Elvira: The Jaws of Cerberus (1992)*
Kevin Shiembieda's *Viking Kingdom* (1991)
Mark Rein-Hagen's *Vampire* (1991)
Jeff Kobe's *Vampire, The Masquerade* (1993)
Viacom's *Dracula Unleashed* (1993)
Psychgnosis' *Bram Stoker's Dracula* (1993)

DRACULA ON CD-ROM

Raymond T. McNally is well known to Dracfans. He has recycled his work, and that of others, in a CD-ROM, *Dracula: Truth and Terror*, with Stoker's novel in full, the film of *Nosferatu*, and more. Film buffs may like the kidded scraps of bad vampire flicks such as *Billy the Kid vs. Dracula* and the list of vampire movies—more than 1000 of them! You may understand, given that fact, why I cannot begin to list in this volume *all* the vampires, as I will undertake to do *all* werewolves in a future volume in this series.

VAMPIRES IN SCIENCE FICTION

As one might expect, the loosening of the grip of religion in our time has moved some writers to replace all or most of the supernatural elements of the vampire story with such popular devices as those common in science fiction and technological fantasy.

There are a great many writers of science-fiction vampire stories. Most of them are not very good. As a sample of a novel interesting as science fiction (and also playing feminist, ecological, anti-colonialist and other political trump cards) I'll recommend Tanith Lee's *Sabella, or The Blood Stone* (1980), fairly early in this mixed genre and still important.

Sabella is a sexy minx who kills her victims not because they lose so much of the blood on which she feeds but because they lose so much semen—she attacks only males—in repeated orgasms. Sabella is a human colonist on a planet called Novo Mars. She eventually submits to a dominant male, Jace, but argues that in doing so she is achieving fulfillment rather than submission. "Don't think me Jace's slave...." The author seems to want to have women's rights and even lesbian superiority and marriage and motherhood. Why shouldn't the modern woman "have it all"? And surely a mother is powerful, nurturing, controlling. The male only supplies blood, or blood products, and a father seldom takes half as much interest—or expends as much time or energy—as a mother does in bringing up the next generation.

One other, and unusually humorous, science-fiction book from the eighties is Jodi Scott's *I, Vampire* (1984). Here vampires and humans are joined by not one but two kinds of aliens. There is some kidding of the vampire genre and of science fiction as well.

RUDYARD KIPLING'S THE VAMPIRE

A fool there was and he made his prayer
    (Even as you and I!)
To a rag and a bone and a hank of hair
(We called her the woman who did not care).
But the fool he called her his lady fair
    (Even as you and I!)

Oh the years we waste and the tears we waste
    And the work of our head and hand,
Belong to the woman who did not know
(And now we know that she never could know)
    And did not understand.

A fool there was and his goods he spent
    (Even as you and I!)
Honor and faith and a sure intent
But a fool must follow his natural bent
(And it wasn't the least what the lady meant)
    (Even as you and I!)

Oh the toil we lost and the spoil we lost
    And the excellent things we planned,
Belong to the woman who didn't know why
(And now we know she never knew why)
    And did not understand.

The fool was stripped to his foolish hide
  (Even as you and I!)
Which she might have seen when she threw him aside—
(But it isn't on record the lady tried)
So some of him lived but the most of him died
  (Even as you and I!)

And it isn't the shame and it isn't the blame
  That stings like a white hot brand,
It's coming to know that she never knew why
(Seeing at last she could never know why)
  And never could understand.

ST. NICHOLAS

A one-man play of this title by Conor McPherson, starring Barry Cox (at The Bush Theatre in London and Primary Stages in New York, 1998) was a tour de force of Irish blather and featured an obscure tale of vampires. Did it all really happen "or did I dream it"? Most unsatisfactory, but once again there was proof that people will sit still for any vampire story.

VAMPIRE SEX

Every year brings more of this in "young adult," "romance," and other sometimes trashy genres. Here are a half dozen titles all from 1996, something for everyone:

Devine, Thea. *Sinful Secrets*
Miller, Linda L. *Tonight and Always*
Reines, Katherine. *The Kiss*
Rowe, Michael & Thomas Roche, eds. *Sons of Darkness* (gay)
Stableford, Brian. *The Hunger and Ecstasy of Vampires*
Tan, Cecilia, ed. *Erotica Vampira*

BOOKS ON THE HORROR STORY

Callois, R. *Puissances du rêve* (Strength of Dreaming, 2 vols. 1966)
Llopis Paret, R. *Cuentos de terrór* (Tales of Terror, 1963)
Lovecraft, H. P. *The Supernatural in Horror Literature* (1969)

VAMPIRE BOOKS OF 1998

Every year sees a large crop of vampire books. As I write, 1998 is not over and already we have (among many others) these 10 titles:

Coffin, M. T. *My Dentist is a Vampire*
Crenshaw, N. *Buffy the Vampire Slayer*
Grant, Linda. *Vampire Bytes*
Hill, William. *Dawn of the Vampire*
Linedecker, C. *Vampire Killers*
Lubar, David. *The Accidental Vampire*
Mayer, M. *The Vampire Barbecue*
Melton, J. G. *Vampire Gallery*
Schimel, Lawrence. *Fields of Blood*
Vornholt, John. *Coyote Moon*

LIBRARY ASSIGNMENT

Vampire literature, as you will have noted in this present book, is copious. Dedicated bibliographers have tried to sort it out for us. See *The Bibliography of Bibliographies* and, among others:

Cox, Gregory. *The Transylvania Library* (1992)
Eighteen-Bisang, Robert. *Dracula: An Annotated Bibliography* (1994)
Finné, Jacques. *La Bibliographie de Dracula* (1986)

HALF A DOZEN HARD-TO-FIND OLD BOOKS

Andrew F. Cross, *Round about the Carpathians* (1878)
H. Heinz Ewers, *Blood* (1930)
S. Hock, *Die Vampyrsagen und ihre Verivertung in der deutschen Literatur* (1990)
Reginald Hodder, *The Vampire* (1912)
Herbert Mayo, *Of the Truths Contained in Popular Superstitions* (2nd ed., 1851)
Dudley Wright, *Vampires and Vampirism* (1914)

MORE DISSERTATIONS

You can see summaries in *Dissertation Abstracts* and scholars can use microfilm copies, etc., of the deeply researched works which graduate students offer for higher degrees. If you are interested in vampires you may be interested in such recent dissertations as:

Boone, Troy Monroe. *Unearthing Plots: Vampirism and Victorian Culture* (University of Rochester, 1994)

Rogers, Susan Lee. *Vampire Vixens: The Female Undead and the Lacanian Symbolic Order in Tales by [Théophile] Gautier, [Henry] James, and [J. Sheridan] LeFanu* (University of California at Irvine, 1993)

Stuart, Roxanna. *The Vampires of Nineteenth-Century Melodrama* (City University of New York, 1993)

Toufic, Jalal Omran. *Vampires* (Northwestern University, 1993)

Zachokke, Magdalena. *The Other Woman, From Monster to Vampire: The Figure of the Lesbian in Fiction* (University of California at Santa Barbara, 1994)

LOVE BITES

Blood is for some people an aphrodisiac and its appearance in deflowering or after a serious love bite a distinct turn-on. In Stoker's *Dracula*, however, the smell of blood on the vampire's lips puts off Jonathan Harker. "In the unconscious mind," writes Ernest Jones, "blood is commonly an equivalent for semen."

As for *Dracula* and sex, there's a whole book or three in that, but here is one sentence form David Punter's *The Literature of Terror* (1980):

> From the bourgeois point of view, Dracula stands for sexual perversion and sadism [I note this author's dichotomy here]; but we also know that what his victims experience at the moment of con-

Perhaps the most unusual performance of Dracula ever staged. Morse Mime in New York presented "The Full Length Silent Performance of *Dracula*," all mimed.

summation is joy, unhealthy perhaps [perhaps?] but of a power unknown in conventional relationships.

ON THE TRUTH OF FICTION OF THE SUPERNATURAL

Immanuel Kant (1724-1804) in his *Dreams of Spirit Seer* writes that he is not "so bold as to deny absolutely the truth of various ghost stories" adding that "while I doubt any single one of them I still have faith in all of them taken together." Throughout this book, which here concludes, I have tried to demonstrate that the vampire myth does in fact contain certain truths about the nature of people.

Farewell. God Bless you. Blessed be.

Index